BOOKS BY ELEANOR CAMERON

The Mushroom Planet Books

The Wonderful Flight to the Mushroom Planet
Stowaway to the Mushroom Planet
Mr. Bass's Planetoid
A Mystery for Mr. Bass
Time and Mr. Bass

The Julia Books

Julia's Magic
That Julia Redfern
Julia and the Hand of God
A Room Made of Windows
The Private Worlds of Julia Redfern

Other Books for Young People

The Terrible Churnadryne
The Mysterious Christmas Shell
The Beast with the Magical Horn
A Spell Is Cast
The Court of the Stone Children
To the Green Mountains
Beyond Silence

Novel

The Unheard Music

Essays

*The Green and Burning Tree: On the Writing
and Enjoyment of Children's Books*

THE SEED AND
THE VISION

The Seed and the Vision

ELEANOR CAMERON

ON THE WRITING AND APPRECIATION
OF CHILDREN'S BOOKS

Dutton Children's Books/Plume · *New York*

Library of Congress Cataloging-in-Publication Data

Cameron, Eleanor
The seed and the vision: on the writing and appreciation
of children's books / Eleanor Cameron.
p. cm.
Summary: A series of essays examining the writing, themes,
influence, range, and critical appreciation of children's books.
Dutton ISBN 0-525-44949-3   Plume ISBN 0-452-27183-5
  1. Cameron, Eleanor—Authorship—Juvenile literature.
  2. Children's literature—Authorship—Juvenile literature.
  3. Children's literature—Appreciation—Juvenile literature.
    4. Children—Books and reading—Juvenile literature.
[1. Children's literature—Authorship.   2. Children's literature—
    Appreciation.   3. Books and reading.]   I. Title.
PS3553.A43185Z475   1993
813'.52—dc20   92-8220   CIP   AC

Published in the United States by
Dutton Children's Books/Plume
divisions of Penguin Books USA Inc.
375 Hudson Street, New York, New York 10014
Printed in U.S.A.
First Dutton edition 1993
1 3 5 7 9 10 8 6 4 2
First Plume edition 1994
1 3 5 7 9 10 8 6 4 2

"The Seed and the Vision" was published in much shorter form as "Writing from Experience" in *The Five Owls,* January–February 1991; "Matters of Character," in entirely different form under the title "Characterization—Some Unforgettables" in *A Sea of Upturned Faces,* 1989; "One Woman as Writer and Feminist," in shorter form in the *Children's Literature Association Quarterly,* Winter 1982; "The Inmost Secret," in shorter form in *The Horn Book,* January–February 1983; "The Pleasures and Problems of Time Fantasy," in much shorter form in *Travelers in Time,* Children's Literature New England, 1990; "The Inimitable Frances," in slightly different form in *The Horn Book,* March–April 1991; "With Wrinkled Brow and Cool Fresh Eye," in shorter form in *The Horn Book,* May–June 1985 and July–August 1985; "Into Something Rich and Strange," in slightly longer form in the *Library of Congress Quarterly,* April 1978, as the annual Gertrude Clarke Whittall lecture; "Of Dreams, Art, and the Unconscious," in considerably shorter form in *The Alberta Learning Resources Journal,* 1986.

Dedicated in loving memory
to Frances Clarke Sayers;
to Dr. Francelia Butler; and
to all women and men who
read to the children

All the little Indians in a half circle around Aunt Emily are getting an imprinting that will last for life. The sound of her voice reading will condition how they look upon themselves and the world. It will become part of the loved ambience of Battell Pond, a mingling in the chromatic wonder of childhood. The small sensibilities will never lose the image of dark woods and bright lake. Nature to them will always be beneficent and female.

WALLACE STEGNER
Crossing to Safety

What the author writes will often fall far short of his vision of the book, but that must not be through failure of willpower or devotion.

JILL PATON WALSH
from a lecture at Simmons College

The individual's dream, whether it be so private a wish that the joyful determination of nesting arctic birds might infuse a distant friend weary of life, or a magnanimous wish that a piece of scientific information wrested from the landscape might serve one's community—in individual dreams is the hope that one's own life will not have been lived for nothing.

BARRY LOPEZ
Arctic Dreams: Imagination and
Desire in a Northern Landscape

Contents

Acknowledgments   xi

Preface   xv

Foreword   xix

I

ON WRITING

The Seed and the Vision   3 ✔

Matters of Character   27 ✔

The Fleas in the Cat's Fur   72

One Woman as Writer and Feminist: Searching for Balance   117

II

ON FANTASY

The Inmost Secret   149

The Pleasures and Problems of Time Fantasy   167

III

IS IT GOOD, WILL IT LAST?

The Inimitable Frances   207

On Criticism, Awards, and Peaches   217

With Wrinkled Brow and Cool Fresh Eye   230

IV

THE UNCONSCIOUS

Into Something Rich and Strange   269

Of Dreams, Art, and the Unconscious   289

References   327

Bibliography   334

Permissions   343

Index   346

Acknowledgments

It was Virginia Haviland, former head of the children's section of the Library of Congress, who urged me to settle on the present title of this book after I'd told her those I had in mind. "Oh," she said, without the slightest hesitancy, "of course it must be *The Seed and the Vision*. That's it!" And so it was. She understood at once the double implication: First, the idea of the child, with all its potentialities curled within it, and one in particular, waiting, full of promise, held firm and constantly becoming richer, more compelling, until the moment of testing arrives. And then the idea of the work itself, the seed from which it grows, and the vision that empowers and nurtures its unfolding into final expression. Virginia died before reading any of these essays, with the exception of "Into Something Rich and Strange," given as one of the Gertrude Clarke Whittall Lectures at the Library of Congress in 1975.

Others, among them my son, David, responded to *The Green and Burning Tree* and hoped for a second collection of essays. None in this volume has escaped untouched following a first appearance, if there was one, and four of the eleven essays are completely new.

To my friend Rita Lipkis, with whom I have been exchanging reactions and opinions for longer than I can believe, I offer here my deepest gratitude for her continual encouragement concerning my vision of the book and for her completely frank judgment of each essay as it came along. So it has been with Pattie Gehrmann after she first wrote me upon reading *The Green and Burning Tree*. My exchanges with her, as in those with Rita, have always sparked further thought, and like Rita's, her enthusiasm for the book as a whole has been unflagging. My thanks, Pattie, and to Stephen Canham, of the University of Hawaii, who gave me his judgment of a good part of the manuscript and spoke just the words I needed in a time of difficulty. To both Christina Garcia, head of work with children in the Beverly Hills Public Library System, and her colleague Kay MacDonald, my great thanks for their piquing observations on reading a section of the manuscript. Both Dr. J. D. Stahl, of Virginia Polytechnic Institute and State University, and Jeffrey Jon Smith read the entire manuscript on its completion, and I am most grateful to them for their sometimes humorous responses and for excellent suggestions, and to Dr. Stahl for his very rewarding foreword.

To my patient and devoted editor, Donna Brooks, my warmest thanks for her sensitive perceptions in reading and rereading this manuscript. We have been en rapport all the way through, and for a writer there can be no greater blessing. To Susan Llewellyn, for whom I particularly asked as copy editor, my gratitude for a sharp-eyed and subtle-minded sweep through to round up all those details that must be questioned and reexamined, details I had become too familiar with to see.

My gratitude also to Josh Weiss, Dutton's managing editor, for his meticulous reading with attention to small points and to the absorbing of a large, general impression. I want as well to thank Sara Reynolds, the art director, whose aesthetic standards and persistent work toward the attainment of what she felt was right for the book resulted in the handsomeness of both format and jacket. And I wish to express my great gratitude to Christopher Franceschelli, my publisher, for having the courage to publish this book in an uncertain economic time.

To another trio of final readers of the manuscript, my heartfelt thanks for taking time out of their own work to read through, in view of long years of experience, these many pages—Betty Levin, Suzanne Rahn, and Paul Heins.

A different kind of acknowledgment has to do with my point of view as a critic. I have been accused in two articles by two writers, much to my amazement, of being a devotee of what was called New Criticism in the 1950s, when it was all the fashion in academic circles. But I am not, and never have been, a disciple of that brand of literary criticism, not to be confused with New Theory, now greatly in favor in present-day literary criticism. How the fashions come and go! Someone once said of Randall Jarrell that "he paid no attention to literary fashion, had no systematic theory about literature, and did not talk over anyone's head." Excellent!

I know quite well that there will be reproachful cries that I have left out many a favorite and/or admired writer, or that I have not given sufficient attention to certain others. No regret could be greater than mine in having, at last and after anxious deliberation, to set aside "Art and the Moral Imagination." It is an essay whose subject means much to me. Certain works of the writers explored in it, writers such as Virginia Hamilton, Natalie Babbitt, Paula Fox, Lloyd Alexander, Sid and Paul Fleischman, Robert Cormier, Jean Fritz, and Mildred Taylor, offer fine opportunities to open up and reveal the depths and many aspects of that subject. But its inclusion would have made *Seed* too long; it could much better be written as a short book on its own, published separately. This I plan to do.

Finally, because I want a certain name to remain clearly in the mind of the reader, I end here with an acknowledgment of someone who shall never be forgotten in the world of children's literature. She is one who, along with Frances Clarke Sayers, pointed out the necessity for scholarly exploration in children's literature generally, as well as in the fields of myth and legend, in folktale and fairy tale. She also, again with Frances Sayers, gave children's literature its present name instead of that shamefully denigrating one the study had had before these two women grasped academia by the shoulder and said, "Listen to me!" She is Professor Francelia Butler. To you, Francelia, I want to say that none of us can offer you enough gratitude for what you did around thirty years ago. You forced the blind or uninformed or insufficiently sensitive to acknowledge that children's literature is something other than "the juvies" that an aspiring writer can learn to produce through some correspondence school where one starts in easy at the bottom of "the writing game," working up to the really tough field of adult novel writing. It is also something other than that represented by those slick little picture books, published in their thousands to be bought in supermarkets. For fine children's literature exists on an entirely different plane of aesthetics, a vast field to be respected and reflected upon: a most rich and irreplaceable literary form. Thank you, Francelia, in the name of both the children and their parents, for our culture must treasure all of its literary heritage, including the literature of childhood, if it is to continue as a culture at all.

Preface

When, in 1968, I gave the manuscript of my first collection of essays, *The Green and Burning Tree,* to an acquaintance widely read in children's books, she couldn't decide what I had in mind to do. She thought I had been trying to write a kind of survey of children's literature and wondered why I had left out picture books, and why I kept bringing up adult literature—a practice she thought had little to do with the subject under discussion and likely to intimidate the student and "give him an inferiority complex."

But since 1968 the whole scene of literary criticism of children's literature has changed profoundly, becoming wide-ranging and scholarly (with reference to that last word, in both the good and the not-so-good senses), where it had been narrow as to point of view, restricted as to references, and almost closed to a frank and explicit discussion of sexuality and its mores.

In 1967 and 1968 the type of essay on a single children's book, or on a genre, to be found today in such publications as *Children's Literature* (the Hollins College annual), the *Children's Literature Association Quarterly,* and *The Lion and the Unicorn* were not appearing in print. And we realize how profoundly the whole picture has changed when we read essays in a *Children's Literature Association Quarterly* special section on structuralism: Anita Moss's study of E. Nesbit's *The Enchanted Castle* and Mark Twain's *Tom Sawyer;* Perry Nodelman's comparison between Toni Morrison's adult novel *Song of Solomon* and

Virginia Hamilton's *M. C. Higgins the Great;* Boyd Davis's Saussurean
comments on Kipling's *Kim,* Le Guin's *The Tombs of Atuan,* and Virginia Hamilton's *Zeely;* and a semiological analysis by Stephen Roxburgh of *Anno's Counting Book,* by Mitsumasa Anno, taking off from
the early essay "Myth Today," by the famous structuralist Roland
Barthes. [1]

  I was puzzled to find Boyd Davis saying: "You will notice that I
am using structuralist approaches as a means of discovery, not as a
yardstick for evaluation." [2] Granted. But what the finest essays on
children's literature criticism *are* about is not simply evaluation but,
most primarily, discovery. All these essays are journeys of discovery,
explorations into the text in order to arrive at a revelation of meaning.
In fact, if discovery were not accomplished and illumination attained,
one could not evaluate. One could neither admire nor be disappointed
if one had not first discovered. One might be confused or uninterested
or unimpressed on a first reading. But following a closer second or
third, the pleasure is to arrive at illuminations somehow passed over
in the first.

  In our day we find ourselves confronted with the very strange picture
of thousands of children's writers, children's librarians, and teachers
of children's literature devotedly at work organizing symposiums,
luncheons, workshops, and book discussions, which we eagerly attend,
enthusiastic and hopeful as we are. Yes, but sometimes, in my lowest
moments, I am reminded of Katherine Mansfield's comment on the
work of one of the writers of her day. "Here, feel of this pot," she
said. "Isn't it beautifully hot? Ye-e-e-s, but there ain't going to be
no tea." Yes, *but*—there sit the children, millions of them, with their
backs to us, watching television or video cassettes, working their
electronic games. One sees a vision, casting its shadow into the years
ahead. As Harold Bloom remarks in his introduction to Robert Burchfield's *Unlocking the English Language,* published in 1991:

  A great dictionary, in another decade or so, is likely to seem a
  grand monument rising out of the compost heap of a universal

electronic culture. We will resort to that monument in the way that the librarians worked at the Museion in Hellenistic Alexandria, hoping to preserve what needs to be preserved, in the coming times of the Fire and the Flood, knowing that conservation needs to be our new Alexandrianism.[3]

Perhaps all of us involved in the children's book world—in writing, in publishing, in teaching its literature and building its collections —hang by a thread, twisting slowly in the winds of change. Neil Postman, in *The Disappearance of Childhood,* says that the most humane creation of the Renaissance was the idea of childhood, and that that idea is disappearing with dazzling speed. Childhood is now, he believes, the victim of the electronic media—a social structure difficult to sustain and, quite possibly, completely irrelevant.*

Yes, but what of those children left to us—eager-minded, imaginative, aware, and sensitive—who may still be led to the printed word in such a way that they will grow up desiring to read, year after year, for pure pleasure, the kind of literature that calls for an intellectual-aesthetic response? It is surely this kind of reading that means that they will have become literate adults in the truest and deepest sense of the word. It is my belief that those human beings—besides parents—on whom the tremendous responsibility rests for the future of literacy beyond mere practical usage are the teachers of children's literature. It is they who send on the future children's librarians and teachers with a knowledge and love of what is good in children's books. And only if these teachers and librarians are well and truly taught can they inspire those with whom they come into

---

*Postman has a new book, *Conscientious Objections: Stirring Up Trouble about Language, Technology and Education,* in which he points out that we have, in the past, considered certain aspects of adult life not suitable for children because they have neither the experience nor the reflective abilities to handle them. "That is why there is such a thing as children's literature," Postman writes. "But television makes this arrangement quite impossible. . . . As a consequence of all this, childhood innocence is impossible to sustain."

contact with their own knowledge of, and openness to, the printed word.

For what we call literature, as opposed to the book that diverts children but offers them nothing they do not already know, is full of revelations, an intensified sense of existence, characters with idiosyncrasies and habits and beliefs, with histories and possible futures that children cannot help dwelling on when the last page is turned. That texture we call the novel offers, at its most treasurable, a passionate, sometimes rapturous meeting between the artist's private vision and the haunting, ambiguous, paradoxical world of feelings and objects, all interlaced. And these interlacings open up intimations about ourselves and the world that we had not guessed at before, or had not seen, or been able to put into words.

I want to show in the following pages how the finest children's literature shares the same elements, the same surges of life and artistry, as the best literature for adults. In dwelling on these elements—the development of story, the sense of place and of time, characterization, style, revelation of theme and vision, sense of reality in both fantasy and realistic fiction—I have been fascinated to discover, in instance after instance, just how, from the earliest reading, from the earliest awarenesses, the writer's worldview subtly enters the work. Somehow it cannot be disguised; the truth of ourselves speaks from the work in ways of which we are very often not aware. And it holds that in writing for either adults or children or the years in between, literature can only be achieved when we work at the top of our bent, mature enough in our craft that all fully realized elements will be fused into a firmly conceived whole—the seed indeed blossomed into the vision, within the writer and within the book.

It is my hope that we who are involved with children will be increasingly concerned to read aloud, to lead them to the riches that lie in wait; that we will never hesitate to read to junior and senior high school students as well as to the younger ones, because *all* of youth needs to be given, not what it already knows, but what it has not yet divined.

Foreword

A Room Made of Windows—this extraordinary title first attracted my attention to Eleanor Cameron's work. From Julia Redfern's journal, the "Book of Strangenesses," through her epiphany and unfolding self-discovery as a writer and a thinking, feeling person, Julia's story did not disappoint me. On the contrary, I became passionately absorbed. So unusual and so evocative, *A Room Made of Windows* is one of those rare novels that address adults and children with equal intensity.

Much later, Eleanor Cameron and I began to correspond, after she read a review of mine that suggested to her that I would be a good critic of her work because I hold views that are opposed to hers with regard to deconstruction and the work of Jacques Derrida. The impulse to seek out a genuinely critical reader is characteristic of her questing, courageous mind.

One of the particular values of *The Seed and the Vision* is Eleanor Cameron's authority and insight as a distinguished writer of children's fiction, a position which gives her criticism of children's literature special interest and perspectives. Her criticism reflects a refined concern with precision, accuracy, and vividness in language, imagery, and characterization.

Cameron's work in this volume is more than an extension of her earlier book, *The Green and Burning Tree*, though it is that also. Her more recent criticism shows growth and development in absorbing and responding to some of the massive changes that have taken place in the language, theory, and methodology of children's literature criticism over the past twenty years. *The Seed and the Vision* displays a reckoning with these changes that will educate and stimulate many of the readers of her earlier book and offer ideas of interest and value to new readers as well. Cameron refers to and incorporates her earlier positions, but she does not rest with those. Rather, she reveals the results of much reading and thought that go beyond what she presented earlier. Still, as before, her great strength as a critic of children's literature is her exceptionally perceptive attention to words themselves and to moods, characters, places, and the subtleties these imply.

The creative process itself and the links between biography and creativity are often the subjects of her investigations, as in her discussions of Lewis Carroll, J. M. Barrie, Virginia Woolf, and her own writing. Her approach to criticism emphasizes appreciation, and as a consequence, her discussions of novels for children often consist of informed close readings interwoven with evaluation. It is a natural and admirable result that she often stimulates a desire to read or reread the books she focuses her attention on.

There are comparatively few children's authors who have also devoted themselves in depth to the criticism of children's literature. Eleanor Cameron is one of the finest. Her work deserves wide attention and response.

J. D. STAHL
Department of English
Virginia Polytechnic Institute and
State University

PART I

On Writing

I'm glad to report that even now, at this late day, a blank sheet of paper holds the greatest excitement there is for me—more promising than a silver cloud, prettier than a little red wagon. It holds all the hope there is, all fears. I can remember, really quite distinctly, looking a sheet of paper square in the eyes when I was seven or eight years old and thinking, "This is where I belong, this is it." Having dirtied up probably a quarter of a million of them and sent them down drains and through presses, I am exhausted but not done, faithful in my fashion, and fearful only that I will die before one comes out right—as though I had deflowered a quarter of a million virgins and was still expecting the perfect child.

E. B. WHITE
Letters of E. B. White

So long as I remain alive and well, I shall continue to feel strongly about prose style, to love the surface of the earth, and to take pleasure in solid objects and scraps of useless information.

GEORGE ORWELL
Collected Essays, Journalism,
and Letters

THE SEED AND
THE VISION

⟡

*My films are my interior studios, and these studios were shaped when
I was a child. All of us collect fortunes when we are children—a
fortune of colors, of lights and darkness, of movements, of tensions.
Some of us have the fantastic chance to go back to this fortune when
grown up.*

INGMAR BERGMAN
The Magic Lantern: An Autobiography

*V*irginia Woolf spent blissful summers as a child in St. Ives on
the Cornish coast in a house called Talland House. So much did
she love it that she made it the place of her best-known novel, *To the
Lighthouse,* in order to evoke that whole world, to bring back what
those summers were like, to conjure up the emotional relationships
of her father and mother and the children. Place was responsible, I
do deeply believe, for *To the Lighthouse,* at least as much as Woolf's
memories of her father and mother, though no doubt the influences
were all interwoven.

She tells how she and Toby and Adrian and Vanessa (her two brothers
and her sister) returned to St. Ives one summer twenty-two years
before the publication of her novel:

In the dark . . . we passed through the gate, groped stealthily
but with sure feet up the carriage drive, mounted the little flight

3

of rough steps, and peered through a chink in the escalonia hedge. There was the house with its two lighted windows; there on the terrace were the stone urns, against the bank of tall flowers; all, so far as we could see was as though we had but left it in the morning. But yet, as we knew well, we could go no further; if we advanced the spell was broken. The lights were not our lights; the voices were the voices of strangers. We hung there like ghosts in the shade of the hedge, and at the sound of footsteps we turned away.[1]

In her imagination she saw her own family's possessions in those rooms where she had played as a child, cried, had tantrums (and she did have them), quarreled, laughed with delight, teased and been teased, heard her father shout at her mother, saw them clasped together, and, in her hallucinatory imagination—like no one else's—saw them all moving through their daily lives. And then went away. There was no use staying about. No, but the seed of *To the Lighthouse* had fallen on rich soil.

I know so well how that is, how it feels, because it was just such an aesthetic chemistry that brought one of my own books into being. Just so did my mother and my son, David, and I go back after many years in search of that brown-shingled bungalow with the white roof, the house that contained, at the back and upstairs, my many-windowed room, in which I lived for little over a year when I was twelve. Thereafter *A Room Made of Windows* took perhaps ten years to get itself ready for the first chapter.

Up in that room had stood a certain desk, made for me when I was nine by the father in *To the Green Mountains,* who had been so often away on his "failing little farm" with the idea of "putting us on Easy Street," as he invariably said. But, I always wanted to know, where *was* Easy Street, exactly? What was it like? What did it *look* like?

In view of his complete lack of feeling for me (as I then supposed) that desk was an anomaly, the most ironic I've ever experienced. For he, who had never shown me the slightest sign of affection since coming home after the failure of the farm, made me something that was to symbolize the central absorption of my life. And I wonder if it would have meant anything to him at all to have known this and what has happened to me as a writer. I have put that desk into *That Julia Redfern* when Daddy—the loving, writing father, he who created himself for the self who is Julia—makes it for her just before he goes off to camp to begin training as a fighter pilot. My own father, in essence, was light-years away from Julia's simply because something in me rebelled against such a re-creation at that time for that particular book. And it took me four years before I was overcome with sufficient understanding, sufficient emotional distance, to write fully and freely and naturally of the man Jason, the father in *Mountains,* as a character belonging within an artistic conception rather than appearing as a raw, realistic representation. The reader cannot know what has happened to bring about the writer's aesthetic maturing, but the results are there on the page.

Because my mother and stepfather and I lived in so many rented flats and apartments after we lost our home on the heights in Berkeley, I wonder if my intense love of home, of leafy, wooded places (I live now in a forest—not a wild one, to be sure), of books—roomfuls of books—might not go back to a certain childhood experience. We knew a professor and his wife, and it was a revelation to me that these people lived in the midst of such beauty, such spaciousness as their home offered, situated in a woodland in the Berkeley hills. I spent hours in their garden, with its gold-backed ferns and buckeye tree and creek that wandered down from higher up, pressing the ferns to the backs of my hands and carving patterns into the silky brown skins of the buckeyes to reveal the ivory smooth underskin. All the while I talked to myself by the creek and made up stories.

Then I would go up to the professor's study, where pillars held up the ceiling—oh, there must have been five or six of them (so I remembered, but actually there were only two). And his huge desk was at the far end of the room in front of floor-length windows that looked down into the wild garden. And all around the walls were rows and rows of little drawers, rather shallow drawers, beautifully made so that they slid in and out silently, with the most lovely smoothness. And these drawers, reaching almost from floor to ceiling around the two walls not taken up by books and windows, were filled with birds, far more birds than I had ever imagined there could be. And with each bird, there beside it lay its egg, pale cream or green or blue, in all shades, some speckled.

They enchanted me, as did the exquisite patterns of the feathers— the cedar waxwing for instance, with the *shibui** elegance of its design and coloring; the brilliance of the South American birds; the iridescence of the hummingbirds, so many different kinds, when I had seen only the Anna. To me, who had seen so few birds, comparatively speaking, all these were miracles, and a miracle, too, was the fact that I could actually pick up their eggs and roll them in my hands, examine them closely. Then there was the ladder that reached clear to the ceiling and on which one could roll oneself along by the little rubber wheels that ran on a track the whole way around. What a wonder that the professor, who was an ornithologist, and his wife allowed this harum-scarum child to be alone in that marvelous room with the birds and their eggs. How could they trust me? But they did, and I do not remember that I ever did any harm. The place seemed almost sacred to me.

Another seminal experience that suggests the influence of childhood on the writer to come. When I was still a child, after we left the house with the room made of windows because my mother had married again, our home on a hillside in Berkeley had a 180-degree view of cities, bay, and ocean. Directly opposite our western windows stood the Golden Gate, where San Francisco Bay and the Pacific intermingle their waters. For me, then, San Francisco was a wondrous, absorbing city, with its enormous wooded park and museum, its cable cars, its swooping streets all giving views of islands, of Marin County across

---

*The Japanese word for understated or muted; from *shibuichi*, having to do with the lustrous gray patina in Japanese decorative sword mounts.

the Golden Gate, and of my own little city over there on the other side of the bay, minuscule with distance.

And the core of my fascination centered on the museum, which evoked for me—though I did not realize it then, staring at the remains of mummies, at Sumerian and Egyptian and Greek and Roman jewelry, at the elegance of chateau rooms brought from France—the poignancy of human beings hundreds or even thousands of years gone. Those who had made and used these objects smoothed them gradually with their hands and clothing, these very mirrors, boxes, tables, chests, chairs, cabinets on which I fed my imagination. What I felt then eventually resolved itself into the firm conviction that the notion of the three tenses of time is an illusion of our necessarily limited senses. Thus, the concept underlying time fantasy became to me not fantastical at all but one having its basis in a reality we cannot normally experience. In *The Court of the Stone Children* I combined this belief—which goes back through the millennia and is shared by all peoples—with my intense and special childhood sense of San Francisco as at once a city like no other and the place where I had experienced my "Museum Feeling."

I gave that feeling to Nina in *Court,* and something else as well that I myself had had as a child. From the handwrought artifacts and the chateau rooms I absorbed a loving appreciation of a certain kind of beauty other than natural: the kind that is humanly fashioned, contained in objects shaped by cultivated perceptions, objects that are expressions of civilizations not engrossed merely in the pleasures of business, the body, and society but in making with patience and devotion what would be the revelation of an aesthetic vision. This spoke to me unconsciously and has never left me.

I go back to Virginia Woolf and *To the Lighthouse,* with which I began, and by way of them turn to mothers and their influence on the writer. Virginia Woolf wrote of her mother:

It is perfectly true that she obsessed me, in spite of the fact that she died when I was only thirteen, until I was forty-four. Then

one day, walking around Tavistock Square I made up, as I sometimes make up my books, *To the Lighthouse,* in a great, apparently
involuntary rush. . . . I wrote the book very quickly; and when
it was written, I ceased to be obsessed by my mother. I no longer
hear her voice; I do not see her.[2]

That fascinates me because at times I have been similarly obsessed.
Virginia Woolf says that she supposes she did for herself what psy-
choanalysts do for their patients. Am I, then, like her, expressing
"some very long felt and deeply felt emotion" and, in expressing it,
explaining it and then laying it to rest? "But what is the meaning of
'explained it'?" Virginia Woolf wonders. I too have been haunted by
my mother and the quality of her life, though I haven't been aware
of any need to "write her out" of myself.

My mother and I were very close, even though we were sometimes
at loggerheads in our younger days and couldn't see the other's point
of view. She was a power in my life, and at times I rebelled against
that power, so perhaps it is revealing that she became, in my later
books, the mother of the child each novel is about. In each of these
later books, beginning with *Room,* she is there in essence—in *The
Court of the Stone Children,* in *To the Green Mountains*—though only a
part of her, as it turned out, in each of the three women. There was
no effort involved; it came about because of place. Place, for me, as
I've said elsewhere, makes story by making possible—indeed, by
making inevitable—certain characters. The mystery to me is why three
childhood places—and times—should have called up three different
facets of the same woman.

In *A Room Made of Windows* she was a mother who was compelled
to say to her daughter that for her children were not enough, because
she did not feel whole without a mate to share her life. In *The Court
of the Stone Children* she was the kind of woman for whom responsibility
comes first, responsibility to circumstance, to making something decent of life; so that Nina thinks of her as habitually saying, "We
must—we must—we must always" do this, that, or the other. The

sense of duty is paramount. In *To the Green Mountains* she was one whose dominant qualities were independence and the ability to manage. In this novel her management of a hotel led her to desire change in the headwaiter's life to the extent that she did change it without discussion with anyone, because she could see so clearly what it ought to be, how it ought to go. And yet my three women, different from one another, are also different from my mother, because each novel magnified one central quality around which others coalesced, so that each novelistic essence is her own person.

There are writers who would never use personal experiences, who never could, perhaps, and others who can use specific events out of their own lives, specific people, as I have in the books about Julia, using autobiography here and there as a catalytic center around which imagined events and characters gather in a way that I, for one, cannot explain. It all seems an act of pure magic to me. I know only this: that childhood is the enchanted cauldron out of which so much arises that there is far more than can ever be used, and I don't mean just facts, just actual happenings, but feelings, moods, longings, intuitions, apprehensions. But of course the results of adult experience also inform books for children. Otherwise the books would not be worthy of being published; for if stories stayed purely within the perceptions of childhood they could not bring more to the child than he or she already knows. They could bring no illuminations in the way that only adult artistry can accomplish. But an intense recovery of the experiences of childhood must be there in the depths of the adult writer if the book for children is to speak to them at all.

In an exchange with one of the editors of *The Pied Pipers: Interviews with Influential Creators of Children's Literature,* Alan Garner said that there were childhood experiences that deeply affected him, and that even to begin to express the whole matter of influencing would take him two hours. He stated most passionately that he did not have a normal childhood—that it was "very dramatic"—and that he had so many illnesses he scarcely went to school before he was eleven. He believed he was "being charitable" when he confessed that his mother "functioned best in a crisis," and that as he grew older he understood that "she precipitated situations by which [he] became ill. Quite unconsciously, of course," but many of the illnesses were caused by "severe periods of mental tension." His mother was a splendid nurse, and though he confessed that it might "sound sick" to say that "she made [him] sick in order to function," he saw this effect with other people as well. "She was a very good nurse and tended to become rather destructive in other situations."[3]

Now, in Garner's *Red Shift,* a book set in three layers of time, the story in the present is carried on by Jan and Tom, teenagers in love and trying to find some place to be alone and warm and comfortable in a cold, wet season. They're suspected by Tom's mother of making love—of which she openly accuses Tom in the most vulgar way. Jan flies out at her because they have not been making love, much as they long to, and the mother is tearing apart, cruelly and insensitively, what they've had together. Later, after having softened toward his parents on the occasion of his birthday, he finds that his mother has been opening letters from Jan and not giving them to him.

In *The Owl Service,* there is a more deeply explored tension between Nancy and her son, Gwyn. Nancy, a housekeeper, had long ago been "the winds of April," according to Huw Halfbacon, once in love with her. Nancy is now lean, knotted, and bitter with memories, with a sense of frustrated destiny. And while Gwyn loathes not his mother's Welshness but her crudeness and illiteracy, at the same time he detests the thick-skinned Birmingham snobs for whom she is keeping house. Furthermore, his loathing of his mother's class, her commonness and what it means for his own future, is all entangled with his fury at her blind, raw, selfish power over him—a fury so intense that his moment of revenge on "the old cow," as he calls her to her face, is one of the jolting scenes of the book.

All this reminds me of Virginia Woolf's disturbing statement: "Every secret of a writer's soul, every experience of his life, every quality of his mind is written large in the works."[4] This may be a slight exaggeration, but as Lyndall Gordon has pointed out in her life of Woolf, our deepest and most wounding experiences find their way overtly or covertly into our fictions. Woolf believed, Gordon says, that "there are only a few essential hours of life. In the lives of most people they would have to be imagined," creating an essence "from which all we know them by proceeds." Woolf, attentive to that essence, captured it and found it to be determined by a "shock-receiving capacity."[5]

Through my experiences as a writer, I know that my own shock-receiving capacity was most vulnerable in youth, and that, as most novelists and poets discover, these shocks leave ineradicable impressions that in some cases are like wounds. They may heal over to some extent, but they are there for life, a point that Selma Lanes brings out in her study of Maurice Sendak's work. If one were trying to verbalize Sendak's major theme on the basis of a close examination of all his books and writings, it would certainly have something to do with his unending exploration of the normal child's burden of rage and confusion, as well as fear of and frustration over the uncontrollable facts of life—adults who don't understand, limitations that restrict and inhibit, situations beyond coping with.

I I

What Robert Louis Stevenson kept from childhood into adulthood is a very curious instance, indeed, of the effect of those earliest years on the writer to come. Stevenson, a most lovable, spoiled small boy, was extremely egotistical and kept this quality all his life, longing not only to be loved but constantly admired until the day he died. Yet spoiled and doted on as he was during childhood, night after night he was ridden by the most frightful dreams. He was born with a chest weakness that kept him awake, coughing again and again, so that through the night hours he watched the bedroom walls swell and shrink, his wardrobe grow to the bigness of a church, then dwindle into a horror of infinite distance and littleness. Knowing what sleep would bring, he fought it off until he was forced to give in, and then the night hag would have him by the throat and pluck him, struggling and screaming, from his sleep. Now his father would pick him up and tell him stories and invent conversations to soothe, comfort, and divert him, little guessing that it was the child's nurse, Cummy— with her morbid visions of righteousness and hell and what the wicked would suffer after death—who was most likely responsible for Louis's misery. His mother was horrified when she discovered later what the child had experienced.

On into manhood the nightmares pursued him, but like Hans Christian Andersen and many another artist, he had by then learned to use his unhappiness and to rely on these dream sequences in his writing. Stevenson had a nightmare that caused him to scream so loudly and with such terror that his wife, Fanny, woke him. She was not thanked, however, for, exclaimed Stevenson resentfully, he had been dreaming a fine bogey tale.

He had, in fact, dreamed his story up to the first transformation of Jekyll into Hyde, including the potion made from the white powder. He got to work the next morning and wrote for three days in a state of completely absorbed silence, during which he finished the novel. He then read it aloud to Fanny and his stepson, Lloyd Osborne. But Fanny didn't share Louis's triumph. She told him head-on that he had entirely missed the point of his own creation and that he had written another piece of sensationalism like his novel *Markheim* rather than the allegory she felt had been intended. At first he was furious with her, and they had the kind of loud and angry row Lloyd couldn't stand, so he had to leave the room. But later Louis admitted that Fanny had been right, threw the nearly forty-thousand-word manuscript into the fire to avoid being influenced by it, and began all over again. In another three days he had rewritten the entire novel as an allegory—a tale that delighted Fanny—after which he polished it for six weeks and then sent it off to his publisher.

Concerning the double nature of Dr. Jekyll, we discover that in

Stevenson's youth he, like James Barrie, had been haunted by a series of dreams in which he led a life that seemed fully as vivid and real as his daytime experiences. He dreamed that he worked by day in a horrible surgery and lived by night on the heights of Edinburgh's Old Town. Finally, he became so obsessed by this double life of his dreams that he went to a doctor, who gave him an opiate, and at this point the dreams stopped. At least, they appeared to Stevenson's conscious mind to have stopped, but they must have been working away in the depths, to burst forth into consciousness at that moment in later life when he had the nightmare of the first part of *Dr. Jekyll and Mr. Hyde.*

I can think of no one in the world of aesthetics, aside from Marc Chagall, Paul Klee, and Franz Kafka, who has in his work more fruitfully involved his dreams and the gifts of his unconscious (which inevitably involve childhood experiences) than Maurice Sendak. Again and again children have asked him, "Where do you get your ideas?"

And at least one answer is that the writer doesn't seem to get ideas as one discovers an apple or a pear, a complete thing. Rather, a feeling or scene gradually begins to haunt the imagination, other feelings and scenes arrive, and then conversations begin to be heard, so that all sorts of implications are seen to be involved. If one waits long enough, one will know when the right moment has come to begin making one's way into a story that nags to be written because it wants to weave all these feelings, scenes, and conversations together—and indeed has already begun to. Undoubtedly it isn't this way with every writer, but here is what Sendak said in an interview with Virginia Haviland at the Library of Congress:

My books don't come about by "ideas" or by thinking of a particular subject and exclaiming "Gee, that's a terrific idea, I'll put it down!" They never quite come to me like that; they well up. In the way a dream comes to us at night, feelings come to me, and then I must rush to put them down. But these fantasies have to be given physical form, so you build a house around them, and the house is what you call a story, and the painting of the house is the bookmaking. But essentially it's a dream or fantasy.[6]

If you spread Sendak's books out on a big table and turn the pages, now here, now there, you get an increasing revelation of the astonishing number of repetitions of certain actions (flying, eating), objects (moons, windows), and creatures (dogs, babies, birds, lions) throughout his work. Among these repetitions that speak to us so powerfully from our own sleeping life is the persistent experience of dream-flying. This element of Sendak's work strikes you at once if you simply sweep your eyes across his pages. In an essay on *Peter Pan,* Michael Egan examines the book according to Freud and therefore interprets it sexually. Apropos of Peter and the Darling children flying, Egan reminds us that, for Freud, this dream experience is symbolic of the sexual act. But Selma Lanes, in her spacious study of Sendak, chooses to interpret the flying figure as symbolic of power and potency (still, of course, easily related to sexuality) and adds that dreams of flying are usual in childhood. But, as a good many of us know, they do not leave off as childhood passes, no matter what they may symbolize.

About moons and windows: "What looks inside and what looks outside?" Why, a window, of course! And a window is an opening that, as Lanes sees it, "serves as the border between the familiar reality of the boy's bedroom and both the real world beyond and the fantasy world within himself." Windows, which we take so for granted, are, when you come to think of it, magical. They give us, as walls do, protection from the vagaries of the weather as well as—to a certain extent—noise. Yet at the same time they open the world to us so that we may contemplate it—that portion of it within our purview—keep watch on it and our fellow creatures even as windows shut us away from intrusion when we choose solitude.

How many nights must Sendak as a small boy have gazed up from his own bedroom window, just as we see Kenny gazing, on the very first page of *Kenny's Window,* at that miraculous, glowing orb floating in the night sky—a silvery orb that is sometimes whole, mysterious shadows visible on its surface; sometimes part of a ball; and sometimes nothing but a delicate eyelash with, at times, just at dusk, the ghostly rest of it faintly to be seen. If he had not been completely enchanted by that sight (and you can feel his enchantment in the drawings on those pages), how else could he have communicated so vividly what the expressions on the faces of Udry's Moonjumpers convey—how the bewitchment of their moon ecstasy is drawing them compulsively into the air.

Babies and nakedness, and not just naked babies, are other compulsive images—and this nakedness, Sendak reports, was at first of considerable concern to some librarians, who have even been known to draw pants on Mickey in *In the Night Kitchen!** Is it to be understood from this that girl children have never in their lives seen naked boy babies—and shouldn't? If in the family, why not in the art of the picture book as well as in the whole world of painting and sculpture, which, as Sendak points out, children inevitably see in museums? In *Outside over There* Sendak seems to revel in the rotund fleshy beauty of the naked babies as much as Renoir reveled in the rotund fleshy beauty of young women. Renoir said that as he painted he stroked their images with his brush—implying, I suppose, with love. Now look at the fantasy sketches in Lanes's book, of which Sendak must have drawn hundreds while listening to Mozart, Brahms, Deems Taylor, Beethoven, Schubert: one series of naked small children after another, flying children, swallowed and regurgitated children, and even naked and flying adults, as in the series in which Papa not only flies but brings a child to Mama on his winged back, the child put into a roly-poly pudding (Beatrix Potter and her Tom Kitten!), eaten, and then mourned at his grave. At which we are taken back not only to Tom

---

*See Sendak's account of this picture book, as well as brief comments on others of his books, in his *Caldecott & Co.*

Kitten, who escaped, but most fearfully of all to "The Juniper Tree," the last fairy tale in the collection *The Juniper Tree: And Other Tales from Grimm*, brilliantly illustrated by Sendak and translated by Lore Segal and Randall Jarrell, in which a bird with a child's spirit sings:

> My mother she butchered me,
> My father he ate me,
> My sister, little Anne Marie,
> She gathered up the bones of me
> And tied them in a silken cloth
> To lay under the juniper.
> Tweet twee, what a pretty bird am I!

And then there is the naked baby flying by outside the window in the Sendak-illustrated version of George MacDonald's *The Light Princess*.

Moons, dreams, flying, windows, babies, nakedness, and, very often indeed, eating and regurgitation.

Concerning eating, Sendak went back to his childhood love of the very shape and smell and feel of books, a love so intense that he tried to bite into *The Prince and the Pauper*, his first "real" book. All previous books had been Disney comics, printed on poor paper "that smelled poor." A ritual began with his sister's presentation to him of that book, the setting up of it on the table, the smelling of it, its fine paper and its shiny, laminated cover. His passion for books and for bookmaking, he believes, began with the total effect of that book upon him and perhaps was indirectly responsible for his peculiar obsession with ingesting and giving out.[7]

III

I've made a discovery with reference to childhood and the writer to come—the seed and the vision—that delights me. The Children's Book Council has, over the years, asked many a writer for children and young people to put down recollections of childhood reading. And what did not surprise me too much in Ursula Le Guin's account was the fact that her reading included a book she has recollected as one of the treasurable experiences of her early years, a book she longed to find and reread—to hold in her hands. In fact, she asked if any of the readers of the council's *The Calendar* (as it was in 1978; it is now *CBC Features*) knew the whereabouts of a copy of this book. It is called *The Rise of the Red Alders,* and she had no idea who wrote it. But then, as a good many of us older people know, we didn't pay much attention to who wrote our books when we were children; in fact, we all thought that authors were dead. How *could* they be alive? we wondered. I must say that the logic of this question escapes me, but so we asked ourselves, if it occurred to us to ask at all.

At any rate, *The Rise of the Red Alders* was about beavers, and here is Le Guin's own description of the story, which I give in full because you will then understand the unique connection between it and Le Guin's innate compulsion to write the particular kind of books she has written since:

The Red Alders were not cute beavers with Disney goggle-eyes, nor were they scientifically accurate beavers. They were intelligent, literate beavers with complex emotional lives and—this may be the particular quality of the book—a long, strange history: a mixture of political power struggles and the rise and fall of nations with half-mythicized tribal lore. This element gave, to its reader of ten or so, a vivid, haunting sense of great extents and expanses of time, lived time. It offered, to the mind just leaving the child's nonhistorical and self-centered world, the mystery and lure of other ages, other civilizations. A child may get the first taste of this in books about archaeology, Indians, ancient Egypt or Rome, or in the *National Geographic,* or—all too seldom in our schools!—in a real history course. I expect many may get it from *The Lord of the Rings.* I got it from a book about beavers.

Is it really a good book? I don't know. As I have tried to describe it, it sounds a bit like Richard Adams' *Watership Down;* but the mood was utterly different, and it was the mood (along with an amiable hero and a good solid plot) that was the beauty of it. It was intense: like a place in the woods, a deep, remote stream-gorge, where nobody else ever comes, and where something mysterious happened a long time ago.[8]

Look what has resulted, the burgeoning of one seed after another to bring forth the creations of later years! "A long, strange history" and "the rise and fall of nations with half-mythicized tribal lore" mixed with "political power struggles" within "a vivid, haunting sense of great extents and expanses of time," all of this told of in one way or another from novel to novel in the four Earthsea books, in *The Left Hand of Darkness,* in *The Dispossessed,* in *Always Coming Home,* and, very precisely and specifically, almost described as it actually was in *The Beginning Place:* "a place in the woods, a deep, remote stream-gorge, where nobody else ever comes, and where something mysterious happened a long time ago." Except that the stream, minus the gorge, was *only* the beginning place, and the deepness and real remoteness comes when we are taken above, far, far from the freeway, into another "expanse of time" altogether, to stream-gorges in a land, Tembreabrezi, which is full of rivers and streams.

The flowering of that early reading is truly astonishing—that particular seed, *Red Alders,* blossoming into special, idiosyncratic visions that Le Guin's giftedness as a writer has been, most fortunately, richly capable of bringing to full fruition.

When I was asked to contribute to "Books Remembered," by the Children's Book Council, what came to mind immediately, without a moment's thinking, were books in three categories that have had a lifelong influence. And this instantaneous knowledge showed me patterns so neat that I distrusted them. But on reflection I couldn't distrust, because there it all was—there it all *is.*

First of all there was Arthurian legend. I've written elsewhere, in

The Green and Burning Tree, how moved I was as a child by the life and death of Arthur, a life and death that haunted me forever after. I wrote that "Arthur's death meant the passing of goodness and courage and idealism, the breaking up of the Round Table, the scattering of the great knights: all of that gone forever, and I remember the un-utterable poignancy I felt—sadness mixed with longing—yet a sense of exaltation, a sense of having touched something very fine and powerful and strength-giving. For me, as a child, Arthur's story was equal to the adult experience of Greek or Shakespearean tragedy." And the idealism and the ethical principles, which were there in the philosophy that compelled Arthur to gather the knights of the Round Table, seem to have stayed with me throughout life and have, I hope, made themselves felt in the books I have written.

The next influence was fairy tales. I consumed fairy tales, English, Chinese, Japanese, all I could come by, in that low-ceilinged, paneled, possibly underlit room in the old Carnegie Public Library on Shattuck Avenue in Berkeley. I loved that room: its windows turned green-gold by the sunlight filtering through bushes and hanging boughs, and the big grandfather clock ticking "comfortably" (I always thought) while I sat there at one of the low tables lost in the happiness of reading.

And the love of fantasy never left me, combining, when I was sixteen and seventeen, with the wonders in the books of that great astronomer Sir James Jeans, so that I could write a sequence of space fantasies for my son, David, many years later. Jeans's descriptions of the universe and its workings I only a quarter, or perhaps an eighth, understood, but they brought me back to his pages all through my late teens, filling me with awe and a profound respect for creation.

Now, of those fairy tales, I was apparently drawn more strongly than I then realized to the Japanese, or was more deeply impressed by them. For it was those tales that must have taken me, on so many afternoons, into the little Japanese shop that I have described in *A Room Made of Windows,* to linger there for an hour or more, minutely examining all the small, magical things that Japanese fingers had made and that were evoked, or precisely spoken of, in the fairy tales. Later my parents opened an import shop and gathered pieces of Japanese art for it, some of which I have inherited, so that I am surrounded by Japanese prints, wall screens, small figures, and other artifacts. They delight me, and whenever I go into an art museum in a city I have never visited before, I make at once for the Japanese section, where I experience something of what the Impressionists must have felt, which they revealed through technique and style in many of their paintings and prints.

The final influence of books remembered came from the animal stories of Rudyard Kipling and the Limberlost novels of Gene Stratton-Porter. After all these years, when I repeat the names in *The Jungle Books,* something eerie still happens—I get the feathery thrill around the back of my neck and down my arms that in Scotland they call a "gru." "Bagheera," I whisper, "Shere Kahn, Mowgli, Darzee, the Bandar-Log, Baloo, Tabaqui, Kaa, the Seeonee wolf pack, Akela, Mang the Bat, Kala Nag, Toomai of the Elephants," and the whole world of Kipling's jungle rises in my mind. The years fall away, and there's no distance at all between the time I was ten and now. How the man could write! And it was then I was realizing for the first time, without knowing it, that the great writer intuits names for his or her creatures—be they animal, bird, or human—that are deeply and beautifully *right,* that will live with us forever after, along with the creatures named.*

The English novelist Angela Thirkell writes of her cousin Rudyard Kipling, who had been her neighbor when she was a child, and how it was when he read aloud:

The *Just So Stories* are a poor thing in print compared with the fun of hearing them told in Cousin Ruddy's deep unhesitating

---

*"I'm sorry, Mr. Kipling, but you just don't know how to use the English language." *San Francisco Examiner,* rejection letter to Kipling, 1889. From *Rotten Reviews: A Literary Companion,* edited by Bill Henderson, Wainscott, New York: Pushcart Press, 1986, page 56.

voice. There was a ritual about them, each phrase having its special intonation which had to be exactly the same each time and without which the stories are dried husks. There was an inimitable cadence, an emphasis of certain words, an exaggeration of certain phrases, a kind of intoning here and there which made his telling unforgettable.*[9]

Despite the fact that none of us has been so inestimably fortunate as to hear Cousin Ruddy read his stories aloud to us, his works have lived differently from Stratton-Porter's. It is true that in our small local library *A Girl of the Limberlost* is still there, the original copy I'm sure, battered and stained and smelly, but Kipling's books take up a whole shelf in many of their editions, old and new. And yet, during her lifetime, Stratton-Porter's books were translated into seven languages and during the last seventeen years of her life, sold seventeen hundred copies a day. (Do you suppose seven really is a lucky number?)

She was one of our first genuine conservationists, and her attachment to the swamp she lovingly called the Limberlost compelled her to risk her own safety photographing wildlife, no matter what difficulties she had to undergo to get the shots she wanted. Her descriptions must have brought place vividly before this child's eyes, because the lasting result has been to cause in me a fierce and bitter resentment when I read of the spoliation of our wilderness and national parks; of the clear-cutting of the nation's ancient forests or any irreplaceable habitat like the South American rain forests; of the ruin of Alaska and the Arctic, which are being littered with the ugly remains of our search for oil.

---

*If you enjoy putting together small corners of literary history having to do with childhood, do read, one after the other, *Drawn from Memory*, by Ernest Shepard, best known as the illustrator of the Pooh books; *Period Piece: A Cambridge Childhood*, by Gwen Raverat; and *Three Houses*, by Angela Thirkell, for their almost miraculous recovery of their little pieces of England in the 1890s. *Blue Remembered Hills*, by Rosemary Sutcliff, and Lucy Boston's *Perverse and Foolish* tell of childhoods but take us beyond their authors' youngest years into adulthood, as the first three do not. Those are pure, unadulterated childhood and imbued with a delectable humor.

There are thirteen of Stratton-Porter's books still in print today, and that sense of place she gave me has stayed with me—apparently for life. Not only the sense of her own particular place where she spent absorbed hours photographing wildlife but, as well, the larger one of what is precious to us in a world whose assaulted beauty we are fast losing and will lose forever unless we fight with all the strength and determination we have to keep what is left. *What is left is ten percent of the magnificent northern forests that were still standing twenty years ago.*

There are, wondrously, some children who still read for pleasure, and this knowledge saves a good many of us when we get into an absolute rut of depression. They may be reading slim formula books, but— and it is the only hope we have—there may come a time when they will graduate themselves through their own inexplicable, unpredictable compulsions, or will be helped to graduate by some concerned and knowledgeable librarian, teacher, or parent, to books that will leave an impression never to be forgotten.

Back in the childhood of Pauline Clarke, author of the delectable *Return of the Twelves,* it was *The Wind in the Willows;* for both Lloyd Alexander and Katherine Paterson, *The Scarlet Pimpernel;* for Paterson, *Jane Eyre* and *Wuthering Heights* as well; for Natalie Babbitt, *Alice in Wonderland;* and for Scott O'Dell, *Treasure Island.*

In her story of the Twelves, in which Branwell Brontë's little wooden soldiers search for safety in a world of giants, is Clarke perhaps remembering just that episode among the adventures of the little animals of the Riverbank in *Wind in the Willows* in which Toad struggles to get out of an enormous human-size jail, and the whole atmosphere of vulnerability and smallness in a world in which the huge ones are in control?

Lloyd Alexander, in every tale of daring adventure and courage he has ever written—and most of his tales are distinctly those—is so clearly recalling, even if unconsciously, that quixotic tale of the marvelously daring Pimpernel, a tale one can hardly bear to put down, just as children cannot put down his. I was told of one little girl weeping over the last volume of the Prydain series, *The High King,* weeping away all to herself in a corner of the children's room and muttering something as well. "I hate him—I *hate* him!" the librarian made out, and leaned over to ask, "But *why* do you hate him?" guessing that she meant Alexander. "Because I can't stop—I can't bear it, but I have to go on—" and go on she did, lost to everything else. And possibly she was being changed. What she was reading was hard to bear, the burden and tone of Alexander's story, or perhaps the spirit of it. But the story would stay buried in her mind and imagination for the rest of her life, just as the spirit of Arthur's story lay buried in mine.

And here is a further revelation about Alexander and the enchanted cauldron of childhood. On the back flap of his latest novel, *The Remarkable Journey of Prince Jen,* we are told:

> After Lloyd Alexander began writing this book, he realized that the six valuable gifts he had imagined for Jen might have been actual objects from his own childhood. For a period of time, Mr. Alexander's father worked in the import-export business and often brought home Chinese artifacts. The author, at one point or another, had in his possession a flute, an inkstone and brush, a kite, and "bowls by the dozens." Once, there was even a sword in the house—although he wasn't allowed to touch it.

There they were, and years and years later, Alexander gathered up all these Gifts of Inestimable Value and, as if he were a genie (which he is), turned them into still another marvelous tale, told not only with beauty of language but with great depth and meaning concerning the human condition, as he did in *The First Two Lives of Lukas-Kasha,* a tale of fifteenth-century Persia.

.   .   .

Scott O'Dell's *The King's Fifth,* a tale of Coronado's search for gold in the Seven Cities of Cibola, in what is now New Mexico, is actually another kind of *Treasure Island.* Or it is, at least, of that type of fiction, though far more on the adult level than Stevenson's tale, and very powerfully conceived.

In relation to childhood experiences and their effect upon our later lives, I am struck by a statement in Annie Dillard's *An American Childhood*—a sentence seemingly in direct opposition to so much she tells about herself in this revealing book. She says: "Young children have no sense of wonder."[10] She does not define what she means by "young children," but she is unequivocal. In *That Julia Redfern,* written about my own early childhood long before I read Annie Dillard's memoir, I called the days I spent in Yosemite "Wonders and Mrs. Woollards," the wonders being my stunned responses to the entire phenomena of Yosemite, and the "Mrs. Woollards" the chances I unthinkingly took in pushing out my experiences in pursuit of wonders. The mother of my friend Maisie Woollard was terrified of my experimental nature and refused her daughter's pleadings to be allowed to come with us. If it was not wonder I experienced at this time, what was it?

The majestic double Yosemite falls: Smashing over upper cliff and then lower in thick spurts and gouts of water—this gigantic plunge, as if it weighed tons, to the final demonic fury of upheaval at the bottom—"this white, visible thunder" was a spectacle that satisfied Julia's soul, though she could not, at that age, have explained why it did. Staring out from the overhanging stone of Glacier Point (enclosed now, but not in my childhood, by a rigid wire fence far back from the edge), far above the valley floor across hundreds of miles, range after range of peaks, then down, she couldn't have enough of looking, couldn't expand her powers of absorption anywhere near deeply and powerfully enough to take it all in. Yet, oddly, she remembered so vividly the birds, how they'd lift their wings and flutter, or simply float out into the illimitable deeps of the air, their tiny bodies, seen from above, seeming to enhance the reality of that appalling drop at her feet.

At night—and now Julia and her family are down on the valley floor again—the flames leapt up from Glacier Point, higher and higher, until it became clear that what they had up there was an enormous bonfire, a bonfire as big as a cabin. When a rain of fire began pouring and pouring over like a waterfall of flame—the burning logs being shoved forward so that the great embers were continually dropping from the edge—they kept, as they descended, the shape of a broad, dazzling falls the entire length of that mile-long rush in blackness against the invisible cliff.

Perhaps twenty minutes after sunset, while the sky was taking on the powerful gemlike blue of early dusk, the forest dimness magically changed. The sky lit up again, becoming a glowing gold that turned to pale salmon, and the gray face of Half Dome, standing stupendous, commanding the valley, split clean through the center by ancient glaciers, turned a rich, deep apricot—the afterglow. And in the night Julia gazes up at the mountain sky, which seems a sea of stars, when all at once one of the most brilliant, the most blazing, swoops straight down across the sky! But could, then, the sun fall and there be an eternally frigid, darkened earth? Could the moon fall? "No, not possible," says Mama. Taking up her words into a kind of ritualistic chant, Julia whispers to herself, curled in her sleeping bag,

> The moon goes round the earth
> And the earth goes round the sun
> And they all go round and round and round
> And none of them *can* fall down.

Which led later on to Sir James Jeans and astronomy, and many years later to the Mushroom Planet books.

·   ·   ·

Barry Lopez is a naturalist and the author of *Arctic Dreams: Imagination and Desire in a Northern Landscape.* When he was a child he was walking along a sidewalk with his mother.

> I stopped suddenly, caught by a pattern of sunlight trapped in a spiraling imperfection in a windowpane. A stranger, an elderly woman in a cloth coat and a dark hat, spoke out spontaneously, saying how remarkable it is that children notice these things.
>
> I have never forgotten the texture of this incident. Whenever I recall it I am moved not so much by any sense of my young self but by a sense of responsibility toward children, knowing how acutely I was affected in that moment by that woman's words. The effect, for all I know, has lasted a lifetime.[11]

I am quoting not from *Arctic Dreams* in this instance but from his *Crossing Open Ground,* a chapter called "Children in the Woods." He lives in a rain forest on the banks of a mountain river "in relatively undisturbed country" in western Oregon. And the neighborhood children come to him. He writes:

> The most moving look I ever saw from a child in the woods was on a mud bar by the footprints of a heron. We were on our knees, making handprints beside the footprints. You could feel the creek vibrating in the silt and sand. The sun beat down heavily on our hair. Our shoes were soaking wet. The look said: I did not know until now that I needed someone older to confirm this, the feeling I have of life here. I can now grow older, knowing it need never be lost.[12]

Just this was akin to my own mystical childhood experience of Yosemite. Nor has it ever been lost.

MATTERS
OF CHARACTER

⟨❦⟩

[Henry Fielding's knowledge of his characters] was but as the knowledge of the outside of a clockwork machine, while yours was that of all the finer inner springs and movements of the inside.

SAMUEL RICHARDSON
to Sarah Fielding
Correspondence

*T*hey rise into consciousness, seemingly out of nowhere. And if they are intent upon being brooded over and realized in all their fullness, our characters haunt us, their authors, and will not let us go until we fail them by proving ourselves incapable of doing them justice or by ignoring them or being indifferent to them.* Triumphant, they use us mercilessly so as to be realized in strangely vivid energies that can, on rare occasions, affect the fate of millions, as did those in *Uncle Tom's Cabin* and in Dickens's novels—imagined lives fueled into being by their authors' anger at society's indifference to the misery of the slaves and the poor. Yet those characters exist only in small black marks—untouchable, invisible, and silent. For even plays are silent until they are drawn from their pages onto the stage. Such is the

---

*See the account of Mark Twain ignoring Huckleberry Finn on page 284.

incomprehensible power of these imagined beings, a power often felt long before the writer sits down to conjure them into print.

For instance, there was the French lieutenant's woman. She first appeared to John Fowles about four or five months before he began writing the novel of that name. He says that her image rose in his mind one morning when he was half asleep,* a woman standing at the end of a deserted quay, looking out over the ocean with her back to him. There she was, just briefly; then she was not. Fowles reports that he is a collector of all sorts of oddities in the way of books and prints, so that the image might have come from one of them, and that "mythopoeic stills" so often float up in his mind that he ignored her image as he has ignored others—as the best way of discovering whether or not they can actually succeed in opening a door into a new world.

But the woman standing at the end of the quay with her back to him did not go away—not at once. She could endure being ignored, at least temporarily. Then gradually she stopped appearing, whereupon Fowles—curiously enough for him, unable to forget her—began trying to get her back, trying to analyze why she had this strange power to arouse his questioning when he had never been allowed to see her face. Because she'd seemed both mysterious and romantic, he asked himself why he sensed her to be not of his own time but of several generations back—why she was always turned away from him as if turning her back on him or perhaps on the Victorian age. And why did she invariably show herself to him standing at the end of an ancient quay? (There was one nearby, which he could see from the bottom of his garden.) She seemed to him to be an outcast for some reason, and he wished to protect her; he began to fall in love with her, though her figure did not impart to him from a distance any particular degree of sexuality. Or was it her stance he had fallen in

---

*So, too, was Mary Shelley hovering between waking and sleeping when she beheld what was to be Frankenstein's dread creation.

love with? He had no idea. But there she was, again and again. And
he knew he must write her story.

As an example from children's literature, I think of the donnée of
Russell Hoban's *The Mouse and His Child*. He had watched one toy
of a collection put under the Christmas tree by his friends Harvey and
Marilyn Cushman—that particular toy being the original mouse and
his child, joined by their outstretched hands. He had watched, for
two or three Christmases, the two little tin figures wound up and
made to dance, and—by degrees, he says—they got hold of him
and would not let him go. He began his book about them in 1963,
and it took him four years to feel his way out into space and over "the
birdshit bridge"[1] beyond the Last Visible Dog, winging his way somehow across abyss after abyss, clinging by his nails to sheer cliff faces,
until he arrived at last, by means of "nothing but bird-droppings and
spittle to work with,"[2] at the final page.

But strangely enough, as time went by, it was *not* the mouse and
his child who stayed with Hoban and urged him to write of them in
another volume. Their story was, apparently, finished. But not Manny
Rat's—the villain of *Mouse,* the head of the Mafia of the Rubbish
Dump, across which, and beyond, Manny had relentlessly pursued
the mouse and his child. As a good many of us thought at the end
of the novel: "I don't believe for a moment that Manny Rat has really
turned into a born-again decent rat."[3]

"No," we said to ourselves, "if only Manny could get back his
'teef,' bashed out during the final battle against the Mafia, he'd be
the same old rat."[4] And sure enough, in an essay so Hobanly titled
"Thoughts on a Shirtless Cyclist, Robin Hood, Johann Sebastian Bach,
and One or Two Other Things," in which Hoban reveals that Manny
had apparently no wish to be done with, he also discovered that there
was more to Manny "than simple villainy." "He [Manny] had given
what was in him to what the world called evil, and he had given in
to what the world called good. In both cases the whole thing blew
up in his face."[5] Manny reassesses his own life, a reassessment *not*

coming of its own free will (important to note) but forced on him by a student revolt at the Last Visible Dog, the inn he himself had helped to rehabilitate from a battered dollhouse. And he realizes at this crucial moment that "his apparent reformation and dedication to good may have had no better motivation than his toothlessness."[6] Whereupon, in an exploratory draft of a second volume, Hoban brings Manny to discover a complete lower jawful of white teeth set in plastic gums, and Manny weeps with joy, murmuring to himself, "Teef! New teef!" Being an extremely clever rat with a most active mind, he envisions "with a satisfying chop"[7] (note the viciousness, still there) the refurbishing of his own useless gums. But how is he to refurbish them? How but by waylaying the Reverend Immenso Joy, whom he sets upon, extracting the poor reverend's teeth with a rock for an anaesthetic. Same old Manny. And how very ironic that it is to a church that Manny now repairs to get on with the work that will turn him into a renewed Manny-style life force—the last place on earth one would think of in connection with such a rat as Manny.

Here, in this place, it is revealed to Hoban that Manny is indeed not a simple villain. For choir practice is going on; there is the scent of coffee and freshly baked brownies, which arouses a sense of coziness in him (physical response); the age and beauty of the building call to him (astonishingly, an aesthetic response). He creeps in through a rat hole, and what now follows is a hymn of praise to organ music, Hoban's personal hymn, flowing forth in all those sentences that fill the next four and a half pages of rather small type, describing minutely the quality of the music. I am tempted to quote at length but will confine myself to the last two sentences before we return to Manny:

He knew then, as the fugue went surging to its end, that he had heard a monstrous and indifferent violence speak its tetragrammaton forbidden; had heard it name with infinite and orderly design the chaos at its core. As the music had gone beyond music, so the thing revealed within it had gone beyond good and beyond evil: it was what it was. And Manny Rat, perceiving that, sank down in a faint.[8]

What is this? Are we back to "the age and beauty of the building called to him"? Or is it that he has been given a vision of the universe that he cannot deal with? But the moment is gone. He returns to consciousness: "He opened his mouth, closed it with a vicious chop, and laughed with pleasure."[9] He gets up and continues his explorations, comes upon the organ, scrabbles up to the bench, from there up onto the keys, and now advances (through the final page and a half of Hoban's essay) to actually bring forth "three high, descending, silvery notes"[10] that sounded sweetly. Having placed the sound and realizing that walking on the "GREAT teeth" (as he called these particular keys) had called up that silvery voice, he explored further, reading "*Swell to Great 16; Swell to Great 8; Swell to Great 4*. What was this if not the printed voice of fate? Swell to great! . . . With a flourish he pushed down all three, expecting thunder and lightning, and found the eight-voiced polyphony as he stepped down the scale very small beer indeed."[11]

How characteristic of Hoban to end this adventure with those four denigrating words coming from Manny's conscious self. How ominously they fit into the picture of a rat reexpanded with enormously refreshed ego—that terrible ego of old.

It would seem, then, that Hoban's new material is revealing to him one of two things. Either he has no farther to go with Manny or he has not reached that particular state of aesthetic awareness in which he can deal with two Mannys—the unconscious one so assaulted by the organ's voice of perception that it could cause him to faint, and the conscious Manny who could call the eight-voiced polyphony "very small beer indeed." What to do with this complex rat, who does not realize his own complexity and—not given to lengthy indulgence in self-knowledge—would never think about it? What possibilities beckon here!

But what Hoban seemed really to want to write about was organ

music. And for that story he will have to wait for other beings to
clutch at him as did the mouse and his child, gentle yet powerful
ones who could bring such a layered character as Manny into their
story. Possibly now, after *Riddley Walker* and *Pilgermann* for adults,
both of which have had a great succès d'estime, he will no longer be
writing for children. For Hoban was writing his essay somewhere in
the early 1970s, and nothing has come of the complex Manny that
we, the public, know of in the beginning of the 1990s.

I I

From an early age I have been haunted by book people—first as a
reader, then as a writer—and I remember so clearly from childhood
the intensity of my relationships with the animals and humans in the
stories I loved best. I suffered and rejoiced with them as if they were
alive—as they were to me, as they are to most reading children—so
that I felt them to be my friends. And this friendship did not stop
when I had come to the last page. There were times when I couldn't
bear to come to the end (I don't know how many times I read the
King Arthur stories and Kipling's tales and Andersen's fairy tales) and
could do nothing but begin all over again. Or, perhaps, in bed at
night with the light out, go on with the story as I couldn't help
feeling it must, because of the writer's craft or, in the case of Andersen
and Kipling, artistry, and, in the case of Arthur, the force of legend.

But of course, as I read, I never once thought of craft or artistry
or legend. Though I myself was a writing child with a view to being
published, I knew nothing of the implications of the word *literature*
(we were not, in those days, talked to in the fifth and sixth grades
about style and plot and characterization) but only how intensely the
people and animals in books could affect me. And if I didn't consciously
think of this knowing, at least I could never do without a book by
my bed.

Ever since childhood, when the writing years began, I have gone
through my days experiencing at least three worlds simultaneously.

There is the world outside my head, in which I interact with other human beings and with animals and plants, trees in particular. There is the world of the receiving mind and imagination with regard to the books I read, in which I live with created characters, not to speak of writers and artists and scientists in their biographies and autobiographies, their letters and essays. And there is the world of the creative mind and imagination in which my own characters continually move and have their being, and which largely takes over during the writing of a new book. Meanwhile, all these worlds are intricately interweaving and influencing one another, richly and diversely.

As a greedily consuming child caught up in story, I was never aware, even though I was a writing child, of just *how* the author's skill had cast its spell over me through some mysterious ability to convey to my senses and imagination, visually and viscerally, another's places, beings, moods, times. What I was reading took on such sharp reality that I could suffer actual physical pain over the wickedness of Mordred scheming Arthur's downfall and death, and immitigable sadness over acts of betrayal by those I had thought incapable of them. Lancelot and Guinevere's disloyalty to Arthur was my first experience, in reading, of sexual betrayal—in this case by two I had admired just below Arthur, especially—oh, especially—Lancelot. And I was moved to a storm of tears over Arthur's death.

Certainly I never thought about structure, that unnoticed yet indispensable, most powerful web that holds a work together in such a way that the child, if the work is a memorable one, is compelled to believe utterly. Surely this tragedy of Arthur had all happened at some time, somewhere. It *had* to have happened.* And so the child reads the book all over again, even though there is sadness in it, and cruelty and tragedy, and tears are shed, and even the ending is known.

---

*And this wasn't simply a childish response: Witness all the books that have been published about Arthur. When the Los Angeles Public Library still had a huge central card catalog, the cards having to do with Jesus Christ and Arthur were the dirtiest of all. Yet as a human being, Arthur is even more elusive in the historical records than Shakespeare, for instance.

Of all the elements that work subtly on one another to make a novel, characterization is, for me, of supreme importance—so long as there is story, so long as feeling suffuses the whole, and so long as a strong sense of place gives one's characters a richly convincing surround in which to exist. It is true that Eudora Welty believes that feeling "carries the crown" among all the other elements—character, plot, and symbolic meaning—while place stands in the shade. But what does one remember in Welty's stories and novels? Her characters! And it is those other elements that support and contribute and make possible the strength of her characters. Without a deep and sure and loving sense of place, I myself have no novel, for place *evokes* characters. It may not be so with every writer, but characters, as far as I have experienced, create story. They make it happen, bring it alive. Otherwise, you have nothing but plot.

No one had a more powerful sense of place than Beatrix Potter. England's Lake District (as well as the countryside of Scotland and Wales) seemed to release her completely from her stultified London life. Whereupon, as she grew older, she developed such a fiercely passionate love for the Lake District, those rolling hills with their long views holding the lakes and villages in their hollows, that they compelled her little books into being. This is especially true of the village of Sawrey, where she bought her first farm, and is vividly apparent in every book she ever created, both in its art and in its writing, and shows how each character grew specifically out of place.* Do give yourself the pleasure of discovering this in *A History of the Writings of Beatrix Potter,* by Leslie Linder, who also translated her minutely code-written diary in *The Journal of Beatrix Potter: From 1881 to 1897;* in *The Art of Beatrix Potter,* with an appreciation by Anne Carroll Moore, showing abundantly both the countryside and the interiors of cottages and old farmhouses; and in *Beatrix Potter's Letters,* selected by Judy Taylor, all published magnificently by Warne; and

---

*For a discussion of the sense of place, see *The Green and Burning Tree,* pages 162–202.

in *The Tale of Beatrix Potter,* by Margaret Lane, also an excellent production by Warne. (And I hope you saw the moving and deeply satisfying BBC production *The Tale of Beatrix Potter,* filmed in both London and the Lake District, quite faithful to her life and in no way fancied up or falsified to suit mass audience requirements.)

At a gathering where they were being asked questions, one of which concerned the importance of place in the creation of a novel, both Lloyd Alexander and Virginia Hamilton confessed that place meant everything. We think of Silver Springs, Ohio, as Hamilton's place (with the exception of New York as the catalyst of *The Planet of Junior Brown*), and Wales as the country that opened up the Prydain series to Alexander, bringing back to him the whole world of Arthur. And yet, for some novelists—even extremely successful ones like Natalie Babbitt—place is not the seedbed that brings forth characters who move story. On the contrary, Babbitt said that ideas come first to her and that she then thinks up the place and the characters who will make a story of the idea she wishes to use.

In my exploration of the novels *The Cartoonist* and *Lucie Babbidge's House,* it appears that the idea of the novel was paramount—that it came first—as we do not get so much a sense of place as the strength of the overriding idea that lies at the center of both novels. We might very well have thought that a garbage dump had put Russell Hoban in mind of *The Mouse and His Child,* so vivid is his evocation of it and its inhabitants. But, as we have discovered, its donnée was something entirely different.

Though the quality of novels for both adults and children depends on depth of characterization, it is one of the elements in which we very often notice a difference in technique between the two. In adult fiction, there can be long authorial explanations of character, as in the work of Anita Brookner, Beryl Bainbridge, Shirley Hazzard, and in Saul Bellow's later works—long, long expositions of the past that bring out family background and show how the protagonist became what he or she apparently is in the present. We are told about, and about, and about—page after page of solid type with only an occasional break. Such longueurs result either in intolerable boredom for the reader or, if done acutely and provocatively, as Gabriel García Márquez does in his *Love in the Time of Cholera,* in richness of understanding and clarity of insight and motivation. But children will not—certainly they cannot—endure these lengthy perambulations. However, in *Sweet Whispers, Brother Rush,* in *Willie Bea and the Time the Martians Landed,* in her Dustland series, and in *Arilla Sun Down,* Virginia Hamilton writes at some length about families and their pasts. I do not mean that rules should be laid down. As in the creation of any art, it is all in the way it is done, and family, very clearly, means a great deal to Hamilton.

In contrast to fiction for adults, in children's fiction, generally speaking, characterization is brought out chiefly through what the characters say and do and think, and through other people's reactions to them. The essence of character is allowed to rise like an almost unnoticed mist from an accumulation of their words, thoughts, and acts in such a way as to leave a clear, final impression. The author's point-of-view explanations are either omitted entirely, even in first-person tellings, or are kept to a few touches—a method that can, in inept hands, result in thinness and shadowy figures, but, in the hands of a gifted writer, in vividness, immediacy, and great economy of effect.

In the next three sections I shall explore, first, characterizations attained through this economy of effect, in which dialogue plays a key part; second, the necessary suspension of disbelief attained wholly through characterization; and third, characterizations of parents that reveal most poignantly the essence of the children resonating against and from them.

I I I

In Betsy Byars's *The Cartoonist,* dialogue and the protagonist's own thoughts create our understanding of character. The portrayal of the mother in this brief novel comes to mind as a fine instance of what I mean by "essence allowed to rise like a mist" (though in her case what rises is more like the acrid smoke from a bonfire), and never from her thought, sometimes from her feelings, but almost entirely through her words and acts, with a bare minimum of authorial comment. As the novel opens, Alfie, the youngest child, is alone in his attic retreat; his mother and grandfather are watching television in the living room; Alma, his older sister, is apparently wandering in and out; and Bubba, his older brother, lives elsewhere. The following exchange begins the first chapter:

"Alfie?"

"What?"

"You studying?"

"Yes," he lied.

"Well, why don't you come down and study in front of the television? It'll take your mind off what you're doing," his mother called.

He didn't answer. He bent over the sheet of paper on his table. He was intent.

"Did you hear me, Alfie?"

"I heard," he called without glancing up.

"Well, come on down." She turned and spoke to Alma. "Who's that announcer that says that on TV? It's some game show. He says, 'Come on downnnn,' and the people come running down the aisles to guess the prices."

"I don't know, Mom. I don't watch that junk," Alma said.

Here we are given Alfie at work on his cartoon, and we feel his deep pleasure and excitement, his burgeoning satisfaction.

"Alfie!" his mother called loudly. Alfie knew that she was at the foot of the ladder now. She rattled it as if she were trying to shake him down. "I'm coming up there and pull you down by the ear if you don't come down this minute." . . . Once his sister, Alma, had started up the ladder, but he had said, "No, I don't want anybody up there."

She'd paused on the ladder. "Why not?"

"Because . . ." He had hesitated, trying to find words to express his meaning. "Because," he said finally, "I want it to be mine."

Later, as his mother keeps at him:

"I don't know what you do up there . . . it's not healthy— no windows, no air."

"I like it just the way it is," Alfie said quickly.

"Well, you ought to be more like Bubba. . . . When he was your age he was outside every day, passing a football, dribbling a basketball—"

"Stealing a baseball," Alma added.

His mother ignored Alma. "You're never going to be on a team."

"That's true," he said.

"But, Alfie, everybody wants to be on a team!"

Thus, out of the opening dialogue, we get a clear picture of this mother, a kind of couch potato (sloppy joes are her most frequent dinner offering), insensitive, stubbornly persistent, fatuous about Bubba (to whose propensities the ironic Alma gives us a quick hint). But Alma's remarks are lost on her mother, who is bent, for some pressing reason, on dislodging Alfie from his refuge. (The reason, we learn later, has to do with Bubba's having lost his job—and what a perfect name Byars has given him, the eternal juvenile.) Here Alfie tries, day after day, to pursue his one joy in this tiny, ramshackle house in which the family of mother, grandfather, sister Alma, and he himself live in all-too-close proximity, with the television booming.

This is the kernel of the story, all compact in the opening pages, from which we suspect that Alfie will prove helpless in the face of his mother's rude, powerful intent. For she does not understand for a moment Alfie's stony grief when he finally learns what is in her mind. So he *draws* up there! She is not interested, does not even look at his drawings, and when she looks at one, has no idea how to hold it. The book is full of sardonic moments: Bubba with his wretched practical jokes, his tangles with the law, which his mother laughs at till the tears roll down her face; Bubba, her ideal of the red-blooded, eternally sports-minded boy, never someone eternally stuffed up, off by himself, *drawing!*

It is a mostly rueful, sometimes cruel comedy, with everyone going on about what interests no one else. And such a woman as this mother has, by her very nature, no way of comprehending a situation out of which arises everything else that drives her to distraction. She, who is lonely, cannot imagine wanting to be alone, wanting to be private, cannot understand that what interests her does not necessarily interest everyone else, that what she wants so desperately—the return of Bubba—is looked on with horror by the others in the little house. Anything crude and unthinking is possible to her (such as making fun of Alfie's pigeon toes and calling other people's attention to them), because she is apparently incapable of ever becoming aware of her own crudity and thoughtlessness. Perhaps we must say of her that she is unwitting in her villainy, but villainy it is to make fun of a child, to completely ignore that child's central drive.

And yet, even though Alfie must, of course, come down eventually, there is something one senses about him, given us in just those words in the beginning. He lies for his art. Then he doesn't answer at all because he is so intent, bent over his paper, so lost to that voice. Then he tosses a bone—yes, he heard. Then he tells the precise truth: He likes "his" attic the way it is; it could be freezingly cold, stifling, airless, muggy, moldy—no matter. He'd never notice. Then again he tells the truth without even thinking, because he knows his own nature: That's right, he will never be on a team. He will never pass a football, never dribble a basketball. He will never, never be like Bubba, whom he cannot endure. He will simply, even forced by his mother to join the team of the family, manage somehow: over in a corner, or in the bathroom, at school during lunch, or off by himself somewhere after school, if he can't have his attic. One feels very strongly that, way down deep, Alfie is as stubborn as his mother, though he himself may not realize it. The seed, from some combination of genes, has been planted. And he has his vision.

I have chosen Sylvia Cassedy's *Lucie Babbidge's House* as a companion to *The Cartoonist* because it is an excellent example of a novel in which our understanding of the protagonist (wholly through dialogue, through her letters, and through her memories) unfolds slowly. This is in great contrast to our understanding of Alfie, whose essence we grasp almost immediately within the first chapter, though we do not really understand more about him as we read to the end. We expect that he will not be able to stand up against his mother, but we do understand throughout the tough single-mindedness that is there.

As for Lucie, we are frustrated in our understanding of her and of the story, which appears to us as a mystery, and may feel that a trick has been played on us when we read into the second chapter. Or we are intrigued by the very unusual approach Cassedy has taken in opening out her story and will understand, according to our own idiosyncratic light (as I have found at conferences) what the whole thing is about, despite mystery and ambiguity. Children will either be intrigued by the unfolding, caught up by the difficulties (some of them intense) that Lucie has to undergo in the face of cool teacher and inimical classmates, ignoring puzzlements for story as they would in reading any mystery, or they will simply reject and cease to read.

No other novel that I have discussed at conferences has aroused so much hard thought except *I Am the Cheese*. It is all very well to discuss a novel on which most agree. But try one like *Lucie Babbidge's House* on a group of readers; in all likelihood contending opinions will abound in the effort to interweave responses to character delineation *and* the unfolding of story.

In many ways Alfie and Lucie Babbidge are a good deal alike. Both are hounded by those more powerful than themselves, Alfie by his mother, Lucie by her teacher and classmates. Both seem powerless (an expression of personality) and yet both are stubborn (a fact of character), pursuing their visions in hiding, sotto voce, because they must—the only way of realizing any sense of self. The vision is the only refuge, from the constant devastation of his mother's voice in Alfie's case, and from the constant devastation of her teacher's cold matter-of-factness or merciless put-downs and the never-ending ridicule of her classmates in Lucie's. Sometimes we get impatient with Lucie, who seems to invite mistreatment, as doormat people so often do. Come back at them! we want to urge the pale, quiet, seemingly helpless child. But she is incapable. And her story is a mosaic in which small groups of stones here and there, or even a single stone, will reveal one more tiny, important clue. So intricate is it all that one wonders how any young reader is going to make sense of the interweavings of such a puzzling tale. Or is this, perhaps, not important?

Consider that there are at least five families to keep track of: the "family" of girls in the school; the family of dolls in Lucie's dollhouse (which, of course, is not hers); Delia Hornsby Booth's family; the Pendleton family; and Lucie's own, with whom we become acquainted through the flashbacks, emerging randomly, during class or when the "Mumma" of the dollhouse family brings Lucie's mother's words to her mind.

As to characterization, Lucie is the only one who grows on us gradually, in depth, while the dolls, given life and simple personalities within her imagination, are far more individual than her classmates. These are scarcely individuals at all, except for a difference in names: Rose, Beth, Clare, Jane, Daisy, Anne. Their dialogue is as undifferentiated as their actions. Often there is no indication as to who is speaking, particularly in times of intense action, as in the assault on the dollhouse, because, apparently, *it doesn't matter*. The girls' part in the novel is nothing more than that of a swarm of stinging bees. They are silly and spiteful and tiresome, their cruelty inevitable, predictable, of a dreadful sameness, so that the reader (at any rate, this one) gets weary of them. Oh, for two or three, at least, who, each according to her nature, would react differently to Lucie from the way the others do! But they have no individual natures. (In *The Lord of the Flies,* there is mass cruelty toward one child, but within that mass there are individuals.)

As for Miss Pimm, she is the prototype of the cold, insensitive teacher, who makes no least effort through kindness to understand Lucie, to get to the root of her strange unresponsiveness, her complete defenselessness.

The central puzzle that teases more than any of the others (and there are other minor practical ones having to do with Lucie's various unexplained absences, questioned only once) concerns the dark green queen stamp that comes on the first letter to Lucie from Delia Hornsby in England—one of the answers resulting from a letter-writing-to-famous-personages campaign set by Miss Pimm. And we are puzzled by subsequent letters from Delia to Lucie because Lucie never writes another to her personage. Next we realize that it is only because of the use of further green stamps (*presumably* further) that the letters to Lucie could be thought genuine, could be thought to be coming from England, and could be delivered to Lucie by an ostensibly convinced Miss Pimm. That is, should we happen to suspect that Lucie is writing all of these letters to herself.*

Finally we are ourselves convinced that these subsequent letters had to be written by Lucie. First, because of the parallels of disasters and triumphs within the two families, Delia's supposedly real one and Lucie's dollhouse family. Second, because of precisely the same kind of straight-faced humor arising out of a play with the literal meanings of words that come from both Phillip and Emmett, the five- and six-

---

*So I believe. But a friend disagrees (and so may others), pointing out that the writer of certain letters appears to be ambiguous and *could* be Delia. But this randomness would seem inelegant within the structure of the novel, serving no purpose that I can see.

year-old boys of the families, one for each, and far too clever a play for that age. But if it is Lucie uttering these clever remarks, then we understand, and they reveal what depths of wryness and deftness with words lie hidden behind her pale, expressionless face and voice. In fact, the whole extent and richness of Lucie's imagination is uncovered entirely through the dollhouse lives played out in the letters, while on the surface: "I didn't read it, Miss Pimm," and "I can't find it, Miss Pimm," "I don't know, Miss Pimm," and "I don't remember, Miss Pimm." She erects, on the surface, the impregnable wall—the Alfie-like stubborn protection of what is private where there is no privacy or understanding or sympathy elsewhere.

But why, if I am right, would the fact escape the merciless Miss Pimm that these letters, supposedly from England, have obviously not been processed there? Certainly not by any post office, with that first stamp cut from the original genuine letter from Delia and pasted grubbily (we can only conclude) onto succeeding letters. Something is wrong, and to add to the puzzlement, we are told that Lucie uses the stamp as a portrait on the dollhouse wall, though it could be removed and returned.

But there has got to be an explanation for what would otherwise seem a failure of logic on the author's part—that Miss Pimm apparently notices nothing amiss when she delivers what are supposed to be Delia's letters to Lucie. That explanation lies in a brief paragraph at the end of Delia's next-to-last letter, in which the writer reveals that she knows her letters are being opened and gives her naked opinion of the opener, the first time Lucie has ever come out frankly against her tormentor. That paragraph reveals as well the depths of hypocrisy in a person who has taken this method of literally slitting (or perhaps, rather, steaming) her way into the thoughts of the hitherto unassailable Lucie. For the betrayer had made it a basic command to the girls: We do *not* read other people's letters and diaries. But Miss Pimm had wanted to keep them coming, and how she must have smiled over the grubbily pasted-on stamp.

On top of the dreadful poignancy of Lucie's farewell to the dollhouse (now that it has been discovered and raped of its dolls, even though she has found and restored them and the dollhouse contents to their places), it could be a disappointment that Lucie's words to Miss Pimm at the end of the book do not measure up to the response one hopes for, as she *is* at last making a reply. For the reader is fully aware by now of her astonishing resources and of the depths of despair, rebellion, and bitter resentment she has experienced. The discovery and invasion of the dollhouse—her one secret source of strength and endurance—has forced on her a spiritual turning point that brings her to acknowledge that the dollhouse must be given up. Therefore we might have expected something more full of cutting meaning than the simple cleverness in her reply to Miss Pimm's everlasting "Pick up your head!"

Yes, but that reply is laden in just its few words with more implications than are apparent on the surface: "How can I, when it never fell off in the first place?" Meaning that no matter how stupid and ignorant, how forgetful and incapable of any mental effort I've made you and these despising girls think me—because I've seen you for what you are, cold, without any shred of kindness or consideration—my brain and imagination have never stopped working. My head has always been on my shoulders, and you know it has, because you've been opening my letters.

Also, Lucie's reply may well indicate that she is going to begin to make use at last—in future confrontations with Miss Pimm and her classmates—of that quick way with words she had given Emmett and Phillip, and some of the imagination she had put into her letters from Delia. It would be the only way to make bearable the years left her at Norwood Hall.

What troubles me in discussions about this curious and challenging novel is that the mystery of the letters and how the structure seems to trick the reader attract the most attention. It is the extreme complexity of structure, like that of *I Am the Cheese*, that concentrates discussion, rather than how the various parts of the novel serve to make possible our gradual understanding of Lucie. To me, however, solving a mystery seems of secondary importance, or less than that, in comparison with the appreciation of the interesting and subtle interplay between the participants in a novel, and how this interplay deeply and convincingly creates character—or doesn't. In the end, we do get a strong feeling of Lucie—a feeling that has caused many readers sharp disappointment. After all the puzzling detail, building to what they could not imagine, that Lucie should come forth with what to them is a distinct understatement, is a letdown from one of whom they'd expected so much more. But it is my belief that Lucie's difficulties have only made her stronger, as her final remark reveals to us.

IV

The following two novels strike me as perfect examples of the way superb characterization attains the reader's suspension of disbelief.

I have already spoken of the importance of place to so many novelists, and Lucy Boston's love of her homeplace, the Manor, was intense. It was not only quite natural for her to relate her passionate indignation over the caging of wild animals in zoos to her identification with Guy, the gorilla in its cage at the London Zoo, but to bring that gorilla somehow into her own garden at Green Knowe at a time when Ping, the Chinese boy introduced in *The River at Green Knowe,* is staying there. In A *Stranger at Green Knowe,* she calls the gorilla Hanno, a stranger so awe-inspiring and so magnificent in his selfhood that in Lucy Boston's hands, he makes the book tower.* It towers, this splendid book, because of its extraordinary communication of the essence of a wild animal leading a threatened life in three homes. The first life is led in the Congo, where it has been captured as a baby by poachers. The last is lived at Green Knowe. In between is a deadly, soul-killing life at the London Zoo, where it is gaped at by humans

---

*It was the Carnegie Medal winner for 1961. And indeed, in his essay "The Darkening of the Green," Peter Hollindale in the British magazine *Signal* (January 1990, pages 10–15) says of *Stranger* that it "may be the greatest of all modern children's books. . . . I am quite certain . . . that in retrospect it will prove the most important."

who seem to the reader far less worthy of respect than Hanno. It towers, above all, because of its conception of the life and death of Hanno the gorilla as something akin to Greek tragedy—a conception inevitably related to the nature and personality of Hanno himself.

In *Stranger* we grow to love Hanno and to ache for him as does Ping the Chinese boy, who cares for him as best he can during the brief, final period in which the escaped animal finds a temporary home in the bamboo thickets at Green Knowe. And because we *do* grow to love him and ache for him, we realize that we will want his death more than we will want his life, because life for him, from now on —after the end of the book, if life were granted him, but not freedom—could mean only the misery of a brutally clamped-down spirit. And what can be more Greek than giving insight, step by step, that shows us how, in one particular instance, for one particular being, death is to be preferred above life, because life could be nothing but a death-in-life—pointless, unendurable, and soul-destroying.

Here is Hanno in his cage at the London Zoo, as Lucy Boston herself had once seen Guy:

As if Ping had really been reading his thoughts, Hanno sprang into action again, hurling himself shoulder first against that door, four hundred and twenty pounds of weight behind each blow, then around his cage on all fours like a whirlwind again and again, as if he were tightening a coil, till at last he stood erect in the center. Reaching to his full height, his arms above his head with clasped hands tense and superb, he began slowly circling round in a tragic dance. Ping's heart missed a breath. Never had he seen any gesture so proud and so despairing. It was like Samson praying for strength to pull the place down.

The poet James Dickey in his book *Self-Interviews* has noted that in conceiving his poems he is caught up most wholly by imagining the impossible and then bringing it into being. He says: "If you want to write about an owl who can teach a little blind boy in the woods to see, then you try to imagine how it would be. You know it's not ever going to happen that way. You know it's impossible. But it's like Tertullian's proof of God: I believe *because* it's impossible. Then you enter into the experience you had imagined and try to realize it. And that entering into and committing-to is what makes writing poetry so damned exciting."[12]

For Lucy Boston—or any great teller of tales—change the word *poetry* to *story* and you have what she has done here. She has entered into the impossible—conceived that a small boy could become the friend of an escaped gorilla—and become so wholly committed to her conception that we believe. And the extent to which she has made us feel the innate quality of Hanno—something we get always through the tenderness and sensitivity of the child Ping—is almost incredible. Here he is gazing up at Hanno at the zoo:

"Hanno," said Ping in his gentlest voice, for Ping had, as it were, fallen in love. The world contained something so wonderful to him that everything was altered. It was not only that Hanno existed, a creature with the strength of a bull, the agility of a spider, the pounce of a lion, and the dignity and grief of a man—too much to take in, all the animal creation in one—but that somewhere there was a country of such size, power, and mystery that gorillas were a sample of what it produced in secret, where everything else would be on the same scale.

Lucy Boston has said that almost all her heroes are dispossessed and looking for what they have lost. This both Hanno and Ping are, Hanno having been captured as a baby in the Congo jungle and Ping having been for some time an orphan refugee in a hostel and now temporarily visiting Mrs. Oldknow in her ancient home. And perhaps here is the profound tie between Hanno and Ping—their being dispossessed, their being strangers in a strange land, with no homes to call their own. Perhaps because of this, Hanno senses and responds to something in Ping that Ping understands and responds to in him: "He had," Lucy

Boston says of Ping, "in his single-minded innocence, no feeling of danger." And so he can bring food to Hanno in the bamboo thicket, come to know his bonfire smell as if he were one of Hanno's little sons, be cuffed by him and quietly watched and accepted so that he can look up with passionate intensity into the great face and study its lordliness, hear Hanno's wicked chuckle, and see how he looked "a very important gentleman taking a picnic in a quiet spot, having shaken off even his secretary," superbly well dressed "with black bearskin sleeves, silver-gray shirt, and opossum trousers, worn with style and pride as if he were fully conscious that he was turned out to strike the fear of God into lesser beings."

Lucy Boston has said of her conviction about this book:

The subject to me was a big one. It had to contain the whole force of my belief that all life, not merely human, must have respect, that a man-centered conception of it was false and crippling, that these other lives are the great riches of ours. In particular I wanted to make clear my immense admiration for this creature so vulgarly shuddered at, and that there was no cosy answer to the wickedness that had been done to him. [13]

There is suspense and often a beautiful, quiet humor in *A Stranger at Green Knowe,* so that I hope the fact of Hanno's death at the end of the book will not discourage anyone from reading his story to children. It has never harmed a child to be moved to tears, should any be so moved, especially if emotion arises not from sentimentality—from the weak, the exaggerated, the false or mawkish—but from identification with truth. This experience may be painful, but at the same time the child will be lifted by this story of the last days of Hanno the gorilla in a home that could not be his for long.

When we consider Margaret Mahy's *Memory* and the nature of Jonny Dart, its protagonist, the whole conception seems extraordinary, especially in view of the almost blind self-centeredness of the average teenager and such yahoos as those in Anthony Burgess's *The Clockwork Orange*. There is his humanity, his stubborn concern, which he tries to escape from time and again but cannot. And this concern hasn't to do with some attractive young girl or stray animal but with a dirty, richly odorous old woman, Sophie West, wandering about in her private world of senility. How can we possibly be brought to believe imaginatively in the reality of Jonny Dart?

Mahy tells us that Sophie West has Alzheimer's. Sophie seems to be going around in a not-at-all-unhappy state of senility, an old widow living alone—yet not at all lonely, except very occasionally when she thinks of the lover she once had—on the upper floor of her own house (for which she is being charged rent by one of the young neighborhood toughs).

How did you meet? we so often ask of those who have happened to come together and respond to one another in a way that will change their lives forever: lovers, husbands, wives, friends who stay close friends for fifty years. It is most mysterious, this momentous crossing of paths. Chance or fate? And such mystical questions as this are apt to haunt Jonny, because of meeting Sophie and because of Bonny Benedicta, his sister's friend, who had always seemed to him to carry around with her an aura of magic, like an almost visible benediction. Certainly Sophie's and Jonny's lives are changed forever by the fact that Jonny gets drunk, hits a policeman, is put in jail, gets bailed out and then bawled out by his father, so that going home is impossible, and finds Sophie wandering the empty midnight streets as he is.

"Are you the one?" Sophie asks him, a question that ends the book as well as opens it. "Her voice was old but distinct, crisp, cultured. . . . 'Are you the one?' she asks again." Jonny doesn't know. But he could go with her, he thinks, just to the corner, sick as he feels, and so walks after her like an obedient dog, "filled with a credulous enchantment." Why "a credulous enchantment"? (*Enchantment* is a key word in the book, having also to do with an interleaving layer of story, which I shall not explore, because I am concentrating on the relationship of Sophie and Jonny.) Because of her voice, perhaps, her elegant voice, or her smile, or because she so sweetly and trustingly takes it for granted that he will want to come with her, being her Alva, her lover of long ago. And when she finally tells him her name, "I'm the angel of wisdom," she says. "Remember the good old days?" She smiles as if she knows they were already old friends and, pushing the empty cart, leads him out of the parking lot and into a one-way street, which turns out to be just that for Jonny. He can never ignore this experience, never go back on it.

Thus the first step in the sometimes willing, sometimes unwilling capture by the amazing Sophie of Jonny Dart, one-time tap dancer. When he was a child of nine or ten, Jonny appeared on TV with his sister, Janine, to dance with great skill as a come-on to engage the emotions of buyers of Chicken-bits cat food. For this, Jonny was loathed by one Nev Fowler (a name that seems here to have a double connotation— the foul fowler going after the chicken-bits boy), who had, in their childhood days, threatened to cut Jonny's throat on some dark corner because of his lighter-than-air cavortings in the public eye.

Unable to go home but also unable to reconcile himself with himself, Jonny is seemingly rescued just in time at this crossroads of a life he has no idea what to do with. And surely Fate (it seems now to deserve a capital letter) has a finger in Jonny's curious capture. For Fate *has* given a certain sign, one we might not think of on first reading, though it is large in reality: a tap dancer led to Tap House, with its enormous old-fashioned water tap, painted purple, keeping watch on the balcony of Sophie's house and beckoning somehow to Jonny, "Come!"

On a good many mornings Sophie steals milk bottles and sometimes the mail from her next-door neighbor, so the neighbor is forced to lock her mailbox. Whereupon Sophie chops it open with her little hatchet. She keeps a great wad of bills tucked under the kitchen sink but doesn't recall the money is there; can never remember that her key is on an old gray string around her neck; puts a small block of cheese in the soap dish in the bathroom but no toilet paper by the toilet; puts soap in the cheese dish in the fridge; and has stowed a banana skin, a grubby hairbrush, the toilet paper, dried cat food, and two or three pencils in the pigeonholes of her desk. Then there are the cats—and the *smell*. As Jonny mounts the hall stairs, after picturing himself disappearing into this house forever and someone in the distant future finding him "hanging from one of the coathooks, dried out, leathery, but still recognizable," he discovers that

> The smell was indescribable. It drove everything else out of his head. His nose tried to close itself in outrage and he began to breathe through his mouth, taking in as little air as possible and getting rid of it as quickly as possible. . . .
> "For God's sake, what *am* I doing *here?* How did I get *into* this? How do I get *out?*"

And in the living room as well, scattered with cats, "There was a revolting smell, coarse, with a chemical edge, suggesting that rubber had been burned there recently, along with contributions from the cats. 'Sophie,' he said, gagging slightly, 'where's the toilet? I need it quickly.'"

He reaches it on the very edge of the fatal instant, and it is these scenes, usually considered private, that Mahy is so superb in depicting for us—not impressionistically, delicately, now you get glimpses, now you don't. Not at all; you get the whole thing. At one unforgettable point Jonny discovers Soph (as he often now calls her) down on all fours, "naked except for her pot hat and unravelling sweater," trying in a fury of frustration to get the plug of a toaster cord into the wall socket, the cord trailing out behind her like a tail. "One mere glance at Sophie's bare bottom and he was outraged. I don't have to put up with this, he thought angrily, as if Sophie had played a malicious trick on him." And later:

"Oh, God, Sophie, put something on!" begged Jonny. "Be one of nature's ladies. You'll freeze."

The closeness of her old skin and bone filled him with a repulsion that was not far from being fear, and which felt like an instinct, too natural to be denied, although he was ashamed of feeling it. Besides, even in her unravelling sweater and pot hat, Sophie still managed to be genteel.

It then occurs to Jonny that this moment could be taken advantage of: *She must have a bath*. She sure as hell *needs* one! And he sweeps her into the bathroom, turns on the tap, then realizes she needs the assistance that only he can give. He giggles, holds out his hand. "Here, Missus, one, two, three!" and in a second or two she is squatting among the bubbles of the green bubble bath he's poured in. After whipping off her sweater and pot hat: " 'Wash all over,' he told her, like a stern father. 'Behind your ears! Everywhere!' Then he left her to it."

But after this he has to help her dress, because she's got her knickers in a twist and must put her hand on his shoulder so that he can hold her pants for her. " 'Look, Sophie, I'm warning you,' Jonny said. 'Be careful, because after this you're on your own. You don't want me to dress you, do you? Not with me taking after Uncle Brian and all that.' 'Oh, no,' she said in a shocked voice, but then spoiled it by giving a naughty chuckle as he left the room." And then:

"What have I come down to?" Jonny asked himself as he peeled an orange and cut it into quarters for her. Over the past year and a half he had developed the reputation, among his parents' friends, for being bad, mad, and dangerous to know, and though he was often surprised when people acted as if they believed it, he was flattered too. He did not want to turn into the sort of man who worried over wet mattresses, baths, and breakfasts; he hated the heavy, harassed feeling that possessed him. Sophie's house felt like a trap closing around him. . . . "I've just got to get out of here," he thought again. "To hell with it!" "But she's a *sign*," said another part of his mind. "You have to go with the signs."

Ah, you might say, it is all (once again) like James Dickey trying to imagine the owl who could teach a little blind boy in the woods to see, all far too much like that. But Mahy has entered wholly and delightedly into this "impossible experience" of persuading you that a lithe, vital nineteen-year-old *would* take over the care—all on his own and with reluctantly growing affection—of a dirty senile old woman. And *if* we believe—why? Because, I think, *Mahy herself believes aesthetically,* and this, let me assure you, is the basic demand of any convincing telling of an incredible tale. Let the writer, even for a moment, lose his or her own aesthetic belief, and *all* is lost.

How does it happen that Jonny stayed long enough to get Sophie clean, to get her flat clean, to get the place so that he can live in it (just for now, he keeps telling himself, just for now)? He would never have dreamed of cleaning like this at home (where he is considered the very source of disorder). What are the steps? Well, first of all, of course, he goes there sick and desperate, unable to go home. Then he finds he has to do some shopping and cleaning because there are only biscuits in the cupboards (an army of biscuits!) and he cannot endure the smell. But above all, he begins to understand that Sophie is being had for the rent of her own house, and he is so furious that he realizes he cannot rest until this cold-blooded larceny is rooted out. One of the many heart-lifting scenes in the book gives us Jonny, filled with a joyous rage—a triumphant, blazing rage—that takes him quite out of himself, leaping from the balcony of Sophie's house right down into the midst of Nev Fowler's gang, almost demolishing himself in the process but also wounding Nev Fowler with delectable thoroughness.

Just as in *Lucie Babbidge's House,* we are made to understand the past through brief flashbacks (set in italics at satisfyingly appropriate intervals) to scenes concerning the source of Jonny's soul-eating guilt over what he believes to have been his part in his sister's death (that interleaving layer of story I am not exploring), and, as well, his relation to Nev Fowler. But—and here we return to the power of private vision—our understanding makes not the slightest difference to the intense originality of Mahy's conception of her novel. And this is not only because of the style of Mahy's writing, which is always poetically idiosyncratic in the best sense and always wittily explicit in its telling details (cats included) evoking place, but above all because of the strong and endearing characterizations of Sophie and Jonny.

"Last night's laid-back hero, the large black cat, yawned rudely and closed his eyes. He looked harder—*denser*—than the other cats, like a visitor from a cat planet with a much higher gravity than earth's." . . . "A night wind, patrolling the city, rushed at him, its paws on his chest, slapping his face with its icy tongue." . . . "Sophie gave him a glance so sweet and clear that he smiled back in involuntary wonder." . . . " 'How about a cup of tea?' said Jonny, taking the coward's way out. 'A good idea!' said Sophie warmly, very much as Mrs. Einstein might have said to the professor on first hearing him speculate on the unified field theory." . . . She "paid for the tea and cakes in the manner of a little girl seriously spending pocket money for the first time. . . . Then she ate the cake, leaving a small mustache of cream." Later on, thinking he has escaped Sophie's magnetic field:

Jonny was filled with great relief. He could have danced. He *did* dance, going forward in a series of silent heel-and-toe taps, filling in the sound in his own mind, building up a pattern of single, double, and triple beats. People in cars joining the long line at a red light stared at him, unsmiling. Jonny, dancing harder, waved both arms at his audience and left them behind, moving onwards in a series of stifled bombashays onto the gravel by the railway line. The ordinariness of everything delighted him. He was dancing his way out of a perverse enchantment, for Sophie's house, with its tribe of cats and its dirt and anarchy was falling away behind him. . . . Sometimes, just practicing, hearing the intricate and inevitable pattern his feet were inscribing on the earth, he had believed he was really drawing it up *out* of the heart of things, and had felt remarkable.

Concerning the "perverse enchantment," from which Jonny is trying to escape, it is cast by Sophie in such an extraordinary way that I do not remember anything in the world of literature for youth that surpasses the unexpectedness of this characterization. In her fantasy *The Changeover: A Supernatural Romance,* Mahy herself has created what is without doubt one of the most evil beings in that world, Carmody Braque, the very spirit of evil, brutal, relentless. At the very opposite pole, goodness is an overwhelming part of what Jonny is. As I have said, Mahy never holds back, and yet she is never voyeuristic. In the following scene, of which I give only a small part, you will see how in less sensitive hands the possibilities are all there for a subtle vulgarity, for a sophisticated knowingness (in the worst sense), which would be unbearable, considering Mahy's audience. But even if one fears a misunderstanding that might hover for a moment or two, it is soon dispelled:

Sophie was standing directly in front of him. She was quite naked. Her eyes were round but she was seeing him.

"Alva," she said in a slow, sighing voice that he had never heard her use before. She was holding something in one hand, but she laid the other hand, her left one, against his cheek. "It breaks my heart," she said, and her voice was still old but not cosy. It was ragged with despair. "I'll never get over it," she told him. "I'll never lose anyone else, never, never, never."

There is much more to this remarkable interchange, in which new depths of both Sophie and Jonny are revealed, and in it I believe that Mahy proves herself such an artist as we have not met in her previous works. Purely and simply, we believe in Jonny and Sophie's experience (though all may not, I will admit) *because of their characterizations.*

V

I clearly recall being advised by a reader of one of my early manuscripts that it would be well to play down the parents I had involved and, in fact, adults in general, as children are not interested in them. But many writers have seen how parents play an overwhelmingly significant role, for good or ill, in books that children read with absorption, and how the characterization of the young protagonist is, as you might say, bounced off or resonated from the characterization of the parents.

Only someone as gifted and as assured of her private vision as Cynthia Voigt could have gone calmly ahead, in spite of Katherine Paterson's Newbery Honor Book *The Great Gilly Hopkins,* with her portrayal in *A Solitary Blue* of a boy imprisoned in his passionate, almost sexual love for his mother, who is what was called in the seventies a flower child. For it is a novelistic conception that repeats in a basic way that of Paterson's novel in which Gilly, a girl child, is imprisoned, if not by the kind of love for her flower-child mother that evokes the sexuality Jeff is torn by in *A Solitary Blue,* then in a love that is just as painful and tearing in its own way over long years of rejection. In both novels we are shown the extreme cruelty of these two mothers, the selfishness and blindness that subject both Gilly and Jeff to slow torture—the continued, persistent deprivation of love and concern when both mothers know quite well how their children long for them. In both novels resolution is arrived at through a series of illuminations. In both there is a saving adult—no, two in *A Solitary Blue.*

At a symposium I happened to say that, as in fairy tales, goodness needs something powerful to push against. There was a discussion about this, and in the course of it, Katherine Paterson remarked that she had particularly wanted to create the character of a thoroughly good woman in Trotter, Gilly's foster mother. To my mind, Paterson succeeded triumphantly, for Trotter *is* thoroughly good but never tiresome, because, for one thing, she has Gilly to contend with. Gilly serves to bring out her toughness, more than equal to Gilly's, which is cruel and defensive on the surface, while Trotter's arises from a deep, concerned, instinctive wisdom. She has also a level outspokenness, the ability to see through to the necessary action without cruelty or callousness. In the end it is her steady persistence that brings Gilly light-years beyond seeing Trotter as only a big, stupid "bale of blubber," as she calls her in the beginning.

Trotter, the latest in a long line of Gilly's foster mothers, is rather appalling as compared to Gilly's memory of her own mother, Courtney, a woman with long, glossy black hair, looking like "the star of some TV show" in the photograph Gilly has of her with the words "For my beautiful Galadriel, I will love you always" written across the corner. Trotter is "a hippopotamus of a woman" with puffy fingers and missing teeth. She smells of baby powder and on occasion of sweat. She could scarcely appear at more of a disadvantage in Gilly's eyes, and, further, she is also the fiercely protective foster mother of little shy, wretchedly vulnerable William Ernest Teague, who stares out from behind Trotter's "mammoth hip" through thick-lensed, metal-rimmed glasses under a topping of muddy brown hair. What a target for Gilly!

However, she will have Trotter to get past, and Gilly's first illumination comes to her when she sees that she is not going to be able to wind Trotter around her finger despite Trotter's innocent-seeming refusal to take offense at Gilly's initial crude remarks interlaced with profanity. And there will be no least possibility of manipulating her. When Gilly starts in on William Ernest: "Listen here, Gilly Hopkins," says Trotter, "one thing we better get straight right now tonight. I won't have you making fun of that boy. . . . Just 'cause someone isn't quite as smart as you are, don't give you the right to look down on them. . . . He's had a rough time, but he's with Trotter now, and as long as the Lord leaves him in this house, ain't nobody on earth gonna hurt him. *In any way.*" Gilly replies with a "Good god," to which Trotter answers: "One more thing. In this house we don't take the Lord's name in vain."

When Gilly goes next door, at Trotter's suggestion, to bring over old Mr. Randolph, who always has dinner with Trotter and William Ernest, she returns with the news that he wasn't there, only "some weird little colored man with white eyes came to the door." This, she is told, is blind Mr. Randolph, but, says Gilly, "I never touched one of those people in my life." "Well, then," snaps Trotter, "it's about time, ain't it?" and "Of course, if you can't manage, I can always send William Ernest."

Gilly is beginning to get the idea. And later, because of Mr. Randolph, it is we, the readers, who get an illumination about Gilly when she chooses to read poetry aloud to him, though it is nothing but vanity, a desire to be at the center, that compels her to choose *The Oxford Book of English Verse* from his shelves and read Wordsworth's "Ode"—"Trailing clouds of glory do we come." "The music of the words," writes Paterson, "rolled up and burst across Gilly like waves upon a beach." And right there we see that there is a crack in Gilly, a girl who has had to put on a seemingly impenetrable facade just to keep getting through the days. And we see that if Trotter ever succeeds in widening that crack, not by forcing it, but by being unfailingly herself, a kind but firm and straight-spoken person, something interesting is going to happen.

Gilly *is* a tough nut. But again she has an illumination. She has made a paper airplane for William Ernest, and he has learned, through Gilly's teaching, to fly it. Trotter is infinitely grateful on behalf of the shy, withdrawn little boy, who hasn't before this dared to do anything on his own. "'Thank you,' said Trotter softly. For a moment Gilly looked at her, then quickly turned away as a person turns from bright sunlight." Gilly takes Mr. Randolph's elbow to guide him home, "taking care not to look back over her shoulder because the look on Trotter's face was the one Gilly had, in some deep part of herself, longed to see all her life, but not from someone like Trotter."

Gilly's next illumination comes from her cool, good-looking black teacher, Miss Harris, but I am concentrating here on Trotter, from whom Gilly has, at this point, stolen one hundred dollars of Social Security money to add to her own ten, plus the thirty-nine she'd stolen from Mr. Randolph. The next one comes after Gilly has said to herself, re Trotter's constant waiting on William Ernest:

Trotter, baby, if you had half my brains you'd know to let the boy do things for himself. If I were going to stay here, I'd teach him how. You want so hard, and you don't know how. Even the birds know to shove the babies out of the nest. If I were going to be here, I'd make a man of your little marshmallow. But I can't stay. I might go all soft and stupid, too. Like I did at Dixons'. I let her fool me with all that rocking and love talk. I called her Mama and crawled up on her lap when I had to cry. My god! She said I was her own little baby, but when they moved to Florida, I was put out like the rest of the trash they left behind. I can't go soft—not as long as I'm nobody's real kid— not while I'm just something to play musical chairs with.

But Gilly has revealed to herself that there is *precisely* that possibility of going soft, and when she is stealing downstairs later in the dark with her packed suitcase, she meets William Ernest. " 'Don't go.' His little face squeezed up at her like his tiny voice." But she pushes past and goes running, running down the hill. All the same, the fact is there: Somebody needs her.

And when Gilly is apprehended at the bus station and it is put to Trotter that it might be best if Gilly stayed at the city jail overnight, there are no recriminations from Trotter, no anger. Only:

"Gilly! Gilly!" William Ernest streaked across the room and began to beat his fists on her knees. "Come home, Gilly. Please come home! Please, please!" The blood vessels stood out blue and strained on his white neck.

The ice in her frozen brain rumbled and cracked. She stood up and took his hand.

"Thank you, precious Jesus," Trotter said.

Trotter bellows "like an old cow deprived of its calf" when the Social Services Agency caseworker suggests it would be best for Gilly to go to another place. Gilly hears, and when she hears as well Trotter say, "Yes, Lord knows, I need her," and the "funny broken sound like a sob" that came from Trotter, and "I like to die when I found her gone," "Gilly's whole body was engulfed in a great aching." But now Gilly has another illumination about Trotter. She might need Gilly to the point of sobbing at the thought of losing her, but Gilly is not to get off scot-free from the stealing. Oh, no. When Miss Ellis has gone, Trotter turns back toward Gilly, and "her face was like Mount Rushmore stone." And Gilly, with work and wages posted as if Trotter had never heard of minimum wage and child-labor laws, is to work off her debt by dimes and quarters.

Now Gilly is confronted with one illumination after another: the moment when she really begins to understand William Ernest, a "crazy, heart-ripping" little guy who goes "pow" and still wets his stupid bed; when she realizes for the first time that *she* needs Trotter, that she wants to stay with her, that she must; that by writing her mother she has opened a door like Bluebeard's wife and looked inside, only to be confronted by the knowledge that she actually loves Trotter—Gilly, who had never loved anyone in her life but Courtney—and that she is going to lose her. For the opening of that door brings not only the knowledge of her love for Trotter, but Gilly's final "seeing," the most agonizing of all for her to accept. Having put into motion the circumstances that cause Gilly's grandmother Nonnie to be sent for, the grandmother in turn sends for Courtney. And when Gilly sees her mother at the airport, the mother she'd been waiting for all these years, the final illumination comes hard and clear.

Can this person be Courtney, her long hair dull and stringy, "a flower child gone to seed"? And Gilly understands now with piercing clarity that Courtney has come for only a few days; she has no intention of staying. But, worst of all, "She hadn't come because she wanted to. She'd come because Nonnie paid her to. . . . Gilly had thrown her whole life away on a stinking lie," the idea that her mother loves her. She wants now to do two things—vomit, then run off. But she can't vomit, so she goes to a booth and telephones Trotter, who speaks these extremely valuable words:

> Ain't no one ever told you yet? I reckon I thought you had that all figured out. . . . That all that stuff about happy ending is lies. The only ending in this world is death. Now that might or might not be happy, but either way, you ain't ready to die yet, are you? And there is lots of good things, baby. Like you coming to be with us here this fall. That was a mighty good thing for me and William Ernest. But you just fool yourself if you expect good things all the time.

But then, "If life is so bad," demands Gilly, "how come you're so happy?" "Did I say bad?" retorts Trotter. "I said it was tough. Nothing to make you happy like doing good on a tough job."

At this point Gilly can at long last tell Trotter that she loves her. "I know, baby, I love you, too." Gilly blows her nose and washes her face in the women's room and goes back to Nonnie and Courtney. "Sorry to make you wait, I'm ready to go home now." But by *home* she means her grandmother's house, not Trotter's, where she longs to be. "No clouds of glory, perhaps," thinks Gilly, "but Trotter would be proud." The last words of the book.

I spoke of parallel situations revealed in *Gilly Hopkins* and *A Solitary Blue,* that of children with coldly uncaring, lying mothers who, without the least sense of responsibility or concern, have left their children at an early age—simply packed up and taken off, with the same devastating result: an emotional wound like a sickness that might have continued lifelong, visited upon both Gilly and Jeff.

However, Voigt's portrayal of Melody (an acidly ironic name), Jeff's mother, is far more damaging to its subject than is Paterson's of Courtney, because we meet Courtney only once, briefly, at the end of *Gilly Hopkins,* while we get page after page of revelations of Melody in the personal exchanges between her and Jeff. For one thing, Courtney is not quite the hypocrite Melody reveals herself to be, ever more appallingly as the novel unfolds, at the terrible and quite visible expense of a son whom she calls, "my Jeffie, . . . the man in my life," of whom she pretends to be so proud (except when she is angry with him), grasping for his good opinion, for his wholly devoted and adoring love.

When Melody leaves Jeff, aged nine and in the fifth grade, and his father, she leaves a note filled with the kind of lies she tells him for the rest of the years they're in contact, saying that she loves him "best, better than anything." Yet, of course, she *is* leaving, because "people everywhere need me, little boys like you who don't get enough to eat and who are hungry every night . . . little animals hunted down and wiped out and air and water made dirty." And it is such a big job that she will not be able to come back to him, so she has to say good-bye to her "little boy, my own sweet Jeffie, from your sad M." Note the Victorian-Edwardian overuse of the word "little," so often evoking a sense of sentimental hypocrisy. And it is increasingly revealing to note the various ways in which Melody unwittingly gives herself away during the progress of the novel.

In the first place, she is very late picking up Jeff at the airport in Charleston (there was a snarl in the traffic, she says) when he arrives for his first vacation after not seeing her for four years. Even with the memory of that traumatic letter she left for him, Jeff waits for her in a state of uplifted joy because at last they're to be together for a whole vacation. At least so he has been led to believe. Further back, I noted the almost sexual tone of Jeff's love for his mother, first brought out here at the airport.

A rush of sweet air washed around him, enveloped him; a voice murmured half-laughing, half sad. "Oh, Jeffie, Jeffie." He closed his eyes as his cheek came to rest on her shoulder and her flowery scent flowed around him. Her arms wrapped around him and he could feel her hands on his back. He tried to grab all the sensations at once, the sound of her voice, honey sweet with its lazy vowels. . . . "Oh, my little boy. . . . Oh, Jeffie, have you been terribly unhappy?" Her eyes filled with tears, which flowed down over her cheeks in a thin line. "I'm so happy to see you," she said, touching his cheek again. Jeff's heart hurt him, it was so full with warmth and sweetness. The warmth seemed to run along his bloodstream. He felt his eyes fill with tears. . . . Her lips brushed his cheek, the palm of her soft hand held his other cheek, and his heart thudded so painfully in his chest that he knew if he had to stand his legs would be too weak to support him.

It is hard for me not to see this paragraph as overwritten: For example, three uses of "around" in the first four sentences, and the double use of "sweet," followed by "sweetness" soon after. Surely "A rush of sweet air washed around him, enveloped him" could have been omitted, for we get "her flowery scent flowed around him" shortly after. There is "honey sweet with its lazy vowels," then "full with warmth and sweetness" a few lines later. It is true that an effect is overwhelmingly produced, and perhaps these repetitions were anything but unconscious.

About sexuality, were it not for that "Oh, my little boy," one might almost take this for the moment before sexual union between lovers who've been apart for a long time. It is a moment of bliss— at least for Jeff—and who is to tell, as far as the Jeff described here is concerned, whether the bliss is sexual or filial? Now Melody is described for us, and I quote most of the paragraph because, like the previous one, I do not recall such an evocation of sexuality in a mother-son relationship in any other novel for young people. And the worst

part is that we intuit, as we read, that Melody is perfectly well aware
of precisely what kind of response she is arousing and even encouraging
in her son.

"Well, what do you think of me?" she finally asked.

"Beautiful," Jeff said. His voice croaked a little, so he cleared
his throat and said it again. "You're so beautiful." He felt like
a man who has been kept in a dungeon for years and years, and
he steps out into the sunlight for the first time. . . . And she
was . . . so beautiful she took his breath away. Her long black
hair curved smoothly down along the sides of her face, until it
was gathered back to form a gleaming circle at the top of her
head. Her eyes—he had forgotten how dark the outer circle of
gray in her eyes was and how the lighter gray shone within that
circle. Her black eyelashes framed her eyes, and her curved black
eyebrows made another circle. Her oval face, her small straight
nose, her smiling mouth, the high cheekbones and the tanned
skin—"I'd forgotten how beautiful you are," he said softly.

Again the lush repetition: the word "beautiful" repeated four times
in the paragraph I have quoted. Voigt writes within the long tradition,
reaching back to Dickens and the nineteenth-century French and Russian writers, of exact descriptions rather than within that of the im-
pressionistic style (brought to our attention by Virginia Woolf
particularly) that gives a brushstroke here, a brushstroke there, con-
juring an evocation through subtle touches observed or thought of by
various participants in the novel, or by its writer. Detail, as given
here and in her Dicey novels, is what Voigt always allows herself. But
I think that few could write for children as Voigt does and retain the
interest of their young readers. Therefore it is intriguing to know that
she retains a devoted following.

Again, here are the intimations of sexuality, all built up to make
Melody's final betrayal the more brutal—and note the word *man* rather
than *boy* in "He felt like a man who has been kept in a dungeon for

years and years." As for the description of Melody, I can't help asking: If Melody left Jeff and his father when Jeff was in the second grade, how could he *possibly* have remembered "how dark the outer circle of gray in her eyes was and how the lighter gray shone within that circle"? It would have been amazing had he recalled from his young boyhood simply the color of her eyes. This is Voigt, one feels, giving her authorial description rather than Jeff's (and we are *inside* Jeff, not outside him, viewing the entire scene); Jeff, in his daze of loving bliss, would be getting, during this first experience after four years, an impression of beauty, of dark hair, pale oval face, and large gray eyes.

From this time on, we note one revelatory detail after another about Melody. On the way back from the airport she says that she uses her friend Max's car whenever he's away, then says that "Detroit doesn't have any of my money, and neither do the fat-cat oil companies most of the time. And that keeps my personal pollution contribution down." Nevertheless she "contributes" whenever it is possible and, above all, useful for her to do so—she will stop at nothing if an act serves her own interests, all of which calls her self-congratulation into question. She doesn't ask if he is hungry, even though it is very late, but stops off on the way home to make use of him to stuff envelopes for one of her projects. Nor does she ask him when they finally arrive. She denigrates his father to him, saying that his brains didn't do him much good and that she had thought she could save him and wake him up, but she never could. Nobody could. In the course of their only whole day together for the rest of Jeff's vacation in Charleston, she tells him what it was like to bear him, how she thought she'd "died and gone to hell," and speaks of the pain and the blinding lights. But later when they brought him to her, she knew the pain didn't matter despite the bleeding and her difficulty breathing. It is then that Jeff says "I'm sorry" for the third of many, many times.

After this Jeff sees little of his mother, "But her presence marked the day for him. . . . Her name, Melody, sang within him, like the music he could sometimes win out of her guitar." We suspect, though Jeff still does not seem to understand the depths of his mother's perfidy, that his letters to her after his return home will never be answered, and that even his especially chosen Christmas gift for her, the most beautiful scarf he could find, will not be acknowledged. But he refuses to face the truth:

> He would be Melody's knight, here in their scruffy little house, like old-fashioned knights who loved their ladies—sometimes without seeing them for years. But the knights were always faithful.

Nor is Jeff's faith shaken until, on his second journey to Charleston, he realizes that he will not be seeing Melody at all. He feels as he does at school, "like a fly in the room. You didn't really mind the fly, you just waved it away. . . . 'Move it, Greene,' one of the boys would say." And it is a part of his psychic wounding that he cannot seem to make an impression, to inhabit any but a peripheral world at school, as he inhabits perhaps an even less than peripheral role in Melody's life, in the Charleston home where his great-grandmother had greeted him so warmly the first time. The truth, he understands now, is that *he is not wanted,* had not really been expected. And part of his slow-dawning illumination is his discovery of how vulgar Max is—Max, the man in Melody's life.

Jeff buys an old barque (as it is called in that corner of the South) for fifteen dollars and rows out to an island, having the night before lain across his bed and cried:

> He felt—rolling over onto his back and wrapping his arms across the pain in his chest and stomach—pain that wasn't even real —as if he had been broken into thousands of little pieces. Broken and then dropped into some dark place. Some dark place where he was always going to stay.
>
> Because Melody was going away, again. Because she didn't

want to stay where he was. And he wasn't sure he could stand that.

He had never suspected how easy he was to break.

He couldn't think of anything he wanted to do. Ever.

And when he takes his boat out, an old, leaking travesty of a boat, we are forced to wonder if Jeff intends to sink it and go down with it. Because when the old black man who sells it to him asks him "Whuffo?"—why he wants it—Jeff replies, "Never mind." And out there on the island is the solitary blue.

We have met the solitary blue once before, when Jeff is on the bus going home from his first stay in Charleston. Here, too, we get precise details in this first description, its "legs like stilts under a clumsy body," its dusky feathers hanging shaggy and ungroomed, perfectly motionless, and "its long beak pointed down from a head both unnoble and unbeautiful. Its beak aimed down into the still, dark water. The heron occupied its own insignificant corner of the landscape in a timeless, long-legged solitude."

And of course we at once understand the symbolism, the second time he sees it, as we may not have the first, in a way that brings both Jeff and his father before our eyes: both solitary, both compelled to remain "half-hidden" psychically because of their wounds, both—especially the father, and Jeff growing up with him—long-legged, and both feeling spiritually shaggy and ungroomed because of their inability to prove themselves needed anywhere, their mental and emotional gaze focused so much of the time on an inner darkness and stillness. In Melody's view they know they are both homely (uninteresting, tedious) and absurd. And both feel doomed to occupy insignificant corners of the landscape in a timeless solitude. "Some dark place where he was always going to stay," we remember Jeff thinking during that night when he was crying on his bed. The last time he sees the heron, he feels it is saying, when he rows away down the quiet creek and it does not watch him go, "Just leave me alone." And Jeff, after his night on the island, feels washed and clean and healed, and as if, could he stay on the island, he might be all right: "Just leave me alone."

Yes, but because of this he and his father must still come to terms, must still find a relationship. And there is a journey going on, a journey being taken by Jeff all through the book: toward his mother and away from his father in the beginning, then slowly, as he begins to recover from her cruelty, away from Melody and toward his father, toward an understanding of himself and of the kind of man his father really is, and a most devastating and dramatic understanding of Melody.

Meanwhile, his father, too, is making a journey, out of the frozen image he has presented to Jeff and to the world—this with the help of his one faithful friend, Brother Thomas (a splendid example of a many-faceted and richly characterized secondary member of the cast) —into a human being who can actually speak of his feelings. And if not with words just at first, then through the action of giving Jeff a guitar, an extremely good one, for Christmas, which says to Jeff: "I love you—I want to please you—I want you to be happy." Later, at Brother Thomas's urging, he writes the book he had always wanted to write, which achieves a success he scarcely knows how to handle. Nor can he deal adequately with the sight of Jeff opening the published book and seeing the words on the dedication page, *For my son*. Here we come on a perfect example of Melody's self-entangling lying. She tells the Professor, when she comes to visit in order to get what she wants, that she "loves" his book, that it's a wonderful book, when a few pages back she has admitted that she hasn't yet had time to read it.

Now Jeff and his father have at last come to a meeting point, psychically and emotionally, an understanding that will save them from a future in which they might have continued as fatally wounded human beings, with servitude to that state becoming ever more habitual. Even so, we note, after coming on "I'm sorry" all through the novel, that the repetitions continue almost to the end, one hundred and thirty-four of them and, on one single page, three, which is so extraordinary that we understand that these are the burden words of the book. For they express how deep-rooted are the mingled pain and regret for so many things that neither Jeff nor his father can help or ever could have helped, except for the Professor's mistake of marrying Melody in the first place. On two occasions near the end, even Melody says she's sorry, when of course she isn't at all, having not the least idea of what it means to imagine the wretchedness being experienced by another, or that she has been the cause of it. They are words spoken simply because it makes her feel good to hear what she supposes they mean, so that in being "sorry" for Jeff and the Professor she is still queen of the castle, looking down on the poor little others, especially her husband and son. She does not see for a moment that they are happier now than they have ever been in their lives.

To attain this meeting point, Jeff and the Professor have been forced to make long and painful journeys, toward each other and into themselves, in an enormous effort to gain understanding. Melody, who travels the farthest physically in her "good-deed" journeys and is about to go to South America, has made no journey of the spirit at all.

V I

In a thought-provoking article, "The Adult-eration of Children's Books," Elaine Moss, a respected English critic of children's literature, wrote of her concern that too many character studies (the kind of treatment, she feels, that adulterates children's fiction with the techniques appropriate to adult novels) and too few good stories for children were being published. She deplores authors who introduce the obscurities and psychoanalytical approaches of adult novels into children's books *at the expense of story.* She would like to see more straight, undemanding adventure stories, and she goes on to say that "if adulteration has taught us anything—and surely it has—it has taught us that children respond to good writing. Perhaps the moment has *now* come for better stories, well written?"[14]

But, one can't help asking, does she believe that editors have ever ceased looking for "better stories, well written" or that serious writers have ever ceased hoping, and trying, to write them? I would say that any story, any novel for children, is improved and made more absorbing through richness of characterization. That richness, arising out of the novel in ways described in this essay, *makes* the stories.

The poet John Ciardi reminds us that novels may stand out horizontally, for everyone alive at this moment, and a very few vertically, for everyone who will ever read them, throughout time. When we think of the complexity of adult novels, generally speaking, compared to the *apparent* simplicity of children's books, it is astonishing to reflect on the vertical endurance of a large body of children's literature. I think that a great part of that enduring power has to do with the vividness, the convincingness, the imaginative truth of their protagonists. We think of the apparently simple preoccupations of the characters created by E. B. White, for instance, or Beatrix Potter, or Laura Ingalls Wilder, or Patricia MacLachlan. Their books, we feel, will go on for decades as opposed to the life span of a good many complex and difficult novels that grapple with far larger issues—political, sociological, theological—for adults. Why? What is the answer? Hasn't it a great deal to do with the singularity of their characters, Henry James's "felt life" that imbues them and that children hold dear? Certainly the answer to the vertical power of Potter's books lies in the imaginative truth of her animal world, despite the fantastical actions of her animals.

Richard Poirier, in his book of essays *The Performing Self,* says of Jorge Luis Borges that he is

> too little concerned with the glory of the human presence within the wastes of time, with human agencies of invention, and he is too exclusively amused by the careers of competing systems, the failed potencies of techniques and structures. We remember the point of his texts, especially since it is so often the same point, but he gives us few people to remember or care about.[15]

What is the use of writing a novel in which there are no characters we recall, and who meant nothing to us as we read?

It would seem that all the memorable children's writers know the following maxim instinctively, intuitively, as all the memorable writers for adults know it: Learn to make yourself akin to people. But let this sympathy be not with the mind—for it is easy with the mind—but with the heart, with love toward them. Reynolds Price, interviewing Eudora Welty, said of her that as her use of radiance mounted, he came to feel that all her work combined to advance a concept of the great writer as a kind of power plant, a large center of energy, radiating for us, and that the fuel is love—a deep and tender fascination with human life.

THE FLEAS IN THE
CAT'S FUR

◆

*"Man," said the critic Kenneth Burke, "is the symbol-using animal."
He might as well have said "Man is the metaphoric animal," for
symbolism is simply a special case of metaphor.*

JOHN CIARDI
How Does a Poem Mean?

Colette gave me my title. She said that clichés in writing are like fleas in the cat's fur and that one must go through one's manuscript and mercilessly nip them out. The trouble is, we're so used to them that even respected writers don't always see them in their own work. Nor do their editors.

For this reason, and because a good many of the rest of us don't see them either, I have been turning over the subject of clichés in connection with the aesthetic sensibilities of childhood, and not only clichés but their mind- and imagination-lifting opposites: vivid and original figures of speech. These figures, as I shall show, are encountered everywhere in the memorable literature of childhood and can be pointed out by sensitive readers and teachers. Of course there are clichés in children's books, but it is only when children move into middle and high school, and are increasingly introduced to literature written for adults, that they begin to swim into a sea of them.

As for television, apart from what can be seen and heard in the usual sitcoms, I was astonished at the plentiful use of cliché expressions in, for instance, the initial episodes of James Burke's long-running PBS series, "The Day the Universe Changed: A Personal View," quite brilliantly original in its purpose of exploring the world of inventions and what they have led to throughout the ages. It is, and I hope will be for some time, a series the more curious-minded teenagers might watch, if not in new shows then in reruns or on their VCRs.

Burke, in the course of his *beginning* monologues, uttered (by my count) at least thirty-four clichés, such as "went over like a lead balloon," "like moths to a candle flame," "dropping like flies," "the plot was about to thicken," "shot up like a rocket," "making hay while the sun shines," and so on and on and on. What interested me was that during a second series, the clichés had considerably diminished in number, as if someone had pointed out his habit to Burke. Yet still he clung to them here and there, one can't imagine why.

But perhaps the use of those tedious expressions was, in the beginning, quite purposeful. It was as if Burke might have felt that the nature of his material, demanding one's full attention in order to follow the thread of his complexities, could hold an audience only on such terms. Possibly he had analyzed Kenneth Clark's television series "Civilisation" and Jacob Bronowski's "The Ascent of Man" and said to himself that if only these programs had been carried off with a more casual, baggy-pants delivery, the everyday sort of person and quite possibly the everyday sort of teenager, not just the eggheads, might have been persuaded to watch and listen. But now he has proved to himself that those everyday watchers, if they are interested in his thoughts, will stay with him, though he continues without indulging himself in one cliché after another. How intriguing that his ideas and connections are piquing and idiosyncratic, anything but clichéd, yet his language in the past emerged as excruciatingly the opposite.

Because a cliché is a brief, precise, neat, direct, and often vivid way of expressing some likeness or thought that has continually called out to be expressed, it lives on, century after century. We don't have to imagine anew: There it is, buried in our minds like a tick in the flesh, only it neither itches nor burns. It is there, comfortably waiting to be used for the billionth time. Josephine Humphreys in her novel *Rich in Love* defends clichés in saying, "On the way home, looking at his gentle face, I actually thought, *time heals all wounds*. I pay attention to clichés because they are likely to be true. Otherwise they wouldn't have achieved cliché status." As for their "truth," they may or may not be true. Time, for instance, does *not* heal all wounds; it may simply keep them buried. For instance, Virginia Woolf committed suicide at the age of fifty-eight partly because of the death of her mother when Virginia was a child.*

So it is all very well to pay attention to clichés in case they may be true, but it is another thing entirely to use them carelessly and tediously in prose. Later in her novel Humphreys uses three. "[Billy] could have left the house forever, and I would have gone on feeling this feeling. 'Walking on air' seemed like an accurate description, or 'on cloud nine,' or 'sitting on top of the world.' It affected my eyesight. When I looked out my window, after the night of the dream, I was shocked." Because of Humphreys's use of quotes, we know quite well that she is aware of these expressions as clichés and is using them on purpose. And in this regard, I find Reynolds Price in his *The Tongues of Angels* (for adults, but an excellent young-adult novel) saying, "And I saw that if I really was going to seize my fate and study in Europe

---

*See *Darkness Visible: A Memoir of Madness* (New York: Random House, 1990), by William Styron, for his discussion of and conviction about disorders and early sorrows and their effects on later life. "Devastating loss figured as a probable genesis of my own disorder; meanwhile, as I monitored my retrogade condition, I felt loss at every hand," he writes on page 56. And on page 79 he comes even closer to what I have said about Virginia Woolf: "The genetic roots of depression seem now beyond controversy. But I'm persuaded that an even more significant factor was the death of my mother when I was thirteen; this disorder and early sorrow—the death or disappearance of a parent, especially a mother, before or during puberty—appears repeatedly in the literature on depression as a trauma sometimes likely to create nearly irreparable emotional havoc." Virginia's mother, the very center and taproot of the Stephen household, died when Virginia was thirteen.

after I finished college, then I'd better put shoulder to wheel as well and see if it moved." Using, but changing a little for his own purpose.

The danger is that the unthinking, purposeless use of clichés in serious writing can result in the subtle vitiation of originality, of the desire to envision freshly, and the weakening of the individual voice, its force and memorable tone. Joyce Carol Oates, in an essay on Thoreau, says of him:

> Quite apart from his mastery of the English language—and certainly no American has ever written more beautiful, vigorous, supple prose—Thoreau's peculiar strength as a stylist is to transform reality itself by way of his perception of it—to transmute it into *his* language. What is the motive for metaphor in any poet—in any poetic sensibility—but the ceaseless defining of the self and of the world by way of language?[1]

Of course, children don't recognize clichés, because all language is new to them; they can have no concept of a cliché. As a friend has said, " 'Quiet as a mouse' can be a wonderful expression when first encountered"—brief, precise, neat, direct, and vivid. It makes the child want to curl up when hiding and *be* a mouse—paws folded, whiskers quivering, nose trembling, bright black eyes intently watching. Therefore it is almost inevitable that children will embed clichés in their own writing unless led to beware of them throughout grammar and middle and high school.*

And if children are using them it is only because they've taken them from us, who've long ago forgotten our first awareness of the visible and sounding universe. We have been content with them all our lives, since we left behind our first startled moments of utterly

---

*A friend asks an excellent question at this point. "Should we teach children to avoid clichés when they are still young enough to take pleasure in them?" I think: Point them out, let the children take pleasure in them, and then remind them that these sayings have been used time without number and that it is better to let the comparisons spring out of one's own imagination.

fresh seeing. "One does not admire things enough: and worst of all, one allows whole days to slip by without once pausing to see an object, any object, exactly as it is," says Sylvia Townsend Warner in her ruthless, endearing, ironic novel *Mr. Fortune's Maggot.*

It may just be a miracle, as Richard Lewis believes it to be, that the few children who really enjoy expressing themselves in the written word—as opposed to those who write only when assigned and then unwillingly—are quite likely to see afresh, in spite of TV sitcoms and adult conversations. Rather than putting into a piece of doggerel that it is "raining cats and dogs," then rhyming dogs with bogs, Ken Dickinson, age ten, writes:

> Raindrops shimmer down dirty glass
> And measle the windowpane.
> The raindrops glide—leaving a motionless road.
> Raindrops fall breaking themselves to tiny china
> and run away like blood.

And because he was a child who had just begun his struggle with the craft of writing, Ken could combine the metaphor of raindrops falling and "breaking themselves to tiny china" with the simile of their running away "like blood." He was seeing the rain for himself, in his own most personal way, which is what we want the child to do.

Sylvia Townsend Warner, perfected in her craft and obeying her own admonition to admire and to see, says that when she woke, she "saw the air between us and the hanging tapestry of trees laced with straight glittering rods of rain, each separate, intentional, like a rain of spears,"[2] ten precise observations in this short sentence knit into three precise images. And exactly so has it appeared to me, gazing out of my window at the deluge, descending with such fierce energy as to seem hurled in enmity at the defenseless earth. In other words, I say to myself with deep satisfaction: "Yes, yes! That's just the way it is!"

Instead of saying of himself that he was "dead as a doornail," Peter Milosevic, age eleven, writes most oddly of death by fever and calls it "Murder."

> The house was haunted like spear
> My heart was underground
> My arms straightened in the fear of death
> Everything tumbled in my eyes
> Till I felt lead stick in my chest
> Till I felt danger
> Crushing into my heart
> It was the black panther
> With dripping spits of fever
> Out of his germy mouth
> Now no longer I could see the earth
> My eyes closed gently
> >   and slept.

Neither Ken nor Peter would have been likely to think of the cliché phrases I have mentioned as possible inclusions in their lines.

To return to the observation that even respected writers don't always see the clichés in their own work, Randall Jarrell, honored poet and author of four books for children, two of which are classics, could write, "She had the worst virtue, omniscience, and would at the drop of a hat have contrasted for you . . ." and later, in the same book, "Her husband lay there like a log." What is astonishing is that these blindnesses were committed in his witty and brilliant novel of academia for adults, *Pictures from an Institution,* full of the most devastating and precise images, piercingly original. And we find nothing but poetic images, most personal to Jarrell, in both *The Animal Family* and *The Bat-Poet.*

Richard Adams, who wrote his first novel, *Watership Down,* for his children with fine freshness of spirit, committed no clichés there that I can discover. Yet in a later novel for adults, *The Girl in a Swing,* he

could say, "come hell or high water," "I would go down with the
ship," "all hell would break loose," "made every shot tell," and on
one page some lethargy of the aesthetic sense allowed him to let slip,
in one ten-line passage, "sink or swim, win or lose," "for better or
worse," "she didn't bowl me over," and "she was desirable, and a nice
girl to boot."

"Out of the blue" is one of the clichés that you see in magazines,
newspapers (including the *New York Times Book Review*), and in books
by both unknown writers and such known and respected writers as,
among many others, Jean Strauss, D. M. Thomas, Laurie Colwin,
Philip Roth, Shirley Hazzard, and Cynthia Ozick.

I I

Ken Dickinson's image of the raindrops, in which the two parts of it
oppose each other, reminds me of three ways in which a figure can
misfire: the failure of internal logic; exaggeration or distortion; and a
mixing and therefore a confusion within the metaphor.

Concerning internal logic: Although Adams committed no clichés
as far as I recall in *Watership Down,* he did contrive there an interestingly
questionable simile in which the internal logic assuredly fails. He
writes: "Then the whole down and all below it, earth and air, gave
way to the sunrise. As a bull, with a slight but irresistible movement,
tosses its head from the grasp of a man who is leaning over the stall
and idly holding its horn, so the sun entered the world in smooth,
gigantic power."

Well, there is the man idly leaning over the stall and grasping the
bull's horn. But why on earth would he be doing *that?* we can't help
wondering; and we should never be tempted to wonder and question
in the middle of a figure of speech. What got into the man? But it
wasn't the *man* getting this fool notion to idly hold the bull's horn.
It was the author *insisting* that the man hold it in order that the image
could be made. But it's a scene we can't use and don't need, and it
ends all wrong. For the tossing slight sideways movement of the bull

freeing itself from the man's grasp results in giving us the picture of a jerking motion, something never involved in the rising of the sun, for the entering is, as Adams notes, one of "smooth, gigantic power." The first part of the image defeats the last and has nothing whatever to do with it.

Josephine Tey, who made herself famous with *The Daughter of Time,* an engrossing tracking down of what Tey believes to have been the true character of Richard III, commits two very strange figures in her first novel, when she has not yet mastered her style. She writes: "Here and there a line of gay, motley child's clothes danced and ballooned in the breeze in a necklace of colored laughter." I jib at having to liken dancing and ballooning clothes to beads on a string, the soft, lively, shape-changing objects to the hard, which can never change shape within themselves as clothing can. Furthermore, I can't liken the necklace to laughter, a string of discrete objects to a sound, which we are asked to think of as colored because clothes are colored. Therefore we are being asked to think of different colors as applied to the sound of laughter, and laughter, I can only suppose, because of the presumed gaiety of childhood. In fact, the more you think about this peculiar, complex image, the more strained and illogical, the more meaningless it becomes, and the more mired the imagination.

Later Tey notes of dresses that they were wrested "from their cardboard shells as one thumbs peas from a pod." But I can't liken peas in their pods to dresses in their boxes because there, again, discrete objects—peas, round and small and hard—are being compared to dresses, large and soft and fluid. Therefore you can't possibly thumb dresses from a box as you'd thumb peas from a pod; you have to lift them out. As in the previous image, the details weren't thought about but accepted en masse after their first arrival.

At entirely the opposite pole, John Gordon begins his short story for children "Left in the Dark" with a stunning interlacing, the picture held together logically and aesthetically by a sense of sewing, the whole rounded out with the result of it, and all satisfying and right and true:

The village seemed to be stitched into the hills. A cluster of houses was held by the thread of the stream, and the stream itself was caught under a bridge and hooked around a stone barn in a fold of the heather and bracken. In the October sunshine the hills looked as soft as a quilt.

The second pitfall in the writing of images, aside from the basic one of not thinking through what comes to mind and therefore running the risk of illogic, results from exaggeration or distortion. In Adams's *The Girl in a Swing,* writing in the protagonist's words of an unattractive furnished room, he says: "It made my teeth feel apprehensive." This is such an awkward expression, and surely so untrue, that we have a notion that he might have written: "It set my teeth on edge," which he thought of as a cliché, and which therefore compelled him to concoct this unfortunate, exaggerated substitute.

Annie Dillard's *Pilgrim at Tinker Creek* is a book I can go back to every few years, open at any page, and immediately become lost, as if I'd never read it, in the delight of Dillard's "seeing" during a period of her life lived on a creek and its environs. It is a book thrumming with images. Dillard thinks, sees, hears, smells, and touches in images. And a group of them, which have stayed with me ever since I first read them, as if they were etched on my mind, are these:

When her doctor took her bandages off and led her into the garden, the girl who was no longer blind saw "the tree with the lights in it." It was for this tree I searched through the peach orchards of summer, in the forests of fall and down winter and spring for years. Then one day I was walking along Tinker Creek thinking of nothing at all and I saw the tree with the lights in it. I saw the backyard cedar where the mourning doves roost charged and transfigured, each cell buzzing with flame. I stood on the grass with the lights in it, grass that was wholly fire, utterly focused and utterly dreamed. It was less like seeing than like being for the first time seen, knocked breathless by a powerful

glance. The flood of fire abated, but I'm still spending the power.
Gradually the lights went out in the cedar, the colors died, the
cells unflamed and disappeared. I was still ringing. I had been
my whole life a bell, and never knew it until at that moment I
was lifted and struck. I have since only very rarely seen the tree
with the lights in it. The vision comes and goes, mostly goes,
but I live for it, for the moment when the mountains open and
a new light roars in spate through the crack, and the mountains
slam.[3]

I respond wholly, much moved by this perfectly knit collection of
images, which bring me a sight involving intense sensation from the
nerve cells running the entire length and breadth of Annie Dillard's
being into mine. Now, you might not go along with that final, "I
live for it, for the moment when the mountains open and a new light
roars in spate through the crack, and the mountains slam." You might
not believe it has happened to Dillard, that she exaggerates for effect.
It's never happened to me (though other sights have mightily transported me in different ways), but I believe this happened to Annie
Dillard, and I'm grateful she troubled to put her full and unadulterated
vision, the sense of it, without holding back, into these particular
words. It makes me think of James Dickey saying that the poet
(substitute here the word *writer*, creating an image) "is not to be
limited by the literal truth: . . . . he is not trying to *tell* the truth: he
is trying to make it."[4] Or is it, rather, I would ask, a matter of the
miraculous, utterly unexpected evocation of the truth? And what,
then, of Dillard's mountains "slamming"? However, she is speaking
here of the *effect* the sight of the tree of light had on her, which is
quite a different matter from any literal reading of the word.

Of Dillard's book *An American Childhood*, one of its reviewers, Noel
Perrin, says that he believes her mystic's "heightened prose can become
mere mannerism and from time to time in this book it does." He
gives as an example her observation about Platonism, discovered when
she was sixteen, that it "had come bumping and skidding down the

centuries and across the ocean to Concord, Massachusetts," on its way
to meet Emerson, says Perrin, and skepticism comes to his mind
unbidden. "Plato's thought? Bumping and skidding? Fine, vivid language, certainly—but would it be either more or less true to say that
his ideas tiptoed daintily down the centuries, or walked in galoshes
through the Dark Ages, carrying an umbrella? In short, isn't Ms.
Dillard overwriting here?"[5] The second pitfall in an image.

Janni Howker is a young English writer whose work I greatly admire
and in whose pages I have found only one, to me, unfortunate image.
Is she creating or evoking the truth when she writes in *Isaac Campion:*
"A primrose sun, my mother would have called it, clouds hung up
like washing"? For myself, I cannot accept clouds hung up like washing, because washing, masses of damp, unwieldy cloth, inevitably
sags in the middle between the pegs, and I have never in my life seen
a sagging cloud. Ah, you will say, but what if the washing is hung
up taut, without a sag? But neither have I seen taut clouds. Light,
airy puffs of them, yes, long stretched-out reaches of them, curdled
meadows of them, dazzling castles with battlements and towers and
heaped up domes of them, heart-stopping black mountains of thun-
derheads. But clouds with sags, or hanging taut, no. All the same,
the writer is not trying to tell the truth, says Dickey, she is trying
to *make* it. But in this case I immediately have a mental picture and
am dissatisfied. I have to question.*

However, it is not Janni Howker *as* Howker telling this story; she
is telling it through an old man's sensitivities and perceptions. Isaac
Campion's, a farmer's. Might he not, then, have spoken about sagging
clouds? I have to doubt it, not one who could be so exact as to say,
"My father had been beaten with the rod of religion by my grandfather,

---

*Two of my readers disagree and feel the figure is just right. Another firmly agrees
with me. And so we see again how subjective criticism can be because of different
"seeings." Janni Howker herself says she's seen clouds hanging exactly like washing.

until all he wanted was to break that rod over his knee," and to say of his own father, so compactly, so painfully and precisely, "I feared him like fire," and then carry on that sense of something burning to, "His eyes were as blue as bonfire smoke." Not just any smoke, but bonfire smoke, and I have seen that blueness with my own eyes. And he speaks of men and women flooding out of the mill, "spilling like black bees out of a basket onto the wet street."

The third way in which a figure can misfire results from the writer having seen double (it is all so much a matter of seeing!) so that he comes forth with a mixed metaphor. Garry Wills, in reviewing Hedrick Smith's *The Power Game: How Washington Really Works,* offers some really splendid examples where Mr. Smith went astray: "The second major incident that stepped on the Reagan parade in 1981, and nearly derailed it, was another self-inflicted wound," says Mr. Smith. Later, Reagan goes to Bitburg to "heal the wound of Normandy and to nourish the balm of Verdun," so that, as Mr. Wills puts it, "Bitburg becomes an unguent-producing tree in Gilead." Still later: "Fragmentation often leaves our politicians wallowing in deadlock," and then, "Access, especially the exclusive access that blindsides other players in the policy game, is a trump card." "Changing games in midsentence," Mr. Wills calls it.[6]

I I I

But Jacques Barzun, critic and biographer, and James Dickey, poet, remind me at this point that I must now get over a bump in the path before I go any further. For I have been speaking alternately of metaphors and similes, as well as of images and figures of speech, when I wanted to use inclusive terms. (Which would have taken in synecdoche, for example, as when Jane Gardam in *A Few Fair Days* writes: "So Lucy and the grandaunts came home together and found as they turned the last corner that the whole world seemed to be gathered on the pavement, their arms in all directions." The part for the whole, a few neighbors referred to as "the whole world.")

In one particular practice, criticism has changed over the years, become relaxed, which is sharply irritating to Barzun. He says, in an essay entitled "A Little Matter of Sense," that

> Actually, a metaphor implies a comparison among four terms. If one says, "the ship plows the seas," the meaning is that just as the plow in its forward motion divides the soil, so the ship moves and divides the sea. Without four terms, no metaphor. Hence there is no discoverable meaning in praising a sculptor for "his way with three-dimensional metaphors" or in saying that in literature the mention of food "serves up many metaphors." Critics whose eye is clearly focused will choose among terms: symbol, emblem, sign, simile, metaphor, comparison, analogy are at hand, all distinct, not synonyms."[7]

But James Dickey would not agree with Barzun on this matter of dividing the figures so strictly. Dickey even calls his Library of Congress lecture on the making and use of images *Metaphor as Pure Adventure*. In it he asks "parts of creation to get together, not with the consent of the Almighty, but simply because [I] ask them to," which of course is what image-making is concerned with, carrying with that act a "passionate and mysterious aura of association."[8] Directly opposing Barzun, Dickey says: "I take metaphor in the broad sense, as denoting any kind of comparison as a basis for the kind of illumination we call poetic."[9] Yes! And when Robert Finch, in reviewing *The Lost Notebooks of Loren Eiseley*, incomparable essayist on bone-hunting and the mysteries of time, says that Eiseley "found metaphors that released a powerful view of man's fate in the modern world," I understand perfectly what he means, as I do when Finch speaks of Eiseley's "welding the force of his personality with the unusual range of his intellect by means of his connecting, metaphorical power, which is the power of the poet."[10] I need not ask Mr. Finch to distinguish between metaphor and simile. I know that he means Eiseley's power to make images of any kind, as I understand Linda Davis when she says of

E. B. White's obituary for James Thurber, that it was "graced with the perfect and perfectly enchanting metaphors."[11] We are not being confined to metaphors in the (four-quadrant) literal sense.

Nor is Marshall Gregory, professor of English at Butler University, being confined when he says in his excellent paper, "If Education Is a Feast, Why Do We Restrict the Menu? A Critique of Pedagogical Metaphors," that "The most powerful and widespread metaphor in education is also the worst: learning is storage."[12] And he contrasts this sterile and spirit-defeating state of affairs with the potent Socratic metaphor of education as something organic rather than mechanistic: education that nourishes plants to reach toward their fullest maturity, their fullest flowering, aesthetically, spiritually, intellectually. What a devastating contrast between this idea and the reality of the educational process in a good many universities today, where the whole idea is the pursuit of "success" by means of stored information, stored facts.

I V

Like Sylvia Townsend Warner, James Dickey looks on the image-maker "as one who feels the world as a gift," and maintains that "almost all metaphors begin with a picture in the head."[13] I'm glad Dickey said "almost." For we must not only consider those that begin with pictures in the head, one object or sight being like another, but with those that involve abstract concepts as well. How refreshing it is, what a delight, to find among the writers of children's books and books for teenagers those who, like Dickey and Warner, experience the world as a gift and who deal with both concepts and the visible universe in a way worthy of being offered to those whose literary tastes are in the process of being formed.

Emotions are continually communicated, as well as abstract concepts that do not always begin with pictures in the head—though indeed they end there—but with an idea, a sound, a scent, an intimation. Russell Hoban has Neaera H. in *Turtle Diary* say, "My despair has long since been ground up fine and is no more than the daily salt and pepper of my life"; and Nina Bawden writes, "her anger grew and grew like a dark flower opening inside her." Paula Fox in her *One-Eyed Cat* translates guilt indirectly into visibility, saying: "When there was a splinter in [Ned's] foot, it was all he could think about; he could forget that every part of his body except where the splinter was felt fine. The gun was like a splinter in his mind." Here, Fox, in an unusual but effective turnabout, puts an explanation of what would ordinarily come at the end of an image at its beginning. Thus, the effect of the splinter, pain, being already dealt with, brings fullest force to the following image, embodying the effect of another object on Ned, the gun lying at the heart of his guilt. Also, my editor reminds me, the order captures the quality of Ned's mind.

Jill Paton Walsh in *Unleaving* puts Patrick's agony of the soul into visibility differently when she says that "the piano is storming through an outburst of passionate notes, raw feeling naked in the sound, like blood from a wound." Once again we are being told about guilt indirectly, but this time in a triple image, for not only is the piano storming, rather than Patrick who is playing it, but raw feeling is naked in the sound, and this naked emotion is pouring out "like blood from a wound." On first reading, one is simply unaware that, actually, there *are* three images bound up in one, and all of them at the very heart of the story, deepening its intimations and bringing the theme of deliberately self-imposed guilt fiercely home to the reader.* In both books guilt is the theme, though in *Unleaving,* other complexities are woven in with it.

In her *Sweet Whispers, Brother Rush,* Virginia Hamilton twice brings fear into visibility. Of Teresa, she says: "Fear crawled up her legs. Cold flopped in her stomach like a dying fish. The flesh froze solid, flaking scales of ice slivers that made her shiver violently," and later, "Fear was sealed inside her like a tatter of paper from her ream. And if you opened the tatter, it would read: This is all the scared I can

---

*And, Stephen Canham suggests, sexual passion as well.

get." In both instances the first image leads on to a second, and in the case of the fish, to a third, like a kaleidoscope turning.

To go from emotions to sound, Paula Fox translates one sound into another when she says that the old man in *One-Eyed Cat* was to be heard "moving inside [his house] like a mouse in a paper sack," his weakness, his age poignantly implied in those few words, his slowness, his continual pausing (perhaps to reflect, or out of weariness) as a mouse pauses to sniff and to listen. Again translating sound into visibility, she says: "At times his speech grew slurred as though a sponge were being wiped over his words."

Both Penelope Lively and Jane Gardam are not only struck vividly with the looks of things and people, but almost always a wonderful wry humor underlies their images. Of certain neighborhoods you pass through in Oxford, Lively says, in *The House in Norham Gardens,* the houses "are growing. Getting higher and odder. By the time you get to Norham Gardens they have tottered over the edge into madness: these are not houses but flights of fancy." Keble College is a collection of "red brick sprawling so copiously that one feels the stuff must have got out of control, unleashing some dark force upon the helpless architect." For Clare, the butcher shop glows with "dark drums of beef, rosy pork. . . . The window display was ready to be painted, a mortuary still-life. . . . The customers were sheep, only one rung up from the meat. . . . Behind [the butcher] the pig carcasses hung from hooks, as docile as the customers. . . . Clare shrank into her coat. Snails must feel like that, pinned down by the blackbird's steely eye. . . . The snail, wincing, glowed pink, crawled out, forgot her purse, had to go back, spotlit by eight pairs of eyes, fell over someone's foot, got stabbed again, escaped."

Jane Gardam, in her witty and endearing *Bilgewater,* the story of a girl growing up in a boys' school, is masterful in her conveyance of the very essence of various characters through imagery or even a single image. She says of Paula Riggs, loved and indispensable matron of Bilge's father's house, that at school functions: "She nods and smiles, this way and that, and all the pork butchers' wives in polyester and

earrings on the platform look like rows of dropping Christmas trees,"
that among her father's friends "was often an amalgam of cobwebs
and dust called Old Price," and that when these aged friends came
to call at seven-thirty precisely of a Thursday evening, they "came
roaming round like elderly, homing snails." Father's headmaster "is
a pewsy man, little and plump, like a dynamo in a dog collar," and
his wife is "rather like a harvest festival . . . an immense storehouse
of a woman, with a large, though indeterminate, face. She's like
someone you've vaguely heard about in a rather bad book." Miss Bex,
the threatening character in the novel, has a "wide, emphatic smile
showing both rows of teeth and the little dampness that collects at
each end of her mouth causes a slight noise as she talks like a singing
tap—a tap whose washer isn't quite gone but will not last much
longer." Father himself, "in one of his more usual moods," looks "as
if he wanted to fly into the stratosphere and consider the meaning of
meaning."

Both Russell Hoban and Rosemary Sutcliff are also masters of conveying in images the quick, vivid impression of a character. Neaera
H., describing William G. in *Turtle Diary,* says that he was "A tall
hopeless-looking man with an attentive face and an air of fragile
precision like a folding rule made of ivory." Of the rat, at the beginning
of *The Mouse and His Child,* Hoban writes that "he smelled of darkness,
of stale and moldy things, and garbage. He was there all at once and
with a look of tenure, as if he had been waiting always just beyond
their field of vision, and once let in would never go away." Sutcliff,
in *The Light Beyond the Forest,* writes of Lancelot of the Lake that "he
was an ugly man, with an ugliness such as women love. His dark face
under the thick badger-streaked hair looked as though it had been
put together in haste, so that the two sides of it did not match. One
side of his mouth was grave with heavy thought, while the other lifted
in joy; one eyebrow was level as a falcon's wing and the other flew
wild like a mongrel's ear."

The very title of Bruce Brooks's first novel, *The Moves Make the
Man,* is an image that has to do with the essence of Jerry, the pro-

tagonist, one that Jerry enlarges upon when he explains his powerful sense of identity with the game of basketball.

> Every evening I came home, and in between, there were my moves. Moves were all I cared about last summer. I got them down, and I liked not just the fun of doing them, but having them too, like a little definition of Jerome. Reverse spin, stutter into jump, blind pass. These are me. The moves make the man, the moves make me, I thought, until Momma noticed they were making me into something else.

V

I should like now to show how the unfolding of a novel's meaning can be brought about through its images. On first reading Zibby Oneal's *The Language of Goldfish*, one may not be fully aware to what extent images are making visual and audible, as though we were inside Carrie's head, the progression of her mental illness.

Goldfish commences with two images, when thirteen-year-old Carrie is on her way to her psychiatrist, Dr. Ross: "The train slowed smoothly, as if gliding on ribbon. . . . The station was contained [on the train window] within her reflected head like a thought." Immediately afterward we get the first picture of one of the theme-objects having to do with the symbol at the center of the story: "Dead leaves were fluttering off the eave troughs, blowing across the parking lot."

A moment or so later, she opens her book to study geometry during the rest of her journey, and we get the first of Oneal's images central to Carrie's difficulty, images that will have to do with both material objects and conceptions: "The neat geometric figures lay solidly on the page. Permanent. Forever the square of the hypotenuse of a right-angle triangle would be equal to the sum of the square of the other two sides. Carrie liked that. . . . She found it beautiful in its certainty. Unlike poetry, which bothered her, math was firm. Meanings didn't shift and change as they did in poetry, as they still sometimes did within her own head." Which is why poetry "bothered" her rather than "bored" her, the verb one reader expected.

From then on, we discover, Carrie's bout with mental illness will be expressed in images. Gradually it is revealed that the pond in the back garden of her home, where goldfish swim and on whose surface leaves fall and float in autumn, is the symbol of childhood. Immediately after her frustrating, seemingly pointless visit with Dr. Ross, she is lying on her bed in the room she shares with her fifteen-year-old sister, Moira. Again there are leaves falling, not floating on the surface of the pool, but down from the hated wallpaper. "Do you ever think of the goldfish, Moira?" "Carrie, for God's sake!" There is no help for Carrie there.

Meanwhile, she is being pressed to go to dancing school, to mingle, to be one of the crowd, to be more "normal," when all she wants is to get on with her drawing lessons in private with her loved and admired friend Mrs. Ramsay, the art teacher at school. And at the moment when her mother tries to make her give up her art lesson for an appointment at the hairdresser's, and when she persists despite Carrie's refusal to agree to both the appointment and the dance classes, Carrie has a second dizzy spell, knowing, without really knowing, "that it was something worse than being dizzy. . . . It was as though things suddenly slipped sideways. . . . Inside my head colors—queer colored shapes—began to tumble around like colored glass in a kaleidoscope. There was a kind of roaring noise. My head began to float. . . . Behind my eyes I saw the colors all beautiful and tumbling."

But she can't go on being a little kid forever, says Moira. And Carrie, lying on her bed, thinks of the pool when they'd first found it as children after moving here from the only home Carrie had ever known. They'd "flopped on their stomachs and looked at the island and the dim green water. A leaf was spinning on its surface." If they were tiny they could use the leaf for a boat and paddle out to the island like Thumbelina and live there forever. What Carrie has come to want most fiercely is for things never to change, as math never does.

Now in her art she discovers a new concept, to draw not the leaf but its movement, imagining "circles within circles gradually growing larger" and therefore, in leaving out the body of the leaf, omitting at the same time "all the confusion of its physical appearance and giving only the geometry of its fall." Thus she expresses her rejection of the physical, which inevitably and most deeply involves sexuality.

At an art nouveau exhibit, to which she goes with Mrs. Ramsay, she studies the work of Maurice Denis and Aubrey Beardsley, thereby experiencing and understanding for the first time the effect of line in art. She studies Denis's first:

Lines that become twisting, curving tendrils, meandering, snake-like. . . . The painting was a jungle of curving lines. . . . The foliage and the figures of women were really simply studies in curve. Carrie stood dumbfounded before the picture. Now that she had seen what was there, she could not imagine it otherwise.

But it is Beardsley's art that cuts most painfully. For there is the

picture of a pond. A strange sort of water lily bloomed on the surface, and leaning over the bank was a woman with trailing hair. Carrie knew how the water would smell—warm and stagnant with rotting leaves. And under the greenish surface there would be flashes of gold where fish were hiding. . . . Then she caught her breath. She saw in horror that the woman was holding a man's head. Just the head. There was no body. His hair was a dozen twisting snakes and from the stump of his neck a long liquid curve fell back into the water.

Salome with the head of John the Baptist. Salome had danced her Dance of the Seven Veils for the mesmerized King Herod after he promised her the head of John the Baptist. "But how could he do that, because of the dance?" Sex is powerful magic, says Mrs. Ramsay. Yes, there is not only the innocent, fairy-tale magic of the language of goldfish, but the powerful magic of sex. Later, at Mrs. Ramsay's, when they are painting together and talking about Herod and Salome, Carrie feels the conversation "tearing a hole in the peacefulness of the room." And when Mrs. Ramsay continues the subject of sex by saying that "it makes an enormous difference," Carrie turns blindly from the sink, letting fall a handful of brushes: "The kaleidoscope pieces began sliding wildly, growing huge, like shelves of rock slipping along a fault."

In the hospital after she has tried to commit suicide, she feels herself surfacing again and again, and we are once more taken back to the symbol of the pond and its dark depths in which she could drown. And then back to the phallic symbols of Beardsley's art when she becomes aware of an enormously fat nurse, with legs "like huge sausages stuffed into her white stockings," sitting nearby, knitting. "Carrie studied her sausage fingers twining pink thread, turning it into a pink snake. . . . the pink snake curled in the woman's lap," like Beardsley's long liquid curve from John the Baptist's neck that fell back into the water.

Much later, when Carrie is well enough to return to school, she buys watercolors and begins to paint, and the first stroke is aquamarine, the color of water, and she paints the island. "What is the island?" she demands of Dr. Ross, but he replies that she will have to discover that for herself.

At last, growing bored with it, she begins timidly doing a border of leaves and vines, "squirrels scampering on branches, a few birds and a mouse. Then faces . . . little figures climbing the vines, faces peeping between the leaves." So that she has now passed through three phases in her art before entering a fourth. Three, as in the fairy tales, the magical number: Having outgrown first the abstractions, then the drawings of line, then the paintings of the island, she comes finally to the drawings of design and minute figures. But as it is the paintings of the island that are the fully expressed and finished work, it is these she brings to Mrs. Ramsay for the art show. And Mrs. Ramsay perceives that they "formed a kind of progression. In each successive picture the details grew clearer. It was as if the cliffs were slowly emerging from mist, as if morning sun were burning off a haze." Carrie emerging from confusion and bewilderment and repression and gaining the physical.

Now the power of sexuality is impressed on her in a most painful and personal way when she hears the gossip that Mrs. Ramsay has fallen out of love with her husband and in love with someone else. But as she is leaving her husband for another man, and not being left for another woman, she will be dismissed from her position. Because Carrie believes Mrs. Ramsay has lied to her, "Anger rose like water boiling inside her. . . . The knowledge [of what has happened] was a thick pain at the bottom of her stomach." But perhaps, as revealed in her paintings, Carrie has, indeed, undergone a progression, because she can determine that there is nothing to do but go and talk frankly to her dearest friend. And in the end: "You will always be my friend, Mrs. Ramsay. Nothing can ever change that." Here, at least, is a firm knowledge she can cling to, a knowledge arising out of the kind of person Carrie has discovered herself to be.

My one regret concerning *The Language of Goldfish* is that we get a growing sense of predictability as we enter into the pattern of Oneal's structure: Always at any mention, any indication of sexuality, any knowledge that now Carrie must herself begin to move toward dealing with it in her own life, we *will* inevitably get the kaleidoscope image, the noise, the rumbling in Carrie's head, the sliding blocks along a fault. And it is undeniably a weakness in a novel when the reader can predict the result of certain situations, when there is ever any sense of convenient neatness in the completion of a new situation. Yes, but what if it is what *would* have happened? But what we look for is subtlety and elusiveness, the kind we get in William Mayne's *A Game of Dark*.

Assuredly, a novel of psychic disorder offers fertile ground for the use of imagery. In fact, there is no more effective way to convey vividly the effects of mental disturbance, as we have seen in *Goldfish* and can see in Mayne's novel, where, through surrealist imagery on the very first page, he begins brilliantly developing our understanding of Donald's instability.

"Something like half an hour" after Mr. Savery has shouted at Donald in class,

> while Mr. Savery stared at him and the board duster folded slowly into a restful heap, falling liquidly from Mr. Savery's hand and leaving its own shadow in the air made of chalk dust, a voice spoke for him, not out of his mouth, but from just above his head, but he knew it was himself speaking. "I feel sick," said the spokesman.
>
> "You'd better go out," said Mr. Savery, oozing forwards from his place by the board and stretching out a hand to take Donald's arm. The chalk dust ghost of the duster swirled angrily around the moving arm. . . . The next to speak was Nessing, who got up from beside Donald, who was startled to see him because he had only been seeing things straight ahead of him, like Mr. Savery at the end of a tunnel of existence, a bright distinctness seen through shadow.

There is never, in *Game*, any sense of patness or predictability. We never know precisely when Donald will slide off into the other world, what triggers that sliding, yet the sense of rightness is always present. However, it can be seen in a moment that *The Language of Goldfish* is infinitely more accessible to the young reader than is *A Game of Dark*, with its sometimes complex sentence structure and the elusive ending, compared to the obviously satisfying and understandable one of *Goldfish*. Despite regret concerning a certain predictability, the reader gradually understands how Oneal's use of imagery, and specifically the use of it with regard to Carrie's art, has been firmly worked out. The central relevance of her art to the problem, revealed in images, interprets clearly how Carrie develops through phases that actually serve to bring about her healing.

V I

As we have seen, very often the pleasure and satisfaction inherent in an image lie in its beautiful concision: William Mayne saying in *A Game of Dark* that "the flame perched on the wick like a bright bird," Natalie Babbitt that Mrs. Tuck in *Tuck Everlasting* was "a great potato of a woman," Rosemary Sutcliff in *The Witch's Brat* that "Rohere's strange, haunted face flew open into joy," Randall Jarrell in *The Animal Family* that the mermaid had a voice "like water gurgling in a cleft in the rock" and "had learned the hunter's words, but said them to the sea's tune," Walter de la Mare in a short story that newspapers scatter scandal "like cats in a chorus," and Nancy Bond in *The Voyage Begun* that bushes were tangled "like old steel wool."

The triumphant quality in any image, whether long or short, always lies not only in its precision but in its ability to take us by surprise, and still more to deliver the shock of recognition. That must be there, otherwise the image fails. And what shock does the cliché ever deliver? Besides delivering the shock of recognition, the rich, suggestive image brings with it an immediate, delighted acquiescence, a sense of peculiarly preposterous justification. "Yes, yes!" we exclaim to ourselves, or burst out laughing as we are sometimes forced to do when we come upon Lively's, Gardam's, or Hoban's dry, ironic, witty images. We feel in them that their creators must have souls that are, in Yeats's phrase, "self-delighting."

And this sense of the usually idiosyncratic, sometimes preposterous quality is noted by James Dickey when he quotes, in *Metaphor as Pure Adventure,* the French poet Pierre Riverdy: "Insofar as the juxtaposition of entities be separated by the greater distance, and yet be just, the metaphor will be thereby stronger."[14] I think at once of Sylvia Townsend Warner saying about listening to Schubert how she got "the sensation of holding the music in one's hand, feeling it flutter and burn and strive there, as though one were holding a wild bird," of being conscious during the writing of *Mr. Fortune's Maggot* that "the shape and balance of the narrative must be exactly right—or the whole thing would fall and break," so that she felt as if she "were in an advanced pregnancy with a Venetian glass child." She saw the church towers in the Norwich countryside rearing themselves "like melancholy teeth in an old jaw," immense crystal chandeliers as flying "like swans in the roofs of baroque churches," and the magnificent cut glass chandeliers in the Valencia Town Hall as being "like frosted walnut trees hanging upside down in the pale blue and pale gold saloon." She saw the roadman's daughter as a "large smooth creature like a bedroom ewer."

William Maxwell, who edited her letters, in which I found these images and innumerable others (for they poured from her in unpremeditated abundance), says of her that though her images "were characteristic of the way her mind worked, sometimes her comparisons were so startling that even she herself might have been surprised by them."[15] I trust that she was not only surprised but entirely delighted with: "I wish you could see the two cats, drowsing side by side in a Victorian nursing chair, their paws, their ears, their tails complementally adjusted, their blue eyes blinking open on a single thought of when I shall remember their suppertime. They might have been composed by Bach for two flutes."[16]

Furthermore, Dickey speaks of dilation around the image: what I would call its plangency, like a musical note, or the deep bronze sound of an enormous Japanese bell, struck, reverberating on and on. The whole sense of Greece somehow opens within us when Paula Fox says of starlight there, in her beautiful *Lily and the Lost Boy:* "The Aegean had been like a great pale flame stretching to the coast of Macedonia, a black line across the water, and the sky had been filled with a milky light as though there had been a silent explosion of stars." At dawn, "The sun would touch the peak of Hypsarion, nearly four thousand feet high, and there the light would flow down the slopes like honey." When Fox writes in *One-Eyed Cat* of how Ned "hated the way the housekeeper spoke in that false, soothing voice, as if she owned the country of calm and he was some kind of fool who's stumbled across its borders," I am at once, under my continued reading, left with a sense of fairy tale in a land where the woman's cool, lying, quiet superiority has affected all the inhabitants and the hero stumbles about, subject to a continuing scorn that is gathering subtly, almost unnoticed, but sensed along all his nerves, into the most tangled difficulties lying in wait for him in the future—as the most tangled difficulties are, in fact, gathering for Ned.

Dickey speaks of this experience as one holding "the passionate and mysterious aura of association. . . . For what the poet [or the writer of any creative work] is trying to accomplish is to discover relationships that give life: mental, physical, and imaginative life, the fullest and most electric sense of being."[17] He says of those relationships that "they carry an emotional charge, a general one which anyone might be expected to respond to, and another one to which any individual, in his particular life situation, is free to respond out of those specific conditions which have resulted in his being who he is,"[18] which is why I responded as I did to Fox's "country of calm," because my mind and imagination have been nourished on fantasy. He says further:

> The true metaphor orients the mind toward freedom and novelty; it encourages the mind to be daring. And at the same time the metaphor furnishes the mind with at least the illusion of a new kind of relational necessity, as well as giving it the joy—the pure joy—of employing faculties that are not used in conceptual language.[19]

These are the truest words one could utter of metaphor, and it is only toward the end of his essay that Dickey says something that, at least with reference to my own experiencing of the arrival of images, I feel must apply to poets specifically rather than to writers of prose. He directs us: "Find your own metaphors." Of course. Anyone else's are of no use to us. "Or better still," he says, "*make* your own."[20] I'm sure this must be possible for Dickey because usually a poem *is* a metaphor worked out most carefully and consciously to express a

central, controlling meaning, while packed with metaphors, all of
which contribute to that meaning. However, he confesses in the paragraphs that follow that he is "not satisfied" with a metaphor he has
been trying to work out. "It is a little too pat, too serviceable, too
one-dimensional."[21] I myself could never "work out" a metaphor, an
image, for I would only end with something "too pat, too serviceable,
too one-dimensional." And I wonder how the writers I have quoted
here have arrived at theirs.

I find, when I go back and read through the rough draft of a page,
that images have come of themselves, often without my being aware
of them *as* images. If one or the other hits me as not expressed in a
quite satisfying way, then I must think, words must be changed. But
they have seemed to arrive like lines of poetry or phrases in it, or like
good puns.*

I imagine that most writers are aware of images coming of their
own will, in their own way, and at times almost as if one calls forth
another, so that they appear in clots. For instance, there are only two
or three mild, almost unnoticeable ones scattered throughout the first
pages of *Charlotte's Web,* and then on one page we find,

> The next day was foggy. Everything on the farm was dripping
> wet. The grass looked like a magic carpet. The asparagus patch
> looked like a silver forest. On foggy mornings, Charlotte's web
> was truly a thing of beauty. This morning each thin strand was
> decorated with dozens of tiny beads of water. The web glistened
> in the light and made a pattern of loveliness and mystery, like
> a delicate veil.

It is as if this was a moment White had been waiting for, the
opportunity to describe, minutely and memorably, this particular
morning and Charlotte's web, the morning on which she does her first
miraculous weaving. It must have been a moment to which White's

---

*See page 213 for Frances Clarke Sayers's triple pun.

unconscious ("the little man in the basement") responded, for there are surprisingly few *separate* images in the rest of the book, though the whole novel is a metaphor for the loss of innocence.

Indeed, it's surprising that while there are many witty and wonderful images sprinkled throughout White's essays, there are comparatively few precise metaphors in his three books for children. But the images in these and in his essays always speak unmistakably of White, of his inimitable ability to combine an underlying rueful humor with a sense of sadness, anxiety, and inevitability; of the absurd, almost clownish quality of his own role; and of tiny human affairs struggling beneath the shadow of a looming, ruthless Fate.

In his "Death of a Pig," written in 1947, five years before *Charlotte's Web* was published, he says that when his pig fell sick, "The alarm spread rapidly. The classic outlines of the tragedy were lost. I found myself cast suddenly in the role of pig's friend and physician—a farcical character with an enema bag for a prop. I had a presentiment, the very first afternoon, that the play would never regain its balance and that my sympathies were now wholly with the pig."[22] Of Fred, White's dachshund, whom he alternately excoriates and admires, and notes always with a clear and loving eye, he says: "You could see him down there [at the pig's pen] at all hours, his white face parting the grass along the fence as he wobbled and stumbled about, his stethoscope dangling—a happy quack, writing his villainous prescriptions and grinning his corrosive grin."[23] When White must give the pig an enema, "The pig's lot and mine were inextricably bound now, as though the rubber tube were the silver cord. From then until the time of his death I held the pig steadily in the bowl of my mind. . . . Deep hemorrhagic infarcts—the phrase began fastening its hooks in my head."[24]

I can't imagine White having to "work out" these images; though, as Peter Neumeyer reveals in his analysis of the stages *Charlotte's Web* went through, he assuredly worked out the book itself once the compulsion to write it had come to him.[25] But these images in the essay seem to me a flowering of the emotional memory of this crucial event, which moved him deeply (he "went to bed, and cried internally—deep hemorrhagic intears"), for he noted two symbolic details at the burial: An enormous earthworm exposed by the grave wall "dug itself deeper . . . seeking ever remoter moistures at even lonelier depths." And just then, "a small green apple separated itself from a branch overhead and fell into the hole. Everything about this last scene seemed overwritten—the dismal sky, the shabby woods, the imminence of rain, the worm (legendary bedfellow of the dead), the apple (conventional garnish of a pig)."[26] This kind of observation, seeing the sadly humorous, the wry symbolism of both objects and atmosphere, and the way in which he expresses it, is pure White. Who but White could confess to "deep hemorrhagic intears"?

Colette's simile, given in the beginning, that clichés are like fleas in a cat's fur and must be nipped out, is so odd and so apt that one knows it to have been a natural emanation, a completely spontaneous revelation of her perfectionist love of, and concern for, both cats and writing. Virginia Woolf, concerning her composition of *The Waves* (as richly conceived a novel, as far as images go, along with *Ulysses* and *Finnegans Wake,* as one could find) said that though she was after certain effects:

> In actual writing one's mind, as you know, gets into a trance, and the different images seem to come unconsciously. It is very interesting to me, though, to see how deliberate it looks to a critic. Of course most of the work is done before one writes, and the concentration of writing makes one forget what the general effect is.[27]

VII

We come now to two facets of this subject about which there can be considerable difference of opinion: first, the use of clichés within dialogue and, second, within the text of a first-person novel told by one not particularly striving for literary effect, not literarily self-conscious, but trying nevertheless to tell the tale as effectively as possible in a relaxed way.

If a character uses clichés in conversation, should the writer muzzle that character? Has the author any right to? Shouldn't the character be let to speak in just the way he or she would, given a particular individuality? On the one hand, if we get too stern, either as writer or as editor, we end by cutting one phrase after another until we scarcely know where to stop. But on the other hand, it strikes me as deadly boring to fill our characters' talk with clichés just because most of us use them unthinkingly. As for certain eccentric characters, would it not be more interesting—and why not take advantage of the opportunity to increase richness and revelation of character?—to use expressions that would do just this rather than the old tedious, exhausted ones? (However, perhaps the author wishes a particular person to be tedious?) The mother in Janni Howker's *Isaac Campion,* while not in the least eccentric, is a farm woman and has a north country, Yorkshire way of speaking. Of Isaac's silent secretiveness, she says: "Yer a deep-swimming fish," and elsewhere, when Isaac wants to run off to find why his father has failed to come home, "No, yer don't. . . . I'm not losing me cavalry because I've lost me scouts."

Eudora Welty's *The Optimist's Daughter* seems to me a well-nigh perfect novel. And perhaps it's unfair of me to regret the very last page where Tish, Laurel's oldest friend, sends her off to catch her plane with, "There now. You'll catch it by the skin of your teeth." What a disappointment! No doubt she might have said it just that way, though there's no *need* for her to have done so. Not another cliché is to be found in the entire novel, nor do we miss them in the give and take of typically shaped Southern expressions, possibly typically Mississippian: "I'd give a pretty to know exactly what that rose is!" And we recall Flannery O'Connor saying that "The best American fiction has always been regional. . . . The writer operates at a peculiar crossroads where time and place and eternity somehow meet. His problem is to find that location."[28]

However, there is an art to using the local or current idiom, which may be the local or current clichés; there is a necessity to *listen* to what one has written. Alan Garner's *The Owl Service* was assuredly created out of the sense of place—Wales in this instance—its legends, its countryside, and its traditions. But most unfortunately, considering the richness of his material, he had been writing for television just before he wrote the novel.

Dialogue, which can be the means of communicating individuality above all else, raises a question here: Can the too-faithful echoing of reality result in an injury to art? In *The Owl Service* the dialogues are even more staccato in rhythm than in *Elidor,* Garner's previous novel. And the number of cliché phrases and expressions is truly astonishing: "Once bitten twice shy," "How now brown cow," "Too much clean living—I'll cut down on the yoghurt," "Holy cow," "How super," "We'll make a packet on the telly," "You can say that again," "We've had a basin-full," "His head's screwed on," "Pull the other—it's got bells on," "For crying out loud." Smart-aleck retorts made their appearance to some extent in *Elidor,* but here their use is carried to such an extreme that they strike us as almost an ingratiation with that ten-to-eighteen age group Garner has said he was writing for: as if he were slanting his book, and this is a regrettable impression. It is no use protesting: "But this is the way people—especially teenagers—talk." Well, at least they did at the time Garner wrote his novel, so that the book is dated because of the use of this kind of dialogue. Art is selective. The artist *must* select, for strict naturalism can prove to be bad art. Oddly enough, Garner says in an explanatory essay that he learned Welsh in order not to use it, to avoid the "superficial in characterization—the 'Come you here, bach' school of writing." And he says of the possible insertion here and there of "a gratuitous, and untranslated, line of the language" that "This is reality laid on with a trowel [the cliché perhaps an effect of his television writing on his style here as well as in his novel?] and it remains external and false."[29]

Garner therefore clearly understood the danger of strict naturalism and might well have looked further into the gratuitous use of another kind of language, using the word *gratuitous* in the legal sense to mean something given without receiving any return value. It is true that the clichés in their dialogue reveal the Englishness of Roger and Clive, and that Gwyn always tries to be less Welsh. But what Garner has succeeded in doing, in his use of a TV type of dialogue, in his unsparing and unselective use of worn phrases in the utterances, quite often as the sole utterances, of those of his characters who use them, is to lessen the number of opportunities for conveying facets of individuality, and to cheapen the texture and therefore the content of his work.

As for clichés used throughout the telling of a first-person novel, I find none, for instance, in *Isaac Campion,* told by the old man about his youth. It is a moving and tender story, giving off most wondrously the essence of this Yorkshire farmer's character, felt in every line he speaks. All the way through, it is his way of seeing that we enjoy, his idiosyncratic utterances, never touched by the worn or the usual.

In *The Moves Make the Man,* Bruce Brooks speaks in a black boy's way through Jerome Foxworthy, but in a way wholly individual to Jerome. I have already quoted his "little definition of Jerome," expanding on the title of the novel. Toward the end of the book he reaches the height of his moves:

No fakeless ball for Jerome. So I slipped my own moves back on piece by piece like they were old clothes I had left hanging up for a couple of months and did they still fit? . . . But now I was hungry for some good old swift deceit, and if the body would be avenged for its servitude and untruth, then I was set to suffer. . . . I threw head so nasty my neck felt like it stretched two inches a day. I slung myself through space blind with speed and could not think for cunning. . . . Every time I went up was pure adventure, I was pure mystery to myself and as long as it stayed that way I was the greatest basketball player on the face of the place in space with grace. . . . The moves piled up and combined into each other and every night I was a new set added to the old, complicated but smooth as air.

I care little for basketball, but Jerome telling of his life with it, his immersion in it, *sent* me (how do I put it more briefly and precisely?) and held me throughout and left me thinking that quite possibly this must be one of the most poetic explications of the game ever written. Each metaphor is precisely right and delivers its own pungent, peculiar shock of recognition.

As it turns out, I could very well be hoist by my own petard. (A cliché? Perhaps: It's an expression that comes from far back in our language—1598 is the date given by the *Oxford*—but possibly not used often enough to have become a cliché.) Andrew as a young man tells his own story in *Beyond Silence,* and I asked a friend to remind me of any lapses by pointing out what he thought were clichés in the novel. He gave me these examples: "pitch black," "pitch dark," "just the tip of the iceberg," "at death's door," "a wave of relief," "in the pit of the stomach," "weep and wail," "keeping it all bottled up," "take a load off your back," "put him in his place," "under his wing," "dead tired," "she had him on a string," "I held up my end," "she never let me down," "she saved my hide," "can't for the life of me," "hadn't thought twice about it," and "a flight of steps."

He then asked if I thought he had defined the word *cliché* too broadly, and I answered that in some cases I thought he had, though it can't be denied that many of those phrases of Andrew's are well-worn. But both he and I like "a flight of steps," for instance, and can't think how to better it. Though of course it would be wise to let the phrase come rather than to *try* to better it. Actually, it is very difficult to decide precisely where the dividing line lies between the obviously worn-out expressions and those that we simply use often but that still can't be considered clichés.

Typically, I never noticed that the phrases my friend pointed out were clichés—they were all in the flow of Andrew's thought. And Eudora Welty, completely relaxed (as if thoroughly enjoying herself in telling *The Ponder Heart* through the first person of Uncle Daniel Ponder's niece), is not at all backward about using whatever clichés she feels her Edna Earle would naturally use. In fact, I wonder if

Welty ever thought about the matter at all. Quite likely she wasn't aware of Edna Earle's expressions as clichés but was being a Mississippi landlady, keeper of a boardinghouse: "Uncle Daniel . . . dresses fit to kill . . . he's as good as gold . . . and in the whole shooting match, I don't care from where or how far they've come, no one can hold a candle to Uncle Daniel for looks or manner." It's an easy, local style, and meant to be that, but *The Ponder Heart* seems to me far less satisfying to read than *The Optimist's Daughter.* I rather often have to rest myself from Edna Earle's insistent way of speaking, as if I might have enjoyed a half hour of actual monologue but would have found it hard to bear going on any longer at one sitting.

On the other hand, in Russell Hoban's *Turtle Diary,* you will rarely find even the most inoffensive clichés throughout the entirety of his first-person tellings. These alternate between the voice of William G. and Neaera H. Here one finds such descriptions—expressed in the typically understated, wryly comic Hoban style, of a certain form of marine life at the aquarium—as, "a poor little civil-servant-looking shark," and oyster-catchers "looking as if they had hands clasped behind their backs like little European philosophers in yachting gear." "The small black faces" of gibbons seem to be "full of Zen," after which he goes into a freewheeling exploration through one image after another of his own self in relation to Zen. "No way to hold the sun in the eye, be held by it, swimming, swimming," referring to the turtles whom he and Neaera H. free into the ocean.

The current slang of any era is closely related to clichés, and it gets just as tiresome if used too often. Yet we all use it: We remember certain eras by the slang they created, as we remember the early 1900s and the twenties especially. But how heavily can it be stitched into any kind of manuscript without defeating the story, without dating it in a way that causes it to lose the timelessness that keeps a book alive? I am thinking of Mary McCarthy's *The Group,* for example, which I finally had to put down after going on with it far past the point where my impulse gave out. In *The Moves Make the Man,* Brooks gives no indication of era through current slang. Jerome, being black, uses black speech patterns, but they are colorful and vigorously expressive. The only phrases that become at all insistent are "your black ass," "my black ass," "your white ass," as in "Get your black ass over here," just as there is a too-generous use, in *A Hero Ain't Nothin' But a Sandwich,* of the word *fuck,* a cliché word of our time if ever there was one.

In Brooks's *Midnight Hour Encores,* I soon became aware of the clichés of current slang and wearied of them long before the end of the book. Nothing is just bad, it's either "crap" or "crapola," again and again. And you don't go to a place, you "hit" it, again and again. As for the word *great:* a car "runs great," "guys felt great," "he's a great detail man," "I had some great music," "great stuff," "the stool feels great," "Great. We're sitting back," "Great. That's cool," "this piece is great," "you're a great kid. I want you to look back and decide I was a great father," with nine more instances to come. *Great* is, in fact, another of the unbearably often reiterated burden words of our time. And I would say that here Brooks is doing exactly the opposite of what he did in handling the voice of Jerome, to the detriment of *Midnight Hour Encores.* It is reminiscent of Alan Garner and his plethora of TV-influenced slang in *The Owl Service.* A touch is enough.

VIII

Like those tiny mammals leading their obscure, hidden lives in the time of the dinosaurs, mammals that would one day become the creatures we are now, there must be all sorts of phrases lying unnoticed within our literature that will one day be alive on everyone's tongue. "As large as life and twice as natural," wrote Lewis Carroll in *Alice,* words first spoken by the king's messenger, and no one just then paid any particular attention. "Oh, frabjous day, calloo, callay!" some of us exclaim when supremely happy (I did, yesterday, at least "Oh, frabjous day!" when I was out with friends walking along the ocean in sparkling weather, and one of them finished, with feeling, "Calloo, callay!"), using what is not yet a cliché in our time but is generally recognized as Carroll's unique expression of joy. "You are old, Father William," I say to myself when weary. "Jam yesterday, jam tomorrow, but never jam today," we say ironically, or even sardonically if bitterness is involved, when it doesn't seem likely that some promise will ever be kept. "It takes all the running you can do to stay in the same place," we say of the dizzying pace of our lives, and "Off with his head!" of someone in disgrace (my Scottish husband told me that north of the border they say, "Aff wi' his heed!" which I like even better.) The Red Queen was responsible for the first, and the Queen of Hearts for the second. Then, of course, we remember Humpty Dumpty's "There's glory for you." Of some cool, smug individual we say: "She [or he] has a smile like a Cheshire cat's," which aren't Carroll's words at all, but he made recognizable the Cheshire cat kind of person.

Most of the time we haven't an idea where or how our clichés originated. Folk sayings, such as "Red sky at night, shepherd's delight, red sky at morning, shepherd's warning"; "A watched pot never boils"; and "A stitch in time saves nine" obviously came out of our folk past when TV weather forecasters and microwave ovens were unimaginable and wives carefully darned their husbands' socks with firm, minute weavings and turned the collars on their shirts. Wallace Stegner, in his *The Spectator Bird*, brings up a cliché that perhaps also came out of our folk past. But he is puzzled and impatient. His protagonist, Joe Alston, says in reply to his wife, who has just remarked that she doesn't go around with a chip on her shoulder: "Speaking of which . . . did you ever *see* anybody put a chip on his shoulder and dare somebody to knock it off? Where do we get clichés like that? *Tom Sawyer* or someplace, I suppose. Maybe once, down in some Mississippi woodyard, somebody made his dare like that, and forever after we have no way to express challenge but that stupid metaphor."

Yes! Why do some sayings stick, foolish as they may be, putting into words what nobody ever does, and others sink away?

Shakespeare was the supreme purveyor of our clichés, as the English journalist Bernard Levin has pointed out:

> If you cannot understand my argument, and declare "It's Greek to me," you are quoting Shakespeare; if you claim to be more sinned against than sinning, you are quoting Shakespeare; if you recall your salad days, you are quoting Shakespeare; if you act more in sorrow than in anger, if your wish is father to the thought, if your lost property has vanished into thin air, you are quoting Shakespeare; if you have ever refused to budge an inch or suffered from green-eyed jealousy, if you have played fast and loose, if you have been tongue-tied, a tower of strength, hoodwinked or in a pickle, if you have knitted your brows, made a virtue of necessity, insisted on fair play, slept not one wink, stood on ceremony, danced attendance (on your lord and master), laughed yourself into stitches, had short shrift, cold comfort or too much of a good thing, if you have seen better days or lived in a fool's paradise—why, be that as it may, the more fool you, for it is a foregone conclusion that you are (as good luck would have it) quoting Shakespeare; if you think it is early days and clear out bag and baggage, if you think it is high time and that that is the long and short of it, if you believe that the game is up and that truth will out even if it involves your own flesh and blood, if you lie low till the crack of doom because you suspect foul play, if you have your teeth set on edge (at one fell swoop) without rhyme or reason, then—to give the devil his due—if the truth were known (for surely you have a tongue in your head) you are quoting Shakespeare; even if you bid me good riddance and send me packing, if you wish I was dead as a doornail, if you think I am an eyesore, a laughing stock, the devil incarnate, a stony-hearted villain, bloody-minded or a blinking idiot, then—by Jove! O Lord! Tut, tut! for goodness' sake! what the dickens!

but me no buts—it is all one to me, for you are quoting Shakespeare.*[30]

But let us go back eons before Shakespeare. John E. Pfeiffer, a lifelong scholar of human evolution, a scientist who can quote the poet Muriel Rukeyser's words, "The universe is made of stories, not atoms," has thought about the very earliest image-making:

The Cro-Magnons probably invented a fair share of high-imagery words in the shaping of their myths. Also, and perhaps on a larger scale, they probably enriched their languages with a burst of new double-image comparisons, new metaphors which in a flash of fresh insight reveal new relationships between familiar things. Brooks run, arrows fly, and tempers flare only figuratively, only in language. These metaphors were poetry once upon a time, bright new perceptions, then clichés—and at last they passed beyond cliché into everyday speech. These and thousands of other comparisons are imbedded in language, ancient but age unknown, perhaps some dating back to prehistoric times. If we could only identify and date the oldest. There is a vast untapped linguistic archeology here.[31]

Yes, because as Pfeiffer says elsewhere, "Cro-Magnon had no writing. But they had symbols, notably in the form of art that came suddenly along with mass hunting and status and personal adornment." He speaks of pieces of antler, bone, limestone, and ivory etched

---

*Gary Taylor, in a June 22, 1990, *New York Times Book Review* essay entitled "Brush Up Your Shakespeare," says that Bernard Levin, in piling up these sixty-two phrases, is not giving us Shakespeare's writing. In almost every case, he maintains, "Mr. Levin is actually quoting the clichés of early modern English, verbal dust gilded over with antiquity. If junk hangs around long enough, it becomes an antique. And if one writer is still widely read when his contemporaries are not, then what is single and peculiar becomes indistinguishable from what was once the common tongue."

with figures, "among them a hunter taking aim at a wild ox, a mammoth engraved on mammoth tusk, and a bone item known as 'amorous pursuits' showing on one side a man following a woman and, on the other, a male bison following a female bison."[32] There we have drawn image-making, it seems to me: "As the male bison follows after the female, so I follow after you."

Furthermore, Pfeiffer tells us, in a small cave called El Juyo, about five miles west of Santander on the northern coast of Spain, after hours upon hours of painstaking uncovering, archaeologists came on a stone that seemed to contain a pair of eyes. Further clearing revealed a hairline along a forehead, a nose, a mustache, a beard on one side of the head, but on the other a sharp feline tooth, which gave it an entirely different aspect, that of a cat, with lines of black spots on either side of the nose to suggest the bases of catlike whiskers. What is more, the human side of the face was so placed that those entering the cave, more than twenty feet away, saw the human side. But in order to see the feline side, they had to come close and examine the head by the light of a torch or lamp. Half human, half beast, this stone face is, its creator seemed to be saying, dual, opposite, double in theme—and so are our natures. Rather than drawn, this ancient metaphor of Dr. Jekyll and Mr. Hyde is stone, conceived some 140,000 years ago.[33]

Concerning the forces and circumstances that encourage metaphor-making today, Pfeiffer tells of Keith Basso, of the University of New Mexico, who has analyzed the process among western Apache Indians, collecting coined metaphors, "private acts of discovery and recognition,"[34] including:

> Lightning is a boy
> Ravens are widows
> Carrion beetle is a whiteman
> Dogs are children
> Coyotes are western Apaches

Butterflies are girls
Burros are old women[35]

"Notice," says Pfeiffer, "that commentaries, the criticisms, are oblique. The humans are always mentioned second in the metaphors. It is gentler that way. To say 'A widow is a raven' or 'A whiteman is a carrion beetle' would be bad manners. Furthermore, it might bring tensions out into the open. . . . Metaphors are open-ended,"[36] he continues, after quoting explanations of these images given by the western Apaches, beginnings that trigger further comparisons and flights of imagination. The comparison of boys and lightning instantly and automatically includes qualities irrelevant at the time and in that context, but potential sources of new comparisons later on.

I X

We humans seem naturally to fall into image-making. Oliver Sacks, in *The Man Who Mistook His Wife for a Hat*, tells of Rebecca, who, at the age of nineteen, was "just like a child" but not a child, because she was an adult and capable of explaining her feelings and her desires through images in the most moving way.

Rather suddenly, after her grandmother's death, she became clear and decisive. "I want no more classes, no more workshops," she said. "They do nothing for me. They do nothing to bring me together." And then, with that power for the apt model or metaphor I so admired, and which was so well developed in her despite her low IQ, she looked down at the office carpet and said:

"I'm like a sort of living carpet. I need a pattern, a design, like you have on that carpet. I come apart, I unravel, unless there's a design." I looked down at the carpet, as Rebecca said this, and found myself thinking of Sherrington's famous image, comparing the brain/mind to an "enchanted loom," weaving patterns ever-dissolving, but always with a meaning. I thought: can one have a raw carpet without a design? Could one have the design without the carpet (but this seemed like a smile without the Cheshire cat)? A "living" carpet, as Rebecca was, had to have both—and she especially, with her lack of schematic structure (the warp and woof, the *knit* of the carpet, so to speak), might indeed unravel without a design (the scenic or narrative structure of the carpet).[37]

Undoubtedly in all of us, writers or not, images must constantly flow in and out of our thoughts, unremarked by us. The other day I was walking in the forest, thinking of a certain dear friend who had suffered so many wracked hours during his last years. "He was sandpapered with pain," I said to myself, and undoubtedly would not have noted the image if I hadn't been generally reflecting on them for this essay.

We humans seem to make images as inevitably as boiling water makes bubbles, unable to help ourselves any more than the heated water can. What is the source of our compulsion always to be saying "like—like—like"; always to be making some obvious, subtle, absurd, or poignant comparisons, and, if not given our own new-minted ones from somewhere in our unconscious, falling back on the old and using them without even being aware of it? Never can we let a thing seem to be itself alone, but must put it in relation to something else. Why? Because we must explain more clearly, more intimately, more precisely, more urgently, by putting the abstract into the concrete; by bringing the sight or concept closer to something more familiar so that complexities can be made understandable, or warm and unforgettable, rather than leaving them cold and mental; by giving sights and sounds and textures a different kind of evocation; by making the serious witty or comic or at least shaping it to bring a smile to the lips. Or perhaps images spring forth purely for the joy or pleasure of it, to call up a memory, to put one piece of knowledge next to another, to make some happening still more moving to the imagination so as to evoke multiple meanings, overtones.

It is fascinating to discern how certain images, appearing throughout a writer's work, can give the writer away, as Virginia Woolf's repeated image of "a fin in a waste of waters," and the recurrence of moths—the fragile moth beating itself to death against the dusty pane, as in her essay "The Death of the Moth," or drawn inescapably to the dazzling light, then consumed in the candle's flame—as in her childhood memory, repeated more than once in her diary and also in *Jacob's Room*—give away the profound torment of her spirit. (Her novel *The Waves* was to have been titled *The Moths*.)

In an essay on Walter de la Mare, Graham Greene comments on how de la Mare could "play consciously with clichés (hemmed like James's between inverted commas) turning them underside as it were to the reader, and showing what other meanings lie there hidden."[38] And one could wonder if de la Mare saw the underside of his own compulsion to repeat the circumstance of bleak railroad stations or the railway journey in his stories, which Greene calls an obsession. In "The Tree" there is the "sole traveller to alight on the frosted timbers of an obscure little station." In "Crewe" he describes its railway station interior in the most forbidding terms, how "the long grimed windows," "the failing, feeble light," "the grained massive black leather furniture" all in all "made for a scene of extreme and diabolical violence." It couldn't have been "designed by a really *good* man." In "A Froward Child," he describes the "sad neutral winter landscape" in which the train lights had come on. In "Ding Dong Bell" the noonday express sweeps in "with a wildly soaring crescendo of lamentation . . . through the little green empty station—its window a long broken faceless facade glint of sunlit glass—and that too vanished. Vanished!"

The same tone pervades de la Mare's poetry—the melancholy, lonely voice; the obsession with death and ghosts, with shadows, echoes, lost children, or children lured away; the deep and penetrating silences after sound. Surely these are all metaphors for de la Mare's own sense of lostness, for they are everywhere in his work. In his poetry in *Peacock Pie* I find thirteen poems at least, including the final one, of which I quote the last verse, that express to perfection de la Mare's sound of melancholy loneliness and desertion.

>   No bird above the steep of time
>   Sang of a livelong quest;
>   No wind breathed
>   Rest:
>   "Lone for an end!" cried Knight to steed,
>   Loosed an eager rein—
>   Charged with his challenge into Space:
>   And quiet did quiet remain.

X

Am I saying finally that all cliché words and phrases should be mercilessly nipped from every manuscript, as Colette advised? Ah, but it *is* all according to the occasion, as even Colette herself, and Virginia Woolf, and Sylvia Townsend Warner, to take three superb writers, reveal to us.

When asked by her hostess at a hotel if she would like a siesta, Colette—telling a story in the first person, herself obviously being that person—replied, "Everything in its own good time. I'm never sleepy the first day," and then reflected that "Her plump person had the effect of making me talk in proverbs and maxims and all the facile clichés of 'popular' wisdom."

Virginia Woolf, the last writer one would imagine being given to clichés, writes in *To the Lighthouse* of Mrs. Ramsay that "She could not help laughing herself sometimes. She said, the other day, something about 'waves mountains high.' Yes, said Charles Tansley, it was a little rough. 'Aren't you drenched to the skin?' she had said. 'Damp, not wet through,' said Mr. Tansley, pinching his sleeve, feeling his socks." Thus, in these few lines, see how she reveals the contrast between a humorous, delightful woman who has indulged herself in a little teasing and exaggeration and this wretched bachelor, who always talked about who was "brilliant but I think fundamentally unsound," and who invariably spoke with the most humorless and scholarly accuracy, never allowing anyone even the most minimal straying from the unimportant but unavoidable fact.

As for Warner, in a short story she characterizes a certain type of lady of easy virtue as one who had, in her own view, "an ardent, selfless, indefatigable passion for the truth; for running it down, and handing it on. She liked facts to be ascertained, nails to be hit on the head, speculations to be shot on the wing, ambiguities to be resolved and pigeonholed."

Ursula Le Guin, in her poem "Inventory," in which someone is going over the aging body for all the signs of age, notes that there has been a

> Replacement of cheek by jowl,
> Of curve by hook or crook.

Clichés are especially unforgivable in poetry, the unthinking ones —where we notice them as we might not in prose. But what a pleasure to find such witty use of these two aged clichés, in which their own age as well as their turned meaning enters in as part of the artistry. Elsewhere, in "Silk Days," Le Guin refuses imagery, at least in these five lines:

> Ironing smells like ironing.
> It isn't really like
> anything. Doesn't need
> a simile.
> Has its own equipment.

Astonishingly (to me, at any rate), friends reading this essay were very protective of clichés, crying, "Oh, but they're a part of our language!" What difference does that make? So are long, pretentious, esoteric words that only serve to distance or obscure the meanings of our sentences. We don't *have* to use them simply because they are a part of our language. We can choose not to. In general, can there really be any choice between the personal and the self-delighting, very possibly the startling or the subtly comic, as opposed to images worn thin as the heel of an old sock? Reflecting on the richness of our language, on the opportunities it offers for mysterious significances that illumine far beyond the obvious, it seems to me that there is nothing to do, in our writing if not in our speech, but throw out the sock.

ONE WOMAN AS
WRITER AND FEMINIST:
SEARCHING FOR BALANCE

*To have and bring up kids is to be about as immersed in life as one
can be, but it does not always follow that one drowns.*

URSULA K. LE GUIN
Dancing at the Edge of the World

There are words that have rung down through four hundred years—those of Elizabeth I, for example, speaking to her counsellors some time after she came to the throne, in 1588. Remember that Virginia Woolf imagined a young woman, Shakespeare's sister, Judith, frantic with frustrated desire to use her lust for writing, going to London and ending there a suicide, for quite apart from writing plays, women could not even take the feminine parts at the Globe Theatre. It is easy to understand, then, that it had to be a queen, and a powerful and headstrong one at that, who could utter these bitter, truthful words so openly in the sixteenth century: "Had I been born crested rather than cloven, my lords, you would not have treated me so."

But along came Aphra Behn, born thirty-seven years after Elizabeth died, who stood up out of a sea of Englishwomen and announced: "I

know who I am, and what I can do, and I will be myself." Those
may not have been her exact words, but her actions spoke for her.
Within the forty-nine years of her life she was dramatist, novelist,
and poet, and when she lost her husband, a Dutch merchant, she
served her country as a spy in Antwerp and Holland. "But the courage
of her!" we have to exclaim, for how many women spies in foreign
countries can there have been in the 1600s? And when she turned to
writing, she used her own experiences, whereupon it was said of her
words that they were as indecent and witty and as bustling with foreign
and amorous intrigues as any Restoration dramatist's. She was the first
Englishwoman to write for a living and the first woman playwright
to write for the English stage, and when she died, she was buried in
the Poets' Corner of Westminster Abbey.

When I remember that I had read *A Room of One's Own* at least by
the 1950s, and that Sylvia Townsend Warner had written the following
words to Nancy Cunard on April 24, 1944, and yet that I did not
become aware of the feminist movement as something abroad in the
land, a part of the very air I breathed, until somewhere around the
early 1960s, I am both puzzled and ashamed.* Here are Warner's
words: "The great civil war, Nancy, that will come and must come
before the world can begin to grow up, will be fought out on this
terrain of man and woman, and we must storm and hold Cape Turk
before we talk of social justice."[1]

I can only see the truth of the matter as lying in the fact that I
knew I was to be a writer from the age of eleven, that there was never
any doubt in my mind: *I could not* be anything else, never only a wife
and mother, as a man is never only a husband and father. I therefore
had a sense of myself very early and never once thought of being
"permitted" (Carolyn Heilbrun's favorite word throughout *Writing a
Woman's Life* and at times in *Hamlet's Mother*) to do as I had envisioned

---

*In the first draft of this essay, which appeared in the *Children's Literature Association
Quarterly* (Winter 1982), I put the date as the mid-1970s. But when I look back
on certain places and conversations, I realize I was mistaken.

with my life. And this sense of self is what is lacking, as we well know by now, in so many women. I had told my husband before we were married that writing was to be my profession, to which he replied, "Of course!" We did not speak of children until nine years after marrying. And I was not bent on proving myself as an individual (feeling no need) but on writing something I felt worthy of being published.

Yet gradually I was becoming aware of two positions composing my outlook with regard to the whole idea of women's liberation and feminist criticism. By then, there was absolutely no doubt in my mind that I'd been a feminist without realizing it ever since I was old enough to respond to the world of society, if I'm to judge by the upwellings that surfaced in the books I've written about Julia Redfern, in *A Room Made of Windows* particularly, and thereafter in other kinds of novels: *To the Green Mountains* and *Beyond Silence*. Julia is myself as a child, though a good many of the scenes never happened. But it is the character and personality of Julia that are unmistakable, her resentments and rebellions, her sometimes misguided determination to do what is challenging even if unwise, to find means of self-expression, to not be put down.

Julia bursts out at her brother Greg one day (in *Julia and the Hand of God*) concerning their grandmother's attitude toward them. And of course it might have been an older sister rather than an older brother who had turned out to be Gramma's favorite, but somehow there's a perception in Julia's mind that for Gramma the male has prerogatives. He's doing something important and he's not to be disturbed, while it's natural that Julia, being female, can be disturbed at any time, called upon to set the table (around Greg's project, and Greg, working on it) and be at Gramma's beck and call the day long, whether she's struggling to write something decent in her ledger or not. And it isn't that Julia shouldn't be expected to help; it's that Greg never is when he's involved in what he most passionately wants to do. Gramma appears to be operating in the tradition of masculine privileges.

It seems to me revealing of one part of my attitude toward feminism that three memories having to do with writing and the relationship between men and women have stayed with me. One memory is of an autobiographical statement by Jacquetta Hawkes, the archaeologist, who said that when she was in the company of her masculine colleagues during scientific discussions, whatever she said seemed to rise like smoke and disappear among the easy, assured statements of the men, that she could not seem to make herself heard in the midst of those loud, confident voices.

The second memory is of a male friend of the family saying off-handedly to my husband, soon after I had had my first book (a novel for adults) published to good reviews, that it was regrettable that none of our group had accomplished anything creatively. (Could he, quite automatically, have been thinking simply of the men?) The third memory is of another male friend observing amusedly, upon my saying that I was brooding another children's book, "Oh, Eleanor, nobody would have to *brood* a children's book!" I asked him if he'd ever written one, anything either for adults *or* for children. To which he replied, still with amusement and a slight lowering of the eyelids as if it didn't really matter, "No-o-o." Even as I recall this brief exchange I'm reminded with a chuckle of George Eliot's words: "A man's mind—what there is of it—has always the advantage of being masculine . . . and even his ignorance is of a sounder quality."

But in the beginning I spoke of an ambiguity in my attitude with regard to feminism ("two positions composing my outlook") and, just above, "one part of my attitude toward" feminism. I've never particularly desired to be called Ms. Cameron, while understanding perfectly that Mrs. is a symbol of second place, a symbol of subjection in the eyes of the women's liberationists, and understanding as well that Ms. comes in handy in writing business letters. And I would just as soon be called madam chairman as madam chairperson. Yet here again is the symbol of inferiority, unless we take "chairman" in the same spirit as we take "the race of man," "man" being used in the general sense, which liberationists refuse to do. And I would have had no desire, in the hottest early days of rebellion, to change my name, had it been E. Newman, to E. Newwoman, or even to E. Newperson. So that clearly I am not a purist—not in these respects, in any case. But I do struggle to avoid the pronouns *him* or *his* or *he* when I am referring in an essay to whomever could be of either sex, for long usage so easily and unconsciously takes over. Lois Kuznets, in a fascinating essay, "Good News From the Land of the Brontyfans, Or Intertextuality in Clarke's *The Return of the Twelves*" takes me to task by putting "(sic)" at the end of my sentence, "whether the child is conscious of it or not, he goes back to his favorite author's *particular way of expressing himself.*" As well she should have, for back in 1967 and 1968 I was not yet struggling to get rid of *his* and *himself.* And of course she had to reveal her awareness of my misuse, and that I should have written, "whether the child is conscious of this or not, it goes back to a favorite author's unique mode of expression, that author's style, the *sound* of it."[2] If one thinks long enough, those *he*s and *him*s and other pronouns in the same category, which we use to refer to either sex, *can* be gotten around.*

And so: a paper on feminist criticism, with relation to some of my women characters, and concerning the extent to which my identity as a writer is connected with my identity as a woman. This was the request of the Children's Literature Association.

When it came, there immediately rose in my mind the image of Elizabeth Rule in *To the Green Mountains,* of whom still another male friend said with obvious dislike, "She's a cold character." "No," I replied, "independent, but not cold at all." "Cold," he insisted.

---

*Leonard Shlain, in his *Art and Physics,* gets around these difficulties by simply substituting *she* for *he* or *her* for *him,* as "the artist leads the viewer to question all her intuitive knowledge about time," on page 225.

Incidentally, it is interesting to see how sexist tradition is built into the Chinese language. In Bill Bryson's *The Mother Tongue,* he points out on page 117 that radicals (or pictographs) of two women mean *quarrel* and radicals of three women mean *gossip.* Of course, men never quarrel or gossip!

"You remember she shows little emotion when Kath tells her that Tiss's church has burned down, after all the work of Tiss and her people to build it, when they had so few resources."

There is a question in my mind as to whether Elizabeth shows, through her daughter Kath's eyes, sufficient emotion or not. But this is revealing: The exchange between Kath and her mother takes only twenty-one lines in a book of one hundred and eighty pages, so that there must be qualities in Elizabeth Rule revealed all through the book that my friend did not care for—her independence, her downrightness, the firm assurance in her attitude to the colored help, whom she would not allow to be called by that denigrating name all black people were still being called in 1917, long after the Civil War, and are still being called by racists. And what made me call her Elizabeth Rule? Why that last name? Simply, it came to me as satisfying in combination with Elizabeth. Perhaps it was not a good choice, considering her force of character; possibly it plays down through evocation what is loving and compassionate in her. Or possibly the unconscious was at work giving me this name as the essential index of her nature, at least in situations such as she was experiencing in running a small-town hotel. For the names that writers give their characters, or are given *to* writers by their unconscious for their characters, are often of considerable interest.*

But I had not set out to create an appealing protagonist. Elizabeth made herself known to me over a period of many years before the book was written, and I wrote her and the child Kath's story only with the idea of telling it, as it revealed itself to me, as truthfully as I could and not to endear Elizabeth to the reader. She is herself, with what I saw as her good qualities as well as her failings, though Elizabeth in 1917 happens to be one of my independent women most nearly matching the picture of the feminist in the public mind today.

---

*See Roland Barthes, "Proust and Names" in his *New Critical Essays*, pages 55–68; and Leon Edel, "The Killer and the Slain," in his *Stuff of Sleep and Dreams: Experiments in Literary Psychology*, pages 308–23.

However, Julia Redfern seems, at the age of twelve in *A Room Made of Windows* (taking place in the 1920s) to foretell the feminist outlook she will become conscious of much later. Her next-door neighbor, Rhiannon Moore, a pianist who lives alone in a big house and with whom Julia has become intimate, says casually one day: "You may not write at all, you know." Julia is filled with shocked disbelief; she feels betrayed by her most treasured friend. Whereupon Mrs. Moore explains:

> "I only want to tell you that just to live with all your senses
> to the fullest, to have a family—"
> "To be ordinary, you mean!" cried Julia. "Well, I'm not *going*
> to be ordinary. That's dis*gus*ting—"
> Mrs. Moore suddenly sank into a chair and laughed until the
> tears came to her eyes while Julia stared at her in bewilderment,
> not knowing what to think.

Yet, says Rhiannon, she knows what Julia means because she herself had that same conviction "centuries ago," yet now she can't express what happiness she has in her son, Oren, what satisfaction in his own career as a pianist, in his tremendous giftedness. She had herself played in public and still composes, but now so much of her pleasure is centered in him. She has handed on something.

Well, says Julia, "*I'm* never going to hand on my ambition to anyone—to a bunch of kids. I'm going to keep it and work on it and make it grow."

Then perhaps Julia could manage better than she, Rhiannon Moore, had done. Maybe Julia could have it all, her work and everything else besides. For the truth of the matter is that Rhiannon, as she tells Julia later, hadn't considered her husband in the years when she was trying to become a concert pianist:

> "And so finally he decided that if my music and my friends
> of that world, who were always filling our house and consuming

my time when I wasn't practicing, were the most important part
of my life, then he would go and leave me to them. Which he
did."

"And did you love him, Mrs. Moore?"

"Very much—very, very much, I discovered after he'd left
and refused to come back. But I'd gone on thinking, you see,
that I could just have my own life without being too much
concerned whether he was happy or not. Or at least I didn't
realize, I saw later, that I wasn't being concerned. I hope you
are never so blind, Julia, as to become that lost in your work.
Never so blind!"

In *Beyond Silence* there is a child who has the same strong sense of
herself as Julia has—Deirdre Montmorency, daughter of the estate
manager in 1890 at Cames Castle in Scotland, though this is a time
fantasy taking place right after the Vietnam War. And there is another
woman in *Silence,* curiously like Rhiannon Moore in *Room,* I see now,
though I hadn't seen it before: Nell Cames, the boy Andrew's mother
in the present time. Because her husband fails, at her desperate urging,
to take advantage of their son Hoagy's indecision about the war in
Vietnam to dissuade him from going, Hoagy comes back physically
injured and spiritually destroyed; eventually he commits suicide. Nell
then turns wholly to her writing, withdrawing from her husband to
the point of leaving their bedroom and sleeping in her study. So that,
in effect, she is no longer married to him but to her work. She is no
longer concerned with him and eventually they divorce. There is a
kind of pattern in my work of the neglected husband, to which Grant's
wife Tissie in *Mountains* contributes in her own way. However, she is
not of the feminist world, the world of longed-for or attained self-
expression, as Rhiannon Moore and Nell Cames are in their demanding
absorptions.

Finally, the other questions that have been asked: "What are your
attitudes toward your characters? Are there differences in your attitudes

concerning the men and the women? Feminist issues are apparent. Was that conscious or not?"

Entirely unconscious. Yet I see, now that the matter has been put to me, that these issues are apparent. I see how my deepest attitudes about relationships between men and women have been expressing themselves. But I could not have harbored differing attitudes toward my male and female characters, for these human beings had all grown in my unconscious over a long period of time, freely, without ever, in any way, being pressed into preconceived sensibilities according to some conscious determination on my part to express a certain current outlook. I have always trusted that these men and women, in their interactions, would reveal a life attitude of mine—a philosophy that would pervade each novel, rising out of observations of the perplexing and mysterious ways in which the human condition twists our impulses and narrows or expands our fateful journeyings.

It is puzzling to me, with these men and women shaping themselves on paper month after month, that I did not for a moment perceive how their thoughts and actions and feelings were stating the main theme of *To the Green Mountains,* expressing something of the utmost importance to me: Thou shalt not try to possess another. And I mean spiritually, emotionally, intellectually. It is as if, in my eyes at least, it is an eleventh commandment, as well it might be. In the epigraph to that book I had put words by Alfred Kazin, "facing a fact until it divides you through the heart and marrow like a sword," which is also enormously important to me but which is assuredly a secondary theme. This I saw in divining the first theme some time after the novel was published.

For me it is human beings *in themselves* that have always mattered. When Albert Schwartz, at the time assistant professor of education, reading, language arts, and children's literature at Richmond College, New York, said of Theodore Taylor's *The Cay* that Taylor maintains a sexist tradition because the only woman in the book is Phillip's weak and fearful mother, I was impatient. It is true that Mrs. Enright is the only woman in the book and that in the beginning she is weak and fearful. However, when the ship she and Phillip are on is torpedoed, she is calm and quiet. But in any case, she comes in only at the beginning and hers is not a rounded characterization. As a writer I am firmly against the idea that because we are now profoundly aware of women's rights and that the feminine self is as worthy of respect and consideration as the male in every way, novelists must remake their characters accordingly. To change them would seem to me a blatant hypocrisy, *if* they have been revealed truly within the circumstances and time of the novel, as is Mrs. Ingalls, Laura's mother, for instance, in the Little House books. Even though, wonder as we might in light of present views, that patiently, with never a word of protest, she once again pulls apart the domestic interior she has created every time Pa wants to strike out farther west because two or three neighbors are drawing in on him. If the conception of my novel were to call for only one woman, and that woman, within the evolution of the conception, were weak (and I am not implying here that Mrs. Ingalls was weak—quite the contrary), then there would have to be one woman and she would be weak. It would seem to me false to contrive a strong one for the sake of the movement. Indeed, the failure in a case like that would lie not in portraying a weak woman but in failing to characterize her consistently, revealingly, and interestingly. That would be the test. However, it would be still more absorbing to show her growth from weakness to strength.

Now I'm thinking of Jean Rhys's heroines, hopeless, hapless, and helpless, self-hating and self-destructive, as Rhys herself was, though she emerged periodically from helplessness in her truly courageous struggle to write the novels that eventually brought her fame and a livable income when she was seventy-six. On the back of the paperback *Jean Rhys,* by Carole Angier, I find the following words: "Rhys was far ahead of her time. In her heroines—surviving somehow in Paris or London, adrift in a *demi-monde* of hotel bedrooms and fur coats, too much drink and with yet another unreliable man—she caught not only the essence of her own life, but something that is timelessly and quintessentially female." I find that insulting. Why is Rhys's picture of heroines adrift in a *demi-monde* of hotel bedrooms and fur coats, too much drink, and with yet another unreliable man "timelessly and quintessentially female"? What possible excuse is there for drawing such a generalization, opposed during all the years women have been fighting for recognition as everything but that kind of female? What is "quintessential" about it? What is "timeless"?!

It troubles me—in connection with story and characterization formed in response to a cause rather than within the natural and inevitable growth of the novel as intuited by the author—that some women writers, in their bitterness and resentment, have made statements having to do with women's aesthetic efforts that seem to go beyond the bounds of reality. They thereby lay themselves open to easy attack by their opponents—quite needlessly, when there are so many legitimate and important issues to be explored.

For instance, I find myself questioning several points in Carolyn Heilbrun's *Writing a Woman's Life,* thoughtful and painstaking as the book is. First of all, I find it presumptuous in the extreme to accuse Eudora Welty of lying (to put it more bluntly than Heilbrun does, but why be delicate when you have a certain meaning in mind?) when Welty remembers a happy childhood. Heilbrun declares unhesitatingly that this is mere nostalgia, a sentimentalized version of what surely must have been years when there was what is now called "buried anger." Specifically, Heilbrun says, "I do not believe in the bittersweet quality of *One Writer's Beginnings,* nor do I suppose that the Eudora Welty there evoked could have written the stories and novels we have learned to celebrate."[3] Welty has camouflaged herself, accuses Heilbrun. I very much doubt it.* Colette had a happy childhood, as far

*Heilbrun should reflect on the first sentence of the preface to *The Collected Stories of Eudora Welty* (New York: Harcourt, 1980): "Without the love and belief my family gave me, I could not have become a writer to begin with."

as adoring her mother and father is concerned, as she confesses in story after story in *My Mother's House and Sido;* yet must we accuse her of camouflaging and sentimentalizing her childhood in view of the novels she wrote as an adult? E. B. White had a happy childhood, as did, apparently, Annie Dillard and Sylvia Townsend Warner. Are they sentimentalizing and viewing with nostalgia, White in his letters that go back to childhood, Dillard in her *An American Childhood,* and Warner in her *Scenes of Childhood and Other Stories?* Is it only those, then, who have had unhappy or wretched childhoods who can be "permitted," in the feminist view, to write memorable novels, non-fiction, and stories? Ursula Le Guin appears to have had a happy childhood, and adds poetry as well as critical essays to her list of accomplishments.

There are so many curious musts and permittings in Heilbrun's *Writing a Woman's Life,* concerning women who will be wholehearted artists, that it is not only the world of men, as I come to see it, that does the everlasting permitting. And Heilbrun wove all these musts and permittings into such large generalizations that I found myself getting oddly wrought up, though I am on Heilbrun's side as a companion feminist. *Why* wrought up? Because, I think, I am not so narrowly a feminist as she, having always been unable to endure generalizations used to pursue an argument, indeed to make them the basis of an argument. So many questionable points can creep in under the baseline!

What utterly baffles me, second of all, is why Heilbrun persists in using the phrase "married off" when she comes to the subject of marriage, as if she loathes the very idea of any woman, possibly gifted, handcuffing herself to a man. I can't think of any woman I know, except my mother, who could ever be looked on as having been "married off"—but then I seem to choose lively, imaginative, and intellectual women for my closest friends. I do think that my mother *was* "married off," by her own headstrong mother. My mother had the handicap of a stiff knee, which never stopped her from doing anything she wanted to, but her mother, believing that Florence had better take the first man who was willing to marry her, bossily saw to it that her daughter went to the altar with a man she could only later divorce. And was Carolyn Heilbrun "married off"? Certainly she seems to appreciate her own husband deeply, for she dedicated *Hamlet's Mother* "For Jim Who Lived Through It All," and in *Writing a Woman's Life* she acknowledges that "James Heilbrun, who lived with me and this book through many years, deserves special thanks for attentions to both beyond all conventional requirements or demands."[4] Bless the man! Was Heilbrun caught in the trap of "the marriage game" when she married him, "abandoned . . . to the fate of a married woman," forced into "proper womanly behavior"?[5] I cannot imagine Heilbrun trapped, abandoned, or forced under *any* circumstances, and I do assure her there are probably millions of women all over this globe just like her in independent spirit. Nowadays, we don't bend easy! And, in fact, since at least the 1920s, millions of women have been acting "against the weight of societal expectations." Vanessa Bell, Virginia Woolf's sister, is a perfect example. She made no to-do about it, living with a lover in the house of her and her husband, Clive Bell (which Bell visited often with pleasure), then casting off Roger Fry and taking on the homosexual Duncan Grant, whom she loved so deeply that she put up with *his* visiting lovers rather than lose him.[6] The big mistake she made was not telling Angelica (her daughter by Grant) that Clive Bell was not her father until Angelica was in her teens, when it came as a traumatic shock.[7] But I really do think Heilbrun ought to give up the phrase "marrying off." We *are* in the 1990s, and the very phrase is 1890-ish!

To continue the subject of false generalizations in which the opponents of feminism can easily pick holes, Ellen Moers says in her most valuable *Literary Women:*

> It is right for every woman writer of original creative talent to be outraged at the very thought that the ground *needs* to be broken especially for her, just because she is a woman; but it is wrong for the literary scholar and critic (creatures by definition

devoid of creative talent) to omit paying their humble toll of tribute to the great women of the past who did in fact break ground for literary women.[8]

Moers's words are justified except for the astonishing statement that critics are "creatures by definition devoid of creative talent," creatures that we somehow feel Moers looks on as men. We need not go on about it; we need only think of T. S. Eliot, Virginia Woolf, D. H. Lawrence, Margaret Drabble, George Orwell, W. H. Auden, Joyce Carol Oates, Gore Vidal, Edmund Wilson, Susan Sontag, Lionel Trilling, John Updike, Cynthia Ozick, Wilfrid Sheed, Randall Jarrell, Delmore Schwartz, Mary McCarthy, and V. S. Pritchett, among others.

I find Margaret Walker, in her essay "On Being Female, Black, and Free," saying that "vice and money" control, among other areas of American life, "publishing, education."[9] Money and the making of it controls publishing to an enormous degree, but necessarily so— otherwise publishers could not do business and could not stay in business (this statement takes into consideration the fact that unheard-of advances to famous writers whose works do not return the advances can drive a publisher out of business). Nor could they continue to publish minor writers whose first works are being brought out, as well as back list authors kept in print despite small sales. But to say that vice *controls* publishing seems to me simply preposterous. How about education? Vice *controls* it? Having read Jonathan Kozol's devastating *Savage Inequalities,* it would seem nearer the fact to say that, in some states, in some cities, the distribution of funds among schools, black and white, is controlled by a racist point of view, a fact as depressing as Walker's statement.

Erica Jong states in an essay called "Blood and Guts: The Tricky Problem of Being a Woman Writer in the Late Twentieth Century" that "women writers (like women) tend to be damned no matter what they do. If we are sweet and tender, we are damned for not being 'powerful' enough (not having 'blood and guts') and if we rage, we are said to be 'castrating,' Amazonian, lacking in tenderness. It is a real dilemma."[10] But I can't see that Jong has been damned to any degree in this way. She seems to have taken her place among known and noticed writers. Nor has Joan Didion been damned, nor has Toni Morrison, Joyce Carol Oates (known for the violence in her novels), Susan Sontag, Katherine Anne Porter, Carson McCullers, Mary McCarthy, Mary Renault, Marguerite Yourcenar, Ursula Le Guin, Sylvia Plath, Marya Zaturenska, Elizabeth Bishop, Louise Bogan (to end with poets—Le Guin is both novelist and poet), or, to go back in time, Virginia Woolf and Colette. Neither tenderness nor violence has damned them, and Flannery O'Connor wrote freely and often, as she had to, of all kinds of violence. More than half the American women noted above have won the National Book Award at least once.

However, Jong later says wisely that "as an artist, [woman] cannot allow her vision to be polluted by the ephemeral dogmas of political movements. It is simply not possible to write a good book that 'proves' the essential righteousness of either lesbianism or heterosexuality, childbearing or its avoidance, man-loving or man-hating. Righteousness has, in fact, no place in literature."[11]

I have been thinking throughout these pages of Virginia Woolf, who wrote her novels with only the unique vision of each one in mind, and who concentrated on that vision to the exclusion of what she had to say *in the form of a message* in *Three Guineas* and *A Room of One's Own,* both concerned with women's disadvantageous position in society. But even to compare these two pieces of nonfiction reveals the difference in effect attained in two different moods of writing. *Three Guineas,* while written with wicked satire and filled with a massive integrity (as critic Bernard Blackstone put it), is a grim book. There is deep bitterness in it, which may be part of the reason why it is being less read in our day than *A Room of One's Own,* written with as strong feeling and conviction but with wit and irony and aesthetic distance. It has become a classic statement of what is best in the feminist movement. However, I have recently reread *Three Guineas* and feel now its "massive integrity" even more than when I read it the first time, when it seemed to me, despite its integrity, wearisome because of its lack of humor, because it drives so hard without let-up. Leonard Woolf, ever his wife's devoted and admiring critic, was cool toward it, as were many of Virginia's friends. But I find its details, point after point, as true now as they ever were. It is a spiky, uncomfortable book—no wonder the male reviewers of Virginia's day sneered at it.

In *A Room of One's Own,* however, she comments on novel writing (despite the arrows she aimed at male pretentiousness in *Three Guineas*):

> It is fatal for any one who writes to think of their sex. It is fatal to be a man or woman pure and simple; one must be woman-manly or man-womanly. It is fatal for a woman to lay the least stress on any grievance; to plead even with justice any cause; in any way to speak consciously as a woman. And fatal is no figure of speech; for anything written with that conscious bias is doomed to death. It ceases to be fertilized. Brilliant and effective, powerful and masterly as it may appear for a day or two, it must wither at nightfall; it cannot grow in the minds of others.[12]

What Virginia Woolf would have thought of the turn the feminist movement—in its women's studies at universities—has taken today it is hard to imagine. A recent practice in women's literature criticism was expressed at one of the MLA conventions, where there was a session on "The Muse of Masturbation," where papers were given on "Clitoral Imagery and Masturbation in Emily Dickinson," having to do with clitoral hermeneutics, and on "Desublimating the Male Sublime: Autoerotics, Anal Erotics, and Corporeal Violence in Melville and William Burroughs." Though one might understand the clitoral part of "clitoral hermeneutics," the implication for hermeneutics is harder to grasp for those outside women's studies. "Clitoral hermeneutics," one discovers, is a synonym for "ovarian hermeneutics." But as related to critical methodology, the explanation is confusing. Apparently certain feminists wish to "valorize" the clitoris rather than the vagina in "the binary opposition of discourse." However, other feminists reject the concept as "pseudophallocentric" and believe that Emily Dickinson's style is "clitoral."[13]

When my feminist friends, both male and female, found this rather exaggerated and even humorous, I referred the matter to J. D. Stahl, of the English department of the Virginia Polytechnic Institute and State University, who wrote the foreword to this book. He took an entirely different view of the matter and was not in the least amused, nor did he think it at all exaggerated.*

Among novels for the young there are two outstanding that I see as feminist, though it could be that the author of the first did not write it in that spirit. They are Suzanne Fisher Staples's *Shabanu: Daughter of the Wind,* and Ursula Le Guin's *Tehanu. Shabanu* is a cruel, passionately felt and evoked picture of a woman's place in Pakistan in our time. Like the dry, merciless sandstorms that swirl across the Cholistan Desert, the story swirls around three crises in Shabanu's life, crises that reveal to the full how much less than little a girl child's sensibilities and desires are taken into consideration when plans are being made for her future, how she is used as a thing, simply a piece in the chess game played to serve her parents' needs. This practice is assuredly no different from the traditional ones carried on worldwide

---

*In response to my letter asking for enlightenment, Stahl wrote: "Since [you have] asked me to respond, and though I find my position as a male critic in this dialogue somewhat problematic, I wish to urge anyone thinking about this issue to consider the sexual discourse referred to here in its context. Part of that context is the theoretical debate that begins with Freud and continues through Lacan, Cixous, Kristeva, Irigaray, and others, about how to 'read' and, more recently, to 'write' the body. This often provocative discourse is valuable, even necessary, I believe, as a means of exploring and clarifying hidden assumptions about gender and particularly about relations between men and women, assumptions that suffuse our language, thought, and literature. To fix on the sexual terminology of criticism in isolation from the rest of the theoretical debate seems to me to distort and misrepresent the nature and the aims of the discussion."

in the past, but Shabanu's story takes place in today's Pakistan, and she is a loved daughter.

The first crisis involves Guluband, the big handsome camel that is the pride of the family's herd. But Shabanu and her family are poor nomads in the Cholistan Desert. Therefore, they must sell part of their herd in order to amass enough money for the dowry of Shabanu's sister, Phulan, soon to be married to Hamir, and then for Shabanu, betrothed already (at thirteen) to Hamir's brother, Murad. Dadi, Shabanu's father, has not promised her that he will never sell Guluband, but to her it is unthinkable that such a thing could happen. They have had the big camel ever since she can remember, and last year at the fairground Dadi turned down fifteen thousand rupees for him. But now Dadi is offered such a price for the group of camels he has brought from his herd, including Guluband, that he cannot resist. "At the center of myself is an aching hole," says Shabanu. "With Guluband, my joy, my freedom, all of who I am is gone. I wonder if I will ever take pleasure in anything again."

But though Shabanu has called Dadi "Liar! Liar!" and does not speak to him for a week, as time passes the coldness of his act callouses over, and she still loves him and knows that he loves her, hard as his hands were when he held her and she kicked and bit him. At the same time she is faced with a second event that not only enlightens her about another aspect of her father but enlightens us as well about Shabanu, whose nature, we now discover, completely rejects the extreme macho, for her the very opposite of exciting and attractive. She happens to come upon a scene of two men fighting, naked except for loincloths, crouching, circling, levering, hurling, flipping, slamming and being slammed to the earth. And one of them, she recognizes with a shock, is Dadi. Though it is he who wins, when Shabanu returns to the women she stares at her mother and wonders, "How can she stand him? How can she let a man who would fight another naked man touch her . . . and do what the camels do?" Is this simply Shabanu's innocence and inexperience speaking, or some innate quality in her that will never submit through compulsion to the most intimate of acts without fury and bitter, lasting rebellion.

At this vulnerable moment she has a talk with her father's cousin Sharma, who has left her husband, who beat her and their daughter because Fatima was not a son. Sharma has no intention of forcing Fatima to marry. "Never to marry," thinks Shabanu. "To stay in the warm, safe circle of women." But her thoughts turn, then, to Murad, "his gentle eyes and his fairness at games. Is any man a good man? If he isn't a good man, I shall be like Sharma—strong and independent."

It is therefore a small strong-minded and stubborn woman-child who has set her face in the wrong direction within Pakistani tradition on the Cholistan Desert, still as oppressive as ever in today's world. And it is when Shabanu and Phulan, with their families, visit the farm of their betrotheds, Murad and Hamir, and come into contact with the young men's landlord, Nazir Mohammed, that Shabanu is forced to experience the extremity of what her father is capable of in his treatment of such a daughter.

One rebellious act on Shabanu's part against the tyranny of Nazir Mohammed, and she has initiated those fateful moves that will bring about Hamir's death and the decision on her parents' part to marry Phulan to Murad (Shabanu's own dear Murad, as she has called him to herself). They promise Shabanu to Nazir Mohammed's older brother, Rahim-*sahib*. It is true that he has fallen in love with her and wishes through lavish gifts to make amends for Hamir's death. But it is also true that he has other wives, that they will be jealous of her youth, that they will harass her and make use of her, and that Rahim-*sahib* may not continue to find her attractive.

For such a nature as Shabanu's the outlook is hopeless, and she attempts to escape to her aunt Sharma on her beloved Xhush-Dal, the young camel she has reared since babyhood and has taught to dance. But Xhush-Dal breaks his leg in a foxhole and Shabanu can only wait for Dadi to come—because he will. Like Guluband, she has been betrayed and sold. And after Dadi has found her and is beating her, it is Sharma's philosophy that enables Shabanu to retain her dignity and her determination never to be defeated spiritually. The inner fortress may be assaulted, but she will keep her reserves hidden. Keep your secrets locked away, Sharma had said, so that Rahim-*sahib* will always have to reach out for them. But he will never unlock Shabanu's. Meanwhile, it is not Shabanu who has been defeated, for when the beating suddenly stops, there is an inexplicable sound, wretched and heartbroken, heard in the desert stillness where there are only a father and his daughter.

What resolution can there be to the subjection of women in countries where familial love is so tragically distorted by tradition?

In *Tehanu,* we are dealing with the fourth and final novel of what had been, for eighteen years, the Earthsea trilogy. In *A Wizard of Earthsea,* the first book, there is no female protagonist. We are wholly absorbed in Ged's search for the Shadow, whose identity he must recognize if he is to save his own life and those of the peoples of Earthsea.

Tehanu takes place on the Island of Gont, Ged's home, where he was born to the name of Sparrowhawk, and where Ogion, the aged master and teacher of his youth, the very great Mage, has just died. Here Tenar lives still, after all these years since Ged had brought her out of the tombs of Atuan, and she knows, deeply and instinctively, that hers cannot be a life with men of power, the princes and rich lords at Havnor Great Port. For she has had no desire for the fame due her as "the white lady" who had brought them the Ring of Errith-Akbe, the Ring of Peace, from where it had lain buried in the Tombs. Still, she is going by the name of Goha, a countrywoman's name, and is now a farmer's widow on her little farm in Middle Valley, up over the hills from where Ogion lies.

It is on Gont Island, at the time of the novel, at her home in Middle Valley, that Tenar has taken on the care of a girl child who was raped, beaten, and burned most terribly on her right side—an eye lost, her cheek a slabbed scar, one hand a club with the thumb as a claw—taken her on and loved her as her own child and given her the name of Therru, which means "burning," "the flame of fire." This is her use name, as Arha was Tenar's use name before the coming of Ged, and as Sparrowhawk was Ged's use name. Later, Tenar will realize, in a moment of despair, what Therru's true name is:

> The child's hair was fine, warm, sweet-smelling. She lay curled up in the warmth of Tenar's arms, dreaming. What wrong could she be? Wronged, wronged beyond all repair, but not wrong. Not lost, not lost, not lost. Tenar held her and lay still and set her mind on the light of her dreaming, the gulfs of bright air, the name of the dragon, the name of the star, Heart of the Swan, the Arrow, Tehanu.

So, for the first time in the book, we learn the true name of the child who will grow into one who could have been called by no other name, her own private, powerful name.

It is the great dragon Kalessin who brings Ged home to Gont, to Tenar, "straight to the Overfell, straight to her. . . . She had been told that men must not look into a dragon's eyes, but that was nothing to her." She helps the almost helpless Ged from the dragon's back (the whole description of the dragon, and of the steps by which one goes up to its back and down, is most marvelous, as though Le Guin herself had lived with dragons), and we realize with a shock, for the first time, that Ged really is, now, empty of power. It is a shock and a sorrow, as it is a trauma to Tenar to realize that he has no wizardry left in him; he is a shell, an ill and ashen man, frail, spent completely, longing only for solitude and a place where he will have no need to speak to anyone. And this is what *Tehanu* is about, the slow recovery of Ged, through Tenar's love (there had never been a time, she tells him later, when she had not loved him; "The girl sitting at the hearth, gazing at the fire, listening, saw the hawk; saw the man; saw the birds come to him, come at his word, at his naming them, beating their wings to hold his arm with their fierce talons; saw herself the hawk, the wild bird. . . ."). And her searching comprehension of him now tells her what his need is, to simply be left alone.

But above all it is about the slow recovery of Therru, who has been so inhumanly treated by those who will come in another season to try to reclaim her that she can scarcely face the outer world, scarcely realize what it is not to be abused, scarcely bring herself to trust. Therefore, it is not only Ged and Therru who must be brought back to a realization of self, as Ged had once brought Tenar, but Tenar herself who through the long months must discipline herself to have the most extreme patience, must learn all the meanings of the word *devotion* she had never, until this time, experienced to the full.

In none of Ursula Le Guin's novels, though she is a strong and noted feminist, have I ever found overt preachments expressing a feminist philosophy. It would *seem* she agrees with Virginia Woolf about the writing of novels that "it is fatal to be a man or woman pure and simple." It would *seem,* and I cannot make my statement stronger, because in *Tehanu* she twice points out—though, be it noted, *through the action of the novel*—that men of power are quite likely not to hear what a woman is saying. (We are taken back to Jacquetta Hawkes, hearing her own voice rising like smoke and disappearing among the strong, assured voices of her masculine colleagues.) In both cases Tenar is in the company of wizards who have come to decide among themselves Ogion's burial place. Aihal, Tenar tells them, was his true name, and this place, she says, in the woods above his home, is where he wished to be buried. Who is *she?* they coldly demand, and later, when she gets through to them that Ogion, having sent for her, had told her on the night of his death his true name, they stare at her. Ogion had told *her?*—the incredulity, the open contempt. " 'I said that name,' she said. 'Must I repeat it to you?' " For, in fact, they "had not heard the name, Ogion's true name; they had not paid attention to her." She was speaking—saying something or other— but it had simply never occurred to them to listen.

On the second occasion it is to one of the great mages, the Windkey, from the Center at Roke, that Tenar is trying to explain why she wonders if more than repairing and healing must take place in this bad time when ominous changes have already become depressingly noticeable; when an evil man could possess such overwhelming power as to be able to invade and deeply endanger the psyche, the civilization, of Earthsea.

The Windkey looked at her as if he saw a very distant storm cloud on the uttermost horizon. He even raised his right hand in the hint, the first sketch, of a windbinding spell, and then lowered it again. He smiled. "Don't be afraid, my lady," he said. "Roke, and the Art Magic, will endure. Our treasure is well guarded!"

"Tell Kalessin that," she said, suddenly unable to endure the utter unconsciousness of his disrespect. It made him stare, of course. He heard the dragon's name. But it did not make him hear her. How could he, who had never listened to a woman since his mother sang him his last cradle song, hear her?

Clearly, it is much on Le Guin's mind, this masculine trait of not really hearing what a woman is saying (though one *cannot* say this of all men!), hearing only the surface sound of the words, but not what they deeply mean: in Tenar's case that she was not speaking about treasure in the narrow sense—Roke and the Art Magic—but about the spirit of the world of Earthsea, its very life. Because the Windkey is not only listening without courtesy and without attention but above all without interest (even knowing, as he does by now, that she had been Ogion's student and confidante). He is not even aware that he is not really listening. "The utter unconsciousness of disrespect," says Le Guin.

Tenar is a strong woman, unafraid to look a dragon, much less a mage, directly in the eye. Yet she belabors herself for not measuring up to her own expectations; she questions again and again her ability to bring up a child she intuits will have a spiritually incomprehensible fate, aside from a future imprisoned inside a body that no one wants to look at. What can become of such a child? "Teach her," Ogion directed Tenar when he was dying. "They will fear her," he said. And, "A woman on Gont." What is meant?

The village people and the farm people believe that "you are what happens to you. The rich and strong must have virtue; one to whom evil has been done must be bad, and may rightly be punished," so that "Not even prosperity would diminish the visible brand of what had been done to her," to Therru. "They will fear her," said Ogion. But was that all? And when Tenar asks Ivy, the village witch of Middle Valley, if she sees Therru as having any gift for Ivy's art— any power in her—Ivy retorts, "A blind bat in a cave could see it" and refuses to take Therru for teaching, because she, Ivy, would be afraid of her, not knowing what she is:

> I mean when she looks at me with that one eye seeing and one eye blind I don't know what she sees. I see you go about with her like she was any child, and I think, What are they? What's the strength of that woman, for she's not a fool, to hold a fire by the hand, to spin thread with the whirlwind? They say, mistress, that you lived as a child yourself with the Old Ones, the Dark Ones, the Ones Underfoot, and that you were queen and servant of those powers. Maybe that's why you're not afraid of this one. . . . I'll give you my advice, mistress, free and feeless. It's this: Beware. Beware her, the day she finds her strength! That's all.

It is a strange thing that neither Ged nor Tenar, in their talks about the relationship of men and women—completely at ease with each other now that they live together as man and wife on Tenar's farm— see the truth of Therru. But they have existed within a tradition of male wizardly powers of Earthsea for so long, a tradition that has been the very breath of this world back beyond their own ancestors' memories, that they cannot recognize what is in front of them. All the same, "Why are men *afraid* of women?" Tenar asks Ged. And Ged sees into this question clearly enough to be able to answer, "'If your strength is only the other's weakness, you live in fear.' 'Yes; but women seem to fear their own strength, to be afraid of themselves.' 'Are they ever taught to trust themselves?' 'No,' she said. 'Trust is not what we're taught.'" And she thinks of the men on Roke, the great wizards, trusting themselves and one another. "Their power is pure, nothing taints its purity, and so they take that purity for wisdom. They cannot imagine doing wrong. . . . Maybe they need some woman there to point that possibility out to them," and then, "'I still don't see why, if there can be she-kings, there can't be she-archmages.' Therru was listening. '*Hot snow, dry water,*' said Ged, a Gontish saying." But still, Tenar reminds him of Ogion's words and how he had said to her, "All changed." But how changed?

Only later, when Handy, the unspeakably cruel one—who keeps Tenar and Therru under his eye because he wants Therru back— helps the men at Re Albi to lead Tenar and Ged down the darkest path of all, do they see what Therru *is:* that she is truly Tehanu, the one who can call Kalessin in the hour of her need and the one to whom he will come; that she, who had been Tehanu since the beginning, is the one who will, through her powers, work the deep changes in Earthsea. The woman on Gont being herself the greatest change of all.

In a discussion of *The Tombs of Atuan,* I was asked why, if Le Guin is a feminist, she had given Kossil, the old priestess of the Tombs, a menacing power over Arha (Tenar), the high priestess, such that Arha was not only the prisoner of the Tombs but in Kossil's power as well—the power of a cold, cruel, merciless woman. Why had a feminist wished to paint such a characterization of a woman?

My answer: Le Guin was writing a novel in which she was putting down what was true to her within the world of this particular novel, and not a generalizing, tractlike work on women's liberation. She was not "making" all women good and all men bad in a feminist preachment. There is the truth of a particular novel (as a writer discovers as the work unfolds under his or her hands) and that truth (whether the writer is aware of it or not) emerges from a worldview. Within it, a writer's experiences of life must speak honestly (if it is a good work) of what men and women are capable of: that women can be cruel and that men can be humane, as well as the truth that through the centuries women have been, on the whole, subjugated. And that we, each of us, men and women alike, for all our sakes, must work with all our powers to right this injustice.

But women must not use generalizations that do not hold true, for instance, that women with families, if they are artists (in the general sense), are holding two jobs while men hold only one. If a man is to earn a living for his family and he wants to write or paint or compose, he, too, must hold two jobs. Le Guin, in her long essay "The Fisherwoman's Daughter," an intensely feminist expression, says most truthfully: "To have and bring up kids is to be about as immersed in life as one can be, but it does not always follow that one drowns. A lot of us can swim." Le Guin swam, as have innumerable other women even without the help of a loving husband, as Le Guin has, by her own admission, had. With his help she managed to bring up three children and, during that time, to write at least ten novels, possibly more, as well as poetry and stories. Giftedness, of course, enters in. Simply wanting, even quite fiercely, to create in a particular field does not in itself imply ability—a fact too often lost sight of in a seethe of resentment against family, the publishing system, and the world. But so it is for a man, too.

Though I had a demanding father to whom it would never have occurred to treat his wife with tenderness and consideration, nor his daughter either for that matter, it had somehow never occurred to me to make an example of him in any of my novels. In writing *To the Green Mountains,* I was not *against* him, and indeed, as I have said elsewhere, the foremost theme of the novel, "Thou shalt not try to possess another," did not come clear to me until, a year after the book was published, I saw that the theme that appears as the epigraph of the book was not the strong, central one.

Jason Rule, as I wrote the book, became simply a part of the pattern that had been shaping itself over many years, and my single purpose was to realize that pattern with all the truth of which I was capable. Story and its ideal expression (for me) was all. Four instances in my books—in *Mountains,* the humiliated Uncle Tede and Clayton Sill, and in the Julia sequence, humiliated Uncle Hugh and as well Rhiannon Moore's husband—speak of the wounds we inflict upon one another by failing or refusing, out of self-love, to imagine ourselves into the other's hurts. Julia will remember all her life Rhiannon's words —"I hope you are never so blind, Julia, as to become that lost in your work. *Never so blind!"*—words that speak for both sexes in terms of mutual respect, consideration, and fairness.

But, you will say, it is all very well to go on about being "never so blind." The disease of blindness, insensitivity, permeates society in every possible way. And it is the result of lack of imagination, which is the only means by which empathy, the ability to identify with another, is attained. Blindness can come about through lack of nurturing, lack of love and understanding in childhood, or through the constant showering of another kind of love, expressed in outrageous indulgence—which is in actuality the satisfying of self-love and which creates a narcissistic human being.

So often this terrible lack is taken out on the weaker ones. To speak of sexuality, we do not hear of gang rape by women upon a man. A daughter cannot rape her father, nor a girl the boy she has gone out with dozens of time and therefore trusts. Nor can young children, male or female, abuse their parents. The deep, urgent, desperate question of our time is still (as it has been for centuries): How is society to be educated in those words *mutual respect, consideration,* and *fairness?* How is each successive generation somehow to be made aware, imaginatively, not to speak of intellectually, what each of us suffers in being denigrated and set in second or third place, whether in physical or emotional ways.*

Here I must go back to what I was thinking about near the end of "Dimensions of Amazement" in *The Green and Burning Tree:* the decreasing play of imagination in our children because of the obsessive power of television, on which follows their increasing lack of ability to handle the English language and the gradual fading out, as they grow older, of whatever imagination they had once had.

R. D. Laing, the British psychologist, wrote in an essay, "The Massacre of the Innocents":

> Let us suppose that we live in two worlds, an inner world and an outer world. . . . By inner, I refer to our personal idiom of experiencing our bodies, other people, the animate and inanimate world: imagination, dreams, fantasy; and beyond that to reaches of experience that . . . I shall call spiritual. . . . The average man over twenty-five . . . is almost totally estranged from inner experience. He has little awareness of the body as a subjective event. He has little capacity to invent what is not, that is, of imagination: he has usually totally forgotten his whole world of experience before the age of seven, often later.[14]

Of course, we know that though Laing uses the pronoun *he,* what is meant is *she* as well. In other words, I thought, one would be tragically lacking in the power to create anything except, perhaps, one's own despair, without even knowing or having any way of knowing what is the source of that despair, that buried anger. Ruskin said that the unimaginative person can be neither reverent nor kind, and J. B. Priestley in *Man and Time* goes even further when he speaks of the adult in whom imagination has withered as mentally lamed and

---

*"Twenty-one thousand women are raped, abused, or murdered a week in the United States—the most dangerous note in the world for women." Peter Jennings, "World News Tonight," October 3, 1992.

spiritually lopsided, in danger of turning into a zombie or murderer.[15] And, one must add, into someone capable of abuse, whether physical or emotional or both.

I am not so foolish as to believe that were a knowledge of children's literature to be required of every potential elementary school teacher, every new generation of high school graduates would be seething with imagination and would be masters of the English language. Yet recalling a recent experience: I have seen, and felt in every nerve of my body, what harm a lack of reading, of being read to, of being told stories by storytellers, can do to children.

After the happiest of responses during an author appearance, with laughter and questions from one group of children after another, I was sent a group who, no matter what I said, no matter how I tried to remind them of fairy tales and other early childhood tales, stared up at me with no expressions of any kind. I do believe those tragic children were incapable of responding. Minute after minute passed, and gradually I grew physically sick under that silence, sick for myself in my abysmal failure and sick for them. I looked down at the table and saw a drop of sweat fall on the papers lying there, and then another, and realized that I was actually ill and had better sit down and ask them to come to me with paper on which I could at least draw mushrooms for each one, to remind them of Tyco Bass, of whom I had been talking. For I had a hollow knowledge that, even in a fleeting situation of private closeness such as this, they would have no questions, nothing at all to say. And yet, as I had thought all those years ago when I was writing *Tree,* I knew how much could be lying in wait to bloom under the desert floor. But where there is no water, the soil remains barren. Imagination had not been encouraged in these children in any way. Was there some possibility that they would develop those qualities of respect and consideration and fairness so necessary to all of us in creating a livable life? What life is truly worth living without them?

For me it is those qualities that sum up and enfold the point of view of what is best in feminism, a point of view that feminists have been working to bring to public consciousness since long before women were given the right to vote (please note that "kindly" word *given*). Assuredly it is the point of view of the humanist as well, for to be a feminist in the highest sense, it inevitably follows that one *is* a humanist.

PART II

On Fantasy

We were all watching the quiz on television
Last night, combining leisure with pleasure,
When Uncle Henry's antique escritoire,
Where he used to sit making up his accounts,
Began to shudder and rock like a crying woman,
Then burst into flower from every cubbyhole. . . .
Extraordinary sight! Its delicate legs
Thickened and gnarled, writhing, they started to root
The feet deep in a carpet of briony
Star-pointed primula. Small animals
Began to mooch around and climb up this
Reversionary desk and dustable heirloom
Left in the gloomiest corner of the room
Far from the television.
          I alone,
To my belief, remarked the remarkable
Transaction above remarked. The flowers were blue,
The fiery blue of iris, and there was
A smell of warm grass and new horse-dung.

HOWARD NEMEROV
"A Singular Metamorphosis"
Collected Poems of Howard Nemerov

THE INMOST
SECRET

✒

Imagination is more important than knowledge.

ALBERT EINSTEIN*
Out of My Later Years

*J*t seems to me that magic, occurring like a sometimes troubled
blessing to a child or to several children in the everyday world
of reality, is, in certain instances, rather like a love affair in the first
stages of discovery. The more secret the magic, the more intense and
wondrous the experience, as it was for Max in *The Return of the Twelves*
and for Peter in *A String in the Harp,* when he realizes he has just been
privileged to be present in the time of the sixth-century bard Taliesin:

> Abruptly it all faded, the light and the lake, the island, the
> voices. Peter blinked at the window streaming with rain beside

---

*Quoted on page 119 of Leonard Shlain's *Art and Physics*. And on page 120, Shlain
tells us that "As a child, Einstein had asked himself what the world would look
like if he could travel astride a speeding light beam, and also wondered how the
wave would appear if he could dismount and travel beside it at the same velocity."
He had to wait until he was twenty-six before he could give the answer.

his bed. The Key was warm under his fingers, but it lay quite still. At least this time he had held onto it, and though he was bewildered and uncertain, he knew it hadn't hurt him in any way. But he couldn't tell anyone about it, he wouldn't know how. And why should he? They all had their own concerns. He would keep his secret. He put the Key carefully back in its hiding place.

Not to be believed and yet, miraculously, having to be!

If the Inmost Secret is kept by the children, its full beauty is far more deeply experienced than would be possible otherwise. In fact, if the secret is allowed by the author to become public or, at worst, to be something that could happen to anyone at any time, the sense of magic is lost (entirely or not entirely, according to the sensibilities of the reader), and the enchantment fades. Thereafter, what had been intense and wondrous descends to something ordinary or, from the reader's point of view, simply unbelievable. Questions as to the actual nature of fantasy begin to arise in one's mind when no questions should: The magic that has happened should all seem believable and right within a certain frame of reference. My belief, it seems clear, rests upon whatever frame of reference is understood in the beginning of the novel.

Let us see how this belief works out in various kinds of modern fantasy and how the authors handle the keeping of the Inmost Secret or the making public of it. However, as I have found that there is some difference of opinion as to precisely what is meant by the word *magic,* I should explain my use of it, as it, together with *secret,* is one of the two words central to this essay.

The first definition in my big *Random House* is "the art of producing a desired effect or result through the use of various techniques, as incantation, for instance, that presumably assure human control of supernatural agencies or the forces of nature," while the third is "the effects produced by this art." Both definitions imply the actions of a wizard, enchanter, witch, illusionist, or sorcerer. Further definitions also imply the presence of a producer of magic. But the meaning I am concerned with here is the fifth: "any extraordinary or irresistible influence, charm, power, etc." But, you will say, this definition still, in a way, implies the action of a producer of that influence, charm, or power. However, I am using the word to indicate an ambience, or the occurrence of unexplainable happenings, the mysterious experiences that one would deem impossible in view of scientific thought. By this, I mean animals and plants speaking, the disappearance of solid objects before one's eyes (yes, illusionists do this, but there is an explanation: It is trickery—the magic in fantasy is not trickery), and/or their movement and speech, all of this as in fairy tales. In fact, anything of an unexplainable nature that happens in fairy tales can happen not because of the will or influence of a sorcerer but because we are in a world where magic is rife and natural.

In the fantasies I am about to offer as examples of my belief, we are in the everyday world and not in fairyland, which makes the magic all the more bewitching and unexpected. In all except E. Nesbit's *The Story of the Amulet* and Penelope Lively's *The Ghost of Thomas Kempe* there are no consciously causative agents. In Lucy Boston's *The Children of Green Knowe,* it would seem simply that magic has always been present for Granny Oldknow and that then the ambience works for Tolly, her great-grandson, visiting her at Green Knowe. It is as if the two of them were what is called sensitives, as perhaps all the protagonists in these novels are. At least we know of no others in *Children,* beside Tolly, Granny Oldknow, and Boggis, the gardener, who are aware of the ghost children. And they are not really what you would call ghosts, but seemingly real presences whose pleasure it is to interact with the three of them in this enchanting and enchanted novel.

In E. B. White's *Charlotte's Web* the magic is simply there, present between Charlotte and Fern, for no known reason. There is no causative agent except, perhaps, this particular time in Fern's life, when she is naively open to so many possibilities. Nor is there any causative agent in White's *The Trumpet of the Swan.* At the opening of chapter six, magic, for no revealed reason, begins happening where there had been no magic before, and keeps on happening. Louis the swan simply starts going public, with his trumpet, and his bag of money around his neck, where previously he had been a normal swan.* In *The Return of the Twelves,* magic takes its eight-year-old protagonist, Max, by surprise as it does Tolly in *Children.*

But as for *The Ghost of Thomas Kempe,* Thomas, having been a sorcerer in his own time, is indeed the consciously causative agent. In crisis, one feels it is purely his frustrated fury provoking the magic, a wild anger beating its undirected way out of him, but it *is* magic he is knowingly and arrogantly working when he causes so many unpleasant (and, in one case, dangerous) events to happen.

In William Mayne's *Earthfasts* and Nancy Bond's *A String in the Harp* it is the time candle in the first novel and Taliesin's harp key in the second that are both causative agents. Yes, but what *made* them so? They seem to be magical objects in and of themselves, waiting to act for whoever is the singularly, mystically right person (or persons, in the case of *Earthfasts*) to use them to a resolving end.

To go back now from magic to the Inmost Secret: I shall consider first a group of three fantasies—*The Story of the Amulet, The Children of Green Knowe,* and Philippa Pearce's *Tom's Midnight Garden*—in which the Inmost Secret is *unambiguously* kept.

In *The Story of the Amulet* there is no question of the children's letting out the secret of their being magically transported back into the ancient times of Assyria, Babylonia, and Egypt, experiences made possible through the condescending indulgence of the temperamental sand fairy, the Psammead.† Most conveniently, the children's father is off in Manchuria reporting the Russo-Japanese War for his newspaper,

---

*I had written, "an ordinary swan," but what swan could ever be termed "ordinary"?
†Who doesn't look in the least like a fairy, and whose likeness by H. R. Millar is so wonderfully satisfying and right that, as Julia Briggs reports in *A Woman of Passion: The Life of E. Nesbit, 1858–1928,* Nesbit thought he must have been telepathic. But he said that his success was all due to her powers of evocation.

and their mother is in Madeira recovering from an illness. Therefore they are staying with Old Nurse in Fitzroy Street, conveniently near the British Museum. And the Psammead, according to a promise made in *The Five Children and It,* has made Old Nurse unaware of him.

In the end "the poor learned gentleman" who lives upstairs over Old Nurse (and who was in actuality based on Dr. Wallis Budge, Keeper of Egyptian and Assyrian Antiquities in the British Museum) is the one contemporary person in on the secret of what has been happening to the children. What with Old Nurse being made magically unaware of what she would consider an impossibly peculiar "pet," whose seen presence would necessitate all sorts of troublesome involvements, and what with the children's parents well away from London, it is clear that Nesbit had no intention of bothering with the complexities entailed by adult nosiness and interference. Indeed, it was a habit of Nesbit's in all her novels not only to get rid of parents but to make sure there would be no relatives around to ask unfortunate questions.

However, adults in fantasies are not invariably nosy and interfering, forcing the opening up of what should remain secret. In *The Children of Green Knowe,* Tolly would have only Granny Oldknow from whom to keep secret his knowledge of the ghost children, for he and the old lady are living alone together at Green Knowe. Of the two of them Boston says: "Tolly was glad Mrs. Oldknow seemed not at all surprised by the hide-and-seek. He was not quite sure whether she thought that he and she were playing a game together pretending that there were other children, or whether she thought, as he did, that the children were really there." And this observation is quite typical of the subtlety with which Boston handles the sensitivities taking place between Granny Oldknow and Tolly throughout the entire book.

Later Mrs. Oldknow complains that it's been an afternoon "when nothing would come alive"—which opens up further speculations on the part of the reader as to just how much she understands of what Tolly knows—and then she goes on to tell another story about one of the children as if she had been there inside the story herself. "I want to be with them," cried Tolly, overcome by the brevity of their rare appearances, which fill him with such strange joy. "I want to be with them. Why can't I be with them?" And when they are talking about Toby's sword and Tolly asks why Toby doesn't want it now, "Mrs. Oldknow looked at him with an uneasy wrinkled face. Then she sighed. 'Because he's dead,' she said at last. Tolly sat dumbfounded, with his big black eyes fixed on her."

Tolly is heartbroken—but now he and his granny, through this exchange, have come to a complete understanding. There had never really *been* a secret to be kept, not hers from him nor Tolly's from his grandmother. It was only that Tolly had at some moment to acknowledge the truth, which he hadn't recognized: that the children were not alive in the sense that he was. However, theirs is a secret known to no one else.

In *Tom's Midnight Garden,* it is true that Tom tries to discuss the mysteries of time, and what the words *Time No Longer* on the face of the grandfather clock in the hall mean, with an uncle whose ability to deal with abstract conceptions is so limited that he can only become angry, for he doesn't like what he can't understand. But aside from this questioning, Tom would never have dreamed of revealing to his aunt and uncle, with whom he feels no spiritual rapport whatever, the experiences opening out to him in the midnight garden. His only confidant is his brother Peter, at home with the measles, to whom he writes long letters marked PRIVATE in large, anxious capitals across the top of intricately folded pages, and with CONFIDENTIAL on the envelope.

Finally, in the end, Tom finds another confidant, most astonishingly, the astonishment flooding Tom and the reader together with the deepest possible satisfaction, because the ending of the story is both aesthetic and intellectual, having the simple elegance of resolution of a mathematical problem.

· · ·

In contrast to the three fantasies just discussed, there are four in this second section—Penelope Lively's *The Ghost of Thomas Kempe*, E. B. White's *Charlotte's Web*, William Mayne's *Earthfasts*, and Nancy Bond's *A String in the Harp*, that may *seem* ambiguous in relation to "secret kept" and "secret revealed." For there is, in all four, a public aspect to the mysterious happenings. But these four never do, actually, give the Inmost Secret away.

In the first book, Thomas Kempe is a tyrannical force—determined to make the boy James his obedient apprentice, he announces his return to the village of Ledsham in letters a foot high. (Kempe is never seen, incidentally, so that the title of the book is a bit misleading.) Thomas Kempe has "come back to this towne," and "The prieste is a liar and a scoundrell." Meanwhile, James is utterly bewildered at what is going on in his own house, for Thomas issues orders to James in the form of notes left about in his room, and when James does not obey, Thomas does damage in the house, which the family blames on James. Having a reputation for telling tall tales, James feels it would be hopeless to reveal the truth, but he does confide in his friend Simon, is only half believed, and then tells Bert Ellison, a builder and exorcist, who tries and fails to exorcise Kempe, a very stubborn individual indeed.

Now, *Ghost* was criticized by a friend of mine because Kempe's return is broadcast by those announcements chalked up throughout the town. For my friend the magic is not only made public by them, but also by the fact that the entire village is brought in on the results of Thomas Kempe's powers when he burns "the wytche's howse"— poor old Mrs. Verity's, a widow who had never harmed anyone in her life. Meanwhile, I reflect on the fact that the great delight of the book is the character of Thomas Kempe, the central point here being that his public image is that of a poltergeist, a piece of dangerously troublesome energy. But his private image is much more precise: an officious, testy, tempery, and finally defeated individual, known only to James.

To me, the beautifully satisfying denouement, when poor old

Thomas finally gives up in the face of crass modernity and begs James to help him find a final resting place, would not have been nearly so satisfying were it not for the particular character of Kempe, who, because of his enormous ego, must try always to exert control. What happens between him and James, and with Bert Ellison, remains the secret of James and Ellison and Simon. Thomas's two public notices, in addition to the large chalked-up announcements, never give away the Inmost Secret.

As for *Charlotte's Web,* while never engaging in the conversations herself, Fern understands what Charlotte and the animals in the barnyard are saying to one another. However, rather than this being Fern's secret in the usual sense of knowledge consciously kept from others, one feels that for Fern it is not something wondrous and incredible happening to her, but rather an experience she accepts as quite natural and which she need not go around telling everyone about. But she does tell her mother, in a quiet moment when they are alone together, that Charlotte's cousin had once caught a tiny fish in her web built across a stream, and about another cousin, a balloonist, who stood on her head, let out a lot of line, and was carried aloft by the wind. Later we are moved to wonder if—having left the world of the barnyard, where there were only Fern and the animals and Charlotte, for the infinitely different world of her young friend Henry Fussy, the boy with whom she has such a happy time at the fair—she may forget that she ever understood the animals. For she confesses to her brother that all she can think of is the fun she had with Henry, and she never returns to the barnyard or to her listening after that dazzling delight of the fair.

There is also in this story the element that relates to *The Ghost of Thomas Kempe.* Charlotte weaves the message "Terrific!" into her web over Wilbur's pen, and then "Some Pig!"—and thus a piece of the magic that is going on *is* made public. But no more than by Kempe's act of scrawling public messages are the townsfolk led by Charlotte's act to know the Inmost Secret: in this case, that the animals speak and that Fern understands. What is more, the public takes the messages as miracles beyond understanding and lets matters go at that, with the exception of Fern's mother. She tells the doctor, to whom she goes for advice: "I don't understand how those words got into the web. . . . Dr. Dorian, do you believe animals talk?" To which he replies: "I never heard one say anything. But that proves nothing. It is quite possible that an animal has spoken civilly to me and that I didn't catch the remark because I wasn't paying attention. Children pay better attention than grownups. If Fern says the animals in Zuckerman's barn talk, I'm quite ready to believe her." He takes it all, Fern's understanding and Charlotte's messages, as simply two more facets of the whole absorbing mystery of life, just as he takes the miracle of the spider's web itself, messages or no messages. And so the Inmost Secret is kept.

Earthfasts, my third example in this section of a secret seemingly made public but, in actuality, whose surface only is revealed, deals with two kinds of magic: traditional and private. The public knowledge of what is going on concerns only the traditional. As for the private magic, the Inmost Secret: David Wix and Keith Heseltine are out in the meadows alone near the ruins of Garebridge Castle, where they witness the spectacle of a drummer boy marching out of an "earthfast"—a hump or rise in plowed land. He is beating his drum with one hand and in the other holding a candle that burns with a cold, spinning, indestructible flame. And the cold flame sets loose traditional magic—publicly known magic—the ancient, sleeping force of this particular corner of Old England. There is a boggart* that had lain quiescent until this moment. There are giants that had stood in the form of Jingle Stones up on Hare Trod but that now, imperceptibly at first and then more swiftly, begin to move and to leave dragging trails behind them. There is some invisible, madly whirling force that causes havoc in the marketplace. Finally, it lets

---

*A goblin, bogey, or mischievous spirit.

loose the private magic, the Inmost Secret, which causes David to vanish and gives Keith the power, when he takes hold of the time candle, to go underground to King Arthur's hall.

Let us take the fantastical elements one at a time. Only the two boys, Keith and David, out in the meadowland near Garebridge Castle, see the drummer boy, Nellie Jack John, emerge from the earth. Afterward he is seen and talked to by one or two others in the village, who take him for what is called a Character but to whom it could never possibly occur that he has come out of an earthfast, out of a subterranean hall underneath Garebridge. In this hall King Arthur has been waiting by the Round Table with his soldiers for his time to come—time that has for them all these centuries been standing still.

All the public aspects of magic in the book, all the traditional magic, we accept. These aspects are the boggart, which has suddenly decided to make its home again with the couple who finally take in Nellie Jack John; the madly whirling force in the marketplace; and the moving Jingle Stones, which, as giants, let loose and eat the local farmer's pigs, and which are traditional within the premise of the fantasy. We accept them just as we accept that people do experience poltergeists.

But the private magic of the book is the incredible secret that is never given away, never made public. It is a secret known only to Keith and David—that Nellie Jack John came out of an earthfast, having been with King Arthur, and that Keith, too, had been with him. However, given David's father's character and sympathy, it seems quite likely, though we are not told, that they will in time tell him. Sympathy is all.

We come now to the fourth book in this second section, Nancy Bond's *A String in the Harp,* a family story wrapped about in magic. Time and again Peter is given the gift of extrasensory perception of the life of the sixth-century bard Taliesin, whose harp key the boy has found. The harp key sings to him when it grows warm and vibrant in his hand, showing him the past. But now others—members of

Peter's family and two young friends—behold scenes in Taliesin's life, and finally the entire village can, if it likes, behold the night scene of a sixth-century torchlight gathering.

When a version of this essay appeared in *The Horn Book,* I included *A String in the Harp* in my third and final group, dealing with those fantasies in which, for me, the sense of magic is betrayed and which are not ambiguous (like those in this second group) as to "secret kept" and "secret revealed." I regretted my doubts about *Harp,* for the answer to what is to be done with the Key is so satisfying, and the scene that reveals it so fine—yet for me the basic premise seemed to have been tossed aside, the inner logic torn, and the magic tarnished. In a succeeding issue of the magazine a letter from Nancy Bond appeared in which she gave her reasons for believing that her novel belongs in the second group. She wrote:

> I don't believe I have in fact tossed the basic premise of the fantasy aside, and torn its inner logic. The instances of "public magic" in the book occur only when Taliesin's story and the geographical location of Peter and the harp key coincide: in the area around the village of Borth, which is in reality saturated with the legend of Taliesin. To Peter alone is given the knowledge of what is happening, the knowledge of Taliesin himself and his story outside this area (where, in fact, the fantasy begins). It is only Peter who can connect the fragments of the whole, through the singing of the Key which only he hears—so he does retain a special "private magic" not given to anyone else, not even his own family. There is, I feel strongly, a difference between Peter's experience and everyone else's; I don't believe what happens to him could or does happen to any other character in the book. He is the receptor and transmitter of the magic; the others are witnesses of a small part of it.[1]

Therefore, one could, according to Bond's very clear and convincing explanation, see how Taliesin's key is a catalyst energizing both the

public and private magic, just as Nellie Jack John's time candle is a
catalyst in Mayne's *Earthfasts*.[2]

Nevertheless, while I gladly accept Bond's explanation, and while
it is I who am bringing up the parallel in the power of the two time
objects, there is to me a basic and fateful difference between the Key
and the time candle that has a direct bearing on another aspect of the
subject of the Inmost Secret. It is an aspect not having to do with
general public knowledge but with knowledge within Peter's family.
The Key grows warm in Peter's hand and sings to him alone before
magic is about to happen, leading to a sense on the reader's part of
the most intense and treasured privacy between Peter and the Key.
On the other hand, the time candle is cold. The flame is cold, and
its effects on David and Keith arouse in them only uneasiness and
uncertainty, though David is fascinated and must lose himself in
looking into the flame. Keith hates it: It is as loathsome to him as if
it were a white maggot, though he finally gives in to its power for
David's sake, so that he may find his friend.

The singing of the Key for Peter and his seeing of Taliesin's past
go together. In *A String in the Harp* Bond says, as I have already quoted
at the beginning of this essay: "But he couldn't tell anyone about it,
he wouldn't know how. And why should he? They all had their own
concerns. He would keep his secret. He put the Key carefully back
in its hiding place." At this point, then, it seems to me that the
singing of the Key, the intense privacy between it and Peter, and the
fact of Peter's telling himself that he would keep the Inmost Secret
are all bound firmly together. And finally Peter keeps the Key on a
silver chain around his neck, for the Key was "too precious to be
separated from."

Then, for some perfectly inexplicable reason, which is for me the
stumbling block, Peter is seized by a strange compulsion to tell his
sister Jen, three years his elder, even though "he had sense enough
to see she was in no mood to believe such an outrageous story." And
I wondered at the time why, if he must share the Inmost Secret, he
wouldn't be more drawn to tell his younger sister, Becky, warmer by

far than Jen, infinitely more outgoing, and closer to him in age. However, after he experiences the great flooding scene, when the Plains of Gwyddno in Taliesin's time (the Low Hundred today) are covered by the ocean, and lives and homes are lost because of the carelessness of the watchmen, Peter tells Jen the Inmost Secret, which she rejects in anger. And when he pulls out the Key and tells her that what she believes to be nothing but a dream all came from his treasured possession, she sarcastically demands of him if he knows how fantastic it sounds. He has, against all reason, against what we must feel would be his deepest intimations and sensitivities, persisted in telling an obviously, crushingly inimical person what is most private to him.

Why? He could have told Becky. He could even have told Rhian, the little Welsh girl who is their neighbor and who is open to the idea of magic, and she would have believed him. Both she and Becky would have loved and treasured the secret as Peter does. So then why *Jen?* This is what is so hard for me to accept, that Peter would have insisted on sharing his Inmost Secret with her. And she remains inimical, glaring, angry, sarcastic, resisting throughout most of the book, and finally takes matters into her own hands. She betrays Peter when she not only goes to their friend Dr. Rhys and tells him Peter's secret (and is astounded that Rhys turns out to be on Peter's side and believes him) but—most insufferably of all—tries her best to tell Dr. John Owen, of the Cardiff Museum, in front of the whole family when they go to visit him there, that Peter has found a harp key, an ancient one, which should certainly belong to the museum rather than being kept a secret by Peter. And her betrayal would have worked except that Becky bursts into tears and is in such a state that she has to be taken outside. Only thus is Peter's secret saved.

Certainly there is no rule in fantasy that says that the keeper of the Inmost Secret may not tell an inimical person! Only it must be believable—the circumstances should somehow make the telling inevitable, unavoidable. And I cannot accept that Peter—given the kind of person he is, given that sense of intense privacy Nancy Bond has made us feel so vividly in the beginning between Peter and the Key

—would actually share his Inmost Secret with such a one as Jen. The shock of it aroused in me a sense of indignation and resentment, though assuredly Jen's knowing, and the intimation that she will betray Peter the first chance she gets, adds tension to the novel.

Finally, the candle in *Earthfasts,* with its cold, spinning, indestructible flame, is utterly impersonal by comparison with the Key. We are never brought to feel that the candle was meant particularly for Keith and David, while we can't help feeling that the Key was meant to be found by Peter alone. Nellie Jack John's bringing the candle into the outside world does cause both public and private magic to begin, but there is no least sense of privacy, let alone an intense and treasured privacy between the candle and Keith and David. One feels it wouldn't have mattered in the least who had come upon Nellie Jack John and the candle—so cold, so impersonal is its magic.

Because of the logic of Bond's explanation of her handling of public and private magic, in which she shows how the Inmost Secret is kept private in the end, I must put *A String in the Harp* in this second section of fantasies that only *seem* ambiguous in relation to secret kept and secret revealed rather than in the next section, where the Inmost Secret is allowed without doubt to become public.

In this third section I am going to try to sort out just why in two fantasies, *The Trumpet of the Swan* and *The Return of the Twelves,* the making public of the Inmost Secret—secret not kept—troubles me.

The Trumpet of the Swan is a very curious novel. In the beginning we are led to suppose that it is going to be a kind of nature story, because of all the facts about swan parents and egg laying, the hatching of cygnets and their care and training—facts carefully researched by White. The only unrealistic element is that the swans talk to one another in English. Sam, the boy, watching the swans and keeping a notebook of their activities, does not converse with them or understand what they say. This whole development of swan life, and Sam's becoming acquainted with the birds to the point where they trust him and become his friends, is Sam's private world. This is private magic, in which we are led to take for granted a certain premise and are just as absorbed and delighted by what is going on as Sam is.

But now, quite without warning, in what seems to be a completely uncharacteristic ploy on White's part, the story takes on a quality of farce that makes me extremely uneasy, as any novel does whose vision seems to go awry. The premise appears to change completely, switching—between the end of chapter six and the beginning of chapter seven—from something private, endearing, and believable (believable within the realm of fantasy) to something public, ludicrous, and unbelievable. At this point Louis, the cygnet born dumb, decides that he must learn to read and write, acquires a small slate and a chalk pencil to carry around his neck, finds Sam's school, and learns with astonishing swiftness. In all this I am not only being asked to "pay something extra,"* I'm being asked to pay more than I'm willing to. Now Louis becomes wealthy from playing his trumpet on a swan boat and in a nightclub, so that a moneybag is added to the collection of objects that dangle and clank from the cord around his neck. The awkwardness and clumsiness and incongruity of this collection seem precisely symbolic of the awkwardness and incongruity of the whole idea of the latter part of the book.

What is more, in the process of going public, both Louis and the story completely lose track of Sam, who has no part in this feverish procession of events. From the point when Louis goes to school, something forced and artificial enters the story. It is as if the book were concocted, instead of having been allowed to blossom quietly in the depths of White's creative unconscious over a period of years as *Stuart Little* and *Charlotte's Web* were. Or it could be that there were two possible novels—one that could carry on from chapter six in the

---

*The words, from E. M. Forster's *Aspects of the Novel* (New York: Harcourt, 1956), concern what fantasy asks of us—but I don't believe that good fantasy does.

spirit of what comes before it, and another that should have a beginning as farcical as what follows it, a beginning in which no Inmost Secret has been prepared for.

The second example of a troubling fantasy is Pauline Clarke's *The Return of the Twelves*. The basic premise of the story is that the Brontës' wooden soldiers must learn to trust their finder—eight-year-old Max Morley—completely and must feel that they can continue to trust him before they will move and speak in front of him as naturally as if they were alone. At this stage, if he picks up one that has been still and wooden, it becomes warm in his hand.

The first question is, shall Max tell his younger sister, Jane? But he *must* tell her, and she treasures the little soldiers and the secret and the wonder of their slowly coming to trust her so that they come alive in her hands as if she were Max. But then the author allows Philip, the older brother, to find out about the soldiers and to see them move and hear them speak. Philip is wholly inimical because he is eager to write—and secretly does write—to an American antiquarian, saying that he knows where the soldiers are and that they can be bought. Now other people find out. The children tell the Reverend Howson, someone sensitive and wholly in accord, who will keep the secret. But then, what secret? For now a farmer sees the tiny figures struggling through the fields to escape to the Brontë Museum, in Haworth. And next, two small girls see them, and then a newspaper reporter finds out. "By Monday afternoon," writes Clarke, "a strange and delightful rumor was spreading through the Morleys' village and the small town of Haworth itself—and even villages farther away. It centered upon Mr. Kettlewell's land, but its exciting possibilities seemed to touch the whole countryside with enchantment."

Well, it may have done just that, but as I read on, I became more and more uneasy, for the soldiers seemed somehow to be losing the first ineffableness of their magic, and I felt a slow waning of enchantment rather than an addition of it. I felt a keen disappointment, despite technical points on the author's side (for instance, Philip is brought round to seem sympathetic). I felt let down. Why? Because it turns out *that anybody could see the Twelves in motion if the person was in the right place at the right time*—a betrayal of the novel's initial premise that this seeing was a rare and special privilege, to be awaited in private with patience and devotion by someone the soldiers had slowly learned to trust.*

In the end it looks as if we are left asking a question, the one E. B. White evoked when he wrote to the *New York Times* concerning Anne Carroll Moore's letter of protest to him about *Stuart Little*. He "detected in Miss Moore's letter an assumption that there are rules governing the writing of juvenile literature—rules as inflexible as the rules for lawn tennis";[3] obviously, White did not think there were.

I do not agree with Miss Moore about *Stuart Little,* although I don't think it compares with *Charlotte's Web*. But the fact is that White did not write simply a piece of "juvenile literature." He wrote a fantasy. I am speaking here of fantasy—a very special category of literature that compares with fiction as a sonnet compares with poetry. Either you have a sonnet if you have written your poem in a certain way, or you don't if you haven't. With fantasy I believe that the author is required in the very beginning to establish a premise, an inner logic for the story, and to draw boundary lines outside which the fantasy may not wander. Without ever having to think about it, the reader must feel that the author is working consistently within a frame of reference, setting a certain discipline (this will vary, of course, from tale to tale). Modern fantasy adds a certain delight: the element of contrast with the everyday world, which provides a kind of reverberation arising from the fact that within this everyday world a little pool of magic exists that possesses a strange, private, yet quite powerful and convincing reality of its own. And the pool of magic seems remorselessly to seep away if the first premise (or promise, you might call it) is not kept, if there is the kind of betrayal in which the story

---

*But in this case, my pleasure in the rest of the novel is not destroyed. See page 221 for a discussion of what I call the "acceptance quotient," which varies from reader to reader.

is handled in opposition to the inner logic laid down in the beginning.

If we set up too many rules about any art, someone inevitably comes along and knocks one or another of them down the mountain, as has happened time after time. But in the case of fantasy I do believe that there is something to think about regarding privacy, even though the unpredictability of art is always rising up to confound us.

THE PLEASURES
AND PROBLEMS OF
TIME FANTASY

❦

It sometimes seemed to Mark impossible that the historic past was extinguished, gone; surely it must be somewhere else, shunted onto another plane of existence, still peopled and active, if only, and available if only, one could reach it.

PENELOPE LIVELY
According to Mark

*I*n a chapter in which she lovingly remembers her five uncles, Gwen Raverat, in her *Period Piece: A Cambridge Childhood,* tells how her father couldn't have enough of history and especially of the past of the British Isles. "He adored a Roman Road," she writes, "or a prehistoric fort, and no one enjoyed a good dungeon, or a fine set of battlements, more than he did. . . . What fun it was, walking with him through the driving rain, over hills and walls and bogs, while he told us stories about the Stone Age inhabitants of the moors." As for Raverat herself:

It used to make me feel quite ill to think that I should never, never see Chaucer or Queen Elizabeth, or Rembrandt, or John Hampden, or whoever was the hero of the moment. I would have given years of my life to spend a day in another century, to see what it was like, and I would still give quite a lot to do so. Once I was overcome by the sad end of a story-book, and was found sobbing in the nursery, saying for all explanation: "Robin Hood's dead! Robin Hood's dead!" My mother could not help laughing a little, but my father quite understood.[1]

Now, Raverat was born in 1885, and E. Nesbit's *The Story of the Amulet* and Rudyard Kipling's time tales, *Puck of Pook's Hill,* weren't published until 1906, when Raverat was twenty-one, so we can regret for her that they came too late for her childhood reading. Because *Period Piece* is about Raverat's childhood only, there is no mention of either Nesbit or Kipling. But if Raverat were a child today, what a revel she would have! If you can't go back yourself, you can at least read about those (not necessarily) lucky children who have.

I've often thought how like an elegantly played game of chess a fine time fantasy can be. In chess each pair of pieces, and the pawns, must always make their own kind of move and no other. But out of brilliant combinations of these moves come completely original games, full of astonishments brought about by a lively mingling of incisive thinking and imaginative foresight. In a minor way, this characteristic of time fantasy led to my fascination with it. But I wasn't drawn simply to this kind of intellectual challenge. Rather, it was supremely the idea of time itself, embodying a wonder and a mystery that so many have felt, as Gwen Raverat did.

"I will wager, I said to myself some years ago, just as if it were an idea fresh to the mind of man, that Time is not a thread at all, but a globe, and the fact that we experience it as thread only must have something to do with our 'doors of perception.'" With these words I commenced an exploration of time fantasy in *The Green and Burning Tree,* which—expressing the idea of the Eternal Moment—followed the genre almost to the end of the sixties.

As I reflect on the time fantasies I have written about previously and reread the ones to be spoken of here, it becomes clear to me that some have sprung primarily out of the author's delight in solving the

complex problems presented by the interweaving of tenses, as in Lucy
Boston's *Treasure of Green Knowe*. In that extraordinary novel, Boston
plays her game of chess brilliantly, but always gives us a vivid sense,
as is her wont, of the interweaving of past and present and of the
innumerable paradoxes of time itself, slipping in phrases, sentences,
paragraphs here and there almost without our noticing. It is as if her
love of the paradoxes of time and the blessings they bestow on her
are the very air she breathes in that Norman Hall she lived in, the
actual, physical embodiment of her fascination with time—"The most
wonderful place on earth," she called it. And so it is this felt atmosphere that has become the invisible surround of the stories themselves.
Without doubt it has been her intense love of her ancient home that
has imbued her fictions with that quality that has made at least three
of them classics in her own time.

And then there are those time fantasies in which the emphasis is
not on the complexities resulting from the mingling of times but on
those strange opportunities that only time fantasy can offer, used by
the author for the enlargement of the protagonist's understanding of
how difficulties and tensions can be struggled with and possibly resolved in some utterly unforeseen way in the world of reality. We
think of Ursula Le Guin's *The Beginning Place,* William Mayne's *A
Game of Dark,* Jill Paton Walsh's *A Chance Child,* and in a less dramatic
but no less absorbing fashion, Penelope Lively's *The House in Norham
Gardens.*

II

Because there are, apparently, a number of opinions on just how time
fantasy is to be thought about, I must speak of this for a moment. I
have always looked on it simply as the kind of fantasy that takes one
or more characters into an age other than our own, or into several
others, as in E. Nesbit's *The Story of the Amulet.*

But I was baffled to find, at a conference whose subject was fantasy,
that *The Court of the Stone Children* was to be discussed at the meeting

on "Inner Space," and I could make no sense of why certain fantasies
had been placed in the sections in which I found them. This brought
home to me strongly not only how we as individuals feel about and
react to certain fantasies, but how we think about them and define
them to ourselves. I haven't an idea of what was meant by "Inner
Space" in this particular instance, or why my time fantasy, along with
others basically unlike it, belonged in that category. Or possibly I
should have remembered Walter de la Mare's words: "Carroll's
Wonderland indeed is a [queer little] universe of the mind resembling
Einstein's in that it is a finite infinity endlessly explorable though
never to be explored."[2]

I I I

So that you will know where I'm headed, I will enumerate the three
different kinds of time fantasy, as determined by what they have the
ability to involve in ways no other genre of fiction can. First, there
is the kind that incorporates *legend* into the working out of the story
in an intrinsic as opposed to an incidental way, bringing the novel's
contemporary characters into close touch with legendary ones, so that
legend is not simply a subject the child has studied, but is all woven
into the vivid life of the story. One thinks of William Mayne's *Earthfasts,* having to do with the legend of Arthur; of Alan Garner's *The
Owl Service,* having to do with the Welsh legend of Blodeuwedd, a
tale out of that great collection of Welsh legends, the *Mabinogion;* of
Susan Cooper's *The Dark Is Rising* series; of Ursula Le Guin's *The
Beginning Place,* rising out of her extremely dim view of our plastic,
technological civilization; of Joy Chant's *Red Moon and Black Mountain;*
and of William Mayne's so very strange *A Game of Dark*—the last
four moving from present reality to currently created legendary lands
and back again. All but *Earthfasts* are, of course, high fantasy as well
as time fantasy (high fantasy being those tales in which it is the hero's
purpose to save his people).

Second, there is a kind of time fantasy that explores the past, bringing *history* into the child reader's mind both directly and by way of osmosis. It is a kind that certain children of this computer age are willing to accept because another dimension enters in—an overtone, a thrilling sense of the unspoken, the evoked—that is not in the nature of realistic novels. I think that the concepts and techniques of the two genres—realism and time fantasy involving history—can most clearly be contrasted and revealed by comparing Joan Aiken's *Midnight Is a Place* with Jill Paton Walsh's *A Chance Child,* both having to do with the beginnings of the Industrial Revolution in England.* How dull that sounds! But Aiken, in her unique, Dickensian fashion, creates an absorbing drama in a straightforward, realistic way, while Walsh takes every advantage of the eeriness her conception offers, so that even after the last page is turned the reader is haunted by this tale of a present-day child entering into a close relationship with children of the past and becoming one with them, in their time, for the rest of his life.

At a writer's conference a young man told our workshop group that he positively ached to write historical novels but knew there was little

---

*It will be noted that most of the writers spoken of here are English. And I think it can be said that we in this country do not produce memorable time fantasy in any numbers as the English do. We remember, too, that Nancy Bond's *A String in the Harp* takes place in Wales, and that Susan Cooper, though she lives in the United States, is English. Jane Langton has produced no other time fantasy beside *The Diamond in the Window,* which arises out of her love of place, the Boston area, where her touchstone people—Thoreau, Emerson, Alcott—lived, with Emily Dickinson not far off in Amherst. But Jane Louise Curry, an American, departing from her fascination with the very early history of America, as in *The Watchers* and *Beneath the Hill,* taking place in America but depending upon the Welsh past, could not resist Britain as setting in three complex, meticulously worked out time fantasies, *The Sleepers, Poor Tom's Ghost,* and *The Bassumtyte Treasure.* The reason for this absorption with the British Isles on the part of Americans who write fantasy of any kind I can only attribute to the rich, deep mulch of history that has been laid down there for more than two thousand years. We go to Britain again and again, still feeling that we have penetrated only a little way, that we have not begun to see and to feel and to know all that is lying there in layer after layer like the time zones under York Minster.

chance of his manuscripts being considered for publication because of present reading attitudes among young people. What to do? I suggested that he might absorb himself in time fantasy as the one way he could possibly realize his compulsion to write history. Even though it is very special genre, demanding certain perceptions, still, I thought, he could study the best and discover if his own way of seeing found satisfaction. One among us commented, "Well, it's *been* done." Of course it has! Again and again. There is scarcely a time fantasy in which the historical matrix is not only necessary for the novel to exist at all, providing the nucleus of the idea and the surround of the past, but in which it isn't of great interest as well.

Third, there is a kind of time fantasy that sits halfway between *pure fantasy* at one end of the spectrum and *science fiction* at the other. Time fantasy puts past and present together in a way that science fiction is not, primarily, interested in doing. Science fiction is far more drawn to life on other planets or to a future on this earth after nuclear devastation, or to a relatively near future, as in John Rowe Townsend's *The Visitors,* or to the kind of future in which man has wretchedly adjusted to life on a dry, dusty, rocky part of another planet. The kind of time fantasy I refer to in this third category incorporates scientific terms and ideas and sometimes psychological ones, as in Alan Garner's *Elidor* and William Mayne's *Earthfasts*—both writers making central use as well of a knowledge of magnetic fields. Yet these novels are indubitably *time fantasy*. And it is intriguing to me to observe that, after years of traditional time fantasy, these two writers should have chanced to come forth in the very same year with novels incorporating the same facets of the world of science. In both, the introduction of scientific aspects is handled so subtly and gradually that one is not at first aware of how a knowledge of scientific phenomena is influencing the story. In my own case, with *Beyond Silence,* I was certain in the beginning that what I was writing was time fantasy, though it gradually became clear to me that it could be interpreted as a novel of psychological trauma. And after publication, when friends and reviewers and one critic had a chance to comment, its underlying qualities of both psychological trauma *and* science fiction were pointed out, though many disagreed and held out for one or the other.*

I V

I have spoken of two different kinds of time fantasy in relation to the opportunities they offer through the interweaving of tenses. And I have discussed another group of three, determined by their ability to involve legend, history, and science (the last, of course, when they touch on science fiction). I now address the pleasures and problems of time fantasy as a whole—a discussion in which I will deal with place and place-names first.

In any memorable novel one has the sense of place interpenetrating all: a deep, wide, firm awareness emanating from the tale that makes us know—whether the place be actual or imagined—that it is intimately and vividly real to the writer's five senses and not simply cooked up or sketched in here and there to provide some sort of background for magical happenings.† It is that passionate awareness illustrated in Lucy Boston's sensitivity to the Manor, already mentioned, and Alison Uttley's to her beloved Thackers in *A Traveler in Time*.

As for time fantasies set in both traditional and nontraditional legendary lands, I can see very clearly that where the creation of names, customs, and situations evoked by different cultures was once a rich and delectable challenge to an author, it might now present problems instead. Certain past usages have been incorporated again and again in published fantasies. For instance, it has always struck me what a hold the tiny territory of Wales, a relatively few square miles, has on

---

*See also, re differences of opinion between critic and author about one of my books (*The Court of the Stone Children*), "Undercurrents: Pessimism in Contemporary Children's Fiction," by Anne S. MacLeod, in *Children's Literature in Education* 21 (Summer 1976), pages 96–102, and then my reply, followed by her reply to me in *CLE* 22 (Fall 1976), pages 94–96.

†See *The Green and Burning Tree*, pages 163–202, "A Country of the Mind," for a full discussion of the sense of place in fiction.

writers of legend-based time fantasy. It has become almost *the* place for that genre of fantasy, which time and again turns out to be high fantasy, with its young hero the savior of *a* people, if not his own.

We all know it is due partly to the irresistible image of Arthur and partly to the nature of the Celts, as so handsomely revealed in Joy Chant's *The High Kings: Arthur's Celtic Ancestors* and Peter Dickinson's *Merlin Dreams,* with stunning illustrations accompanying Chant's searching text and Dickinson's splendid stories. Then there is the extraordinary nature of the Celts. As Joy Chant sees them, though the Celts were illiterate, they "were members of the most verbally alive culture there has ever been and had skills of ear and mind lost to literate people."[3] Their bards, poet-priests, were, as she says, "keepers of the soul of the people,"[4] and that soul has had, since early times, a continuing over-the-shoulder awareness of the dual nature of reality, of unity in disunity, of the simultaneity of life and death, and of time as an eternal moment rather than as something comprising a separate past and future.

For me the sense of Celtic place is a most memorable quality in all these legend-based time fantasies: Cooper's *The Dark Is Rising* series, Garner's *The Owl Service,* and Bond's *A String in the Harp;* the authors' devoted attention to details of the Welsh countryside, the character of the people, and the way the Welsh speak and think and feel reveals their genuine love of the land and its unique qualities. Indeed, it would seem that this specificity of detail can only be born of a deep love of (or perhaps I should say intense reaction to) the place one is writing about. (The Welsh must have felt this, in addition to admiration for the legendlike sweep of Cooper's sequence, in giving her the Tir na n-Og Award.)

Naming is a subject that follows close on the heels of place and, like place, offers its full share of pleasures and problems. In Bond's and Cooper's and Garner's novels, as we are in the world of the Welsh past (the world of the bard Taliesin in Bond's case, and the *Mabinogion* in Cooper's and Garner's), at those points where its people enter the present there need be no created names. But as for created worlds, only in time fantasy would Hugh and Irene of contemporary America walk from the freeway to the mountains in Le Guin's *The Beginning Place* and find themselves in a place called Tembreabrezi, which for Irene becomes her "ain country" and whose ground she kisses for the very love of it. Here they are in the midst of men and women named Aduvan and Verti and Lord Horn, Trijiat and Dou Sark, Palizot and Sofir. Oliver and Penelope and Christopher in Joy Chant's *Red Moon and Black Mountain,* out for a bicycle ride in contemporary England, find themselves in the place of the Hurnoi tribesmen, in Kentor lands, on the Northern Plains, in the realm of the Kendrinh and the land of the Vendarei. Oliver himself finds he has become O'li-vanh. I am fascinated, incidentally, by Chant's spelling of various Hurnoi names, making wide use of apostrophes and *h*'s, and I know that could I hear them, I would quite possibly hear them differently than I would be able to speak them—as if I were attempting amateurishly to speak a foreign language.

This was brought home to me sharply when I heard the tape of Le Guin's songs for her astonishing novel *Always Coming Home*. She wrote them both in English and in the language of Kesh, a people who "might be going to have lived a long, long time from now in Northern California."[5] And when Todd Barton sings them, I realize how utterly clumsy and unbeautiful has been my own pronunciation (though I could never have dreamed, before I heard him say the words, just how they *could* be said).

Surely *Always Coming Home*, taking place in California a thousand or so years hence, is one of the supreme examples of a wholly created world, down to the last acute accent, which is used widely over certain letters in Kesh words. Le Guin has written in "A First Note" that "The difficulty of translation from a language that doesn't yet exist is considerable, but there's no need to exaggerate it. . . . The fact that it hasn't yet been written, the mere absence of a text to translate, doesn't make all that much difference. What was and what may be lie, like children whose faces we cannot see, in the arms of silence. All we ever have is here, now."[6] And concerning this whole subject of creation, of naming, Le Guin has other interesting things to say, because she has done so much of it.

About the attitude that colors her work, an attitude handed on to her by her anthropologist father, she writes that among its elements must be "a curiosity about people different from one's own kind; interest in artifacts; interest in languages; delight in the idiosyncrasies of various cultures; a sense that time is long yet that human history is very short—and therefore a kinship across seas and countries; a love of strangeness, a love of exactness."[7] Exactness—yes!—as to the nature and naming of animals and plants and foods and customs and dress and languages and the looks of different peoples and the names of islands and ports. That is what we feel so strongly in the Earthsea books as well as in *Always Coming Home,* and that is what reminds us of Henry James's conviction that the supreme virtue of a novel worth considering is its truth of detail, its air of reality, its "solidity of specification." Think of all those musical unheard-of yet satisfying names that slip with such naturalness from the tongue! Say aloud to yourself, "Tembreabrezi." And that sense of both strangeness and naturalness is, I think, one of the tests of good fantasy—that evoked sense of absolute rightness.

V

Which brings me to my next mingling of pleasures and problems. This is the repetition, the echoing of certain names, details, techniques, personalities, resolutions, and constructions that we find in time fantasies—repetitions and echoings that seem increasingly to be handed down within the genre, which truly test the freshness of each new fantasy. For instance, in Meredith Ann Pierce's *A Gathering of Gargoyles* (not time fantasy but simply high fantasy, though the problem holds for both), we see how Pierce's Orm and Pendar echo from Le Guin's Orm Embar and Pendor, and the precognitive riddling rhyme, which structures Pierce's book, is of the kind found first in Cooper's sequence and then in Jane Louise Curry's *The Watchers,* and in her *The Wolves of Aam* and *The Shadow Dancers.*

Because the eternal or timeless moment is always the powerfully felt presence in any time fantasy, a fate will almost invariably be laid down for the young protagonist in those novels that are also high fantasy. I am reminded of the sequence in Ingmar Bergman's film *Wild Strawberries* in which the elderly protagonist dreams of his own funeral carriage moving along a warped and deserted street where a giant watch hangs overhead, a watch with no hands and a blank face, symbolizing timelessness. And it is exactly this element of a premonitory sense of dream, in which events seem insanely warped yet exude a sense of dreadful logic, that is present not only in *Elidor* but is echoed in so many time fantasies. It is there when Garner prepares for and carries off the moment in which the children are, apparently through their own decisions, led to that fateful crossroads of incidents that eject them from our plane of existence into another that has awaited them since the days of the starved fool. It is there when Roland discovers the empty fingers of Helen's recently lost mitten clutched in layers of smooth-growing turf and, underneath—in a situation only possible in time fantasy—the cuff frozen in ancient quartz. It is there when the children are shown an ages-old parchment on which the fool had foretold their coming and painted their small pictures in figures of medieval beauty. Here, in these last two details, are the first hints of Garner's captivation by the idea of the timeless moment, which is repeated, and comes to fuller fruition, in *The Owl Service.*

In that novel the element of fate lies brooding within the conception of a series of three triangles, the first formed in legendary *Mabinogion* times by Blodeuwedd; by her lover, Gronw Pebyr; and by her betrayed husband, Lleu Llaw Gyffes. The second is formed centuries later by another triangle composed of Nancy; her husband, Huw Halfbacon; and her lover, Bertram; and in the next generation by Nancy's son, Gwyn; by Alison, whom he loves; and by her stepbrother, Roger.

Garner takes full advantage of the fact that Ardudwy is a valley to make it a reservoir in which force, power, energy (Blodeuwedd's wild agony at being imprisoned) builds up until it must find violent release through whatever humans are in a particular emotional state with regard to one another. Both Blodeuwedd's imprisonment and the valley's desolation have continued over the centuries because hatred and murder have been the choice. And it is Huw Halfbacon's fate, as protector of the valley, to hold within himself the weight of the legend, to take on its burden in order to protect his people from it, and to see that young Gwyn does not escape its inheritance, because Blodeuwedd, a creation of magic, exists in timelessness.

In the *Dark Is Rising* sequence Will of course has been seen for centuries as the Old One of our time, to be taken into that company of a rare few that includes Will's uncle, Merriman Lyon, and King Arthur. Cooper writes in *The Grey King* that movement through time held no difficulty for an Old One, and in *Silver on the Tree,* in a conversation between Uncle Merry and Arthur, the former foresees that Arthur will be victorious at Mount Badon. For he is one who knows from his own experience that although the past is a road that leads to the future, the future can affect that past because past, present, and future coexist.

In Cooper's five books, a tremendous undertaking, the author is engaged in presenting the curious situation of Will Stanton, who finds that—while to his family and friends he is just about like any other boy of twelve—he is in reality the last of the Old Ones, not yet come into his powers, a member of a small group of the Forces of the Light. These forces are caught up in various skirmishes with the Dark, preparatory to a final, desperate coming to grips, though there are no physical battles as in Chant's *Red Moon and Black Mountain.* Instead there is a series of momentarily frightening and astonishing crises in which each side uses various forms of magic to temporarily checkmate the other, so that a great deal of appearing and disappearing goes on.

Cooper says that there are rules by which the Light and the Dark pursue their ends. And in fact there are innumerable regulations throughout the sequence for what the Light and the Dark may and may not do. But one unfortunately feels that the rules have been created especially for whatever difficult situations evolve, while in the world of reality there are no rules for the carrying out of human evil. Nothing is too terrible for humans to do to their fellow creatures. If a cruelty can be imagined, someone will perpetrate it. And the truth of the human condition must be evoked in fantasy; it is no escapist genre. What we ask, for children at least, is that cruelty and violence be presented with aesthetic distance and discipline.*

Another basic problem: In Cooper's books, there appears to be a lack of real force and depth in the workings of the Dark. Magic is too often used to effect appearance and disappearance, and for ease of solution, so that one is disappointed whenever it seems that the human resources of wit, intuition, and intelligence could have been called upon rather than, primarily, magic, with the brief rules that continually protect and sustain it.

In *The Dark Is Rising,* Will Stanton finds the six signs of power with astonishing ease, considering that he is being tested as an Old One; each of the signs or its hiding place is indicated to him in some undemanding way. In *The Grey King,* in which the supreme test comes, Will simply repeats a Welsh triad when one had expected so much of this determining scene, thinking that here at last he would be faced with a moment that would challenge his powers to the utmost. In *Silver on the Tree,* among other scenes showing machinations of the Dark, the horrible beast, the Afanc, simply sinks away and disappears after delivering its frightening moment, and the dancing horse skeleton is dispelled by a flight of blossoms. Words used in *The Dark Is Rising* to describe Merriman Lyon's handling of a situation "with swift enchanted ease," accurately describe the handling of a great many situations.

---

*A friend asks if this means that aesthetic discipline is, in this case and cases like it, also a form of ethical discipline. I would say that indeed it is.

The problem of timelessness as a moving force is common to all time fantasies. In Cooper's conception of Uncle Merry, it is woven through the whole five-novel sequence. For Merriman Lyon, all times coexist. Therefore it has always been a puzzle to me that Lyon should be heartsick and reproachful when Hawkin, whom he has deliberately used in the service of the Light in the coldest and most unfeeling way, should turn on Lyon and go over to the Dark. What could Lyon expect when Hawkin discovers that Lyon has betrayed him throughout the ages! Having experienced all times as one time, as coexistent, Lyon would have known from the beginning that Hawkin, in his searing bitterness, would turn to the Dark once he knew the truth. For if Lyon, Hawkin tells himself, could act in this fashion, how did he differ in his actions from those of the forces of the Dark?

As in Cooper's fantasies, and in Le Guin's and Tolkien's, Henry James's "solidity of specification" as to place is what we also feel strongly in Chant's *Red Moon and Black Mountain*. And this is a matter of wonder when one considers the extent of detail in all of them: the admirable precision with regard to customs, legends, music, clothing, housing, and very often plants and animals; the precision with regard to the various peoples and their ethnic characteristics and the kinds of magic they live with, all of which I have already noted at some length in the case of what was, at the time, the Wizard trilogy, now a quad-rilogy, with the addition of *Tehanu*. These are pleasures indeed.

I have a reservation about *Red Moon*, and it is that it takes Chant two or three or even, some might say, four chapters to overcome a certain awkwardness of phrasing and timing of movement to become thoroughly at home in her novel and complete master of it. But once set on her path, with firm assurance regarding conception and technique and a vigorous and vivid style, she achieves a remarkable evocation of Kendrinh, the Starlit Land.

A young brother and sister and their older brother, Oliver, are brought without warning out of our time into Kendrinh, this other world. There they are to carry out certain tasks that will, if they succeed, accomplish the defeat of Fendarl, the disgraced and fallen Enchanter of the Star Magic. Oliver, an untried youth when he finds himself one of the Hurnoi tribesmen, knows that he is appallingly unready to deal with the task laid on him: through testing and self-discipline to become Tuvoi, the Chosen One, destined to lead his companions into battle against the supremely evil Fendarl.

Like Rosemary Sutcliff, Joy Chant has the gift of presenting, magnificently and with utter conviction, the various massings, advances, retreats, and regroupings of forces on both sides of the battle. And we are down to the bone of human suffering—fantasy is not an escapist genre, we are reminded here. When the tribe is burning its dead, though he has defeated Fendarl, Oliver knows the hollowness of victory. How can it be victory when so many loved companions have died in agony and are gone forever?

The chief beauties of the book lie in the rich evocation of the life of the tribe, but most of all in Oliver's gradual growth through the sternest testing to wisdom and insight, and to that last moving moment when he knows that he must offer himself of his own accord, that he must leap into the bottomless pit and thus bring to an end his life as a Hurnoi tribesman. Oliver "drew a deep breath and raised his arms. Then savoring the sweet terror of doing just what he desired, he laughed and sprang out from the edge."

An interesting point is the contrast between Cooper's handling of the children's recollection of their out-of-time experiences and Chant's. At the end of *Silver on the Tree*, Merriman Lyon tells them that the final magic is to occur when they, all except Will, see him for one last time. All that they know of the Old Ones shall withdraw into the "hidden places" of their minds, and they shall never again know anything of them except in their dreams. At the end of Chant's novel, the author's decision, or perhaps her instinctive compulsion as she wrote, was a different one. The Lord of Life and Laughter, the Leader of the Great Dance, Iranani, offers Oliver a goblet, whose contents, if he drinks, will cause his memory of the past to be clouded in order to save him pain. But Oliver turns the goblet away, saying he will not drink. And when he returns to our world and to his brother and sister, Nicholas and Penelope, who have been with him in that Other Place, they know, as he does, that they have come back through a door that opens only one way. "Oliver, was it all true?" Penelope asks, and Oliver replies that it was. She says with a slow smile, "And they'll say to us [at home], 'You didn't go far.'" For they had only been out for a bicycle ride. They will go on, with Oliver's leather brow band embroidered with the mark of the Hurnoi to hold in remembrance. They will grow up remembering the wonder and the terror and the joy they have known with Oliver in that other world.

V I

The likenesses in structure, symbolism, and evocations between William Mayne's *A Game of Dark* and Ursula Le Guin's *The Beginning Place* are so astonishing that I want to parallel them briefly. Consider these facts: Mayne gives us a boy who turns from a life that has become insufferably oppressive and made almost unbearable by the continual reproaches of a mother who has no understanding of her son's unhappiness or of his sense of worthlessness. But now Donald begins finding himself, time and again, without warning, in a no-color legendary land, where it turns out that he must kill a dragon, called the Worm. The people of this other place take it for granted that there is only one way to kill the Worm, but when Donald finally succeeds in this completely alien task, he succeeds because he *is* totally alien, alien to that mindless, unquestioning tradition among these medieval people who "know," because it is tradition, that there is only one decent, honorable, acceptable way to kill a dragon. And Donald, in his turn, because their way is hopeless, knows that there is no other possibility but to kill it in his own outrageous fashion, whether he himself is killed or not, or disgraced and thrown out of the village for succeeding in doing what has to be done.

Now, a dragon has traditionally been called a Worm. Here, in

Mayne's novel, the creature's identity carries a phallic connotation, connected with Donald's father's wretched illness, which fills him with revulsion and despair just as the villagers are filled with revulsion and despair by the Worm's slime, stench, and mercilessness.

In the case of Le Guin's Hugh, in *The Beginning Place,* we have a young man who—precisely like Mayne's Donald—turns from a life that has become insufferably oppressive and made almost unbearable by the continual reproaches of a mother who has no understanding of her son's unhappiness or of the sense of worthlessness that haunts him. "I haven't got anything," says Hugh, "and I'm not anything." He is a checker in a supermarket and has no one to love or be loved by. Like Mayne's Donald, Hugh, when he hikes in from the freeway to the Beginning Place and climbs upward, finds himself in a strange legendary land, Tembreabrezi, where it is known that he must kill a dragon. And it turns out that he, too, like Donald, must kill it in an unorthodox fashion—for of course he has never met, let alone killed, a dragon in his life.

Both Donald and Hugh find maturation and release in the killing of their dragons, which differ in the following respect: Donald's dragon, the Worm, a phallic, masculine image, can be identified with his inability to love his father, while Hugh's dragon can be either a "he" or a "she" according to who is perceiving it—as "he" by Hugh and as "she" by Irene, the young woman who leads him to it. So that we realize that these two are seeing it as some unconscious restriction within themselves that must be recognized and resolved. Hugh and Irene, who have met at the Beginning Place, are both oppressed (as is Mayne's Donald) by guilt, by the inability to love, and by a terrible sense of placelessness in a technological world—of belonging nowhere and of having no one to love as they desire to love. And it is only when Hugh discovers a sense of himself, respect for himself, that both Hugh and Irene find release in discovering love for each other on the long journey home to what we call reality. Very clearly, these "other places" in the novels are refuges in their protagonists' unconscious from stress, guilt, and an acute inability to deal with an unbearable

situation. The weather is always colorless in the world of the unconscious. We are not aware of weather changes. In the legendary land,
it is always twilight, the twilight of the unconscious.

These two novels reveal the closest parallels of both structure and
symbolism I have come across in the world of time fantasy, indeed in
children's literature. But does it matter in the least? I shall speak of
this a bit later.

V I I

One writer's reaction to *A Chance Child,* by Jill Paton Walsh, brings
me to the subject of tricks in time fantasy. When she handed the
book back to me after I had lent it to her, she said only: "Up to the
old tricks, I see. It would have been far more effective if Walsh had
just told the story straight as a historical novel. I can't imagine why
all the fancy business of Creep's going back in time to the days of
child labor. Why not just have put him there in the first place?"

I knew it would have been useless to try to explain my strong
response to the novel. I realize that there are those who enjoy and
understand memorable time fantasy, who see why the materials of
certain ideas work better as time fantasy than as a straight novel; and
that there are those who prefer a certain kind of factual logic and
common sense to work all the way through a novel, in realistic fashion.

But to my way of thinking, in this particular case, for Walsh to
have told the story straight, with Creep in the first chapter a child of
the Industrial Revolution in England, would have destroyed the special
vibrant edge that her handling has created. It is an edge provided by
Creep's linkage with the past, by the intensity of Christopher's search
for his small, brutally treated bastard brother, and by the shock of
finding—carved in the moss-covered stone of a canal bridge—Creep's
name, crossed by a deeply notched and grooved iron bar. How long
has that bar been there? Christopher asks a workman. "Oh, maybe a
hundred and fifty years. . . ."

And there is that other moment that only time fantasy interwoven with history can offer: that moment, after Creep's inability to laugh and to eat, and his invisibility to all but children in that Other Time, when an enraged mother in the cotton mill beats one of the terrible masters with a billy roller, and everyone, *including* Creep, begins laughing, sending up huzzahs, and breaking out into great gales of mirth. Then "Blackie ran to Creep, and put her arm around his shoulder. Creep suddenly wailed aloud, with his two hands pressed to his belly. 'Oh, Blackie, I'm so hungry! I'm clemmed to death!'" So Creep becomes vulnerable again because he has returned to humanity, and will work out his human life in the past and be fulfilled in a way he might never have been in the present—nor could have been in his invulnerable ghostliness.

Finally there is that moment when Christopher finds a verse, hidden behind bushes, cut below Creep's name in the stone:

> Time as it is cannot stay,
> Nor as it was cannot be.
> Dissolving and passing away
> Are the world, the ages, and me.

"What does it mean?" asks Pauline. "What he said he meant by it," says Christopher, who has been searching through the old records, "was that those are his words to us, and so Farewell." And all of this hauntingly poetic overtone would have been lost entirely if *A Chance Child* had not been time fantasy. And it is the same with K. M. Peyton's *A Pattern of Roses* and Penelope Lively's *The House in Norham Gardens* and Philippa Pearce's *Tom's Midnight Garden,* all of which could be told straight. Yet how could one tear these conceptions apart and redo them with the same quality of overtone? A different overtone, of course, but not *that* one.

It could be, though I hadn't thought of this before, that some people—perhaps many—dislike time fantasy because they believe it has to do with tricks. Certainly John Cech, who teaches children's literature at the University of Florida and who is therefore firmly embedded in the field, seems uneasy with the genre. For in a review of Betty Levin's *The Keeping Room* he says:

> The author could have made this novel into a time fantasy or a literal ghost story, but her plot is more convincing because she has chosen to play it straight without tricks. The uncanny penetration of historical events into our present is believable and all the more mysterious because it is realistically presented.[8]

I agree wholly with his words "uncanny penetration" and "believable." But I wonder if Cech thought that Walsh, for instance, might be judged as having presented an unrealistic, unconvincing picture of the beginnings of the Industrial Revolution in England for the very *reason* that *Chance Child* is time fantasy, for the very eeriness of finding Creep's name carved in stone over a century ago?

But there are different kinds of reality! One of the paradoxes lying within the nature of fantasy is this: Though it contains assumptions no sane person would be willing to admit, and though it assaults and breaks the scientific laws of our world, all fantasy that lives and continues to live possesses a strange, private, yet powerful and convincing, reality of its own.

In any case, there would seem to be a certain misapprehension regarding the writing of fantasy, at least according to my own experience. A writer does not begin to be aware of a certain novelistic conception and then coolly decide which genre it should be written as: historical fiction, ghost story, or time fantasy. For me the nature of a novel comes unarguably as *itself;* I could not have *chosen* that either *Court* or *Silence* be straight historical novels, ghost tales, or anything but time fantasy—they had been that from the beginning. However, could Cech be right in a way? Betty Levin tells me that *Keeping Room* started out as a time fantasy but turned into a contemporary novel reaching back into the past. And it was only as it unfolded under her hands that she could no longer see it as time fantasy. Perhaps, then, you could say that she had "chosen"? But it seems to me instead that the material itself, by some mysterious process having to do with the writer's sensitivity, revealed its true nature, its own kind of reality. Now if you call that choosing, then John Cech is right. But one could say that it is not so much a matter of choice as of enlightenment, given by the material itself. It seems to me that one feels one's way. Says the poet Eric Barker,

> I go by touching where I have to go,
> Obedient to my own illumined hand.
> I part the darkness and I follow slow.

VIII

Can it be said that there are tricks in the following fantasies? I think not; these three—*A Pattern of Roses, The House in Norham Gardens,* and *Playing Beatie Bow*—seem to me to offer nothing but pleasures.

After K. M. Peyton's Flambard series, set in reality, what a happy astonishment it was to come across this beautiful novel of hers, *A Pattern of Roses,* when I had no idea she had a gift for fantasy. While the present-day boy and girl Tim and Rebecca are eminently believable and appealing, it is Tom Inskip of the past and his pathetic fate that touch us deeply. Tom is a boy imprisoned within the rigid and seemingly impenetrable barriers of class distinction that still held in 1910; he is chained to the humblest, hardest tasks—yet, strangely enough, he has a compulsion to draw. He thinks nothing of it: Simply, he finds some curious satisfaction in catching the look of certain scenes and would have gone on unreflectingly living out his modest life, working to the very limit of his powers, day after day, wearing himself out to a possible early old age but finding release and comfort in his drawing. That is, had it not been for the selfish whim of Hattie, who lives in the Big House.

Meanwhile, Tim in the present is very much aware of Tom's life, for he has in his possession a tin box full of Tom Inskip's drawings, which he treasures and thinks about, recognizing the scenes Tom had drawn. And it is the artistry of this time fantasy that, though Tim in the present never emerges into Tom's life in the past, we are most believably shown how Tim becomes sensitive to Tom Inskip, his ways, his moods, his unspoken longings. Furthermore, through this awareness, Tim finally knows he must follow his vision of fulfilling his love of patterns and shapes and forms by working with iron at the forge instead of becoming a businessman, his father's ambition for him. This is not the traditional time fantasy in which the protagonist experiences, through being there, a time other than his or her own. Rather, in scattered chapters, we are given glimpses into Tom's short life in the past, so that we see how the lives of the two boys are drawing closer and closer together on two levels of time, until they meet in the final dramatic crisis of Tom's death.

It is a most moving piece of work. And I wonder if Peyton ever happened to read *Journey from Obscurity,* by Wilfred Owen's brother, Harold. Sylvia Townsend Warner says of it:

> It is a book of the utmost integrity—and horror: the account of a childhood spent in the direst respectable poverty, struggles to be clean in filthy surroundings, struggles to be well-behaved among degrading companions. It is like an accusation pressed into my heart to realize that while I was growing up in a world that seemed all promise these children, my contemporaries, were writhing up, no other word for it, in a morass of squalor and emotional destitution. Art saved him. He found that he could draw, made his way into a night school, and knew at last a reason to exist.[9]

But, alas, Tom knew nothing of night schools—it would never have entered anybody's head to tell him; he was nothing, why on earth should they?—and was not allowed to live long enough, as a result of Nettie's whim, to find out on his own, to become aware of a reason to exist. This sensitive and gifted child simply went down, and the icy waters closed over him.

. . .

One of the pleasures of Penelope Lively's artistry is her preoccupation not only with the Eternal Moment, but with time's varying effects on our lives, with the ways in which these effects differ from person to person, and with those strange moments when we become sensitive to the past at the same time our lives are going on in the present. Lively's purpose has not always been to write time fantasy in the tradition of Nesbit and Pearce and Boston, but rather to give each incident making up the patterns of her novels the plangency of double and triple echoes from acts in the past influencing the present.

David Rees, in his *Marble in the Water,* says of Lively's *A Stitch in Time* that it is "probably her most important and memorable book."[10] I disagree. For me *The House in Norham Gardens,* which I must have read four times over a period of years, stands ahead of *A Stitch in Time.* For me it even stands ahead of that little gem *The Ghost of Thomas Kempe,* in subtlety, in depth, in symbolic meaning, in its wider evocations and implications regarding the human condition, as well as in the sheer, accomplished artistry of giving each level of rising emotion and awareness, on the part of Clare Mayfield, of double and triple echoes from the past. One finds this vision of time and life throughout Lively's work, in her novels for adults as well as for children.

I wonder if Lively is an admirer of Virginia Woolf's *The Waves.* For in *Norham Gardens* we find that in order to bring in her other world of the past, the world of a hidden valley existing out of time in a New Guinea jungle, Lively has used Woolf's method of a single paragraph set in italics at the head of each chapter. These paragraphs advance both the movement and our understanding of the story. In *The Waves* each italicized paragraph describes an advance in the time of day, while in Lively's novel each italicized paragraph gives us another view of a timeless New Guinea, of the days being lived out in utter remoteness, of the making of a tamburan—a sacred object used in native ceremonies. And toward the end of the book they reveal the slow, threatening advance, step by step, of the outside world's encroachments, until at last the modern world of technology breaks into the quiet villages and they become completely lost to their past.

In the midst of a bitterly cold English winter, Clare Mayfield, living with two much-loved elderly aunts in a huge old house in Norham Gardens in Oxford, comes across the tamburan stored in the attic, one of the objects brought back from New Guinea by an anthropologist great-great-grandfather. It is the shape of a shield, with strange, compelling eyes, a nose, and a gaping mouth painted on it in dull colors. Or so they seem at first. But as the days pass and the weather grows ever more bitter, the colors deepen and become richer. And Clare sees at times dark people moving confusedly beyond the bushes and in among the trees in the garden, people who cry out and seem to want something. She has troubled dreams of finding herself in a long dress, pressing her way through jungle, and is conscious of some mysterious compulsion. She becomes paler and thinner, possibly because of the stresses of trying to get back and forth to school in the wet, icy weather and of not eating properly. Or could it be the continuing demand of the dark people among the trees?

Finally she decides that it is the tamburan they want, and in a dream undergoes the struggle of carrying the tamburan up a jungle mountainside and down into the valley. But when she arrives at one of the villages, she finds that the people no longer recognize the tamburan as having any value, and she knows that she has come too late. It has lost its ancient meaning and become simply a slab of wood.

The beauties of the book are many. There is the style, full of utterly original metaphors—one can't imagine Lively using a cliché. There are the wonderful little passages on Clare's feelings about time, on the architecture of Oxford and Norham Gardens. There are the fine characterizations: of a busy, officious, self-satisfied aunt, of the two old aunts Clare lives with, existing at once in their past and in this present, and of the two boarders, the working girl Maureen and John Sempembwa, a detribalized African (as he puts it) who gives the book another echo. There is the uncommented-on contrast between the heat of the jungle, where the dark people are crying out to Clare, and the freezing cold of the English winter she is living through. And of course there is the infinitely melancholy symbolism of the tamburan itself.

Penelope Lively won the 1973 Carnegie Medal for *The Ghost of Thomas Kempe*. She won the English National Book Award in 1982 for her novel for adults *The Treasures of Time*, a fine book but one that, for me, does not displace *Norham Gardens* as far as pure artistry is concerned. Her novel *Moon Tiger*, strong and bitter, won the Booker Prize for 1987, and in this and in her sad and penetrating *Passing On*, also for adults, she again and again sees the past in the present.* Indeed, in *Moon Tiger*, told by Claudia, who wishes to write a history of the world woven through her history of herself, she says that chronology irritates her. "There is no chronology inside my head. I am composed of myriad Claudias who spin and mix and part like sparks of sunlight on water. The pack of cards I carry around is forever shuffled and reshuffled; there is no sequence, everything happens at once."

Nowhere is the contrast between Lively's writing for children and her writing for adults more delicately apparent than in the following passages, one from *Ghost* and the other from *Passing On*. Each brings out the same observations concerning the continual loss and renewal of life within the Globe of Time; what is more, each uses precisely the same material. But the difference in effect emerges most poignantly because of the two protagonists' difference in age and experience.

Here is the well-nigh perfect ending of *Ghost:*

> He looked at the branches near his head and saw suddenly that the new leaves were already there, sharp folded shapes, shiny brown tips of beech and chestnut and elm. He walked on, with Arnold somewhere not far away, and the old leaves fell silently

---

*At the Children's Literature New England Summer Institute at Newnham College, Cambridge University, August 1989, Lively stated that she would no longer be writing books for young people.

around him and piled up under his feet and above them the branches held up the new ones, furled and secret, waiting for spring. Time reached away behind and ahead: back to the crusading knight, and Thomas Kempe and Aunt Fanny, and Arnold: forward to other people who would leave their names in this place, look with different eyes on the same streets, rooftops, trees. And somewhere in the middle there was James, walking home for tea, his head full of confused but agreeable thoughts, hungry and a little tired, but content.

And here is the end of a chapter in *Passing On:*

In fact he was waiting for the place, its calm and its unconcern, to make him feel better. To make him feel less alone, less disturbed, less hungry. He was howling once more, within. And the place did nothing, nothing at all. It simply went about its business. And its business, of course, at this fecund point of the year, was that of survival—survival and reproduction. As Edward looked around he saw everything determinedly perpetuating itself—buds forming, leaves unfurling, seeds setting, the whole place off again on the same mindless, uncaring cycle, while Edward stood there in the midst of it, quite alone.

I began "The Inmost Secret" by saying: "It seems to me that magic, occurring like a sometimes troubled blessing to a child or to several children in the everyday world of reality, is, in certain instances, rather like a love affair in the first stages of discovery. The more secret the magic, the more intense and wondrous the experience."

But in *Playing Beatie Bow,* by Ruth Park, an Australian, fourteen-year-old Abigail Kirk feels anything but wonder and delight at finding herself in the Victorian age in her own city of Sydney. For unlike Tolly in *Children* and Tom in *Midnight Garden,* who continually enter the past and return, and unlike Peter in *Harp*, who beholds the past but takes no part in it, Abby becomes a prisoner of the past, like Creep in *A Chance Child*. But while Creep, despite the bitter hardships of his experiences, would have had a horror of returning to the present, Abby is fierce in her passionate determination to do precisely that.

In Abby's case the time object is an old Victorian lace collar. And because she is part of an apparently foreordained pattern, her possession of the collar is fatal: It is the controlling power that sends her off into the past, chasing little monkeylike Beatie Bow, who—out of her own time—watches her game being played in the present. "Why?" she demands of Abby later. "Why do they play it? How do they know my name?" And she unwittingly leads Abby down the wretched stinking alleys of a Sydney that Abby would never have dreamed existed and cannot recognize.

What makes this third pleasurable time fantasy memorable is, for one thing, the way in which Park creates the slow, almost imperceptible stages of change in Abby, as Le Guin did with her Hugh in *The Beginning Place*. From being a resentful "hot-headed rag of a child," she gradually comes to accept what she must do to carry out her part in the family's daily round, and then goes beyond mere duty to the courageous, determined saving of a life that does not seem worth saving and, with a wisdom beyond her years, realizes she must keep secret her love for the man who belongs to someone else. She must not change the past, and because she does not change it, her own life in the present finds its happy denouement.

Here, once again, with regard to the resolution of both story and theme, we see the pleasures of beautiful craftsmanship and original conception, in this case weaving toward a conclusion in which we understand why the children knew of Beatie Bow today and how Abby becomes, in the most astonishing way, an integral part of the family she had once hated.

IX

In the following three novels I could find nothing that amounted to outright trickery, but in Penelope Farmer's *Charlotte Sometimes,* Lucy Boston's *The Stones of Green Knowe,* and Robert Westall's *Devil on the Road,* the mechanical use of the time object seems to me to represent a version of it.

I cannot call up another time fantasy, though there may be one, in which two people exchange times, with the difficulties that would naturally result, as they do in *Charlotte Sometimes.* The author must deal honestly and strongly with these difficulties in order to make the fantasy believable. Also, the idea of the time object is new—the same bed occupied by two girls, each in a different decade but in the same boarding school: Charlotte in our time, and Clare in World War I.

Farmer's is a dangerous position, and she was courageous to take it on. One of the greatest dangers lies in the fact that she must convince us that Clare's friends in the boarding school at the time of World War I would fail to recognize that Charlotte is not Clare—especially Emily, a friend of both girls. This detail I could not believe. Surely everyone who knew Clare would notice certain details in Charlotte's physical makeup, movements, moods, and ways of speaking and would note the sound of her voice, her handwriting (here the teachers are involved), her knowledge of various subjects, and areas of ignorance outside her studies. Furthermore, and this is most important, there would be something indefinable about Charlotte—as there is something indefinable about each of us—that would surely give away the truth that this is not Clare but someone else entirely: "Yet no one noticed that I'm not her and she's not me."

And then, by far the less difficult of the two ways to write about another time was to send Charlotte into the past rather than deal with Clare in a future that would have terrified her almost beyond endurance, which Farmer acknowledged. At least Charlotte of our time had read about the past, heard about World War I. But Clare would be bombarded by one frightful strangeness after another, and I kept urgently wanting some sign of this in the messages she left for Charlotte, but there is no hint of Clare's reactions, which would have added a needed edge to the impact of the story.

Finally, we are never completely satisfied as to the deep-down reason for this entire happenstance. The girls sleep in the same bed on the night of Saturday, September 14, 1918, in Clare's time, and Saturday, September 14, in Charlotte's. But this occurs all the time to any one of us, sleeping in other people's beds. Hundreds of girls must have occupied those beds in the boarding school in different eras. I wanted something of deep, rich, personal significance to those two girls to account for the fact that they, of all the girls who had occupied that bed, should exchange times.

However, Farmer is almost always original in her grasp of possibilities that bring us up short with surprise and usually with satisfaction. For instance, Charlotte, in her own (our) time, finds *Twentieth Century Europe* and slams the book shut so that she won't know how World War I turned out. Of course she might never go back again, but in a strange, wistful way she hoped she might. And then imagine holding in your hands your own journal, written in another era in which you could not possibly have lived and containing a message from someone you don't know, in sensible actuality, who is more than forty years away from you in the past. Furthermore, Charlotte realizes with a shock that Emily, Clare's friend, could still be alive in her own time, and she is not at all sure she wants to meet this elderly woman, having known her as a ten-year-old under circumstances Emily would most likely neither understand nor believe. And how could Charlotte, should the subject arise, know that Clare had died long before Charlotte could have known her?

Farmer's depiction of place is vivid: On almost every page, scattered with colorful images, we are drawn into the school and its surroundings through sights, sounds, smells, and textures. But above all we are moved by the poignancy of the relationship between Charlotte and Clare and the subtle details with which it is made real.

In the end it is the bed that troubles me—the precise neatness with which it delivers each girl to the other's time at exactly the right moment: the mechanical usage of the time object.

It was no surprise, when Lucy Boston's *The Stones of Green Knowe* was published, that it should prove to be a novel not only of the past and present interlaced, as her other novels have been, but of the future also. Again and again we are reminded of Boston's belief that "all of time is one time," not only because of Roger D'Aulneaux's experiences in time but because of his bone-deep, passionate love for this, to him, incredible stone house his father is having built, a great Norman hall to replace the old wooden Saxon one. (Note that the Norman name D'Aulneaux has become Oldknow in this later century.)

Here, almost at once, we come upon those artifacts that are the time objects (though Roger uses only one of them), the stones of Green Knowe, carved into the shape of crude, child-size chairs by ancient, unknown hands. Concerned as he is for the continuance of his home, he wishes, sitting in the Queen chair, that he could know the answer to his most urgent questions: Will Green Knowe last? How long? How will it look in the future? What will its still unborn owners do to it? Will they love it as he does? "'O my house,' he thought. 'Live forever.'" And surely it is Lucy Boston speaking.

Because of a lack of subtlety in the method by which Boston puts Roger five hundred and forty years ahead in time and later eight hundred and fifty, one can't place this late novel of hers on a level with *The Children of Green Knowe* and *Treasure of Green Knowe,* jewels of time fantasy. For Roger has only to sit on the stones and wish, and he is at once taken to the age of Linnet and Toby and Alexander, whom we find in *Children*—in which time he also meets Susan and Jacob of *Treasure*—and then precisely into the present to meet Tolly. Because the stones obediently act as transports, we miss the deftness and wit and unobtrusive technique of *Children,* in the scenes when unseen hands tug at what Tolly is sitting on; when he simply goes outside and finds Toby and Linnet and Alexander under the big copper beech; when Alexander plays on his flute in his time and Tolly plays on Alexander's flute in the present and they hear each other's accompaniment as if they were playing together (reminding me of the double use of Hattie's skates in her time, in *Tom's Midnight Garden*, both Tom and Hattie gliding over the ice on them together); or when blind Susan knows instantly that Tolly is finding himself unexpectedly in her time, though Jacob can't see him.

Nevertheless, when all seven children from the different layers of time meet under the beech tree in *Stones,* and Tolly meets his great-grandmother Granny Partridge (old Mrs. Oldknow) as a young woman, we are delighted at Boston enriching and adding overtones to friendships blossoming over a period of eight hundred and fifty years. And when at last the stones—which Roger reverences almost as if they were sacred—are given over to the fate of so many ancient objects that are both movable and historically valuable, the act is wrenching to the reader and traumatic for Roger. But with this final scene the stones almost move out of their mechanical role as transporters into a role that is symbolic of changes often mercilessly wrought within the eternal moment.

In the late seventies and early eighties a new toughness seems to have entered time fantasy, as if Robert Westall in *The Wind's Eye* and *Devil on the Road* and Andrew Davies in *Conrad's War* had been intent on overcoming the idea that fantasy is, after all, on the whole, for girls. The mother in *The Wind's Eye* is an objectionable, aggressive, swearing woman, while the third tricky novel under discussion, *Devil on the Road,* begins, "My name's John Webster, and I'm on a drug. Not speed or grass, or even alcohol, the oldies' friend (though I like beer). My drug's Chance." Lady Chance, he calls her, and she defeats him in the end.

John's motorcycle is his companion throughout the book; and his discussion of motorcycles, his struggles with traffic, and his devoted care of his machine, as though it were in fact a living friend, will be entered into feelingly by any motorcyclist. And is it Lady Chance or the motorcycle itself that keeps John from being able to reenter the swift, tight traffic on England's A12, so that he is forced to turn back into a particular side road, where he comes upon a modern reenactment of a pike battle between Cromwell's forces and those of Charles I— the era John is about to experience? Here he finds what appears to be a barn, in which a wealthy farmer seems bent on having him stay, and here too he comes upon the cat that is the time object in *Devil*. For, as John puts it, his homely cat, whom he comes to love most dearly, "could make time jump." And it can make the motorcycle jump—or not jump, as desired—by some mysterious will. The cat's? One time object, then. Not two, though the book's title seems at first to refer to the motorcycle.

In the fields higher up behind the barn, led there by the cat, whom he calls News, John sees a cage hanging on a gibbet and in the cage a skeleton flittering with rags of old flesh; and there are far too many trees—thick, pressing masses of them. Here he also comes on a young woman, Johanna, who will draw him into a maze of interlacing powers. Having become passionately determined to set her free of the hatred of Matthew Hopkins, Witch Finder General, who is intent on "swimming" her with the rest of the wretched women he has rounded up, John tries—and fails—to blow up the man and his brutal colleagues.

What is impressive in the book is not only Westall's power to convey place and time but, above all, to convey the outlook of those who lived in that dark time. Indeed, John is doubly shocked at the end, when Johanna reveals facets of her own outlook of which he would never have believed her capable—she who had seemed to him both clear-minded and humane:

"But you're not *really* a witch—you're a lady."

"Did you not read of Canewdon, Cunning Webster? Where they did always have three witches in silk and three in cotton? Do you listen?" She moved her legs together under her skirt, and there was a rustling of petticoats. "Do you hear my silk, Cunning? There are far more witches in silk than cotton. But they are never hanged. Who dares look for witches in great men's houses?"

But later, when John asks in despair, as the existentialists used to, "Why me?" Johanna answers:

"You did look for me, Cunning, before I did look for you. What do your friends at the university seek? Drink, sport, the bodies of young women? Why was not that enough for *you?* Why did you set out to look for Lady Chance?"

"Oh, my God!"

"I do not mind you calling upon God. Only Hopkins and his like did think we were against God. Do God be more wroth with us or Hopkins, Cunning?" . . .

"But how do you *do* it—all your witchcraft and seeing the future?"

"I shall tell you why you *cannot* do it. Because you fill your hearts with thoughts of engines and money. And because you fill your houses with boxes that flicker the same dream over and over again, and benumb your brains."

John is both fascinated and repelled by this ambiguous, complex young woman—by the faint, deeply personal odor of dirt, sweat, and smoke that Johanna in our time cannot rid herself of, no matter how often she washes her body and hair. And, not being wanted in his bed, she leaves him.

It is this quality of story that Westall—completely outspoken as we know him to be from reading *The Machine Gunners*—handles so well. For he is willing and able always to follow down to the end the implications of all that he has created, bringing out in convincing detail the facts of the times, the looks of objects, the emotional climate, the climate of the senses of these people: the poor, filthy dying woman, whom Johanna visits faithfully out of compassion and whom John, sick in his soul and in his gut, feels forced to kiss.

All so good. Why, then, do I have a reservation? Why do I feel that time fantasy has been mechanically manipulated into an area that is neither fantasy nor science fiction? I did not begin to sharply resent the fact that the cat News could "make time jump" until the latter part of the book:

> Again the column began to ascend the hill. And the soldiers came and galloped past the line of witches. Like an action replay of a World Cup goal on telly.
>
> I gasped. It seemed the cat had made me master of time itself. I tried it again and again, like a kid.
>
> Then I began to use my brains.
>
> I had the advantage. Hopkins was the prisoner of time. I could make him perform the same action a hundred times, always the same. But *I* was free; I could do whatever I liked. . . .
>
> One last thing remained. Could the cat force the whole mass of gear over the time gap, out here in the open barn, without benefit of trapdoor? . . . Let's go, girl! And I want five hours to work before Hopkins comes. . . . Somewhere in the hedge, all the fuses would meet. Ten-minute fuses, because I'd timed old Hopkins up the hill on one of his action-replay journeys. And in ten minutes he would just be reaching this tree.

It is all so aesthetically grating that I almost gave up at this point. Even with Westall's superior ability as a writer, he never seemed to notice his failure to match the subtlety of influence inherent in the time objects in the finest time fantasies—objects that have their own secret will. Again, in Westall's *The Wind's Eye*, there is the children's mechanical use of the Viking ship *Resurre*, which moves to an always-convenient wind according to the strict needs of the plot as well as the ever-convenient coming and going of the mist around St. Cuthbert's Island—it is as if it were a light to be flicked off or on by a switch.

When we read Westall's excellent *Blitzcat,* the story of a female cat, Lord Gort, during World War II, we are certain the writer must be a cat person. And this certainty is reinforced by his short story "A Walk on the Wild Side," in his collection *The Haunting of Chas McGill,* which—because of the relationship between the cat and its "owner" —reminds me of Colette's novel *The Cat.* Therefore, what a pity it is, this wretched misuse of News, whom one cannot help finding as endearing as John Webster does. The scene in which John takes the starved, diseased, even ugly little animal he has just found to a starchy young know-it-all veterinarian, who only wants the cat dead, is perfect. And John's satisfaction is ours as we watch it gain weight, glossiness, gaiety, and lovely lithe movement under his care and love and feeding. It makes the trickery involving the cat all the more unworthy.

X

Ideally, any particular element in a time fantasy—for example, an old person who remembers the past, scenes of the past alternating with the present, or records of the past such as letters or a journal—works in terms of the flow of inevitability the story had for its author. It speaks of how it grew as a part of the writer's private vision of his or her novel, characteristic of and right for it, embedded so deeply within the structure that it could not be torn out and replaced by some other element dealing with the communication between past and present. Nothing that has grown, slowly and surely, can be torn apart without ruining the delicate web composed of all the elements of the novel. Delicate, yes, but a web that must at the same time be so firmly woven, with so satisfying an inner logic, that one never stops to think, as one reads, of the technique by which this firmness and sense of satisfaction was achieved.

If you can say of a book that, aesthetically speaking, it is a living thing because of the various influences it exerts, then the air it breathes, the air that sustains it, is its creator's private vision. The essence of private vision is the deepest mystery of all. Technically it has to do with theme; certainly it makes itself felt through conviction and point of view. It is of course secreted in none of these elements alone but in all of them combined in such a way as to defeat a wholly satisfactory summing-up. Private vision is an expression, emerging either consciously or unconsciously from the writer's deepest attitudes and convictions about life. Jill Paton Walsh is aware of its presence and of the necessity for a continued striving to fulfill it, as stated in the words I have quoted as an epigraph of this book: "What the author writes will often fall far short of his vision of the book, but that must not be through failure of willpower or devotion."

Particularly in the genre of time fantasy, it is unfailingly intriguing to me to note how private vision acts on the basic constructs of various fantasies to situate them so far apart in my mind that I am not even aware of their likenesses as I read; I do not think about their similarities until I actually analyze the novels, as I have done with Le Guin's *The Beginning Place* and William Mayne's *A Game of Dark*.

I have noted that Donald in *A Game of Dark*, Hugh in *The Beginning Place*, and Oliver in *Red Moon and Black Mountain* all feel sickeningly incapable of carrying out the task laid on them, of taking on the role of hero. And Will in *The Dark Is Rising* sequence cannot help thinking of himself, again and again, despite Uncle Merry's knowledge of him, as a perfectly ordinary English schoolboy. If we are to consider dream laced into the structure of the novel, no two fantasies could be more dissimilar than Jane Langton's *The Diamond in the Window* (astonishingly, New England transcendentalism is the moving force in this novel) and Penelope Lively's *The House in Norham Gardens**—in both of which dreams play such essential parts that neither could exist

---

*For a discussion of other time fantasies involving dreams, see *The Green and Burning Tree*, pages 94–95, about Edward Eager's *Knight's Castle;* and pages 125–26 about Alison Uttley's *A Traveler in Time.*

without them. Tim in *A Pattern of Roses*, Peter in *A String in the Harp*, and Clare in *Norham Gardens* are all aware of the past and its patterns, but they take no part in the resolution of events in the past, except that Peter finally realizes what he must do with the harp key to save it from being taken into public hands.

And Donald in the legendary world of William Mayne's *A Game of Dark*, Hugh in Le Guin's *The Beginning Place*, Oliver in Chant's *Red Moon and Black Mountain*, and John in Westall's *Devil on the Road* are all characters who have been awaited. There are no parchments with the young protagonists' likenesses painted on them in medieval beauty as in Alan Garner's *Elidor*. But it is known in the first two novels, as a legend or racial awareness is known, that these young people will come at some unspecified time and slay the marauding dragons; that they will lead the Hurnoi tribesmen to victory over the evil power Fendarl in *Red Moon;* and that they will do away with the Witch Finder Hawkins in *Devil*. The only difference between *Devil* and the other novels, as far as public precognitive awareness is concerned, is that John fails.

But there is no end to originality, to the power of a unique point of view to give us something new and treasurable and mind expanding. In this respect I am reminded—by some words in Barry Lopez's remarkable *Arctic Dreams: Imagination and Desire in a Northern Landscape*—of an astonishingly different understanding of time from ours, born into the child through tribal tradition. Lopez says that Hopi is a language that

> has only limited tenses . . . makes no reference to time as an
> entity distinct from space. . . . It is a language that projects a
> world of movement and changing relationships, a "continuous
> fabric" of time and space. . . . All else being equal, a Hopi child
> would have little difficulty comprehending the theory of relativity
> in his own language, while an American child could more easily
> master history. A Hopi could be confounded by the idea that
> time flowed from the past to the present.[11]

Lopez then quotes Benjamin Lee Whorf, who cautioned that all observers "are not led by the same physical evidence to the same picture of the universe."*[12]

It is those most sensitively attuned to the mysterious phenomena of life and time, who have quite different awarenesses than most of us, and who have the ability to express richly and clearly what they intuit, who will give us the impressive time fantasies of the future. There are so many paths to follow, so many unexpected crossings, extraordinary possibilities, that who knows what strange wonders still lie waiting in the dark to surprise and delight us, to set our minds and imaginations moving toward entirely fresh ways of seeing?

---

*Whorf, in "An American Model of the Universe" in *The Philosophy of Time,* says that "The Hopi language contains no reference to 'time' either implicit or explicit. At the same time [it] is capable of accounting for and describing correctly, in a pragmatic or operational sense, observable phenomena of the universe. . . . The relativity viewpoint of modern physics is one such view, conceived in mathematical terms, and the Hopi Weltanschaung is another and quite different one, nonmathematical, linguistic."

PART III

Is It Good,
Will It Last?

The motives for criticism are even more puzzling than the motives
for art. The systematic reflection upon another's creativity; the
exploration of the subtleties of a work that lie, in a sense, mute
within it; the dialogue with an invisible and perhaps skeptical
audience asserting that a work is more resourceful, more astonishing than a casual reading can suggest—all contribute to a
critical impulse.

Criticism speaks, as Northrop Frye has observed—and all
the arts are silent. Their expression is only of themselves and
never for themselves.

JOYCE CAROL OATES
The Profane Art: Essays and Reviews

I can see and hear Ransom and Jarrell now, seated on one sofa,
as though on one love seat, the sacred texts [Shakespeare] open
on their laps, one fifty, the other just out of college, and each
expounding to the other's deaf ears his own inspired and irrec-
oncilable interpretation.

ROBERT LOWELL
Randall Jarrell, 1914–1965

THE INIMITABLE
FRANCES

Now it seems to me that we who have chosen to be the medium between
children and the written word are very much like the Emperor of
China. We, like him, belong to a privileged class, with as great an
inheritance as his, with as much responsibility and variety in our
lives. Like him, we have heard the nightingale.

FRANCES CLARKE SAYERS
Summoned by Books

No matter how large the room, you could always spy Frances
Clarke Sayers at once in any gathering as that tall, beautiful
woman in the big hat. The big hat was her visible trademark. Surely
she knew she was stunning in whichever one she chose to wear for
the occasion; she *knew* how to present herself.

In the old days, when I was a clerk in the literature department of
the Los Angeles Public Library, librarians were thought by some to
be intellectual snobs, quite possibly fake—"the duchesses," one irate
patron labeled them in a letter to the *Los Angeles Times*—in flat shoes
and navy blue dresses with little white collars. This outfit was, presumably, thought of as the librarian's uniform. But Frances always
came before us in anything but this navy blue outfit. And she could
speak!

She had a style, very much her own, of hesitating here and there within the flow of her words, so that one felt she was trying to express her thought in a way that would be as fully revealing and satisfying as possible. This gave the impression that she was speaking extemporaneously, and yet when you read her "Lose Not the Nightingale,"* you realize how meticulously she prepared herself to speak in public. If she used notes, it was scarcely apparent. She spoke at a reflective pace and almost always with gleams of mischievous humor that shone out between memorable observations very personal to Frances. Her style was in the pacing of her thought.

She had been a librarian for years and then a teacher of children's literature at UCLA in two different periods, during the second of which I knew her.† And I, as well as many others, thought that she might have been an actress, for she possessed a very special ability, only partly realized. Not only was she a most gifted and impressive teacher of her subject, she was an absolutely superb storyteller. Her unforgettable voice—rich and resonant and with a slightly southern glide to it—could hold any audience, either child or adult, mouse-quiet and convey a most subtle appreciation of the nuances of a story. These she brought out to the depth and extent of their possibilities, not by large gestures or movements of the body (abhorrent to the skilled storyteller, when all attention should be concentrated on the story itself) but by the rhythms of her telling, the variations of tone and emphasis. To me she always evoked the impression that a story came out of her very essence, that she was the magical spider spinning her web out of her own imagination and experience, though she would have been the first to remind me that her art lay in faithfully handing on, simply as the medium, what the ages have given us.

I first heard her tell a story, which happened to be "Molly Whup-

---

*See *Summoned by Books*, pages 52–67. Though these essays were written through four decades, they are as vigorous and urgent about what it means to be in the profession of librarianship now as they were then.
†See Ethel L. Heins, "Frances Clarke Sayers: A Legacy," *The Horn Book* (January–February 1990), pages 31–35, for an overview of Sayers's professional life.

pie," to a huge auditorium of children of all ages, from kindergarten through the sixth grade. They had arranged a throne for her, surrounded by green, leafy branches, so that she would be seated in a bower. And though she would much rather have stood at the front of the stage, she graciously accepted the honor of being queen of the occasion. And she held her audience, which is for some reason much more difficult to do seated than when one is standing stage front. During that entire story there was not so much as a whisper from any child, scarcely a wriggle (I was listening and watching intently), all eyes fixed on her face as though under a spell. For she was assuredly a spell caster, an enchantress.

And she was this too in her teaching, because of an unusual elegance of delivery in her lectures, a most powerful conviction in all she said that the best in children's literature was indeed literature and not "kiddy lit"—the stock sneering phrase of her days at UCLA. For instance, you would hear from the adult side of the English department, What could there possibly be in the subject to deserve graduate study? Plenty! Frances would have shot back. And she would have wagered she could convince any of them—at least those who had vivid enough memories of their own childhood and enough of the ability to identify with that self of years long gone, to perceive truth and illumination in the writing of the finest children's fictions—of this fact if only they would come to one of her lectures. But of course, she would have said, too, that without those memories, without that ability, the case would be hopeless. And she would have given them her dry, ironical, questioning sidelong glance.

One of those professors took her up on her wager. Dr. Lawrence Clark Powell, former head of the UCLA library, cheerfully admitted that for years he had resisted her influence and avoided her at conferences because what she purveyed was "kid stuff." Another victim of the intellectual snobbery that then infused English departments (and still does, in certain universities), he finally decided that he might as well listen to her just once, and she reached out to him in the back row with her infinite power of projection and caught and held him, and he recognized at last her scholarship and vision—"her gift of celebration," he called it.

Unfortunately, I never had the privilege of being one of Frances's students (what I have said about her teaching has been reported to me by one whose work in children's literature has gone on fruitfully long past retirement). I had heard her speak many times, but it wasn't until I read those fine, brief pieces of hers at the beginning of each section of the third edition of *Anthology of Children's Literature*[1] that the conviction came to me that this was exactly what I had a passion to do: consider children's literature as a whole, with critical discussions of specific titles to illustrate my points just as critics do in essays on literature for adults.

This was centuries ago, back in the 1960s. I had long before become enamored of literary criticism while working in the literature department of the Los Angeles Library. It seemed to me, and I fervently hoped, that what I had in mind was something quite different from what Lillian Smith, in *The Unreluctant Years,* and Paul Hazard, in *Books, Children and Men,* had done. And it was Frances who forced me to set down the words of my first essay when she asked me to become one of a group to travel up and down the southern California coast as well as inland to Riverside, giving one-day seminars on "Excellence in Children's Books." And you can tell what a power of persuasion there was in the woman (money would have to be put out!) when I say that the project was launched under the auspices of the UCLA Department of English and the School of Library Science—this during the era of "Kiddy Lit."! Frances planned three aspects of her subject: "Who Defines Excellence?"; "Who Creates Excellence?"; and "Who Chooses Excellence?"

Our company, set to travel in our own tour bus, consisted of professional women in the library, editing, and writing world of children's literature, with the addition of Scott O'Dell. We called ourselves Les Girls, and Scott didn't mind in the least. On the contrary, he was highly amused and had a splendid time: all these women to himself to entertain with his bottomless supply of literary anecdotes (he had written novels for adults before his *Island of the Blue Dolphins,* knew Hollywood well, and had obviously been quite a man-about-town). The only thing that bothered me was that, throughout my talk on the final day at UCLA, Scott walked up and down, up and down the corridor just outside the lecture hall. Which meant that I had to watch him pacing nervously back and forth (appearing and disappearing as he came into sight and vanished beyond the two big open doors at the back, which I faced) while trying to keep my mind on my talk, not read from a prepared paper but given with the help of sparse notes.

What was borne home to me on that happy journey was that Frances's particular variety of wit and her mischievous, sometimes sharp humor were never apparent enough in her writings. What a pity! If you ever experienced an evening with Scott, you can well imagine how those two, Scott and Frances, couldn't wait for one to finish his or her anecdote so that the other could top it.

I should add (and Frances would be the first to delightedly agree) that she had her paradoxical moments. Certainly Marie, her sister, who loved her better than anyone else in the world, would agree as well, she who—usually sitting at Frances's side on the big sofa at the end of the living room in their Ojai home—would be heard to mutter sotto voce into her hand from time to time: "Oh, *come* now, Frances!" or "Well, it wasn't just *exactly* like that. . . ." This when Frances, at the very peak of her creative recollecting and entirely carried away, would be off on some highly dramatic or exquisitely funny moment, deaf to all hints of objection or doubt. Surely she was like Virginia Woolf in this (Marie her Leonard): You *couldn't* just leave a story lying there in all its flatness, filled with those precise, dull, gray facts, when it offered so many juicy opportunities to be made suspenseful and astonishing and vivid—in short, wholly delectable, the kind to bring shouts of laughter from her reveling audience. And those involved in her story could never have dreamed at the time that what they were living through would turn out to be this dramatic tale, and that they themselves were so colorful, so quick, so brilliant. Marie could mutter into her hand all she liked; her mutterings only added to the whole satisfying effect.

But although Frances had a sharp sense of humor, sometimes that sharpness—devoid of humor and filled with bitterness and indignation, as in her famous piece on Walt Disney and the way he presented the classics in "his" *Snow White,* "his" *Pinocchio,* "his" *Alice in Wonderland,* "his" *The Ugly Duckling*—revealed to the full her conviction about quality in children's literature and how it can be cheapened.*

At one point during our Les Girls journey we landed in a certain city and were greeted by some Higher-Up from the board of education. In Frances's eye he must have been far more administratively able than literarily knowledgeable. For after his welcoming speech, during the course of which he assured us what a very fortunate thing it was that we had chosen to come to his city, Frances, quite unexpectedly, raised a finger and pressed it to his shirtfront. "Yes," she agreed sternly, though with a teasing sparkle in her eye, "but are you sure you *deserve* us?" We were all so taken aback, no one knew what to say, least of all the poor administrative gentleman, who thought he had greeted us most warmly with precisely the proper literary quotations and references.

She could be quite outspoken in both word and gesture. When my husband and I made our first visit to her and Marie's home in the

---

*See "Walt Disney Accused," *The Horn Book* (November–December 1965), pages 602–7. This article is an interview, conducted by Charles W. Weisenberg, then public relations director of the Los Angeles Public Library. It came about because of Frances's acerbic letter to the *Los Angeles Times* concerning California Superintendent of Public Instruction Max Rafferty's praising of Walt Disney as "the greatest educator of this century." Her opinion of Disney's treatment of the classics (not including his nature films) being the exact opposite, her letter to the *Times* was, as she herself called it, "a blast of anger." Her letter opens the interview.

Ojai Valley, back in the hills between Ventura and Santa Barbara, I had a moment of misgiving the instant we arrived because I had forgotten to warn him that Frances greatly disliked being kissed (at least at the time she did). Sure enough, on coming up to her and Marie at the entrance, he leaned over and kissed Frances lightly on the cheek, though I don't believe he'd ever presumed to do so before. At once, up came a finger and curled itself around an apparently slightly damp spot he'd left there, wiping it abruptly and distastefully away. He *saw*—his first action an unfortunate one! But the moment was lost, we were wafted in, plunged into talk and laughter and nothing was said about the incident until, on the way home, Ian himself brought it up. "Ah, well," he said. "One lesson learned when visiting Frances."

But what fun we'd had! It was then that we discovered her love of puns; particularly triple ones. She and Marie, she'd told us, had gone to the home of a friend who'd just acquired a nanny goat named Amelia Earhart, and Frances at once, without a moment's hesitation, cried: "Oh, a flying buttress!"

Frances also brought me my first experience of professional irk, the kind in which any of us can get caught up in the process of the mingling of egos. Because of Les Girls, Frances wanted to talk over with me my part in the arrangements, and she asked me to have lunch with her at the university club so that we could become acquainted over a quiet meal first—just the two of us, she said—and then go into the lounge and get on with practical affairs. I was more pleased than I would have admitted: She had long been my ideal of the professional woman in the world we shared, and I looked forward day after day to our date. What a pleasure it would be to talk over the authors we both held in high esteem, ask each other about books read and what the other thought of them, perhaps suggest new ones and exchange experiences in writing. There was no end to all we could speak of—and there would actually be so little time.

But no sooner had we settled ourselves over our salads and coffees and had begun that excited, searching exchange I knew would take place the moment we got together than along came BB, young, handsome, completely sure of himself and pleased with what he was sure of, newly published and utterly fascinated by Frances, whom he admired, one could see at once, at least as much as other people did. "*Fran*-ces!" he cried, advancing with outstretched hands, "*what* a serendipity! Would you *mind*, my dear? May I join you?" There wasn't a chance that he wouldn't. Nothing could have kept him away from this nice little opportunity to confide in Frances—Frances, of all people!—his hopes and plans and ideas for a new manuscript.

I glared at him. But it was no use. He wasn't looking at me. She murmured something polite and down he sat, and from that time on it was his luncheon—well, his and Frances's. I sat and simmered, and though she turned to me anxiously from time to time, trying to get me to join in, I was silent. She should have objected in the beginning, I was thinking, said, perhaps, "B, I'm sorry, but Eleanor and I must take this opportunity to—etc., etc." But that moment had passed. Finally, following dessert, he got up, humbly asked our forgiveness for having so rudely interrupted what had no doubt been meant to be a private occasion, and hurried off to whatever appointment waited. "*Well!*" cried Frances, "I've been a bad girl, haven't I?" What could I say? I'm sure she must still have been Mrs. Sayers to me at that time—I did not take easily to first names of people in my professional life. "Well, it *was* too bad," I admitted. Then we grinned at each other, partly over the nature of B, finding himself far more entertaining and expressive than usual in her unexpected company, and Eleanor, "nur-r-rsing her wr-rath to keep it war-r-rm" (see Bobby Burns, "Tam O'Shanter").

In that handsome home in Ojai, the dining and living rooms opened into each other—high-ceilinged, wood-paneled (it was an entirely *woody* house)—one end of the dining room covered with books from floor to roof. The outside walls of both rooms were almost completely windows, looking onto a patio surrounded by a profusion of greenery with, in the low places, views of the thickly wooded hills beyond. In the hills, here and there a chimney would be sending up blue wandering smoke if the air was that of fall or winter or coolish spring. The other two walls were covered with original paintings from children's books, sent to Frances by the artists, and with Japanese art. The space over the couch at the far end was covered with a troupe of artfully arranged original paintings. The inner wall, its back to the entrance hall, held a large brick fireplace with a piece of Japanese carving standing nearby. On the floor was a silky golden green carpet, the color of leaves translucent with sunlight; and all the comfortable chairs, there and in the dining room, had coverings in colors that harmonized with the Japanese art on the walls. The whole feeling was one of quiet spaciousness, comfort, and invitation, a place where the eye wandered to take in one aesthetically satisfying effect after another.

It must have been there that Frances insisted, one afternoon, that I was wrong about emotion in criticism. "No, no, Eleanor! Criticism does *not* begin with emotion; it begins with thought." "But Frances," I said, "we are made up of both emotion and thought, and when we read a book, any kind of book, we can't help, during our very first impression of it, feeling a certain reaction. Sometimes that reaction can be overcome later, on a second reading, or it will be modified as we get into the book, our understanding of it expanded and deepened, or by the passage of years during which we've changed and matured. Criticism isn't good criticism unless it's thought through. But emotion will still be there, somewhere." "Then that part isn't criticism," insisted Frances. "The only part that is *real* criticism is that part which is thought."

So we went—on and on, up this road and down that, each (I, at least) having the kind of experience that only afterward is recognized as having been thoroughly and deeply satisfying. Ian and I invariably had so much to talk about that the journey home from Ojai to Los Angeles seemed magically short.

And always—always, no matter how Frances and I disagreed, as we sometimes did—I was reminded of Lawrence Powell's words that what she had treated us to over that triumphant period of almost thirty years was "a celebration of books." A celebration that actually changed the course of criticism of children's literature, showing us how all literature could be brought to its consideration and that that criticism need not be kept within narrow bounds but must be enhanced and deepened and challenged by a knowledge of every kind of worthy book you could lay your hands on.

On Criticism,
Awards, and Peaches

➊

There is nothing more important than writing well for the young, if literature is to have a continuance. . . . They will inherit the earth; and nothing that we value will endure in the world unless they can be persuaded to value it too.

JILL PATON WALSH
from a lecture at the Library of Congress

*Y*ou would have thought his favorite reading might have been Saki or Oscar Wilde, considering their worldly, ironic, and at times sardonic wit. But, no, not at all.

When Noël Coward was a small boy he would save his pennies until he had a shilling and then stop by a secondhand bookshop on the way home from school and buy a bundle of successive issues of the *Strand Magazine,* containing all the installments of one of E. Nesbit's children's novels. When a certain purchase revealed that several issues were missing, he stole a coral necklace belonging to a friend of his mother, pawned it, and bought the book from the army-navy store. Nesbit loved that confession when, in her late years, Coward made one of his devoted pilgrimages to her out in Romney Marsh at Jesson St. Mary, where she lived with her second husband, Thomas Terry Tucker ("The Skipper"), and told her the tale of his wickedness.

Something in the tone of her humor, a certain toughness, tartness
(rather like Beatrix Potter's), answered something in his tone, kept
into adulthood. He adored her and everything she wrote all his life,
and at his death *The Enchanted Castle* was found lying on the table
beside his bed.

From his home in Jamaica, where he lived in retirement, he wrote
in a letter in 1956:

> I am reading again through all the dear E. Nesbits and they seem
> to me to be more charming and evocative than ever. It is strange
> that after half a century I still get so much pleasure from them.
> Her writing is so light and unforced, her humour is so sure and
> her narrative quality so strong that the stories, which I know
> backwards, rivet me as much now as they did when I was a little
> boy. . . . E. Nesbit knew all the things that stay in the mind,
> all the happy treasures. I suppose she, of all the writers I have
> ever read, has given me over the years the most complete sat-
> isfaction and, incidentally, a great deal of inspiration.[1]

It is plain, then, that Coward would have smiled at any criticism
of her work—justified or not, in his view—because he had gotten
beyond that kind of consideration of it. And now that he was in old
age, he could say that what he enjoyed was "her actual talent and her
extraordinary power of describing hot summer days in England in the
beginning years of the century. All the pleasant memories of my own
childhood jump at me from the pages—aspects of a writer's art that
one becomes increasingly aware of in later years."[2]

How amused and untouched he would have been to read Humphrey
Carpenter's words that she was actually "a Victorian in disguise"[3] for
all her pretensions to being a Fabian (a good example of Victorian
hypocrisy, I assume), when all her child protagonists come from the
middle class, unlike the child protagonists in the novels of Charles
Kingsley, George MacDonald, and Mrs. Ewing, who, as Carpenter
points out, come from the families of the poor. "Any deep concern

with changing the existing social order is notably lacking from the Nesbit books."[4] In his view she was, in fact, nothing but "an energetic hack,"[5] this fact revealed in two scenes that, taken together, illustrate his point. At the end of *The Railway Children* there is the "tear-jerking moment"[6] when Roberta, reunited with her father, cries out, " 'Oh, my Daddy, my Daddy!' That scream went like a knife into the heart of everyone on the train." Unfortunately, Nesbit uses exactly that same cry (though without the cliché to describe its sharpness) in a scene in *The House of Arden*. "In one flash she was across the room and in her father's arms, sobbing and laughing and saying again and again—'Oh, my daddy! Oh, my daddy, my daddy!' "

But perhaps such a repetition was natural, at least in Carpenter's view, for to him Nesbit was incapable of memorable characterization, and one must admit that this is in a way true, except for Oswald Bastable in *The Story of the Treasure Seekers* and the other Bastable books and the Psammead in *The Five Children and It:* individuals not searched through but whom one at least remembers, though Carpenter notes that the Psammead's personality is strongly reminiscent of the feisty Cuckoo and Raven in Mrs. Molesworth's *The Cuckoo Clock* and *The Tapestry Room*. Her preoccupation was always with the exciting working out of story. But Humphrey Carpenter is cool and dry and denigrating about E. Nesbit in every way and at every possible opportunity throughout the twelve pages of his chapter on her in his *Secret Gardens*. "She is an author," he says in his final sentence, "whose methods are comparatively easy to copy, and many have done so, though whether to the ultimate benefit of children's literature seems questionable." But who *are* these copiers of Nesbit? If he means (though he does not say so) that she set into motion the genre of time fantasy in children's literature with *The Story of the Amulet,* then he is quite right, for it could be that, without her, we would not have had the absorbing and rewarding works of Lucy Boston, Philippa Pearce, and all the other time fantasists of whom I have spoken in "Pleasures and Problems." In view of what I have written there, it is plain that I most strongly disagree with his dismissive words. The power of private vision is all.

Indeed, Julia Briggs, author of the engrossing *A Woman of Passion: The Life of E. Nesbit, 1858–1928,* says of her, quite contrary to Carpenter's opinion:

> If her books, taken all in all, are not uniformly well written, they nevertheless give an impression of a rich and vital inner life, of a response that was never less than passionate to her surroundings, family and friends, to her reading and the social milieu in which she lived. . . . She never forgot that pain, embarrassment and anxiety are the usual accompaniments of all real adventures, nor—though her characters were so independent and enterprising—that all children . . . are ultimately at the mercy of adults. . . . While her rapid shifts of attitude and mood, her wit and versatility, and her refusal to conform to a single approach or expectation make her writing difficult to analyse conveniently, they are also the source of its richly varied and wonderfully animated vision.[7]

This is quite a statement if one is to consider her, as Carpenter does, simply "an energetic hack." But Edmund Wilson recalls his early reading of Nesbit with great warmth and speaks of the boy's uncle in Faulkner's *Intruder in the Dust* being as ironic and delightful as the uncle next door in Nesbit's story of the Bastables. And C. S. Lewis, in his *Surprised by Joy,* says of *The Story of the Amulet* that it first opened his eyes to antiquity, "the dark backward and abysm of time," and that as an adult he "could still read it with delight."[8]

My point concerning E. Nesbit and these opposing opinions of her work is to emphasize in a specific way the subjectivity of criticism. Pamela Travers is irritated by Hans Christian Andersen's sentimentality (though only certain of his stories can be accused of that—many of them are cruel in the extreme), but I recall reading of Isak Dinesen, on her way to bed, asking herself, "Where is my Andersen?" Both she and Coward had gotten beyond the consideration of their favorites as subjects of critical discussion.

A good many of us who are reading animals have our favorites, comforting or illuminating or both. To them we return again and again and about them an objective discussion of faults, weaknesses, and lacks would be of passing interest only. We might make certain admissions, but these would in no way affect our overall enjoyment of the works under fire. Here enters what I call the acceptance quotient. As a friend of mine accepts, for instance, the troubles I have with Sylvia Cassedy's *Lucie Babbidge's House* but still considers it an endearing and moving novel, so I accept my own trouble (at the end) with Pauline Clarke's *The Return of the Twelves* but am still devoted to it. There are works that, despite whatever small or large faults they may have, are accepted by their admirers with unfailing warmth, even love, because the books nevertheless give them lasting pleasure.

In view of the fact that criticism (in the large sense) is such an extremely subjective matter, considering that we each bring an entirely personal collection of convictions, recollections, knowledge, and sensibilities to any work and must therefore bring our coolest thought to it as well, I must ask myself: For whom does the critic write, and why?

It is a question answered very firmly by Alfred Kazin. After commenting on "the critic-as-popularizer, the critic consciously mediating between the work of art and the public," he then goes on to say: "But no critic who is any good sets out deliberately to enlighten someone else; he writes to put his own ideas in order; to possess, as a critic, through the integral force of his intelligence, the work of art that someone else has created."[9] Samuel Pickering, Jr.,* author of *John Locke and Children's Books in Eighteenth Century England*, agrees with Kazin. "Ultimately we all write for ourselves," he says, and adds that the writing is "for our pride and the sense of accomplishment."[10] On first reading Kazin's words, particularly about a critic being no good if the critic sets out deliberately to enlighten someone else, which

---

*The teacher who inspired Tom Keating, the screenwriter of *Dead Poets Society*, to develop the Robin Williams character.

assuredly sounds condescending, and Pickering's writing for our "pride and sense of accomplishment," I at once became self-questioning.

When I write criticism, I say to myself, what am I trying to do? Why am I writing at all? Why have I persisted in going through the at times enormously frustrating and difficult process of trying to explain, with as much truth and clarity and precision as I am capable of, what I think and intuit about some book I admire, or one that seems to me lacking in certain essentials necessary to a memorable piece of work?

I agree with Kazin that first of all I must put my thoughts in order, for if I can't explain myself to myself, I can't explain to anyone else. But why, having thought out my ideas and reactions very clearly— or so I imagine—do I then have the compulsion to put them down on paper? For one thing, to clarify still further a subject that haunts my mind (and has haunted it for some time, to judge by the number of notes I've made). And perhaps, having gotten down a first draft, to discover that I must change my mind here and there, that I must go deeper, that I must refine, that I must clarify again—and again. For in the process of writing, something either devastating or electric happens. Either I find that certain "certainties" become not so certain and demand more examination, having been put to the test of visibility—that is, of being spelled out on paper—or else door after door opens. In the midst of the tussle with syntax, with searching for precisely the right word, for the one mysteriously right mode of expression that will satisfy that judge residing in my inner ear, I discover new implications, perhaps new pathways into that cave of meaning lying at the center of the work in hand. It is a most exhilarating experience, this making unforeseen discoveries in the testing of one's own intellect and aesthetics, and proves the truth of the question: "How do I know what I think until I see what I say?" Though for me the line should go, "How do I know what I *really* think until I see what I say?"

For another thing, all the time I'm writing, because of the very fact that I *am* writing, I'm reaching out. I am, in effect, saying, "I wonder if you agree, or disagree, and why." I'm hoping to arouse a reaction, not necessarily one of hot disagreement (though I've experienced this, with letters flooding in to *The Horn Book* at the time of my "McLuhan, Youth and Literature"[11]) but one that invites and leads to further thought, perhaps even creates new illuminations in the reader that I hadn't come upon myself. *There* would be a fruitfulness! Or, if the reader of this criticism hasn't read the work being explored, perhaps there will be a compulsion to get it and read it with fresh and attentive mind and imagination. Concerning Pickering's "pride and sense of accomplishment"—yes, of course. But even more, for me, the possibility of inviting further perceptions and intuitings and recognitions. We don't have to agree! In fact, disagreement can lead to openings and understandings that might not have been possible otherwise.

Concerning openings and understandings, Professor Pickering says in his essay "The Function of Criticism in Children's Literature," from which I have quoted, that much of this literature "is understandable at first reading and does not lend itself to multiple 'close readings' or interpretations; and textual scholarship, in contrast to historical research, is relatively unimportant," being "irrelevant to the large affairs of life."[12] No, of course there are not many *Alice in Wonderland*s or *Huckleberry Finn*s. None but the two of them! But I don't believe that this makes scholarship (in the large sense), close readings, and interpretations unimportant. As a matter of fact, comparatively little textual scholarship, published for the general profession, is being done in children's literature. Peter Neumeyer's papers in *The Horn Book*— one on E. B. White's *Charlotte's Web* and the other on his *The Trumpet of the Swan*—are fine examples of such work.[13]

To speak of close readings, the most memorable children's and teenagers' books are not always penetrated on one reading; indeed, I should say, rarely. One could name Ursula Le Guin's Earthsea books, Jill Paton Walsh's *Unleaving,* William Steig's *The Spear and the Piccolo,* Russell Hoban's *The Mouse and His Child,* Katherine Paterson's *Jacob Have I Loved,* Robert Cormier's *I Am the Cheese,* Virginia Hamilton's

M. C. Higgins the Great, William Mayne's *A Game of Dark,* James M. Barrie's *Peter Pan,* and Alan Garner's *The Owl Service* and his *Red Shift.**
Those who run through a book, merely for superficial pleasure, *might* think that they "get" the story. Get the top, perhaps, as children get the top of Hans Christian Andersen's fairy tales, while a world of pain and regret and longing lies underneath, as it does in "The Ugly Duckling," a symbolic tale of his own life, and in his merciless story "The Shadow," which Ursula Le Guin penetrates in her Library of Congress lecture entitled "The Child and the Shadow."†

For the critic it is always a matter of rereading, which can be, inevitably, a revelation, if the book is a rich one. On a closer second or third reading, the pleasure is to arrive at understandings that prove one to have been all but blind the first time through—as I realized I had been on rereading *The Tombs of Atuan* after my first quick devouring. (Indeed, not only did I *not* appreciate the book that first time, owing to my blindness, but found it a letdown after *A Wizard of Earthsea.*) I reread Le Guin's *The Beginning Place,* of great interest to me, in order to compare it with William Mayne's remarkable *A Game of Dark,* a book I positively disliked on first reading and only later appreciated. Evaluations mysteriously, almost magically, change and open out under these circumstances, and discovery must come first.

---

*I am referring here to Paterson's ending of the book, which has puzzled a good many, who view it as "an unnecessary appendage." But see Sarah M. Smedman's " 'A Good Oyster': Story and Meaning in *Jacob Have I Loved,*" in *Children's Literature in Education* 14 (1983), pages 180–87. Concerning Robert Cormier's many-layered *I Am the Cheese,* see Perry Nodelman's "Robert Cormier Does a Number," in *Children's Literature in Education* 14 (1983), pages 94–103. For William Steig's *The Spear and the Piccolo,* see Anita Moss's exploration in *Children's Literature* 10 (1982), pages 124–40. For a Freudian and fascinating interpretation of *Peter Pan,* see "The Neverland as Id: *Peter Pan* and Freud," by Michael Egan, in *Children's Literature* 10 (1982), pages 37–55. Concerning *The Owl Service* (but not *Red Shift*) see my "The Owl Service: A Study," *Wilson Library Bulletin* (December 1969), pages 425–33.
†See Le Guin's *The Language of the Night.*

One tries to see into the text for what it is actually saying, not what one thought it said, or thought it should have said, or got the impression it said, or seemed to remember it saying. One notices details that the author has woven into the work most subtly, details easily missed on first reading. There could be a single word (the kind I call "the burden word") used again and again, not out of carelessness but for some definite purpose, as Le Guin uses the words *shadow* and *power* under varying circumstances in *Wizard.** There is the word *see* in all its meanings, physical, spiritual, and aesthetic, as instrumental in the awakening of the young girl Tenar, renamed Arha, the One Priestess of the Tombs in *The Tombs of Atuan*. As I've confessed, I was quite blind in the beginning until I, like Arha, began to experience one awakening after another.

A student, reading quickly for duty or pleasure, might not notice words and instances in the light of spiritual, intellectual, and aesthetic growth, and would then miss their purpose, thus failing to achieve the whole import of the novel. I note the words *blood* and *bloody* expressed again and again under varying circumstances in Mollie Hunter's *A Sound of Chariots* (excluding "bloody" used as an expletive by Bridie's father). The repetition speaks to me of the horror and the deep-lying traumatic effects of war suffered in the British Isles through two and three generations in our time. They were there in Mollie Hunter as she wrote, welling up quite unconsciously as one situation in the novel after another called for them. Interestingly enough, when Bridie comes to the age of menstruation, which is a milestone for any young girl, the words are never uttered. So that it would seem they arose, in this novel, specifically from the trauma of war. When I asked Mollie Hunter about this, she replied that she was quite unaware of what she had done and seemed genuinely astonished at my discovery.

In Cynthia Voigt's *A Solitary Blue* the two-word sentence "I'm sorry" is repeated so often—sometimes twice on a page and once, even three

---

*See my "High Fantasy: *A Wizard of Earthsea*," in *Crosscurrents of Criticism*.

times—by the protagonist, Jeff, and his father that one cannot help
noticing, and then counting, the number of repetitions—one hundred
and thirty-four of them. At this astonishing total, we realize that
these two words speak again and again of the central theme: What
damage a cruel and profoundly wounding indifference to a loving
husband and son, coupled with a cold-blooded using of both, can do
to them, and how such usage and indifference affects the relationship
of the two to each other. I can think of no more powerful exposition
of this theme, involving of course the deepest loneliness, in children's
literature.*

In his essay Professor Pickering speaks of the irrelevance of "textual
scholarship to the large affairs of life."[14] Whether we agree or not,
we cannot absorb critically *A Sound of Chariots* and ignore the relevance
of one of its themes to a towering contemporary concern: what war
does to those who have been mutilated by it either physically or
spiritually or both. We cannot examine critically Robert Cormier's
two best novels, *I Am the Cheese* and *After the First Death,* and ignore
the intensity with which he presents his theme of the awful reality of
blind, cold-blooded power in three worlds today: those of government,
terrorism, and the military. We cannot explore critically *Watership
Down* and *The Mouse and His Child* and ignore their themes of the
effects of power on the defenseless. But even seemingly private fictions
like *The Wind in the Willows* and *The Tale of Two Bad Mice* are woven
through with their authors' attitudes to the large affairs, as pointed
out by Humphrey Carpenter in his chapters on Grahame in *Secret
Gardens* and, concerning Potter's little books, in Suzanne Rahn's essay,
"Tailpiece: *The Tale of Two Bad Mice.*"[15]

One more point in this overview of various kinds of criticism is
Professor Pickering's firm belief about historical criticism:

---

*See "Matters of Character," pages 61–69.

I have found historical studies more useful than other kinds of criticism and believe that children's literature benefits more from the products of criticism founded on historical research than any other basis. What is needed now is more criticism that provides titles, dates, and publishing history; that traces trends and the development of ideas; and that discusses the growth and evolution of genres.[16]

There can be no doubt that that kind of criticism has great value. But I believe that the teaching of contemporary literature, the exploration of fine works by new writers coming into their richest assurance—opening all this to future children's librarians and teachers of children—would suffer grievously if there were few or no perceptive critical studies of modern works worth critical attention. Virginia Woolf comments on this point in her essay "How It Strikes a Contemporary" when she asks: "Is there no guidance nowadays for a reader who yields to none in his reverence for the dead, but is tormented by the suspicion that reverence for the dead is vitally connected with understanding of the living?"[17]

I think, too, that for the serious writer a certain atmosphere of expectation is created in which one can become aware, through reading penetrating criticism of one's fellow writers, what new high-water marks are being established by which one can measure one's own work.

Which brings me to the Newbery Award. It seems to me unfair and completely misleading to try to choose the *one* so-called most distinguished book of the year in children's literature out of a sea of fiction, nonfiction, and poetry for *both* children and young adults. I cannot imagine that the Newbery committee could have thought that Jerry Spinelli's *Maniac Magee* is superior to Le Guin's *Tehanu* or Staples's *Shabanu*. But *Maniac Magee* is for children, while *Tehanu* is for young adults or, one should say (as one could of *Shabanu*) for anybody. But the committee had to choose, whether the book was for children *or* for young adults. And what of all the other fine novels for young adults, all the fine nonfiction written for both categories, and what of poetry?

I believe that the far-too-large Newbery committee of fourteen— in which vote after vote has to be taken among so many contending opinions that if you did win the Newbery you would have to wonder how many votes were taken on how many books before they finally wound down to yours—should be broken into committees of three. If there were three judges for children's fiction, three for children's nonfiction, three for children's poetry, three for young-adult fiction, and three for young-adult nonfiction (by the time of high school, young adults are probably reading adult poetry), only one person would have to be added to the present fourteen-member Newbery committee.

Doesn't it seem burningly unfair to writers, not to speak of the almost impossible burden of judgment on the committee members, that they are trying to decide among bananas, lemons, oranges, plums, and peaches as to which is the *one* finest fruit of the year?

To go back now to that question I asked near the beginning: For whom does the critic write and why? After searching myself, after explaining my thoughts to myself as best I can, it seems to me that, indirectly, I write on behalf of the children. Because it is the children we work and hope for, most desperately. There are two wonderful sentences in *Maniac Magee,* apropos of his working every lure he can think of to get little Russell and Piper McNab to agree "in the prayer-dark seed of their kidhoods" that *they must keep going to school.* He thinks:

> But they were spoiling, rotting from the outside in, like a pair of peaches in the sun. Soon, unless he, unless somebody did something, the rot would reach the pit.

Yes. And I would never have written this book if it weren't for the children, and you would not be reading it. For we want, most fervently, as many of them as possible to go on reading, to be literate in a way that means reading will affect their lives, will give them a view of the human condition they would never have without it, that will become a companion to them all the rest of their days.

WITH WRINKLED
BROW AND COOL
FRESH EYE

❧

*If God were a writer and wrote a book that Randall did not think
was good, Randall would not have hesitated to give it a bad review.
And if God complained, I think Randall would then set about showing
God what was wrong with his sentences.*

ROBERT WATSON
Randall Jarrell: The Lost Years

*T*he poet Randall Jarrell, author of three fantasies that have
found a lasting place on children's bookshelves, was also an
impassioned critic. Robert Lowell said of him:

With wrinkled brow and cool fresh eye, he was forever musing,
discovering, and chipping away at his own misconceptions. Getting out on a limb was a daily occurrence for him, and when he
found words for what he had intuited, his judgments were bold
and unlikely. Randall was so often right that sometimes we said
he was always right. He could enjoy discarded writers whom it
was a scandal to like, praise young, unknown writers as if he
were praising and describing Shakespeare's tragedies, and read
Shakespeare's tragedies with the uncertainty and wonder of their
first discoverers. [1]

Mention of Jarrell's cool fresh eye, his willingness, despite his passion, to discover, to chip away at his own misconceptions, reminds me of two instances out of my own experience. The first reveals an attitude that abruptly stops discussion, and the second, a furious unwillingness to discover and to chip away at point of view, or an irritation at having to.

An acquaintance of mine, in charge of the children's section of a large bookstore, greeted me one day by eagerly demanding what I thought of *The Trumpet of the Swan.* Having looked forward to another book of the same quality as *Charlotte's Web,* I had been less than enchanted, and I suppose that an expression of mingled doubt and disappointment came over my face. For I had no sooner begun to answer by saying, "We-e-ll, I think—" than my acquaintance shot back in pure and obvious disgust, "Oh, you stinking critic!" Thoroughly shaken, I realized that I had, in the space of a second, been anticipating a companionable, possibly vigorous, thus inspiriting and even illuminating give-and-take about *The Trumpet of the Swan,* in which I might get to the bottom of my troubled reaction to it and might discover a point of view I couldn't have arrived at alone. Yet even though I now saw that such an exchange was out of the question, I asked, "I wonder—how do you judge a book?" To which the answer came at once: "Why, by my emotions, of course."

It was a revelation that this acquaintance, despite long years of work as a children's librarian before coming to the bookstore, knew so little of criticism that she thought she could react purely through her emotions—*and stop there.* That is the important point. She apparently believed that any but an emotional response leads one down a false path: the path of cold intellectuality; of niggling, carping, and fault-finding; of "harsh and captious judgment," which, as a matter of fact, is a second dictionary definition of criticism. She would have agreed with the book salesman who said to me, "I'm an anti-intellectual. I go to a movie and come home in a warm glow of pleasure and appreciation—then read some criticism of it only to find all sorts of reasons why it isn't a good picture, and sometimes I have to agree. I *hate* criticism!"

Both my acquaintance in the bookstore and the book salesman would disagree entirely, I take it, with the proposition that if there is—as Benjamin DeMott maintains—the necessity in art of a reflective intelligence, then in the criticism of that art there must also be at work a reflective intelligence. Otherwise the entire intention of a piece of art in all its facets is not being absorbed. Even Paul Klee, whose paintings seem wellings of pure imagination and the unconscious, spoke of "the thinking eye."

And apropos of pure emotion and stopping there (as opposed to the reflective intelligence), it is, of course, the cause of those hot arguments about not only politics and religion but the arts as well. It seems that our convictions about these matters, especially, have their roots so deep in our makeup, planted so deep in the soil of a certain inheritance, our upbringing, our emotional attitudes, our intellectual mind-set from childhood, that we ourselves can scarcely understand all that is contributing to a sometimes fierce defense of what we believe.

Certainly it would have been fascinating to know what, exactly, lay at the bottom of the outpouring of furious, sometimes despising mail that flew in to *The Horn Book* after the first part of "McLuhan, Youth and Literature"[2] appeared, in which I explained my reaction to Roald Dahl's *Charlie and the Chocolate Factory*. It seems almost as if, considering the previous spate of outraged mail that descended on the magazine after the appearance of Frances Clarke Sayers's "Walt Disney Accused,"[3] both Disney and *Charlie* had grown into some sort of icons in the public mind. And taste was felt to have been questioned.

Then, of course, in both cases, there was the confusion of popularity with quality, a confusion revealed to its fullest apropos of children's enthusiasm for the book. "Doesn't Mrs. Cameron know anything about children at *all?*" demanded one appalled correspondent. A teacher, obviously equating popularity with quality and believing wholeheartedly in children's critical insights, had his entire class write to me after he read them the Dahl section of my essay. And the letters were all so much alike—with EC being called, again and again, "an old Veruca Salt," which made me chuckle—that I could only suspect the children had been well primed before they wrote their letters, though I'm certain that most of them assuredly resented me for not loving *Charlie* as they did.

The point is that the teacher did not recognize that criticism meant for adults cannot possibly speak to elementary school children because they read their books with emotions to the fore. In fact, it could be that for ninety percent of them, emotion is almost the entire ingredient of their reaction. As for adults, a friend wrote me from Switzerland half agreeing with my attitude toward the book but reminding me of Dahl's record in World War II. Still another wrote of Dahl's care of his wife during a paralytic stroke. But what these points in Dahl's favor, concerned with his active life, have to do with the quality of *Charlie,* I will never know.*

Of course, the most regrettable part of the whole business of getting into a fury when someone disagrees with us about a greatly admired piece of art is that illumination can never happen: Further expansion of understanding, the opening up of our point of view, is stopped short, and there we sit in our pit of stubborn conviction as hedged about as we ever were. Furthermore, as most of us really know, it is infinitely more fun to have a good lively discussion in which we find out something because of what we ourselves or the other person has been led to say in the thick of the moment, rather than stomping off in a temper. And of course it is usually something other than simply the book itself that is involved—one's whole ego is entangled in the matter.

Joyce Carol Oates is inclined to profit from such give-and-takes. She says, concerning such hot discussions, that initial responses and immediate opposition have at least the advantage of provoking her to

---

*See Paul Heins's clearly thought-out editorial on the subject of critical cross-purposes, the confusion of the popularity and the literary qualities of a book, in *Crosscurrents of Criticism,* page 97.

further thought. Though a quarrel with others, in Yeats's famous definition, may lead to rhetoric, rhetoric itself may lead to something more valuable. Yes, as long as we give the other person time and are ourselves allowed time to get out an opinion. And as long as we *listen* and the other person does us the courtesy of *listening*.

After the essay "The Inmost Secret" appeared in *The Horn Book*, Nancy Bond was moved to respond in the magazine, differing from my point of view on her *A String in the Harp*. I replied, admitting the validity of her defense. Whereupon Paula Stakenas wrote in to say, "I have been teaching at the college level for several years now, and at times I just long for someone to challenge the statements I make so that we can enter into a dialogue and perhaps discover something new together."

On this subject, Richard Sewall says, in his *Emily Dickinson,* that he learns even as he disagrees, and that his desire is to "keep the dialectic alive." Beautiful words: "keep the dialectic alive," even though we may at first be divided by taste, which is completely subjective.*

All of which brings us to the point that we, as critics, must be firm in our reasoning, must have gotten to the bottom of our feelings about a book, to the bottom of that gut reaction that any reader will have on first launching into a new work. On this subject I once said, in answer to Roald Dahl's indignant reply to my "McLuhan, Youth and Literature," that "those who are concerned with children's reading

---

*Dr. Karen Hoyle, curator of the Kerlan Collection at the University of Minnesota, wrote me on the subject (after I had been there to give a talk): "I want to add a personal note about your comments on book reviewing in the reading room in November. I especially liked your encouragement of debate. Some people verbally ask for it, but then try to smash another's point of view." At one of the sessions during a summer symposium at the Center for the Study of Children's Literature at Simmons College, in Boston, I had given an exploration of Philippa Pearce's *The Way to Sattin Shore*. As I had voiced some doubts about various aspects of the novel and knew that the book had been generally highly admired, I said, at the end: "Now, *have at me!*" And *have at me* they did. And nothing could have been more rewarding. Why do we hold back from being disagreed with?

realize that they must think about a book as well as have feelings about it, even though criticism—indeed, *because* criticism—like poetry, begins with emotion."[4] As I have related in "The Inimitable Frances," she replied to that statement: "Criticism does *not* begin with emotion; it begins with thought."

I believe that there are two ways of looking at the matter. I can see that she meant that until one begins thinking about a work of art, one is not practicing criticism. Intellection is the starting point. But it seems to me that one can never entirely rid oneself of that first reaction unless, if this reaction is negative, it is a work that one could potentially respond to. I am not alone in my belief. The critic Frank Kermode speaks of "that emotional stimulus from which criticism begins."

And I meant by "even though criticism—indeed, *because* criticism—like poetry, begins with emotion," that one must be intensely aware that one's first response will be so largely subjective that one must search out what it arises from, since this response cannot fail, even if subliminally, to enter into one's critical judgment. One's whole bent, all one's predilections, all of one's intuitions cannot help but determine how one is going to start thinking about a work. This intense awareness of, and the sought-out reasons for, the impulsive reactions will contribute to a balancing of various considerations in the written response. On the other hand, C. S. Lewis said that he was so deeply opposed to the idea of love affairs between children that he simply refused to review or to write criticism of books dealing with such circumstances, undoubtedly because he knew that he could not overcome his antipathy and therefore could not attain enough distance to be fair.

A further point concerning criticism is brought out in that statement of Robert Lowell's quoted in the beginning, when he spoke of Jarrell's finding "words for what he had intuited." I believe that an unerring intuition more often than not enters into good criticism, the kind that comprehends without words the writer's vision. The Australian critic Susan Moore has written me:

I feel that although I have not written fiction before, I will be able to, and that my unconscious will do its work, as it does when I write criticism. Things flood onto the typed page, things I didn't know were there, once I feel I've grasped the *whole,* the essential Updike or Hazzard or Singer or Bellow. I have to have the whole, conceptually, first. Possessing it makes me feel so emotionally secure that I can let detail come pouring out, in the order it imposes, with the fullness it imposes.[5]

I think that those of us who write know exactly what she means by "things I didn't know were there," in writing both fiction and criticism. And a University of California study has found that most creative thinkers are able to move freely back and forth between intuitive thinking and logic, combining the best output of both sides of the brain.

I I

Something the critic must be aware of: the danger of being so devoted to some critical theory that one could be tricked, even unbeknownst to oneself, into forcing a work to answer to that theory and judging the work accordingly. The work itself should lead: the writer, not the critic, is the artist.* Of forcing, the French structuralist critic Gerard Genette has said in his study of Proust:

It appears to me foolish to search for "unity" at any price, and in this way to force the coherence of a work—which is, we know, one of the strongest temptations of criticism, one of the most banal (not to say vulgar) and also one of the easiest to satisfy, requiring only a bit of interpretive rhetoric.[6]

---

*Contrary to deconstructionist thinking. For one using that approach, the critic is all; the writer of the work is of no importance whatever.

These are harsh words, and only one's own thorough knowledge of a work could shed light as to whether or not the interpretation is justified, where the investigation is as dense and complex as Michael D. Reed's, for instance, in his essay "The Female Oedipal Complex in Maurice Sendak's *Outside over There*." But even with Sendak's book beside me so that I could follow along from page to page, and having some knowledge of the Oedipus complex, I had to think that perhaps my difficulties in understanding arose from not having read such a work as Otto Fenichel's *The Psychoanalytic Theory of Neurosis* to relieve my sense of claustrophobia inside Reed's symbol hunting. But I did not for a moment feel this sense of forcing the symbolism through Freud in reading Michael Egan's illuminating and satisfying "The Neverland as Id: Barrie, *Peter Pan,* and Freud."

In Jonathan Cott's *Pipers at the Gates of Dawn,* in his interview with Sendak—in which Sendak reveals the entire, enormously intricate growth, from seed to the realization of his vision, of *Outside over There*—I was struck by the following words:

> Sendak says that *OoT* was his attempt to make concrete his love of Mozart, and to do it "as authentically and honestly in regard to his time as I could conceive it, so that every color, every shape is like part of his portrait. The book is a portrait of Mozart, only it has this form—commonly called the picture book. This is the closest I could get to what he looked like to me. It's my imagining of Mozart's life. . . . When I was dreaming the book, what I was imagining was the most real thing I've ever felt."[7]

As I explore *Outside over There* once again, it is difficult for *me* to see the book as this. But I accept Sendak's vision; he has created a symbol of his loving response to Mozart that we can hold in our hands.

In quite a different mood, there is Betty Levin having fun while being serious about what she obviously feels is a preposterous application of Freudian theory in David Holbrook's interpretation of C. S.

Lewis's Narnia series. In her comments she in turn gives an ironical interpretation of Arthur Ransome's Swallows and Amazons series. Deadpan, she points out as one example that in *Pigeon Post* poor Titty Walker, discovering that she is a natural dowser, is horrified. For she is only a small girl, already in awe of tomboy Nancy Blackett, and her gender is emblazoned by her name. The dowsing rod having raised Titty to a new phallic awareness of her own powers, here is Dorothea reacting to Titty's remarkable transformation:

> I'm making you a boy, and you do that business with the stick all by yourself and you've got a spade with you and you start digging. It's at night and the moon rises through the clouds, and all of a sudden you've dug deep enough and the water comes spouting up into the moonlight.

Levin gravely observes that innumerable boys and girls have been subjected to this disturbing sexual symbolism, while parents and librarians, "complacent and hearty," have approved such material for adolescents.

Assuredly Beatrix Potter regarded some of Graham Greene's remarks about her works as both forced and absurd. In a most delightful essay, in which he treated her oeuvre as seriously and with as much detailed observation as he would that of the writings of some admired novelist for adults, he divided her books into periods.

> Looking backward over the thirty years of Miss Potter's literary career, we see that the creation of Mr. Puddle-Duck* marked the beginning of a new period. At some time between 1907 and 1909 Miss Potter must have passed through an emotional ordeal which changed the character of her genius. It would be impertinent to inquire into the nature of the ordeal. Her case is curiously similar to that of Henry James. Something happened

---

*But he meant Miss (or Ms.) Puddle-Duck, the first name being Jemima.

which shook their faith in appearances. . . . With the publication
of *Mr. Tod* in 1912, Miss Potter's pessimism reached its climax.[8]

Miss Potter was much annoyed and no doubt looked on all this analyzing of her little books, together with suppositions about her private
life, as pretentious. Greene added a note to his study of her oeuvre:

> On the publication of this essay I received a somewhat acid letter
> from Miss Potter correcting certain details. *Little Pig Robinson,*
> although the last published of her books, was in fact the first
> written. She denied that there had been any emotional disturbance
> at the time she was writing *Mr. Tod;* she was suffering however
> from the after-effects of 'flu. In conclusion she deprecated sharply
> "the Freudian school" of criticism.[9]

I found myself in accord, on the whole, with Susan Sontag's essay
"Against Interpretation." And I remembered Mary McCarthy's piece,
"Settling the Colonel's Hash," an essay she wrote after being hounded
by students and instructors who insisted on finding all sorts of symbolism in her story "Artists in Uniform" and asked her to give an
interpretation. She replied that the story happened to be completely
true, that there were no literary symbols in it, and that "to disentangle
a moral philosophy from a work that evidently contains one is far less
damaging to the author's purpose and the integrity of his art than to
violate his imagery with symbol-hunting, as though reading a novel
were a sort of paper chase."[10]

There is, to be sure, Russell Hoban's rubbish dump, which he himself has called a symbol of the world in microcosm. But E. B. White,
for instance, found himself constantly protesting against symbolisms
the public found in his work: "In the course of my long literary life
I've learned that some readers just can't believe that a writer can ever
be objective: they read something deep or symbolic or sinister or
political into every work."[11] That was a note to Dorothy Lobrano
Guth, the editor of his letters. To John Detmold he wrote: "As for

your noting an allegory, there is none. *Charlotte's Web* is a tale of the animals in my barn, not of the people in my life. When you read it, just relax. Any attempt to find allegorical meanings is bound to end disastrously, for no meanings are in there. I ought to know."[12] Unforgettably, he adds further on in his letters, in one to Gene Deitch: "It is a straight report from the barn cellar, which I dearly love, having spent so many fine hours there, winter and summer, spring and fall, good times and bad times, with the garrulous geese, the passage of swallows, the nearness of rats, and the sameness of sheep."[13] That sentence is typical White, in its rhythm, its spirit, and its evocations.

Surely a grim and purposeful symbol hunting on the part of the reader can do great injustice to a novel, reducing it to nothing but a puzzle to be solved in a certain way, when there is so much else to be considered and enjoyed.

However, with this point still in mind, when it first came out, I read *Aspects of Alice*—a collection of various interpretations of *Alice in Wonderland* and *Through the Looking-Glass* by Freudians, Jungians, philosophers, writers, and others—and was intrigued. I read, too, some of the works of Jung and wrote an essay on my understanding of Ursula Le Guin's *A Wizard of Earthsea,* in which I saw her brilliant and moving use of Jung's idea of the Shadow, although she hadn't read Jung at the time she wrote the book. I had to give a psychological understanding if I was to do justice to the novel, and I could not feel I was forcing a response in doing so, despite my dislike of this kind of interpretation before I had read Jung.[14]

I had gotten bored with Freudian critics finding phallic significances in every novel they read and had reminded myself, on first reading Mayne's *A Game of Dark,* that in legend a dragon was often called the worm and did not see it at all as having a particularly Freudian significance as one of my friends insisted it had. But on rereading, I saw very clearly the relationship between the Worm—if it did indeed have a phallic and therefore masculine significance—and Donald's father. The Worm is described as pale and legless and emitting a stench, just as Donald's father is "white against a white pillow" in his terminal illness, unable to walk and therefore legless, and emitting the odor of the sickroom and approaching death. Given the choice of which world he shall continue to live in, Donald chooses reality rather than the world of his unconscious, where the Worm had dwelt. Having killed it, he is enabled to come back to himself from the hatred and guilt he had harbored, associated with both his father and the Worm, which had been lying in wait to defeat him utterly.

Le Guin's essay "Dreams Must Explain Themselves" admits to symbolism in *The Tombs of Atuan*. The subject is sex, she says, and rebirth.[15] Therefore, my understanding of the novel is as follows: The child Arha, who becomes the Eaten One at the age of five, is reborn at the moment of death of the former high priestess. Brought up with such sternness and rigidity that she is spiritually, aesthetically, and morally numb, she finds her greatest pleasure in memorizing her way through the complete darkness and silence of the Tombs. And Ged, the Wizard of Earthsea, with his wizard's staff (the phallus), strikes the Red Rock Door (the hymen), an entry to the Tombs, and enters the Tombs (the womb) to bring Arha's being, her numb senses, to warmth and self-awareness, to full sensitivity, so that she is willing to be led by him—both progenitor and midwife—out of an unfulfilled existence into the daylight of fully realized life. At an early stage of their relationship, the exquisite dress Ged conjures around her in the depths of the Tombs is a baptismal gown, symbolically speaking, blotting out her stiff, harsh black one. For it shows Arha her true self, her feminine self ("it glittered softly, like rain in April," and April is the month of rebirth, just as rain is the catalyst making it possible), which she had not been conscious of before. This episode is a dramatic step on her way to rebirth into seeing and feeling life, a rebirth in reality and not within the superstitions of her people. Soon after, Ged calls her by her true name, Tenar, for the first time.

A colleague of mine, one of the speakers at a conference, read this paragraph to the conferees as an example of exaggerated and amusing psychological interpretation, and said that he was quite sure Le Guin must have been being mischievous. I explained to him afterward that if the interpretation was absurd, he mustn't blame Le Guin, for it was mine, and that I very much regretted not having made the fact clear when a shorter version of this essay was published in *The Horn Book*.[16] I had not included the words "Therefore my 'seeing' of the novel is as follows," and his mistake in attribution was quite understandable. I then sent the essay to Le Guin and she wrote back: "Thank you!" I do not think she would have been mischievous under these circumstances, nor have I ever known her to be mischievous when the matter was serious.

Peter Neumeyer, of San Diego State University, not normally a Freudian reader of texts, has written me of his Freudian understanding of Virginia Hamilton's *M.C. Higgins the Great*. He sees the now-famous pole as a symbolic artifact central to the oedipal rivalry going on between M. C. and his father, Jones, in their silent vying for the admiration and approval of the mother, Banina. It is an object to which M. C. turns at every crisis, something he's mastering ever more strongly in his climbing of it as his father grows more impotent and as M. C. begins to supplant him in the household in one way after another. Jones's inability now to climb the pole is revealing of Jones as descendant and M. C. as ascendant in this study of generational conflict, of mingled love and hate between father and son, whose confrontations provide much of the impetus of the story.

Assuredly critics, using their Freudian and Jungian knowledge, can have no idea if they may be imputing all sorts of purposes and meanings the author never intended, interpreting in a way that was never a part of the author's *conscious* awareness. But this is not a restriction. However, it *is* fascinating to read Le Guin's awareness of her own purposes, and Maurice Sendak's explanation of what went into *Outside over There* on the one hand, and also to read letters, journals, autobiographies, or autobiographical fictions that shed astonishing light on what the authors were not aware of. This is certainly so in the case of *Peter Pan*, into which Barrie introduced so much of himself without ever being aware of what he was revealing—something we understand in reading

Andrew Birkin's *J. M. Barrie and the Lost Boys* and Michael Egan's essay "The Neverland as Id: Barrie, *Peter Pan* and Freud."

When *Watership Down* was called a political novel, Richard Adams replied that it is simply "a little story about rabbits which I wrote for my children."[17] One has to take with a very large grain of salt that Adams really believed he had written *only* "a little story about rabbits." When asked if a novelist isn't bound to be blind to some of the statements his books have made, he said:

> Oh, yes, indeed. A novel is like a dream, do you see, and once the unconscious is let loose . . . The dreamer is very often the very last person who can see any sense in a dream. And the novelist, I suppose, is the last person who can see the implications of his novel.[18]

Though Adams has more than once said that he wrote *Watership* for his children, he undoubtedly wrote it for them in the same sense that Carroll wrote *Alice* for Lorena, Edith, and Alice Liddell, telling the children what must have been the basic story on car rides just as Carroll must have told the little girls only the basic story of *Alice* on their boat rides ("the original tale was little more than half the final length"[19]) and attaining the final version with added characters, poems, allusions, evocations, and underlying meanings.

I I I

With regard to the critic's style and words: In his introductory comments to *Science Fiction Studies* #7, a collection of critical essays on the work of Le Guin, Darko Suvin compares her writing to that of Philip K. Dick and says that "while Dick is a 'romantic' writer, whose energy lashes out in a profusion of incandescent and interfused narrative protuberances, Le Guin is a 'classical' writer, whose energy is as fierce but strictly controlled within a taut and spare architectural system of narrative cells."[20] What *is* a narrative cell, anyway? None of this gets me anywhere at all in a deeper understanding of the real essences of Dick and Le Guin.

Patricia C. Willis, in her introduction to *The Complete Prose of Marianne Moore,* says of Moore's style that "the compression dictated by the single-paragraph format resulted in the tour de force precise diction and the inventive splicing of quotations that make these reviews extraordinary reading."[21] The following sentences occur not in the "single-paragraph format" but in the course of a long piece of Moore's on poetry. And we find in Moore's comments on *Alice* some of that "tour de force precise diction," evoking a sense of that bizarre—certainly that most unique—mode of expression that is distinctly Moore-ish and surprising, not to say inimitable, in her poetry:

> Seeming to some in childhood incomprehensibly epic in character, Lewis Carroll is to mature taste, appropriate *espièglerie.* Overcoming all sense of the somnambulistic predetermined formlessness of a conscious trance, certain qualities are beyond cavil. There are the personable, self-contained, human completeness of the rabbit, and the attentive uncontradictoriness of Alice. A precision of unlogic in Lewis Carroll, is logic's best apologist— a hypothetically accurate illogical law of cause and effect. And the connection between the kitten as precipitating the dream and the fact that all the poems are about fish, is most precise.[22]

One can predict that this is *not* the kind of prose that those who care about clear and immediate comprehension will accept without a distinct reaction. On the one hand there may be those who are intrigued by, and smile over, it, as they do over Moore's poetry; on the other, there may be those who will be sharply irritated and even those who will throw the book down, muttering, "Why can't the woman come right out and say what she means?" (But of course she *is* saying what she means!)

If one could in any sense call Moore's mode of expression a compressed or tour de force style, the following—analyzing telephone conversations—would be an extreme and wearisome example of the pedagogic:

> As social phenomena, conversations are structured episodes of interaction: the mutually interdependent production, distribution, and consumption of shared symbols and their meanings, along with the resultant reciprocal influence of interactants or conversants upon one another; taking each other into account as the lines of communicative action shape, and are shaped, by the partners and the normative environment in which they and their conduct are located. It is in such transactions that organisms become persons, and persons become social actors: putting forth selves to be ratified and confirmed or disconfirmed and denied by their audience of others while at the same time receiving or rejecting imputed identities assigned to them by these responding monitors.[23]

Aside from the wordiness, I could argue about the generalization that conversations are "structured episodes" of any kind when they're so often unstructured to a delectable degree, filled with sideslips, double takes, and complete misunderstandings so that answers bear no relation whatever to questions. Furthermore, I must say that I resent the notion that I'm nothing but an organism until I speak aloud to someone. Like all of us, I very often carry on arguments and explorations within my own mind. Is this the activity only of a non-person organism?

The following passage is very typical of the current style in literary criticism:

> In creating a distinctive choric voice, *Between the Acts* both returns to the ancient choral band and creates a new comic mode. The

new collective voice emerges through a subtle manipulation and transformation of three comic modes—a satiric, amiable, and liminal. Woolf inhibits her satiric impulse by modifying the satire with elements of amiable comedy and expands the amiable comedy with elements of liminality to create a subversive and revisionary mode, the art of the whole community.

What is melancholy is to hear echoings of these last two styles in the criticism of children's literature. Unlike the sound of Marianne Moore, they are not the voices of particular individuals but impersonal ones issuing formal statements from inside the Institution, from within the Discipline. Where, in so much modern academic criticism, are there images and colorful, even witty turns of phrase, as in Virginia Woolf's "Modern Fiction" (speaking of Woolf), in which she is responding to Hardy's novels in her own unmistakable accents, or as in the rapier wit of a Randall Jarrell? Carolyn Heilbrun, in *Writing a Woman's Life*, illustrates my point to perfection. She is quoting from Teresa de Lauretis, who is speaking of consciousness-raising, recommending the habitual "political, theoretical, self-analyzing practice by which the relations of the subject in social reality can be rearticulated from the historical experience of women." "To put it simply," adds Heilbrun, "we must begin to tell the truth, in groups, to one another."[24]

Another touch: Joan Murray and Robert Fulford comment on Jane Jacobs's seminal *The Death and Life of Great American Cities*, a book with no academic reputation behind it and no basis in theory, that David R. Hill criticized it for Jacobs's failure to meet the criterion of "empirical verifiability" with conclusions "operationalized for quantitative research." But the wretched part is that, even so, he had to acknowledge "that she had forced a rethinking of orthodox ideas and changed the assumptions behind city planning."[25] A final touch: Did you know that the practice of putting a colon in the title of a book is known, in some academic circles, as "titular colonicity"?

George Steiner (Extraordinary Fellow of Churchill College, Cambridge, and Professor of English and Comparative Literature at the University of Geneva) gets quite fierce on the subject of style in his latest work, *Real Presences*. He refers to the

> often repulsive jargon, to the contrived obscurantism and specious pretensions to technicality which make the bulk of post-structuralist and deconstructive theory and practice, particularly among its academic epigones, unreadable. This abuse of philosophic-literary discourse, this brutalization of style, *are* symptomatic. They, also, tell of hatreds and bewilderments sprung of absence (the *Logos* being in *absentia*). But it is not the symptoms which are of the first importance. What I want to do is to clarify, with full awareness of the multiplicity of currents involved—the Marxist, the Freudian, the Heideggerian, the absurdist—the theological and metaphysical repudiations which lie at the heart of the entire deconstructive enterprise.[26]

Not that I'm asking, with reference to Virginia Woolf and Randall Jarrell as critics, that we continually echo the past. But in connection with those two quotations before George Steiner's, I was amused to read a recent confession from Peter Dickinson, prolific writer of novels for both youth and adults and the style of whose mysteries for adults is usually termed "elegant." He says:

> Now I read very little fiction at all. Bad books make me angry and good ones tend to block my own work. I read, much slower than I used to, books on almost any scholarly subject in which I might be interested. My only need is that they be written in living English.[27]

I can't help wondering if, in part, it could possibly be the mode of expression of the New Theorists, particularly the deconstructionists, that is to blame for the nonliving English that Dickinson abhors. For somewhere along the way students of literary criticism are going to run into the works of the big names. And the style of most New Theorists tends to be dense, wordy, with meanings so layered as to become ever more obscure. The effect is intensified by their habit of leading into byways off the main path before curving—by tedious, often untranslatable, always-complex thought processes—back again to what one had thought (if one can be even faintly certain) to be the central theme.

George Steiner, on the contrary, while he demands one's concentrated attention in *Real Presences,* is nevertheless *understandable,* no matter how difficult the subject.

Roland Barthes, the celebrated master of that branch of New Theory called structuralism, has his own longueurs. But he is someone in whose work Nadine Gordimer, the South African author of many a novel passionate in the cause of the blacks in her country, finds great satisfaction. Concerning Barthes, she confesses that for her "his brilliance, with its element of divine playfulness, made and makes enthralling reading—for those of us who share at least sufficient of his cultural background to gain aesthetic pleasure and revelation from his cited word 'signifiers.' "[28]

However, speaking of longueurs, the student of children's literature criticism, having decided to venture into a study of structuralism, could get a puzzled start if he or she happened to read the structuralist exploration of Jules Verne's *The Mysterious Island* as carried out by Roland Barthes. His essay is entitled (almost ironically, from the reader's point of view, as one presses one's way through certain definitely Barthean patches) "Where to Begin." He warns that the student must be sufficiently well-read not to be astonished by side trips from the central path of exploration, misleadingly collected, by his own admission, under the label *structuralism.* He then continues through various other warnings to the final fact that one must accept that it isn't a matter of acquiring an explanation of the novel, what you would call a positive result, its "truth" or "determination," but something quite other. One must enter through the "play" of the signifier. One must accomplish, through one's search, its *plural*.*

One then comes to the word "gestual," but almost immediately one understands that this must be a typo for "gestural," for he goes on to state that the *first gesture* is what must be made in the involvement with the text. But the reader is at first puzzled because Barthes is enormously given (as are most New Theorists) to the use of the unusual or little-known or little-used word. Also he has misnamed Cyrus Harding in the novel as Cyrus Smith, so that here, too, one is puzzled and hunts through the novel thinking that one has perhaps slipped up on a character. And what *luck* that Harding is an engineer, for, as you will recall, the six colonists who have landed on the island will die if they are not rescued or shown how to rescue themselves.

At one point Barthes works his way through a paragraph concerning the transformations the colonists must undertake with completely unpromising objects that must be turned into useful ones in order to exist on the island. It is a paragraph scattered with parenthetical phrases and subjunctive clauses, and it is composed, by far more than half, of a sentence so long that one must go back and puzzle one's way through again. One *could* say that the transformation process being examined in this passage, which turns objects from their original shapes and essences into much-needed objects of practical use, must be not only scientifically possible but, in order to increase the reader's suspense, these objects must also be distant from one another in their nameable actualities. Examples: seals (the marine mammals) from forge bellows and candles, seaweed from nitroglycerin, and balloon canvases from windmill blades.

But one who values the individual voice must admit at once that this very plainly and uninterestingly worded synopsis of mine, con-

---

*Pluralism: "A theory or system of thought which recognizes more than one ultimate principle. The theory that the knowable world is made up of a plural of interacting things." *Oxford English Dictionary*.

siderably shorter than the original passage, lacks entirely Barthes's peculiar tone, his learned impressiveness characterized by numerous parenthetical interruptions, and the use of such words as *bricolage* and *Dasein*. However, one can't even be certain that a search for their meaning has yielded Barthes's precise and intended one. *Bricolage:* a serendipity resulting from pottering around? In my French dictionary, the word *bricole* is given, meaning a collar or strap or sidestroke, but *par bricole* means "indirectly." And *Dasein:* an object's determinant being, its essential being?

Throughout his *New Critical Essays,* in which "Where to Begin" appears, Barthes constantly uses such words as *onomastic, diachrony, heteroclite, propadeutics, aleatory, coenesthesia, anacoluthea, syntagmatic, ascesis, ideolect,* and *hypersemanticity,* as well as *Dasein, semic, diegesis,* and *precellence* (the last four not to be found in the 1988 *Random House Unabridged*).

Considering that most New Theorists seem to require esoteric words, it is delightful to read V. S. Pritchett in his *The Myth Makers* on Victor Brombert's criticism of Flaubert. Of Brombert's style, he says:

> The effect is pretentious and may, one hopes, be simply the result of thinking in French and writing in English; but it does match the present academic habit of turning literary criticism into technology. One really cannot write of Flaubert's "dilection for monstrous forms" or of "vertiginous proliferation of forms and gestures"; "dizzying dilations"; or "volitation"; "lupenar" when all one means is "pertaining to a brothel." Philosophers, psychologists and scientists may, I understand, write of "fragmentations" that suggest "a somnabulist and oneiric state." But who uses the pretentious "obnuvilate" when they mean "dim" or "darkened by a cloud"? Imaginative writers know better than to put on this kind of learned dog. . . . Literary criticism does not add to its status by opening an intellectual hardware store.[29]

For his structuralist colleagues Roland Barthes was one of the most important, if difficult, of the modern critics and theorists, so that they would scornfully brush aside this intrusion of Pritchett's comment as having anything at all to do with Barthes's own compulsions, his style being an expression of his essence. Barthes may not be pretentious in the style of Brombert. Yet surely it would be wearying, even at length defeating, for the student who seriously wants to *begin,* to be constantly met with rarely used words, some of whose definitions elude research.

I V

Unlike the critic who is simply that, the writer-critic can be in the position of trying to see through to the intentions and underlying meanings of fellow writers and of being, meanwhile, faced with a request to respond to a critical study of his or her own work. I have found myself looking back on, for instance, *Beyond Silence* as both creator and objective critic. I disagreed with my critic in some instances, agreed in others. And I saw for the first time certain parallels between this time fantasy of mine and others of the same genre, some parallels pointed out to me in criticism and others revealed to me because of the new point of view I was being forced to take. I was able to see into my own work in ways that hadn't occurred to me before, finding myself in an entirely different relationship to it than I had previously.

Robert Scholes says, of writers speaking of their own work, that interpretation must justify itself by bringing something external to the work, if only the subjectivity of the critic, which is different from that of the artist. Which is why he believes interpretations of their own work by artists are rarely attempted and seldom valuable. This may be so, but at least I could see that the experience I had had in critical explorations of fictions in the same genre as mine helped me to view my own book with sudden objectivity in relation to other fantasies, *which then led me on* to further insights concerning time fantasies in general.

An editor once told me that she didn't believe that writers should be critics. While writer-critics must maintain cool heads when it comes to taking criticism themselves if they differ vigorously with others, they must also be capable of full appreciation of the work of fellow writers, as well as being capable of clear analysis. I am speaking here of criticism in the large sense, and appreciation is the better part of criticism. Critics who do nothing but criticize in the narrow sense are boring and unrewarding representatives of their profession.

There is as well the possibility of outright blindness to a peculiar individuality that contrasts sharply with the writer-critic's own. Being a writer, working within a certain mode, one could be sunk too deep within a private point of view to attain insight and aesthetic distance and to consider an entirely different outlook and method sensitively. For instance, I myself am no devotee of science fiction and was not eager to read Peter Dickinson's *Eva* (for young people, but I would say for anyone). But because of its brilliance, its feeling, its truth to the writer's vision, I am struck all over again, having read it twice, by the fact that everything depends on how a work, representative of any genre, is conceived and carried out. One must judge the book, not the genre.

The ideal writer-critic of children's books should be able to take under the critical umbrella novels as different from each other in structure and conception and tone (and perhaps as different from one's own in style and import) as Virginia Hamilton's *M. C. Higgins the Great* and Beverly Cleary's *Ramona and Her Father,* Robert Cormier's *I Am the Cheese* and Mary Norton's *The Borrowers,* Alice Childress's *A Hero Ain't Nothin' But a Sandwich* and Jill Paton Walsh's *Unleaving,* Robert Westall's *The Machine Gunners* and Jane Gardam's *The Hollow Land,* and to appreciate the unique kinds of artistry in each. What is touching is to learn from Virginia Woolf's diary how keenly she felt about the reviews and criticisms of her books. Surely she must have been reflecting her own attitude in reviewing when she wrote that no creative writer can swallow another contemporary. The reception of living work is too coarse and partial, she added, if you're doing the same thing yourself. "When Desmond praises 'East Coker,' and I am jealous, I walk over the marsh saying 'I am I.' I must follow that furrow, not copy another. That is the only justification for my writing and living."[30]

V

But it is inevitable, aside from Virginia Woolf's questionable generalization that no creative writer is able to swallow a contemporary, that each of us will have trouble with certain conceptions per se, and that because of our very natures there will be degrees in our ability to see various works with a sympathetic eye. A friend of mine, usually an excellent critic, can't appreciate Le Guin's *A Wizard of Earthsea* and so hasn't tried the remaining three of the sequence because, as he puts it, he can't abide "the clank of chains sort of thing." By which he means, I imagine, heroic or high fantasy and not fantasy in general, for he greatly admires Hoban's *The Mouse and His Child* as well as Randall Jarrell's *The Animal Family*. And you will recall my saying earlier that, such was his prejudice, C. S. Lewis knew that he could not possibly review fairly a novel whose subject was a love affair between children.

In my own case, my difficulty is with certain kinds of fantasy, of which William Mayne's *Antar and the Eagles* is a prime example. In it eagles teach a boy of six to fly with wings he has made, and to speak "eagle." Given these two facts alone, we are at once on treacherous territory because we are dealing with magic and reality mingled in a most peculiar way.*

---

*"But what about your own two boys in *Wonderful Flight?*" asks a friend. *They* made a spaceship, which they then took to Tyco M. Bass, the fantastical little character in this space fantasy. But he did not teach them to fly it. He himself had made his own peculiar spaceship fuel, atomic tritetramethylbenzacarbonethylene, which he put into the ship, in a particular receptacle he had ready for it, and hitched up the

My objection here is related to the difficulty—having to do with the machine itself—I experience with H. G. Wells's *The Time Machine,* an objection I explained in *The Green and Burning Tree,* in which I compared Walter de la Mare's poem "Jim Jay" with the machine. Jim, a human, never heeds that the wind of his particular, personal time is spent and so slips farther and farther into the past, until at last, "much too frightened to help himself," he becomes a speck "slip-slipping by," and come the morrow, the neighbors say, "He'll be past crying for; / Poor Jim Jay."

Protesting E. M. Forster's idea that "fantasy asks us to pay something extra,"[31] I was moved to say: "It never occurs to me to even reach for my pocket. I *see* poor Jim Jay, I see his flapping handkerchee, and that's Yesterday he's dwindling into as sure as I'm holding *Peacock Pie*" (de la Mare's collected poems for children). However, as for the time machine: "I could not believe, and I cannot now believe, that a shape of physical matter, with a temporal man astride its temporal back pushing and pulling levers, even though the whole be constructed of such exotic materials as ebony and quartz and crystal, can be the means of exploring a concept. It is the combination of the temporal and conceptual at which I boggle."[32]

And it is the awkward, illogical way in which fantasy and reality are intermingled at which I boggle in *Antar,* the story of a boy kidnapped by eagles so that he can, as a human, steal back from the king's palace the egg that will hatch into the eagles' future king when their present wounded one dies.

Mayne himself says that eagles do not think as humans do, yet gradually one of them, Garak, teaches Antar to speak their language. And they call him Gadar, which means *goose* in their tongue, because Antar seems to them stupid and incapable in so many ways. But this

---

fuel lines. He then introduced into the ship his absurd oxygen urn, which went "Pheep, pheep!" all the way to Basidium and back. In other words, as Ursula Le Guin caught on, I was having a bit of gentle fun with the whole idea of two small boys building something that could actually be used for such an adventure as our space effort labors over, year after year, and on which we spend billions.

is a wholly human conception—to connect the propensities of an animal or bird with the propensities of a human, and to call the human by the animal's or bird's name, as *donkey* for someone stubborn, *pig* for someone greedy, or *goose* for someone dull or foolish.

And Garak says, as though trying to be simple for Antar's sake, as we would speak to a foreigner, "Gadar fly. Keek fly," and yet speaks a page or two later in the same scene of how "humans moult in the night and grow new plumage" when Antar is taking off his boots. He goes on: "Now I have seen it. You have another hand on each leg. Have they been there all the time?" How does the eagle know that we call losing feathers moulting, and, above all, that this process would apply to Antar taking off his boots? And if Garak can use the words *moult* and *hand* and *leg*, why doesn't he know the word for feet? And how, not thinking as humans do, can he speak of "a great weight lost" when he looks at the boots and apparently realizes that their removal is going to make flying easier for Antar because the boy will be lighter? Later Garak says "Eggs are not hatched in a day," which is a variation on an old folk saying among humans. Any bird knows instinctively that it must brood its chicks for many days and nights, but here Garak is applying the instinctive knowledge to Antar's impatience. And he speaks of gliding and of a pinnacle and of lead, copper, gold, and silver and that these must be dug out of the earth.

In a fairy tale there would be no need to teach Antar the language of eagles, or to find a way around certain words, such as *feet,* because we are in a magical world in which there is traditionally instant communication between humans, animals, and birds. The circumstances would not arise in which it would seem absurd that the eagle knows the names for certain things but not for others in the same class, and the names of certain activities or states, such as moulting, gathering speed, or being wounded, but not the word for mining. Again, while speaking of guns, bows, and spears, and of a roof, fire, and the egg involved in the story, Garak cannot speak of the box or cupboard where the egg is hidden, saying of this place that an eagle could only call it a nest. (One finds, incidentally, a different kind of illogic in the naming of things time and again in Richard Adams's *Watership Down,* in which there are rabbit names for certain objects but not for others, and the same sense of incongruity and awkwardness in White's *Trumpet of the Swan,* but for different reasons.)

As for the making of wings, which Antar must do, he sticks feathers through the cloth of his coat and the eagles show him how the feathers lie and overlap one another. They pierce the holes and comb the plumes straight, but Antar at the age of six must find thorns and splinters to lock the shafts of the feathers into the coat. He then sews the feathers in place "with the thread from his shirt, using a piece of bone to make a hole, threading through and pulling tight." Finally he makes a tail (with no details given at this point), but there is no way to make it "stretch and turn like that of an eagle." However, even with these clumsy makeshifts the eagles somehow teach Antar to fly. But why the makeshifts?

If this were pure fantasy, we would not *have* to ask why Garak knows certain words, used with certain meanings, sometimes quite abstract, but not others of the same class, and why Antar must sew himself wings and a tail in order that the eagles can teach him to fly. If this were pure fantasy with no awkward intermingling of realism, we would not wonder that a boy of six could make himself wings and a tail that would enable him to be taught. There is no such bumbling about in fairy tales or in *Peter Pan* because we are (given the unalloyed tone of the tales, where we are entirely in the world of magic) taking it for granted that Peter Pan can take the children by the hands and fly off with them. No making of wings is needed.

As this is clearly meant to be a fantasy, why do the eagles not simply speak to Antar, as pots and pans and animals and trees do to humans in the handed-down fairy tales and in the created tales of Hans Christian Andersen? But why, you might ask in return, *must* one write fantasy of this kind, the story of Antar, in the tradition of the fairy tales? Because we feel, in this case and others like it, that the necessity for mechanical process is denying fantasy, is confusing it.

V I

To continue the writer-critic situation, in an exchange between Jill Paton Walsh and John Rowe Townsend in which they were discussing writers as critics, Townsend spoke of letters sent to him (as editor of a children's book page) complaining of so many reviews being done by writers and suggesting that, because they were writers, they couldn't be trusted to be impartial.

Were they at that time suspected of being too enthusiastic out of a kind of defensiveness in the face of the general denigration and ignorance of children's literature?* I, for one, believe that those writers who feel no defensiveness whatever about being writers for children and youth but who are devoted to the genre and who are happy to be writing within it, or who are writing for their own pleasure the kinds of books that children happen to enjoy, make the best writer-critics in the field. But I think that very often, as reviewers, we *are* enthusiastic in a most unself-conscious, sometimes overly generous way, when later that initial outburst will simmer down to greater objectivity. In fact, this quality of outsize and sometimes unjustified overenthusiasm marks the difference, I believe, between the judgments of the reviewer and the critic. The critic can take time for longer, more balanced, and cooler reflections, and usually writes some years after the work under consideration has been published.

What seems dangerous are the glowing adjectives and nouns, as always, in any kind of writing. A writer-reviewer, in her review of Jane Gardam's funny and moving *A Long Way from Verona,* spoke of Gardam as "a genius" and the novel itself as "a towering phenomenon." Much as I admire Jane Gardam and her work and watch with pleasurable anticipation for the appearance of each new novel, I cannot see her as a genius or *A Long Way from Verona* as a towering phenom-

---

*As of 1992, the time of my rewriting this essay, the situation seems greatly improved.

enon. On more than one occasion in *The Art of Maurice Sendak,* Selma
Lanes calls Maurice Sendak a genius, and I am sure that many would
agree with her. I would ask those who do if they can think of him
up there with Picasso, van Gogh, Cézanne, Rembrandt, or Michel-
angelo. I cannot, because I hold the word *genius* in the most special
regard.

In her introduction to *New Women and New Fiction: Short Stories Since
the Sixties,* Susan Cahill begins by saying, "Genius tends to take your
breath away. Prepare, reader, for breathlessness." And she speaks of
the "talent" of twenty-one writers, of this talent's "rock-like strength,
that astounds."[33] But to my mind the word *genius* is not interchange-
able with talent.

And Buckminster Fuller, himself a brilliant man, goes so far as to
say: "Every child is born a genius, but is swiftly degeniused by unwitting humans and/or physically unfavorable environmental fac-
tors."[34] Which seems to me an extraordinary remark.

But perhaps it is—surely it must be—all according to our definition
of the word. Justin Kaplan thought that the person of genius "works
in a dazzling darkness of his own which normal modes of explanation
hardly penetrate, and to describe Mark Twain as he neared the age of
forty-eight, one has to evoke the same rich symbols that occupied his
imagination."[35] Clive Bell, speaking of Virginia Woolf, said:

I can imagine myself as bright as Roger [Fry]; I cannot imagine
myself in the least like Virginia or Picasso. With Roger's understanding and mental processes mine were of a kind: I thought
and reasoned and invented and arrived at conclusions as he did,
only I thought and reasoned and invented less well. But Virginia
and Picasso belonged to another order of beings; they were of
a species distinct from the common; their mental processes
were different from ours; they arrived at conclusions by ways
to us unknown. . . . The point is that half an hour's conversation with Virginia sufficed to make one realise that she had
genius.[36]

Lucy Boston agrees with Clive Bell that the true geniuses belong "to another order of beings," imaginatively and intellectually, arriving "at conclusions by ways to us unknown." She writes,

> I have rarely met what I now use the word genius to stand for —something different from high talent, brilliance, originality, megalopersonality or inspired non-conformity. All these can be eccentric, even lop-sided, but genius is concentric, unforced and of sublime clarity. I would like to think that life moves towards the production of such human beings, but I believe the old tree throws off its miracles at random throughout the ages.[37]

I could not put my own belief as to the quality of genius any more succinctly or clearly. It is all very well for a friend to write me that my belief is far too narrow and excluding, and that there are degrees of genius. But as far as I am concerned, either one is a genius, or one is not. There is no use being loose and including, for in that way the word loses all significant meaning.

Finally, Donald R. Howard in the preface to his huge, fascinating life of Chaucer, says: "For Chaucer's mind we have the stunning evidence of what it produced—on which we see the mark of genius. But genius is the most elusive of qualities—it is the part of a subject's mind we can least hope to grasp or understand. So we are back again with his works."[38]

Perhaps there are dozens of geniuses around, in the same state as Cézanne in his early days of struggle, of whom Zola said, "Paul may have the genius of a great painter, but he will never have the genius to become one." Of course we know that he *did* have the genius to become one, "but he was maddened by his incompetence for, having more temperament than technique, he could not give expression to his vision."*

---

*Said Cézanne: "Patience is the mother of genius," reporting the advice of his friend Honoré Gibert when Cézanne had grown depressed and discouraged. Cézanne was, on the instant, anything but a patient man but over the years, infinitely so.

If we say of Gardam that she is a genius, what word have we left for Shakespeare or Tolstoy or Chaucer? And how can we say that *War and Peace* and *Hamlet* and *The Canterbury Tales* and *A Long Way from Verona* are, all *four,* towering phenomena? We can't! Such statements are treacherous in the extreme and lie in wait to embarrass us when we come on them later in an old review or piece of criticism.

VII

Someone has said that the critic of children's books should learn to be childlike. Certainly one must have the ability to identify with childhood, not only to remember vividly what it was like to be a child but to actually be able to relive certain moments and recognize intimately the true atmosphere of the child's world as opposed to the contrived and the feigned. I have said that in my own novel writing I am always very much aware that myriad impressions of childhood are still there in the depths.

I was never so struck by the truth of this as when I was writing about Julia Redfern at the age of six, when she was trying to save a mouse from the wrath of her aunt Alex, who had set one of the uncles after it with a broom with the firm intent of squashing it. From complete identification with Julia I came to with a jolt when I happened to go into the kitchen, saw a mouse whisking into a cupboard, opened the cupboard, and smelled the mousy smell. Instantly, from going around in a trance inside my adult body as six-year-old Julia —rebellious, disobedient, and wholly on the mouse's side—I became Eleanor Cameron, housewife, and went immediately into the garage for a mousetrap.

The jolt from one age to the other with well over half a century between was so instantaneous that I stood for a moment realizing in the depths of my being what had happened to me. And I felt positively ashamed, as if I had betrayed Julia. This is what it means, I thought, to be completely the child inside the adult, yet writing with adult craft a novel that must satisfy my highest aesthetic standards: the double vision.

Quite possibly this was what was meant about the critic of children's books having to learn to be childlike, and yet I doubt very much that one can *learn* that state of being. Writers for children seem to be profoundly oriented, for some mysterious reason, toward that other world. Indeed, it is because they are so oriented, so attuned, with so many of the impressions of childhood still inside and crying out to be expressed, that they become writers for children or, as I have already put it, are capable of writing for anyone the kind of literature that children enjoy. What they have to say flows most naturally, most instinctively, from that world.

Therefore, the writer-critic of children's books assuredly has an edge on the critic who has never felt compelled to relive those emotions and awarenesses as the children's writer does. But if someone devoted to criticism is capable of this reliving—and I don't mean remembering with nostalgia—then it matters little whether he or she is a novelist or not. For once the writer-critic turns from fiction to criticism, the work of others is approached by the same path as the critic who is not a novelist but who nevertheless identifies with childhood. It is the pedant who has left childhood behind forever, who cannot remember it, who has no sympathy with it, who looks on children's literature simply as another discipline to be approached like any other or with condescension—that is the one whose words seem like nothing so much as the crumbs of wood left by termites.

But all scholars are not pedants, thank heaven. What fun T. S. Eliot must have had writing *Old Possum's Book of Practical Cats!* And he himself was quite capable of reliving what it was to be a child, of completely empathizing with the essence of child:

For whom the candle is a star, and the gilded angel
Spreading its wings at the summit of the tree
Is not only a decoration, but an angel.
The child wonders at the Christmas Tree:

Let him continue in the spirit of wonder. . . .
So that the reverence and the gaiety
May not be forgotten in later experience,
In the bored habituation, the fatigue, the tedium,
The awareness of death, the consciousness of failure. . . .[39]

The poet Louise Bogan reported in one of her letters about T. S.
Eliot, with whom she was sitting at a luncheon:

> We talked, during the end of the entrée and *through* the coffee
> and ice cream . . . and, finally, of the *cat* poems! I asked if he
> had enjoyed writing them; and he said that he had tried them
> out on "various young listeners." My favorite, I remarked, was
> the cat who taught the mice how to crochet. O yes, said he;
> that, among others, had "scandalized my adult readers."—One
> adult reader, namely [the critic] Allen Tate, was being visibly
> scandalized, just across the luncheon board.[40]

V I I I

Now I am remembering my friend the anti-intellectual book salesman
who hates criticism. I can well imagine him asking if we actually *need*
criticism in the world of children's books—if criticism of the extremely
academic variety may not destroy the pleasure of its young students.
I can well imagine him asking if Susan Cooper wasn't right when she
said to the critics: "Be careful how you treat the magic of books. . . .
The imagination doesn't need shoes. It goes barefoot"—referring
here to the story of the shoemaker and the elves.* One could agree
with Cooper over the writings of the pedantic critic, the kind I spoke
of above. But the critic devoted to literature and the pleasures and
illuminations it can give must still point out what troubles the search-

---

*See Lois Kuznets's response from out of academe, "Susan Cooper, a Reply," in
Signposts to Criticism of Children's Literature, pages 109–13.

ing mind, and it must be accepted that we shall never, never agree with one another on every point. No matter how disinterested the writer tries to be, one has the most trouble reading with an open mind a criticism of one's own work; then inevitably emotion rather than intellectuality rises to the fore.

Cooper's was a heartfelt address, words she had to speak (or shout) in her desperate resentment of critics who write of "using" a novel (in the beginning she stresses fantasy but later seems to include any kind of fiction), who speak of "effectiveness," "didactic intent," "messages," and "information"; who use such words as *criteria, value, attitudes, behavior, issues, competency, tools,* and *genre*. She calls *tool* a "doom-laden word."[41] She says that these practical standards of consideration of an imaginative work are not aesthetic but moral and "force thought on the author in an area where thought is destructive of the imagination."[42] She quotes John Rowe Townsend as saying that it is dangerous to consider the social, psychological, moral, and educational impact of a book and call it criticism. She quotes as well Ingmar Bergman, concerning the creation of his motion pictures: "I'm an artist, not a moralist."[43] She believes that all the approaches mentioned above are "dangerous and even destructive to any artist who lets them influence his future work." She could, she says, have simply gone back to her attic, closed the door, and got on with her writing, but she was so disturbed over the harm these approaches could do to young writers and to children subjected to pedantic, purely factual teaching that she was forced to speak out.

I agree with Cooper, in her shying away from extreme academicism and from all kinds of critical jargon. And I can share her anxiety over those approaches that "force thought on the author in an area where thought is destructive of the imagination."[44] But no critic, I must add, could destroy continually burgeoning imaginations such as those that envisioned the stories of the Borrowers, or the Moomintroll novels, or the great Gilly, or such a girl as Dicey, or such a child as Ramona. So that Cooper must be speaking of the kind of criticism that would endanger the young, unestablished writers who are not yet aesthetically strong enough to remain uninfluenced by the pedagogical on the one hand or the temptations of mass marketing on the other. In times such as these, when mass marketing is taking over, it must be very difficult indeed for the young writer not to be lured over into that other world, where popularity, easy reading, and the idea of the novel used as a tool in the classroom are the main focuses. But as soon as private vision is abandoned and the idea of usefulness replaces it, the initial perception fades and with it, in all likelihood, the possibility of a fine novel.

However, further on, in the last paragraph of her essay, I am troubled. For here Cooper as good as says that in addition to not needing or wanting the words of the didactic, pedagogic, pedantic critic, she does not want even the words of the thoughtful critic who might admire her work in many ways but who still wishes to inquire about certain aspects of it that either puzzle or intrigue, or who might in admiration ask about sources she has used in her research. Therefore it would seem—as she confesses to having done research—that she herself has thought, as well as written, at the behest of her imagination and the unconscious, for one does not do research without thought. All she wants, she says at the very end, is the kind of direct response that the children give her plays when they see, listen, laugh, cry, or say "Oooooh!"[45] The children are enough, she says. They are the ones to whom she listens to discover whether they are bored, angered, or brought to enchantment. And that kind of compulsive response is all she, as an artist, ever asks for.

For myself, I am rewarded that someone took the time necessary to try to understand. I may not agree with every facet of that criticism, but there is always the chance that I might understand something I hadn't before. And I don't *need* to agree. I don't remember coming anywhere near being destroyed, though I have on two occasions been indignant.* But you take these occasions in your stride as all part of the

---

*See Ursula Le Guin's essay "The Only Good Author?" in her *Dancing at the Edge of the World: Thoughts on Words, Women, Places,* in which she takes up the subject of being criticized.

adventure of being published; as I've said somewhere else in these pages: We're not innocents; we know what we're in for! And an adult's thoughtfulness gives me something the child's direct response (much as I delight in it) can't possibly give, something that answers my own thought in creating the work in the first place. For though I tell later of the power of the unconscious as I have experienced it, it goes almost without saying that always, after I have absorbed what has been given me—by memory, thought, the unconscious, and imagination—over a considerable length of time, I read over the manuscript minutely again and again to test thoughtfully what I have written—as I know Cooper does.

We *are* thinking beings as well as imaginative, intuitive ones, so that it seems inevitable that the best critical writing comes from the recognition of how wrinkled brow and cool fresh eye companion and balance one another, unconfined by the need for some "correct" critical approach (which may remain "correct" for only a decade or two), approved, rigidly theoretical or ideological or any kind of narrowly restricted approach dictated by some school of critical theory. A. S. Byatt, the by-now-famous author of the brilliant *Possession* and *Still Life,* said in an interview: "Now, if you get literary theorists, they only talk to other literary theorists about literary theory. Nothing causes them to look out." Hear, hear! Let us look out. Let us not be dictated to. Let us respond to a piece of writing as fully and honestly as we can out of our own searchings in life and in reading, out of our own observations and feeling and thought. And that goes for the writing of fiction as well as of criticism: the need for the private vision.*

---

*Once again, I turn to Joan Murray and Robert Fulford's essay "When Jane Jacobs Took on the World" (with her *The Death and Life of Great American Cities*). In it they refer also to Paul Goodman's *Growing Up Absurd,* Rachel Carson and her *Silent Spring,* Betty Friedan's *The Feminine Mystique,* Marshall McLuhan's *Understanding Media,* and Ralph Nader's *Unsafe at Any Speed.* As Murray and Fulford put it: "Each of these books presented a fresh voice that we did not know we needed until we heard it. . . . This is the role of the great amateurs: to see clearly the issues that academic specialists cannot see because they are limited by the blinders of their institutions and their disciplines." See the *New York Times Book Review,* December 16, 1982, page 28.

PART IV

The Unconscious

Somewhere inside we do know everything about ourselves. There is no real forgetting. Perhaps we know somewhere, too, about all there is to come.

JANE GARDAM
Crusoe's Daughter

I think a good deal about the Phoenicians and the Druids, and how I was a nice little girl here, and ran along the top of the stone walls, and told Mr. Gibbs after tea that I was full to the chin. Do you like yourself as a child? I like myself, before the age of ten, that is—before consciousness sets in. Still I expect I muddle it all up after Cornwall.

VIRGINIA WOOLF
letter to Saxon Sydney-Turner
The Letters of Virginia Woolf

INTO SOMETHING
RICH AND STRANGE

❧

Full fathom five thy father lies;
Of his bones are coral made:
Those are pearls that were his eyes:
Nothing of him that doth fade,
But doth suffer a sea-change
Into something rich and strange.
Sea-nymphs hourly ring his knell:
Hark! now I hear them—ding, dong, bell.

WILLIAM SHAKESPEARE
The Tempest

Composed almost four hundred years ago, the words in this epigraph for me express symbolically how the unconscious absorbs our experiences, buries them, turns them through slow transformations over the years—during which time they may, in their original form, be entirely forgotten—into treasure that emerges from the depths to be used by the artist in ways he or she could never have foretold. So perfect is this symbolism that one would think that Shakespeare, that majestic sub-creator (to use Tolkien's word), knew precisely what is now known about the unconscious: how it is a fathomless sea, perhaps literally boundless, holding innumerable experiences, both individual and racial, knowledges and intuitions of which the conscious mind is not aware, and how it nurtures them, turning bones into coral and eyes into pearls, as it releases them to the thinking mind.

269

Did he never wonder, William Shakespeare, with a kind of awe, where it all came from, scene after scene that assaulted his imagination as if he had lived each one? Did he never ask himself what there was in him that compelled this profusion and held him slave to it? For the writer—or any artist—literally cannot help the compulsion. There would seem to be some ruling power that drives creation and gives the stuff of creation. Charlotte Brontë wrote, in her preface to the second edition of *Wuthering Heights,* when she was troubled by Emily's characterization of Heathcliff: "But this I know: the writer who possesses the creative gift owns something of which he is not altogether master—something that at times strangely wills and works for itself."[1] Consider Flaubert's sense of doubleness when he tells of having to get up and fetch a handkerchief at the death of Madame Bovary because he had been so moved by his own writing that tears were streaming down his face. There was the Flaubert who wept and the one who had made Flaubert weep—two deeply united and yet, as it were, separate beings. One could think of the other as Faulkner did of his creating self in a letter to his friend Joan Williams:

> And I now realize for the first time what an amazing gift I had: Uneducated in every formal sense, without even very literate companions, yet to have made the thing I made. I don't know where it came from. I don't know why God or the gods, or whoever it is, selected me to be the vessel. Believe me, this is not humility, false modesty; it is simply amazement.[2]

Flaubert and Faulkner must often, I should think, have reflected on "where it came from," the source of their art. Whether Shakespeare did or did not, we shall never know, but surely we can at least say that he did not call it the unconscious. When did that word come into use? I asked myself. And what I found in Lancelot Law Whyte's *The Unconscious Before Freud* made me uncertain as to just what Shakespeare might have intuited. For Whyte says that the idea of the unconscious was conceivable around 1700 *and by some long before that;* was being talked about in the 1800s; and was being used effectively in the 1900s, thanks to the efforts of a great many creative individuals.

I use Jung's term the *unconscious* rather than Freud's the *subconscious*—for Freud a dark basement of repressed desires—because I respond to Jung's concept. For him the unconscious is a world as vital and real as the conscious world of the individual—at least half of his total being, and far wider and richer than that of his thinking ego. From the unconscious, says Jung, comes advice and guidance that no one and nothing else can give; its language and protagonists are symbols, and its way of communication is through dreams, or the creations of artists, or the fairy tales, myths, and legends that have come down to us over thousands of years from the memories of our race. Dreams—like art, like myth and legend and fairy tale—speak in poetic images.

My husband has been ill, and because of a doctor's mistaken prescription for therapy, which has resulted in increased pain, he says, "He has ruined me." That night I dream that I am in a ruin and turn to speak to my husband but he is no longer there; he has vanished, and I go over to a fallen wall to hunt for him, but I have lost him. I then see him on my right in front of a fireplace in a long, narrow, roofless room. He is sitting in a yoga position as if given over to contemplation. I go to him and he turns into a small oriental figure of fired red clay like the Japanese figures on top of my bookcase, still sitting in a position of calmness and serenity, of meditation, as though trying to attain wisdom. But now suddenly he becomes a little girl of nine or ten and I realize that she is to be my child, and that I have been given her in place of my husband. We are going along a crowded street in Los Angeles and she looks around in amazement, saying that she somehow recognizes this street though she cannot remember ever having been here before. I tell her that of course she recognizes it, as she is in reality my husband, who used to live and work in Los Angeles. She bursts into tears and I try to comfort her by saying that I will love and care for her and that she is not to worry about anything.

And I myself know that only through my own patience and devotion will she be transformed back into my husband.

What does it remind you of? Yes, a fairy tale. In the true fairy tale, as in the true dream, says Fredrik Böök, in his life of Hans Christian Andersen, there lies always the force of the dark message.

I have felt for a long time that my dreams are a significant part of my life and have written down those I could recall with startling clarity. Some have stayed with me since childhood: The earliest I have remembered in every detail since I was nine. And I can see how two series of dreams point, each in its own way, to what must be an unconscious preoccupation: a sense of being lost, of which certain dreams of de la Mare's spoke to him also. I was comforted to know that he, too, had had this sense, though why he had it he never told, so far as I know, and I am mystified about myself. In my conscious life I have never felt overwhelmingly lost, only as if I am continually searching. At times struggle is involved (or is this only in connection with writing? I can't be sure, but then writing can be not only a struggle to express one's deepest meaning in the text but as well a search for meaning in the experiences of one's life, which can go deeper and deeper as the years pass), so that possibly this is my "lostness": not having yet found what it is I am searching for. But I would add that I need the struggle and the search; life would be pale without them, and I am accustomed to living with uncertainty.

Cathy, in *Wuthering Heights*, says: "I've dreamt in my life dreams that have stayed with me forever after, and changed my ideas; they've gone through and through me, like wine through water, and altered the colour of my mind."[3] De la Mare says that that is surely the voice of Emily Brontë herself and that, with some qualifications, it had been his own experience as well. Yes, and mine, though I had not realized how much dreams meant to me until I remembered how often I have introduced them into the texture of my books—or how they have woven themselves in!—not as embroidery, something that could be picked out, leaving the weave intact, but as a necessary part of the whole.

There are two premonitory dreams in *The Court of the Stone Children*, inextricably knit into the pattern of meaning because of the central idea that if time is an eternal present, as I believe it to be, precognition is inevitable for those whose narrow human slits of awareness are widened on certain occasions; they know ahead what—according to human time sense—has not yet happened. There is, also, near the beginning of the book, Nina's dream of lostness in which, trying again and again to telephone home, she exclaims to the telephone operator that time is passing, to which the cool voice replies, "Time is a river without banks. If there are no banks, there is nothing for time to pass." Chagall's painting *Time Is a River Without Banks* hangs in the museum where Nina has seen for the first time the girl who has come out of time to fulfill her own dream of precognition and to inadvertently bring about Nina's. And when Helena Staynes, one of the curators, says to Nina, "And what do you make of the painting?" Nina answers, "I don't know. I wish I knew what it meant. It's like a fairy tale—or a dream." And Mrs. Staynes says, "Yes, it is. You've hit it exactly. . . . If you try to make sense of it by means of logic, you can't, because Chagall is always remembering his childhood and so, probably, his childhood dreams, and the feeling of losing himself in fairy tales."

To the Green Mountains begins with a dream, Kath's, of coming back in summer to a mountainside on which—and now, even as I sit here writing these words, the repetition strikes me for the first time—"she has an intimation not only that she is alone in this vast solitude but that she is lost." Here I am again. I keep saying it and keep saying it, one way or another; I seem to make opportunities for saying it. "An intimation that she is lost" but "that she has climbed this path before and has come to her longed-for destination. No, she cannot say that. Rather, she has looked down upon it, though always the moment of actual arrival has been denied her." And with Kath once again looking down on her grandmother's house, down there in the valley, and the loved figure she can never seem to reach, she wakes as always, just before beginning the descent.

Two more dreams come into the book, both, now that I come to think of them, of lostness: the first of Kath being abandoned in a city theater by Tiss, the black girl whose valued friendship she has lost at the time of the dream, and the second of finding herself at her grand-mother's house at last but realizing that there is no one there. "The garden was all gone to seed. There were no curtains nor even any blinds, and the porch was dusty and littered with old papers and dead leaves, and nobody answered the door." A terrible kind of lostness: to reach a place, after years of effort, where someone much loved has been waiting, only to find that that person has not been there for a very long time, died or gone away, and no one has told us when, to where, or why.

Near the beginning of *A Room Made of Windows* twelve-year-old Julia takes from her desk drawer an unfinished story, a dream she has written down and now tries to continue as best she can, but it will not round itself out. It ends, simply because it will go no further, with the man she feels she knows in some intense and personal way going out of the tall dark house into which she and a mob of unknown people have pursued him. He turns and hands her his mask, which she takes, and in terror she slams the door against him, but she cannot lock it because the lock has been broken by the mob who had forced it open to follow him with some evil intent. At the book's end, Julia realizes the man was her dead father, and it is Rhiannon Moore, the musician who lives next door, who interprets her dream and tells her what will be meaningful to her later as a writer—having been handed her father's complex qualities of passion, persistence, and intensity in the symbolic form of his mask. This dream of Julia's is based on an exceedingly long and complex one I had as a child only a little older than twelve, and that I wrote down and still have in my possession.

What has astonished me in connection with my own discoveries of a preoccupation with lostness is the case of the dreams of Walter de la Mare, surely one of the kindest and gentlest men who ever lived. Yet, as one discovers on reading his stories and poems, there is more often than not a haunting sense of the powers of evil or an obsession with death, ghosts, and graveyards—with people like Seton's aunt, who prefers the company of the dead and who absorbs the living as a mantis absorbs insects; and others, like the dreamy, absentminded grandmother in "The Riddle," whose old oak chest swallows up the seven children, never to be heard of again.

De la Mare dreamed that though he had no reason for murdering her, he had killed his sister and then claimed that he had not. When he went back to the upstairs room where the murder had taken place, he did not recognize it; yet he went immediately to a chest, opened the bottom drawer, and groped about for the clothes he had been wearing to prove they were clean and that he was therefore innocent. But when he withdrew his hand, it was sticky with blood. He also related dreams of two other murders he had committed. In the second he saw an old woman sitting in a chair. To the side of the chair was a door with a space beneath, and he knew that beyond was a hall where there were people who would hear any audible movements. Nevertheless, with no sense of revulsion, he leaned forward and plunged a knife into her, then noticed, when the blood began to flow, that it would run along the sloping floor toward the space under the door. At once he found a cloth and a leather bucket (why a medieval object? one wonders—and yet, as a friend observes, it is exactly right for this particular dream, and recall that the floor was sloping, as floors do in medieval houses, sloping this way and that) and began to sop it up, then turned abruptly at some sound and knocked the bucket over. Now he looked out at the apparently dawn sky beyond the tall Gothic windows and noted the red in it—precisely the color of the spilled blood making its way toward the door—whereupon the dream ended. How could anyone explain that dream? demanded de la Mare. Who had constructed a story at once so complex and yet so coherent?

There you have it again, the intimation of some power at work, in this case giving the dreamer his dream; the ghostly provider for the creating mind, as Faulkner implied concerning the novelist and what he writes; some larger, collective unconscious, possibly, as Jung believed, speaking to the individual unconscious. Graham Greene asks, in his novel *The End of the Affair:* "I say 'one chooses' with the inaccurate pride of the professional writer who—when he has been seriously noted at all—has been praised for his technical ability; but do I in fact of my own will choose that black wet January night on the Common in 1946, the sight of Henry Miles slanting across the wide river of rain, or did these images choose me?"[4] The Bushman, cocooned in his ancient wisdom, says of human life, "There is a dreamer dreaming us." And Joan Aiken, at the end of her 1971 Library of Congress lecture, tells of a marvelously complex and coherent dream of which she says, "I didn't have it, it had me. Words won't convey its blazing intensity."[5]

Three experiences of Graham Greene's are curious exceptions to Jung's belief that dreams are extremely personal expressions of the unconscious, meaningful to the dreamer alone, rather than artistic expressions, and that only the conscious can, through the process of discrimination, turn what the unconscious gives us into art. Greene notes of his story "The Root of All Evil" that he dreamed the entire thing and woke laughing, and that he did not change a single incident, nor did he after dreaming "A Sense of Reality." In the novel *A Burnt-Out Case,* identification with character went so far that Greene actually dreamed Querry's dream. About this he is certain because the memories and symbols and associations of the dream belong specifically to Querry, so that the next morning Greene could put the dream without change into his novel, where it bridged a gap that for days he had been unable to close.

Jung believed that we do not create our dreams but that they happen to us, as experiences happen to us, which would perhaps explain the complexity and sophistication of that childhood dream of mine about the mask, seemingly too old for me, a version of which wound its way into *Room.* Does, then, what we seem to create as novelists "happen to us" in the same sense, *if* we draw on the depths and not merely the surface of story, cobbling up a plot? Elizabeth Bowen has written of Katherine Mansfield that "there were times when [she] believed a story to have a volition of its own—she seems to stand back, watching it take form. Yet this could not happen apart from her; the story draws her steadily into itself."[6]

The question of whether what we create happens to us may find a response in several facts. First, what we ourselves write can instruct us, giving us revelations of which we were previously unaware, symbols and themes can later be discovered that we did not realize were there; and the completed work can say something to us that we did not realize it would say. Second, characters are discovered. They are given, either gradually revealing themselves as the work progresses or presenting themselves entire as though they had been waiting, existing like living beings "full fathom five." Only if one were to construct creatures to fit a plot, to be used purely for the purposes of the plot, would one be aware of mechanically putting them together out of bits and pieces, all of which would have nothing to do with the unconscious. Third, what we write can seem to coalesce into fascinatingly interwoven patterns without conscious effort on our part—that is, all seems to weave together, sometimes with astonishing rapidity, as though the weaving had already been accomplished. Fourth, the unconscious has the ability to recall to the conscious mind, under pressure of the author's writing about a certain time and place, scenes and events long forgotten.

Now, to enlarge on the ability of the writer's work to instruct. One of the most remarkable instances of this is brought out by Mark Schorer in a few paragraphs on Emily Brontë. He makes no mention of the unconscious, however. Quite the contrary. He speaks of Emily's somnambulistic excess, generated by years of writing about a world of "monstrous passion, of dark and gigantic emotional and nervous energy,"[7] which was for Emily the ideal world. It was one she had lived in since childhood, the natural atmosphere of her most private being, as set down in those interminable stories she called her Gondal Saga.

What Emily wanted to do in *Wuthering Heights,* according to Schorer, was to persuade us of "the moral magnificence of . . . unmoral passion."[8] She wanted us to accept at their own valuation such demonic beings as Heathcliff and Cathy. But then, says Schorer, because of "a mere mechanical device"—technique—and because "technique objectifies,"[9] the novelist Emily Brontë revealed to the girl Emily the absurdities of her own conception. Her technique, as the novel progressed, exposed those absurdities for what they are, so that in the end we are persuaded that it is not Emily Brontë who was mistaken in her estimate of her characters but they who were mistaken in their estimate of themselves. Technique alone, Schorer believes, taught Emily that the theme of the moral magnificence of unmoral passion is a false one, and that it was not what her material meant as art.

Now I can well believe that Emily Brontë's novel instructed her as to the truth. But I am not willing to believe that it was merely technique, merely "mechanical device" that persuaded Emily of the hopelessness of idealizing a world of demonic passions, together with its values, as she had at first thought to do.

The heart of the matter, it seems to me, the secret of what happened to Emily Brontë, is that her aesthetic intuition, her unconscious, call it what you will, chose as place for her novel not the imaginary world of Gondal she had lived in as a child and adolescent but Haworth country. And with that choice, because Emily knew Haworth country and Haworth people as she knew her own home and family, she was compelled to plunge into reality rather than, once again, into fantasy, as she had done in the Gondal Saga. Whereupon the full force of her conscious and unconscious knowledge of the peculiar Haworth breed of human creature forced truth into the final pages of *Wuthering Heights*, despite the fact that Heathcliff remains a melodramatic figure throughout the novel. And that truth is that unmoral passion could not possibly call up a tale of moral magnificence, but could only resolve into, as Schorer puts it, the "devastating spectacle of human waste"[10] that *Wuthering Heights* turned out to be.

Glenway Wescott believes that writers of fiction learn from their material as the work unfolds, learn from "the phantoms of memory and from the powers and accidents of art."[11] They do indeed learn from their own material, but I think that a good many of "the powers and accidents of art" are flowerings of the creative unconscious—sudden, inexplicable revelations that can make the work of writing a novel an utterly absorbing adventure into hitherto unknown territory of the self. Ursula Le Guin wrote, at the time she was working on *The Farthest Shore:*

> I finally finished a second draft last Friday, but have been fairly cross-eyed since. I have been working on a third volume—a trequel?—of the *Wizard,* and what happened was that Ged got the bit between his teeth, as it were, and started telling me things I didn't know, and doing things I hadn't intended him to do, and he changed the whole end of the book, and fouled me up good and proper. Damned strong-minded wizard.[12]

Related to the power of the unconscious to instruct is its ability to reveal symbols and themes the writer has not been aware of. It is my books that have shown me that the theme of possession (or attempted possession) of one human being by another and the unhappiness, frustration, and bitter resentment it can bring are apparently preoccupations of mine. In *Room* the theme grew out of place because it was in Berkeley that I myself was a selfish child. Julia, in her youthful blindness, tries to possess her mother, and it is not until she is faced with her mother's words—that for her, children are not enough—that Julia is forced into the knowledge that she must allow her mother her own life, must allow her to be her own person and not simply an extension of Julia, existing solely for Julia's comfort and satisfaction.

Concerning the theme of possession in *The Court of the Stone Children,* the book has as its central event in the past the rejection of Napoléon's tyranny by Antoine de Lombre, because of which he is shot. But there turns out to be another preoccupation, something I had felt during the writing but had not consciously enunciated to myself, and that a friend told me was of central significance to her, because she is an artist: Nina's preoccupation with the museum's works of art.

As in *Room,* and certainly in *Mountains,* whatever significance is there, indeed the very story itself, grew out of place, because place is something without which my unconscious cannot conceive a novel, and I should think this might be the case with a good many writers. If the seed of the story finds no particular place to fall, no particular environment to breathe in and get light from, it dies. Place makes story by making possible certain characters out of which story grows.

As for character creation and the unconscious, I had thought from the beginning, many years ago when I wrote *Mountains* as a one-act play, that Tissie, the black woman, would come up to Elizabeth Rule's hotel room, intent, out of jealousy and hatred, on threatening Elizabeth and possibly in her rage doing Elizabeth actual harm. But what was my astonishment on arriving at that chapter to find that Tissie was *not* going up to Elizabeth's room, Tissie having revealed herself to me during the writing of the book as not at all the kind of woman who would threaten another human being. Once it becomes clear to her just how the law books Elizabeth Rule has brought her husband are going to affect her life with him, she simply never has anything to do with Elizabeth again. Nor with Kath, the child who loved her and who had loved being with her. A friendship, unquestioning and trusting all those years, vanishes as if it had never been. That was the truth about Tissie as she revealed it to me.

I do not see how the fact can be other than that in the depths of the creative unconscious the whole, given character must exist. Tissie, my Tissie—the real one—must have been there inside me the entire time as a completed person, so that she could gradually reveal herself in one aspect after another under the pressure of various circumstances. If a novel has been allowed to grow slowly in the imagination, the writer should never have to wonder what a character would do under this circumstance or that. One will know, infallibly and unerringly, without having to stop and think. And it has often seemed to me that if one did have to cast around in order to find the answer, then that character must not naturally and deeply be one's own, and that a serious flaw is likely to be woven into the novel, a flaw that could become increasingly serious—subtly at first but with increasing proof of artificiality as the novel progresses.* For the writer would constantly run the risk of having that character, purely for the sake of imposed story, do something that would run contrary to his or her inmost nature. Unless, of course (and this is most likely if he or she is a "made" character) that character is presented so shallowly that there would be no inmost nature. But even minor characters in memorable novels have inmost natures. The writer perceives them and, even if they come into the novel only briefly, will have got a distinct sense of their essences, as Walter de la Mare had of the old sailor, the Oomgar, who befriends little Ummanodda Nizza-Neela in *The Three Royal Monkeys,* and Cynthia Voigt had of Jeff and his father's dear friend Brother Thomas in *A Solitary Blue.*

Concerning the third ability of the unconscious, to cause a coalescing of novelistic events into complicated patterns without apparent conscious effort on the part of the writer, I think of Virginia Woolf walking around Tavistock Square when she made up, "as I sometimes make up my books, *To the Lighthouse;* in a great, apparently involuntary, rush. . . . I wrote the book very quickly."[13] But despite the apparently involuntary quickness of conception of her novel, we know that it was not a visitation out of nowhere. She was forty-four when this happened, and when she was nine, on vacation in Cornwall at St. Ives, across from the Godrevy Lighthouse, we learn from the *Hyde Park Gate News,* which she produced for her family, that Virginia and her two brothers Thoby and Adrian were invited for a sail to the lighthouse on a day of "perfect wind and tide for going there" and that "Master Adrian Stephen was much disappointed at not being allowed to go."[14] And so for thirty-five years that day of perfect wind and tide, and of the keen disappointment of the little boy who had

---

*I do know that each of us has different experiences. But I place great emphasis on the novel being allowed to grow naturally, like a plant, as Philippa Pearce puts it. Nothing should be forced.

had to stay at home, had remained in her unconscious. It must have been her unconscious, for she gives no hint in her account of the book's inception that she recalls the incident she recorded when she was nine. Yet surely that day and its intense joy, for her, must have lain there weaving itself into a novel all that time, ready to break forth. "One thing burst into another. Blowing bubbles out of a pipe gives the feeling of the rapid crowd of ideas and scenes which blew out of my mind, so that my lips seemed syllabling of their own accord as I walked. What blew the bubbles? Why then? I have no notion."[15]

When the first urge for a book comes rushing in, when it comes quickly like this, it is a kind of bliss (and I do not mean that this guarantees its goodness). Then either the book is written immediately, as in the case of *To the Lighthouse,* or one goes about the daily business of living, knowing that the unconscious is at work and that over a period of time the book is getting itself ready to be written. Later, after writing has started, the presentations of the unconscious continue, sometimes in long, pouring spurts when the conscious and the unconscious seem in perfect harmony and the right tone, the right voice, is found without effort. Or with struggle, when the conscious is striving to find the tone that will satisfy. In fact, I often picture myself as an objective editor or judge.

This sense of inevitability seemed suddenly apparently lacking in William Mayne, usually a superb artist, when he wrote one ending for the British edition of *The Jersey Shore* and another for the American. Perhaps he had not waited long enough for his unconscious to tell him the ending he would stand by no matter whether it was for a British or an American audience. Certainly for me, the American (written later) is the right and the good one. So strongly did I feel this that I somehow knew that the main character, Art, would be killed in battle after the written part of the story was over, so that I was not in the least surprised when I was told by his editor that Mayne himself had, in fact, known that Art would be killed beyond the novel's ending. But I never for an instant felt this in reading the final chapter of the British edition.

It is true that the self can be objective only to a degree in judging its own work, because its aesthetic judgment contains both the conscious and the unconscious. But the cooler the self is in listening and judging—in other words, the greater the aesthetic distance that can be attained—the better the work. The material can be hot, but the judgment must be cool. And by "hot" I do not mean a scene of violence but that the writer has been cutting to the bone of truth, whether the scene be light or somber, comic or harsh. Cutting to the bone is always the hope, rather than skirmishing over the surface because one hasn't the knowledge, the ability, the wisdom, or the patience to hit the bone itself. If I know I am skirmishing, then I know further that it is a matter of waiting in order to be given insight, which is the voice of the unconscious. And whenever it is a matter of waiting, I am depending on and trusting to the unconscious to send its message. Is it, then, that the unconscious knows better than the conscious mind? It would seem so, and when I go astray, when I am struggling, it is because I haven't waited long enough, have not kept the channel clear, or have misinterpreted.

And it is always a matter of waiting, never of forcing, because forcing is fatal. (In fact, I believe that forcing is fatal no matter what we do.) Katherine Mansfield felt that for her "each idea for a story had an inherent shape, that there could be no other for it, that it was for her to perceive that shape, and that it was far more a matter of perception than construction."[16]

Carson McCullers tells us that for a whole year she worked on *The Heart Is a Lonely Hunter* without understanding it at all. Each character was talking to a central character, but why she did not know. "I'd almost decided," she has written,

> that the book was no novel, that I should chop it up into short stories. But I could feel the mutilation in my body when I had that idea, and I was in despair. . . . Suddenly, as I walked across a road, it occurred to me that Harry Minowitz, the character all the other characters were talking to, was a different man, a deaf

mute, and immediately the name changed to John Singer. The whole focus of the novel was fixed and I was for the first time committed with my whole soul to *The Heart Is a Lonely Hunter.*[17]

Vladimir Nabokov has spoken of inspiration at work,

mutely pointing out this or that, having me accumulate known materials for an unknown structure. . . . I feel a kind of gentle development, an uncurling inside, and I know that the details are there already, that in fact I would see them plainly if I looked closer, if I stopped the machine and opened its inner compartment; but I prefer to wait until what is loosely called inspiration has completed the task for me.[18]

He looked on the structure of a book in process, "dimly illumined" in his mind, as comparable to a painting on which he could work at any point—never from left to right or from top to bottom but on any part that involved him most strongly—and keep working until all the gaps were filled in. I myself am currently having this exact experience.

Related to Nabokov's sense that the whole work must somehow preexist in the unconscious ("the details are there already") is Graham Greene's observation that in the course of writing a novel "somewhere near the beginning for no reason I knew, I would insert an incident which seemed entirely irrelevant, and sixty thousand words later, with a sense of excitement, I would realize why it was there—the narrative had been working all that time outside my conscious control."[19]

Mark Twain, too, firmly believed that a novel should come of itself, that his unconscious was vitally involved and that if it did not freely give him its material, there was no point in continuing. The case of *Huckleberry Finn* with relation to waiting and the work of the unconscious is surely one of the strangest on record. For it was not only the writer who waited, in the beginning, but later the unconscious that had to wait, when it wanted only to give.

Mark Twain began work on "another boy's book," as he called it, in 1876 but was not engrossed; indeed, he started the writing, he said, simply to be at work at something, liked it "only tolerably well," and intended either to pigeonhole or to burn it when he had finished. But long before he came to the end, he set it aside and continued to ignore it for four years. In 1880 he took it up again, remained unenthusiastic, and abandoned it once more. Then in 1881, following that memorable visit to the Mississippi that was to make the great river central to *Huckleberry Finn,* Mark Twain suddenly became imbued with such a frenzy of creative energy that the book flowed from his pen day after day. However—and this is the inexplicable part—even though the unconscious was at last working full force in a way that would have overwhelmed any lesser writer with gratitude, Mark Twain allowed the most unimportant projects—such as book publishing— to tease him away from his work, so that in full spate it was forced to wait while he vitiated the hot, rich energy that should have gone into it without interruption.

When at length *The Adventures of Huckleberry Finn* was completed, Mark Twain began to realize to some degree what his unconscious had granted him. Yet even so he could not have guessed that his book was to be one of the seminal forces in American literary history, a book that was not particularly valued by its author until the response to it began growing, and that had had to wait interminably on secondrate affairs before being given its completed expression.

Finally, to speak of place and the unconscious, how it brings back sights and sounds and events long forgotten: *Mountains,* a book that waited so long to be written, rose out of the deepest layer of any book I have so far attempted; it came out of the years of very young childhood. Nothing that happened in it actually happened except for one or two small events; only the place is as it was, and a certain situation—the fact that I lived in a hotel with my mother between the ages of three and five, and that she was the housekeeper. It was a book that had a long, slow parturition partly because I was uncertain of how it should be written, from whose point of view. And some element of my uncertainty came from the fact of having left Ohio behind so many years ago. Could I relive my place?

I was about to begin writing when, in the scheduled order of events, I had to go East. There was no reason why I should not stop off in Ohio and take the train to that tiny spot on the map I have called South Angela. I stood at the desk in the airport having, so I thought, completely made up my mind as to what I intended doing. "But do *not* do it," something said. "Trust to the aesthetic impulse." Which meant, it seemed to me, that all the impressions of childhood are still there in the depths and that creation can do its best work, the most aesthetically satisfying work, with what is part of the unconscious and can freely combine with imagination, rather than with what has been freshly observed and recorded. Whether I was right or not I shall never know. But I could never have foreseen all that would rise to the surface in the act of writing—scenes, details of street and countryside and the interiors of houses, gestures, sounds, smells I had not thought of in all those years. Much had already come to me, but it was the act of writing that brought me, finally, what I needed for a full evocation of place.

To sum up: The unconscious would seem to give the novelist, if it is allowed to, the material of the novel—its characters, the voices speaking, its landscape, its construction, its theme or themes—and while it would seem to be the work of the conscious to discriminate as to expression, as I have said, words will sometimes come in an apparently unpremeditated flow that seems like a blessing. However, these words must be looked at later with a cold eye to determine their rightness. For style *is* content; meaning subtly tilts from word to word, and each part of the novel—each word, sentence, paragraph—depends on every other part like the cunningly stressed beams leaning together without nails in the tower of the cathedral at Ely. Only by the use of certain words, these and no others, can the writer express a private way of seeing. Only by working toward those words and not being satisfied until they are found can the writer do justice to whatever the unconscious has given.

I said above: "the unconscious would seem to give the novelist, if
it is allowed to . . ." But how does one open oneself to the offerings
of the unconscious? If a seed has been planted, if within the novelist
something is unfolding, it would seem that receptivity should be
maintained, a state of general and attentive awareness for as long as
one senses it necessary, for years perhaps. By never forcing. By in-
tellectualizing as little as possible. And if there is a block, by waiting
in unparticularized expectancy. Intuiting the whole seems infinitely
preferable to making aggressive determinations. For this latter state
of mind means that thinking will take over in such a way that the
novelist begins writing character sketches, drawing up schemes and
outlines, making diagrams of plot structure, and writing out family
histories. All this is a far cry from the poetic process involved in the
secret and silent, slow and natural growth that will eventually, in its
own good time (if the work is right for the novelist), offer its own
solutions. Yet I cannot be dogmatic about this as the only way, for
John Rowe Townsend reveals himself in *The Thorny Paradise* as one
who—among many other highly successful novelists for both adults
and children—does make all the intellectual preparations. However,
it may not have occurred to him to tell us of nonthinking phases such
as those Alan Garner underwent in his work on *Red Shift,* during
which years went by between writing bouts while he waited to be
given further enlightenment about the way in which his novel should
be told.

In discussing an essay by Mary Hanle, Silvano Arieti, in his study
of creativity, quotes her as saying: "We cannot get creative ideas by
searching for them, but if we are not receptive they will not come."[20]
Creative work, she believes, demands both a passionate interest, in
which ideas are actively welcomed, and a certain degree of detachment.
This paradoxical state she sums up as one of "detached devotion," a
phrase which seems to me to be precisely right.

Gerard Manley Hopkins's privately created word was *inscape,* a word
that for him was charged with meaning just as for him the world was
"charged with the grandeur of God." And because it was, he believed

that the only way to do justice to it, in Conrad's sense of "doing justice to the visible universe," was to observe minutely, to take in and express the inscape of every created thing, the essence of it. Slowly his word *inscape,* the central word in his vocabulary and the motif of his mental life, came to mean an inner country that required a devoted seeing-into. It is the way in which he explored and expressed his private vision, his singularity. Nowhere has he written more poignantly of his belief than in these lines:

> As kingfishers catch fire, dragonflies draw flame;
> As tumbled over rim in roundy wells
> Stones ring; like each tucked string tells, each hung bell's
> Bow swung finds tongue to fling out broad its name;
> Each mortal thing does one thing and the same:
> Deals out that being indoors each one dwells;
> Selves—goes itself; *myself* it speaks and spells;
> *Crying What I do is me: for that I came.*

I believe that in listening for the voice of the unconscious the artist is enabled to make something worth the highest effort, for what is made in this way will speak truly of a uniqueness, a personal inscape, something no one else on earth can give. *"What I do is me: for that I came."*

OF DREAMS, ART,
AND THE
UNCONSCIOUS

The most beautiful experience we can have is the mysterious.

ALBERT EINSTEIN
Out of My Later Years

*J*ust as "No man is an Iland, intire of itself; Every man is a peece of the Continent, a part of the maine," so no writer, no artist, can possibly be entirely an island, a Crusoe wholly alone (though assuredly Cézanne and van Gogh came near to that state). There *are* Crusoes who treasure a certain vision, which must remain inviolate if they are to tell their private version of it, if they are to communicate honest perceptions and vulnerabilities and refuse to tinker with what they sense as the deepest truth of their work. Yet they can never be wholly Crusoes in that they are born within their own times and respond to them. But if they open themselves to the work of the unconscious and receive its messages with gratitude, they may also, almost eerily, become aware at times of the collective unconscious, that limitless ocean surrounding their individual islands, which allows their work to touch a common chord, as do all memorable pieces of creation.

Be it cosmic or human, the act of creation remains a mystery. We speak familiarly of the big bang as a theory of universal creation and of DNA as the essential primitive matter of the living creature. But we do not know why or how the livingness is breathed into creation, how life and consciousness emerge from matter. No more do we understand the why or how of the act of creation in the human mind and imagination. We understand certain activities of the neurons and brain cells, but when it comes to the final human ability to create what has never before been expressed, in a certain unique, idiosyncratic, sometimes unforgettable way through the mediums of stone, wood, paint, sound, or words, we must stand silent.

Freud spoke of the subconscious at work, and Carl Jung of the collective unconscious common to all, "the foundation of what the ancients called 'the sympathy of all things,' " expressing itself through dreams and art, which are so intimately related. We all of us have dreams, most of which mystify us—when we can remember them. But some of us express compulsively in paintings, in symphonies, plays, poetry, novels, and shaped forms, what the unconscious has given us and wonder why we are so driven to bring into being these particular creations in just a certain, particular way. We may never know; we will *probably* never know, because the workings of creation are buried very deep indeed.

I propose now to continue the exploration, begun in "Into Something Rich and Strange," of the part dreams and the unconscious have played in the work of writers.

In his introduction to Jung's *Man and His Symbols,* John Freeman speaks of the conscious and the unconscious within an individual learning to know and to respect and to accommodate one another, and says that for Jung: "Man becomes whole, integrated, calm, fertile, and happy when (and only when) the process of individuation is complete," that is, "when the conscious and the unconscious have learned to live at peace and complement one another."[1]

Of the workings of the unconscious and its relation to dreams, Jung believed that, at the moment of dreaming, the dreamed-of event may still lie in the future, for it is only our consciousness that does not yet know; the unconscious seems already to be informed and to have come to a conclusion expressed in the dream. Also, the unconscious is poetic, speaking in symbols, guided by instinctive trends, "represented by corresponding thought forms—that is, by the archetypes."[2] And he gives as illustration a doctor who describes the course of an illness using the rational concepts of infection and fever, while the unconscious, expressing itself through dream, is more poetic, presenting the diseased body as man's earthly house and the fever as the fire that is destroying it.

Franz Kafka had, from childhood, felt utterly diminished—mentally, physically, emotionally, socially, and spiritually—by his big and autocratic, muscular, loud-voiced, immensely successful father, a man who sneered and jeered most cruelly at any of Franz's efforts to do anything. Kafka tells of a dream in which he (represented in the third person) and his father are facing a sheer wall. Up this wall his father runs so easily that he seems, as Kafka put it, to be doing it almost in a dance, but he offers no help to his son, who climbs agonizingly, with tremendous effort and on all fours, often sliding back again, as if the wall had become steeper under him.

A dream or vision of Virginia Woolf's is another example of a dream speaking in symbolism of what is to come, one which assuredly offered a symbolic image of some deep emotional stress that was to be expressed in one way or another throughout her life. She tells us in the essay "A Sketch of the Past" that

> I dreamt that I was looking in the glass when a horrible face— the face of an animal—suddenly showed over my shoulder. I cannot be sure if this was a dream, or if it happened. Was I looking in the glass one day when something in the background moved, and seemed to me alive? I cannot be sure. But I have always remembered the other face in the glass, whether it was a dream or a fact, and that it frightened me.[3]

Earlier in this particular essay, Woolf said that at the age of six or seven she had got into the habit of looking at her face in the hall mirror, but only if she was alone, for she was ashamed of doing this. Somehow a strong feeling of guilt was attached to the act, and she felt as an adult, looking back, that that feeling of shame went very deep, perhaps inherited from the puritanical Clapham Sect, of which there were members in her family. But she also connected it with the fact that when she was very small her much older stepbrother had explored her body, and that she had dumbly disliked and strongly resented this, so that she felt at the time of writing that there must be something instinctive in the feeling that certain parts of the body are private. "It proves," she wrote, "that Virginia Stephen was not born on the 25th of January 1882, but was born many thousands of years ago; and had from the very first encounter instincts already acquired by thousands of ancestresses in the past."[4]

These words speak clearly to me of Jung's idea of the unconscious. He says of it that on the one hand there is the personal unconscious, which gives us our little dreams, easily forgotten, if remembered at all, and, on the other, our big dreams, which come from a much deeper level, from the collective unconscious, and that reveal their significance, aside "from the subjective impression they make, by their plastic form, which often has a poetic beauty and force."[5]

The force of Woolf's dream or vision and the fact that she never forgot it would seem to point to the fact that it came from deeper levels, and that therefore it spoke of something larger and more inclusive than the personal, as Woolf herself seemed to recognize in speaking of her thousands of ancestresses of the past. However, it remains that she could never powder her nose in public or be fitted for a new dress or come into the public eye wearing it without being frightened. She experienced "raptures and ecstacies spontaneously and intensely,"[6] she says, so long as they were not connected with her own body. Therefore, she must have been ashamed of it. She was a frigid wife to Leonard Woolf, much as she loved him, and there is no overt sex in her novels, only implications in *Orlando* and in a brief passage in *Jacob's Room* and near the beginning of *The Years*. That dream or vision would seem to have spoken symbolically of a central trait in Virginia's character—her shame concerning her body and a sense of extreme privacy about it—which revealed itself in her novels.*

I I

As I began weaving together this account of various writers and their awareness of the workings of the unconscious in their writing, it became clear that, in the cases of many writers who, like Woolf, were in close contact with the unconscious, they not only exhibited a certain doubleness but also that this doubleness is revealed in the protagonist of their most famous work. We think of the case of Mary Shelley and her *Frankenstein,* Robert Louis Stevenson and *Dr. Jekyll and Mr. Hyde,* Louis Carroll and his *Alice,* and James M. Barrie and his *Peter Pan.* You might call this situation, collectively, "The Case of the Fractured Four." I shall not speak at length of *Frankenstein* or of *The Case of Dr. Jekyll and Mr. Hyde* because Joyce Carol Oates has already done so most admirably in her *(Woman) Writer: Occasions and Opportunities.* But I would like to explore Carroll's doubleness in connection with Alice and Barrie's in connection with Peter Pan.

What the Reverend Charles Lutwidge Dodgson, known more generally to the world as Lewis Carroll, would have made of the pronouncements of the critic-psychologists in our time regarding the two *Alice*s is hard to imagine. He might have been disgusted, amused, irritated, or even, quite possibly, given his logical, exploratory mind, interested. Certainly we ourselves can't help but be fascinated by those findings collected in *Aspects of Alice: Lewis Carroll's Dreamchild as Seen Through the Critics' Looking-Glasses* (edited by Robert Phillips), con-

---

*See Louise DeSalvo's *Virginia Woolf: The Impact of Childhood Sexual Abuse on Her Life and Work* (Boston: Beacon Press, 1989), laying Woolf's avoidance of sex in her novels wholly to childhood experiences and taking no notice of deeper levels of the unconscious, which could speak of something larger and more inclusive than the personal.

sidering all the evidence they offer for their authors' beliefs. And no matter how he explained those events in the *Alice*s that the psychologists have plucked forth for layers of meanings, he did recognize quite clearly the work of the unconscious in his own writing:

> *Alice* and the *Looking-Glass* are made up almost wholly of bits and scraps, single ideas which came of themselves. In writing out [*Alice's Adventures under Ground*], I added many fresh ideas, which seemed to grow of themselves upon the original stock, and many more were added when, years afterwards, I wrote it all out again for publication; but (this may interest some readers of *Alice* to know) every such idea and nearly every word of the dialogue *came of itself*. Sometimes an idea comes at night, when I have to get up and strike a light to note it down—sometimes when out on a lonely winter walk, when I have had to stop, and with half-frozen fingers jot down a few words which should keep the new-born idea from perishing—but whenever or how it comes, *it comes of itself*. I cannot set invention going like a clock, by any voluntary winding up; nor do I believe that any *original* writing (and what other writing is worth preserving?) was ever so produced.[7]

Furthermore, he said in his introduction to *Sylvie and Bruno:*

As the years went on, I jotted down, at odd moments, all sorts of odd ideas, and fragments of dialogue, that occurred to me— who knows how?—with a transitory suddenness that left me no choice but either to record them then and there, or to abandon them to oblivion. Sometimes one could trace to their source these random flashes of thought—as being suggested by the book one was reading, or struck out from the "flint" of one's mind by the "steel" of a friend's chance remark—but they had also a way of their own, of occurring, *a propos* of nothing—specimens of that hopelessly illogical phenomenon, "an effect without a cause."

Such, for example, was the last line of "The Hunting of the Snark," which came into my head . . . quite suddenly, during a solitary walk; and such, again, have been passages which have occurred in dreams, and which I cannot trace to any antecedent whatever.[8]

Now if Carroll had been speaking only of *Sylvie and Bruno,* Joan Aiken would be justified in the following criticism of his method, but he was speaking of his writings in general. She quotes this paragraph of his in her Library of Congress lecture and says that it seems to her to be "an absolute blueprint of how *not* to construct a children's book."[9] But, you see, Carroll did not "construct" his books; he let them "well up," as you will find Maurice Sendak does. For it isn't a matter of sticking one's visitations together, of making "a children's book out of 'odds and ends,'" as Aiken concluded from Carroll's remarks he must have done. Sendak has had precisely the same experience as Carroll. Concerning *Outside over There,* which he gives as an example of how inspiration arises, he said that the Lindbergh kidnapping obsessed him; a girl in the rain—a character in one of his childhood books who imprinted herself on his brain when he was six or seven—obsessed feelings about his own childhood always obsessed him. They seem to be very disparate, Sendak said, but somehow as an artist you have a kind of faith that they *will* come together. The unconscious has such a need to make an artistic whole that you just have to wait. And of course Carroll was always willing to wait. There was never any question.

In my essay "With Wrinkled Brow and Cool Fresh Eye," I confess that for many years I was impatient with psychological criticism, feeling that many a novel has been completely misrepresented by false interpretations and ridiculous psychological assumptions. Furthermore, I thought, how can we possibly know what the writer had deeply in mind during the writing? We can't. Yes, but then, it might very well be, neither did the writer. Concerning *The Hunting of the Snark,* which Martin Gardner sees as having an existential meaning,

Carroll wrote toward the end of his life: "I'm very much afraid I didn't mean anything but nonsense! Still, you know, words mean more than we mean to express when we use them; so a whole book ought to mean a great deal more than the writer meant."[10] And when one reads some of the revelations the critic-psychologists have seen in *Alice in Wonderland* particularly, revelations that tell so much about that staid, conservative Reverend Dodgson, one can't help suspecting that there must have been a doubleness in the person of Dodgson-Carroll from which the unconscious spoke very clearly. As far back as Carroll's own time, anyway, that doubleness was there for Harry Furniss, his illustrator for *The Hunting of the Snark*. With Dodgson the mathematician Furniss had a wretched time, for Dodgson "would take a square inch of the drawing, count the lines I had made in that space, and compare their number with those on a square inch of an illustration made for *Alice* by Tenniel! . . . In fact, over a criticism of one drawing, I pretended I could stand Dodgson the Don no longer, and wrote to Carroll the author declining to complete the work."[11] (But of course we know that Furniss eventually did.)

Consider the details of this doubleness. One individual, the Reverend Dodgson, exchanged his clerical suit and black top hat for white flannel trousers and a straw boater when, as Lewis Carroll, storyteller, he and his friends took small girls boating and on picnics. Dodgson, in the senior common room at Oxford, was difficult, complaining, and pedantic. Carroll, when he entertained his little guests, was the most delightful companion and teller of tales imaginable. Dodgson was prissy and conservative. Carroll loved nothing better than photographing small girls in the nude, well aware of what Mrs. Grundy would think of him. Dodgson wanted every atom of attention due him for his modest inventions—his new ideas for controlling carriage traffic, for making notes in the dark, for keeping book covers clean by putting jackets on them, for keeping track of one's correspondence—and always wanted to see his light verse published. Carroll never dreamed of publication and fame. Dodgson had a stammer (therefore he was the Dodo in *Alice:* Do-do-do-Dodgson), while Carroll, at ease with little girls, lost his stammer almost entirely in their company. (But not completely, otherwise he would not have injected himself into the earliest version of *Alice* as the *Dodo*.)

Jean Gattégno, despite at least fifteen other studies and biographies of Carroll by various authors, still had a multitude of thoughts concerning Carroll and his creations, and he explores various aspects of Carroll's doubleness in his *Lewis Carroll: Fragments of a Looking-Glass*. First of all, he asks in his foreword if the author of *Alice* is a different person from the reverend mathematical lecturer of Christ College, Oxford, and answers: "I'm afraid I don't know the answer to that. In Carroll's case, the pseudonym represented far more than just a pen name: it transformed Dodgson's entire life."[12] However, he denies that it split it in two, for you can't consider either Carroll or Dodgson without considering the other. Peter Alexander, a professional logician, agrees. In his opinion, "Without Dodgson the pedantic logician, Carroll the artist would have been of considerably less importance: there was no discrepancy." And to this Gattégno adds an intriguing possibility:

On those few occasions when [Carroll] reached certain intellectual high points (or what seemed to him high points), the satisfaction he felt was as profound as, and similar in kind to, what he felt after spending the afternoon with an enchanting little girl. A joy of discovery, of invention: this is an element we must be very careful never to forget in any effort to capture the personality of Lewis Carroll.[13]

But now Gattégno takes up a further fascinating aspect of this question when he speaks of the possibility of identifying Alice with her creator, a possibility that kept impressing itself on me during my readings of *Alice,* considering two facets of her nature in connection with the two facets (or modes) of Carroll's: the prim, conservative, fussy, narrowly creative one, in company with the joyous, Mrs. Grundy-snubbing, classic-creating one.

Think of Dodgson, bossy and complaining, both aggressive and determined in wanting details taken care of exactly as he wished them to be in the senior common room, and pushing for recognition of his inventions and the publication of his light verse. Then think of Alice, who in Gattégno's opinion "is, above all, determination and aggression; there is no gentle, passive femininity about her. She knows where she wants to go, and it is none of her doing that she is not getting there more quickly. . . . Whatever concession she may make to 'good manners,' she always 'answers back.'"[14]

But surely if Gattégno wants to consider the metamorphosis by which Carroll becomes Alice, he must take into account the fact that Alice is as complex and changeable as her creator, containing within herself certain gentler traits, shyness and timidity, long associated with femininity. This practice of gender stereotyping is now highly suspect (though I must acknowledge it in order to speak to Gattégno's point in this particular instance). For the male, be he child or man, can be just as shy and timid as the female, though of course it has been traditional to present the male as aggressive and determined and knowing his own mind on the one hand, and the female as shy, timid, and not knowing her own mind on the other. All of which may have been very handy for the gentlemen, but which, as has been forced on their attention, is nonsense. Both male and female can appear either shy or aggressive on the surface with the opposite very much the truth: "He had a curiously womanish face, and in direct contradiction to his real character, there seemed to be little strength in it. . . . In the society of people of mature age he was almost old maidishly prim in his manner."[15] So Isa Bowman, one of Carroll's closest friends, described him.

To give examples of Alice's complexity and to oppose Gattégno's picture of her as all "determination and aggression," I find her replying "shyly" to the Caterpillar, and later "timidly" and "pleading in a piteous tone." Time and again she either speaks or acts "timidly," complains of being "never so ordered about in all [her] life, never!"

but makes no remonstrance as she follows along after the Gryphon, waits "patiently" and later answers "meekly." Above all, in chapter ten, when she offers to tell her own adventures, "'beginning from this morning,' said Alice a little timidly," she adds the provocative and revealing remark relating to this whole subject, "but it's no use going back to yesterday, because I was a different person then."

So Carroll felt this changeability in both Alice and himself. She is an idealized image of himself, says Gattégno, and if Carroll experienced

some intensely passionate feeling for the real Alice, it was not for the child but apparently for the idea of her at that particular age when his literary creation first came into being. For Carroll, this was perhaps the only time when he closely engaged with the self he wished to be, because Alice at prepubertal seven evoked the time before he went to school, an idyllic time which he seems to have remembered as one of perfect happiness.[16]

She "was not someone external to himself: *she was inside him,*" says Gattégno. "Alice is the direct figure of his sexuality because she is one of the explicit expressions of his sexuality and his own childhood personality. . . . Alice is a figure of identification."[17]

Humphrey Carpenter, in his absorbing *Secret Gardens: The Golden Age of Children's Literature from Alice in Wonderland to Winnie-the-Pooh,* sees Carroll-Dodgson in two distinct modes. This is immediately understood from the title of his Carroll-Dodgson chapter, "Alice and the Mockery of God," whose six words compactly oppose the writer Carroll to the Reverend Dodgson the don. Carpenter's thesis is that something is missing from all the imitations of *Alice,* "something which underlies the mathematical-logical comedy, and operates on a deeper level than it."[18] And that something is the constant awareness and communication of the threat "of Nothingness or Not Being, which at the very least is death and at its worst is something more frightening,"[19] and which lies just around the corner in both *Wonderland*

and *Through the Looking-Glass*. It is this characteristic that gives the books their driving purpose, "even a sense of desperate urgency, that is utterly lacking in the bland *Alice* imitations by other writers."[20]

Carpenter begins by noting Alice's fall in the novel's beginning, which could have ended in death but instead brought Alice one reminder of extinction after another. Following the shutting up like a telescope, the shrinking that might end in her going out altogether like a candle, the uncertainty as to just who she is, the possibility of drowning in her own tears, the baby in the Duchess's kitchen that ceased to be human, there is the Mad Hatter's Tea Party, which explores the arrival at a second form of nothingness. The first, you will recall, was that exploration, whose end the Gryphon couldn't face, when Alice pressed him and the Mock Turtle concerning the lessons that "lessen from day to day." Now, the time is always six o'clock at the party, so that the Hatter and Hare are condemned to an endless repetition: the setting up of endless riddles that have no answers and the final using up of everything. " 'Suppose we change the subject,' the March Hare interrupted, yawning," for the same reason the Gryphon had interrupted Alice with, "That's enough about lessons," when faced with the awful and unavoidable conclusion of Alice's questioning: the arrival at nothingness.

As Carpenter points out, only the Cheshire Cat seems immune to the threat of extinction, because it has "command over its own non-existence."[21] Humpty-Dumpty in *Through the Looking-Glass* would seem to be another free individual, as Carpenter puts it, for whom one might have hope, for Humpty-Dumpty claims "the ultimate power—words mean just what he chooses them to mean."[22] But because *Looking-Glass* is more "ruthless" than *Wonderland*, Humpty-Dumpty is not spared, and the last we and Alice hear of him is that heavy crash "which shook the forest from end to end."

Carpenter has seen fascinating instances of doubleness in Carroll. For instance, that the *Alice* books, though they are presumably comedic, are continually occupied not only with Nothingness, as illustrated above, but with violence and death, and especially with a mockery of Christian belief to an astonishing degree, when Carroll himself was the Reverend Dodgson! As examples we are reminded of how he turned Isaac Watts's "How Doth the Little Busy Bee" (a hypocritical expression of the virtue of work when you think of the state of child labor in those days) into "How Doth the Little Crocodile." He turned "'Tis the Voice of the Sluggard" into "'Tis the Voice of the Lobster" and revisioned the enormously respected "Resolution and Independence" by Wordsworth, which ends,

> "God," said I, "be my help and stay secure;
> I'll think of the Leech-gatherer on the lonely moor!"

into "Jabberwocky" (again proving how the great fantasists have a special gift for names):

> One, two! One, two! And through and through
> The vorpal blade went snicker-snack!
> He left it dead, and with its head
> He went galumphing back.

Galumphing! A combination of words—*gallop* and *triumphant*—to describe the act of moving heavily and clumsily. We use the word to this day. And one has only to read "Resolution and Independence" to wonder with an irrepressible smile how many staid British mothers and fathers, dignified and faithfully churchgoing, with high-minded convictions of what was and was not "suitable" (at least to all appearances), must have been horrified to recognize what their Reverend Dodgson had done to Wordsworth! And then, if they knew him in the latter part of his life, must have gone on wondering what on earth had happened to him when they read the following on the subject of "Irreverence." For surely they are lines in which the reverend would seem to be bitterly reproving his younger, Carroll mode.

No type of anecdote seems so sure to amuse the social circle as that which turns some familiar Bible-phrase into a grotesque parody. Sometimes the wretched jest is retailed, half-apologetically, as said by a child, "and, of course," it is added, "the *child* meant no harm!" Possibly: but does the *grown man* mean no harm, who thus degrades what he ought to treat with reverence, just to raise a laugh?[23]

So much for Alice! The elderly Dodgson will not leave Carroll even that escape hatch: of speaking in the voice of a child, or of various other beings.

But Carroll went on to another kind of more nearly blasphemous (my word, not Carpenter's, though surely Dodgson's) sort of mockery when he used the words DRINK ME and EAT ME on the bottle and cake Alice finds before she enters the garden. And it is *not* the paradise of the Garden of Eden, *not* an enchanted place, but a heartless parody of heaven where the Queen of Hearts is forever screaming "Off with her head!" Carroll's choice of words inescapably reminds Carpenter of Article XXVIII of the Anglican Creed, "Of the Lord's Supper," which states that Holy Communion is to be regarded as "a sign of the love that Christians ought to have among themselves one to the other" as well as "a Sacrament of our Redemption of Christ's death." Here there is a particular echo out of Article XXVIII: ". . . and when he had given thanks, he brake it, and gave it to his disciples, saying, Take, eat; this is my Body which is given for you. . . . Drink ye all of this; for this is my Blood."

Carpenter offers the answer proposed by Elizabeth Sewell in her book *The Field of Nonsense,* "that both the parodies and the anguished piety spring from the same thing, the fact that Dodgson's religious beliefs were utterly insecure. . . . And indeed we find a distinct suggestion of insecurity in religion in his refusal to proceed fully into Holy Orders."[24] I can only take it further: If there had been no insecurity in Dodgson, the *Alice*s and Carroll would have been entirely wiped out. And if there had been no admixture in Carroll of Dodgson's type of fussy mind, which loved to play with logic and language and make puzzles and invent things—the type of mind that provided that exceedingly necessary tension between the two extremes of Dodgson and Carroll—there would have been no *Alice*s as we know them, and surely no *Alice*s as unforgettable.

In December 1915 James Barrie had a nightmare that he afterward used as the core of a play, *The Fight for Mr. Lapraik*. Mr. Lapraik is schizophrenic, and Barrie often spoke of himself as having a divided personality, recognizing what he called his writing half, which lived with the uncontrollable, "unruly" other half (whom Barrie called M'Connachie, a name that was to become a curse to him in later life). Yet the two combined to create the most incredible, lavishly triumphant success any writer could possibly hope for in *Peter Pan*. The nightmare recurred, a nightmare of "some vaguely apprehended interloper who was, and yet somehow was not, himself." As Barrie himself described it in his notebook:

At last I rushed from the darkness to my mother's room [she has been dead for many years] & cried to her abt my degenerate self—[the] thing I have evolved into was trying to push me out of bed and take my place. Till the moment of telling I had no idea what the thing was.[25]

And the play, which for some reason never evolved beyond the typescript, concerned a young Mr. Lapraik, who, as a ghost, comes to tell his now elderly wife that he is her husband. When she asks who her present husband is, the ghost of the young Lapraik replies that it is the man he himself has grown into, a man who has apparently lost all the "fine ideas and conduct and aspirations of twenty-five years ago." And he tells her how he had once lain asleep and awakened to find "something bending over me, pushing me stealthily. . . . I knew that that degenerate thing I had become was trying to push me out of this shell that is called me, to take my place."*[26]

When Barrie read his nightmare-induced play aloud to his friends the Asquiths, Asquith remarked on the "unforgettably eerie" sense he had of how Barrie was able to enter completely into the struggle between the two personalities, one good and the other evil, for the possession of poor, ordinary Mr. Lapraik. " 'I can't describe,' Asquith said, 'the disquieting tricks he played with face and voice, nor how visibly and audibly he split himself into the two Mr. Lapraiks.' "[27] And Michael Egan has pointed out in "The Neverland as Id: Barrie, *Peter Pan,* and Freud" how the two sides of Barrie are mercilessly revealed in *Peter Pan.* "Apparently," says Egan, "he had unusual access to his own unconsciousness," and since Barrie could not "have been familiar with psychoanalytic thinking, given the exigencies of place and time, we must conclude that he achieved all this by scooping unwittingly, as it were, into the bubbling turmoil of his own half-formulated wishes and ambitions."[28]

---

*It is intriguing that, in both Mary Shelley's and Robert Louis Stevenson's novels, just such a scene occurs of a "degenerate other half" standing at the bedside of its creator, not necessarily trying to take his place, but *there.* For we read in *Franken-stein,* remembering that Frankenstein is the name of the creator and not the ghastly thing he has created: "He [Frankenstein] sleeps; but he is awakened; he opens his eyes; behold, the horrid thing stands at his bedside, opening his curtains and looking on him with yellow, watery, but speculative eyes." How that word *speculative* haunts us!

And in Stevenson's tale, the lawyer Utterson, who tells the tale of his friend Jekyll's disintegration and downfall, and knowing that Jekyll's other self, Hyde, has trampled a child, sees in his mind "a room in a rich house, where his friend lay asleep, dreaming and smiling in his dreams; and then the door of that room would be opened, the curtains of the bed plucked apart, the sleeper recalled, and lo! there would stand by his side a figure to whom power was given, and even at that dead hour, he must rise and do its bidding."

In Stevenson's unconscious, surely there lay the memory of that scene in *Franken-stein,* made vivid and immediate by his own dreams, by something in him that *understood.* In all three cases, it is the shadow self, the unconscious self, that awakens its other half to look on what it has willfully brought into being.

Now, adding to what Egan has drawn out of his explorations concerning the relationship of Barrie, *Peter Pan,* and Freudian theory, I should like to lay a basis for some of the facts of Barrie's haunted, in many ways tragic, life, facts all bearing on his doubleness, so that the reader will understand more clearly a number of the details so perceptively brought out in Egan's critical analysis.

At the end of *Peter Pan,* you may recall, after Peter and Tinker Bell have brought Wendy and Michael and John home, Mrs. Darling finds her children all cozy in their beds again. Peter and Tink fly off, Mr. Darling (who had consigned himself to the doghouse all this time for having chained up Nana, the guardian Newfoundland, with the result that Peter was able to steal the children away), comes joyfully forth, and he and his wife and children resume their former life. The years pass, and:

> As you look at Wendy you may see her hair becoming white, and her figure little again, for all this happened long ago. Jane [Wendy's daughter] is now a common grown-up, with a daughter called Margaret; and every spring-cleaning time, except when he forgets, Peter comes for Margaret and takes her to the Neverland, where she tells him stories about himself, to which he listens eagerly. When Margaret grows up she will have a daughter, who is to be Peter's mother in turn; and thus it will go on, so long as children are gay and innocent and heartless.

Thus ends the tale of *Peter Pan,* with Peter destined to go on forever, himself gay and heartless certainly, but innocent we must question, for after all he *has,* in certain moods, become Hook. And he has long ago forgotten Wendy, Jane, and Margaret and even Tinker Bell, for there are so many fairies to take Tink's place and so many new little daughters to take Wendy's, Jane's, and Margaret's. For Peter there is virtually no time, except in flashes—only an eternal now and what he desires in it, with no regard for anyone else. And that is the end of "that terrible masterpiece,"[29] as the real Peter called it.

And terrible it was.

There were once five small boys, the cherished sons of Arthur and Sylvia Llewellyn Davies—George, John (Jack), Peter, Michael, and Nicholas (Nico), in order of age. For these boys Barrie wrote *Peter Pan*. He adored them *and* their mother, and would have been devastated to know that because of his terrible masterpiece the following headlines appeared on the front page of one London newspaper after another on April 6, 1960: BARRIE'S PETER PAN KILLED BY A LONDON SUBWAY TRAIN, THE BOY WHO NEVER GREW UP IS DEAD, PETER PAN STOOD ALONE TO DIE, PETER PAN'S DEATH LEAP, PETER PAN COMMITS SUICIDE, THE TRAGEDY OF PETER PAN. As the *London Daily Express* explained:

> Until he died at 68 [actually 63] Peter Davies was Peter Pan. He was the Little Boy Who Never Grew Up; the boy who believed in fairies. The name was the gift to him of playwright Sir James Barrie, and Peter Davies hated it all his life. But he was never allowed to forget it until, as a shy, retiring publisher, he fell to his death on Tuesday night.[30]

There are inaccuracies in these lines. Peter Llewellyn Davies was *not* Peter Pan until he died—he loathed the idea; he *did* grow up; and he did *not* believe in fairies.

Remember Peter Pan's words: "To die will be an awfully big adventure." Andrew Birkin, in his *J. M. Barrie and the Lost Boys: The Love Story that Gave Birth to Peter Pan*, reveals what an enormous release death must have looked to Peter Davies. And behind the Llewellyn Davies family's part in the creation of *Peter Pan* stands another small boy, James Barrie himself. For when Barrie was six his older brother, David, died: David, whom their mother, Margaret Ogilvy, adored for his cheery nature, for just his special way of standing with his legs apart and his hands in the pockets of his knickerbockers, whistling. Beside him, the quiet Jamie was nothing but a shadow. Margaret Ogilvy's grief over David's death was "a catastrophe beyond belief,"[31] wrote her younger son, something she never got over, and Barrie was devastated, not only by the loss of David but by his mother's refusal to recognize him as someone worth loving and being comforted by in David's place. "When I became a man," wrote Barrie in his notebook, "he was still a boy of thirteen." And from the fact that Margaret Ogilvy "drew comfort from the notion that David, in dying a boy, would remain a boy forever," Barrie drew inspiration.[32]

Though it took thirty-three years, the idea of that ever-youthful boy proved to be the seed, planted in Barrie's unconscious at the age of six, a seed that grew and flourished into the apparently immortal being Peter Pan. "Apparently immortal" because he is still vividly alive in all our minds more than three-quarters of a century after Barrie's novel was first published, in 1911. His story goes into edition after edition, one of the more recent a special one illustrated by Trina Schart Hyman in 1980.

As for Wendy, she was Margaret Ogilvy. Barrie, who finally in desperation brought himself to his mother's attention by putting on the persona of his brother (even whistling and standing with his legs apart), was already beginning to play many roles and to experience the doubleness that proved to be a quality of the peculiar giftedness that made *Peter Pan* and others of his writings possible, but that at the same time bewildered and affronted so many of those who knew him and whom he loved. Wanting now to get inside his mother's childhood, he questioned her closely about her early years.

She told him of her mother's death—a death that made her the mistress of the house at the age of eight, scrubbing and mending and baking and sewing and becoming mother to her small brother, but in her childishness suddenly pelting outside to play dumps and palaulays with the other children. Thus it was, in Barrie's imagination, that she became after thirty-three years Wendy, mothering Peter Pan and the Lost Boys in the little house in the Neverland. Invariably, he confessed, "I soon grow tired of writing tales unless I can see a little girl, of whom my mother has told me, wandering confidently through the pages. Such a grip has her memory of her girlhood had upon me since I was a boy of six."[33]

Barrie's doubleness, as we shall see, manifests itself both in the character of Peter Pan and that of James Hook, the tyrannical pirate captain of his "dogs"—his cringing, terrified, subservient crew. And interesting, isn't it, that Barrie should have given his own first name to that cruel, heartless, and yet somehow, most subtly, in certain moods, attractive man—as Wendy sometimes found him. It is as if Barrie were saying in effect, "Look, here is the M'Connachie side of me, the dark, unruly side—*Hook!*"

Of *Margaret Ogilvy,* the story of his mother, a story questionably true to the facts of her life, George Blake wrote, "For all his understanding of women and children, we have to deal here with what seems to be a case of refined sadism."[34] And in his own semiautobiographical novel, *When a Man's Single,* he said, "My God! . . . I would write an article, I think, on my mother's coffin."[35]

Now, Barrie was a very small man and mourned that if only he had been six feet three his one aim would have been to become a favorite with the ladies, whereupon he would never have bothered turning out reels of printed matter. But as he was small and shy, never flirted in his life, and never "had a woman,"[36] he might have foreseen that his marriage to Mary Ansell would be a failure.

Meanwhile, Barrie, like the cuckoo bird that takes over another bird's nest (though Barrie could never have actually cuckolded any man), was insinuating himself into the Llewellyn Davies family because of Sylvia and the boys. "There was never a simpler, happier family until the coming of Peter Pan"; so wrote Barrie in the novel itself. And here is Barrie's description of Sylvia: "tip-tilted nose, wide-spaced grey eyes, black hair and a crooked smile." As for Mrs. Darling in *Peter Pan:*

> She was a lovely lady, with a romantic mind and such a sweet
> mocking mouth. Her romantic mind was like the tiny boxes,
> one within the other, that come from the puzzling East, however

many you discover there is always one more; and her sweet mocking mouth had one kiss on it that Wendy could never get to,
though there it was, perfectly conspicuous in the righthand corner. . . . Mr. Darling . . . took a cab and nipped in first, and
so he got her. He got all of her, except the innermost box and
the kiss. He never knew about the box, and in time gave up
trying for the kiss.

But here is Barrie's mocking description of Mr. Darling:

Mr. Darling used to boast to Wendy that her mother not only
loved him but respected him. He was one of those deep ones
who know about stocks and shares. Of course no one really knows,
but he quite seemed to know, and he often said that stocks were
up and shares were down in a way that would have made any
woman respect him.

Mr. Darling was always worrying about money—he had to. They
were not at all well off, which was why they had Nana, a "prim
Newfoundland," for a nanny instead of a respectable nurse in a starched
apron and cap, wheeling a very fine perambulator. This troubled Mr.
Darling,

who had a passion for being exactly like his neighbors. . . . No
nursery could possibly have been conducted more correctly, and
Mr. Darling knew it, yet he sometimes wondered uneasily
whether the neighbors talked. He had his position to consider.
Nana also troubled him in another way. He had sometimes a
feeling that she didn't admire him. "I know she admires you
tremendously, George," Mrs. Darling would assure him, and she
would sign to the children to be specially nice to father.

What could have been more devastating than these pages in *Peter
Pan,* not to speak of the description of Sylvia with that tiny inmost

box of hers and the sweet mocking mouth with the one kiss that Mr. Darling finally had to give up trying for? The brazenness of Barrie is beyond belief.

However, still worse is to come. At the end of the novel, when the children and the Lost Boys have come home and Peter and Tinker Bell have flown off, Mr. Darling is "curiously depressed" when the boys line up in a row in front of Mrs. Darling and "their eyes [ask] her to have them." He is depressed because "he thought they should have asked his consent as well." Possibly Arthur Llewellyn Davies had the traits Barrie ascribed to him to one small degree or another. The point is, however, that Barrie was having the cruelest, the most M'Connachie kind of fun at Arthur's expense.

But Barrie was inscrutable. During 1906, the terrible last year of Arthur's life, when he had developed cancer of the jaw and had to have an operation that dreadfully disfigured his handsome face, Barrie could not do enough either for him or for the family. Several years after Arthur died, Sylvia too died of cancer,* and Barrie adopted the boys and devoted the rest of his life to them, or as much as they needed of it, for there was always his work. His one misery, aside from what he had suffered over the loss of Sylvia and would suffer over subsequent losses, was not "being at it." It is no wonder that later pictures of him show a deeply saddened, sunken-cheeked and hollow-eyed man, for first George was killed in the war, and then Michael drowned, a possible suicide.

Concerning Barrie's doubleness, which made him the most amusing, enchanting, generous companion in the world when he felt like it, Cynthia Asquith said: "His subconscious was more than a collaborator. It could, too often did, take control. He might make myriad notes before he began to write, but he never knew quite what would emerge."[37]

---

*Sylvia and Arthur could not have read the published *Peter Pan and Wendy*, which came out in 1911, but their friends and relatives would have.

. . .

It would seem that there are three aspects to Barrie's sentimentality ("so-called," Asquith would say): There is what she would call the silver-coating of his writing with the hard reality underneath; there is the aspect that, according to his friend Sir Walter Raleigh, is his "satire which doesn't quite come off"; and there is his excruciating self-indulgence in exaggerated sentiment, the kind of thing that made Anthony Hope exclaim, on leaving the theater after the first performance of *Peter Pan,* "Oh, for an hour of Herod!"[38]

Yes! And what I dislike as well in *Peter Pan* is Barrie's habit of talking over the heads of the children to the adults, winking knowingly in describing Tinker Bell as "exquisitely gowned in a skeleton leaf, cut low and square, through which her figure could be seen to the best advantage. She was slightly *embonpoint*." As for using French, Hook raises his hat with "ironical politeness" to Wendy when escorting her to the place where the Lost Boys are being gagged, and he does it "with such an air, he was so frightfully *distingué,* that she was too fascinated to cry out. She was only a little girl." It makes no difference that the child reader hasn't an idea in the world as to the meaning of the French word, or of the sexual overtones the scene arouses for adults. It was not written for children.

And of course Tinker Bell is in love with Peter and is furiously jealous of Wendy, but no doubt, as he has "a voice that no woman has yet been able to resist," and no doubt makes a habit of "gnashing his little pearls at her" (as well as at Mrs. Darling), she continually forgives him. As Wendy always does, being "every inch a woman," and when she teaches Peter about kisses: "She made herself rather cheap by inclining her face toward him." In return he tells her about fairies. "So I ran away to Kensington Gardens and lived a long time among the fairies. . . . You see, Wendy, when the first baby laughed for the first time, its laugh broke into a thousand pieces, and they all went skipping about and that was the beginning of fairies."

When it comes to sentimentality, everything to do with fairies and babies brings out the worst in Barrie, though his use of stars comes close: "A moment after the fairy's entrance the window was blown open by the breathing of the little stars, and Peter dropped in. . . . They [Mr. and Mrs. Darling] would have reached the nursery in time had it not been that the little stars were watching them. Once again the stars blew the window open, and that smallest star of all called out: 'Cave, Peter!' "

It can be seen how Barrie loves the word *little* (used again and again in *The Little Minister, The Little White Bird,* and *Peter Pan*), as did a good many of his fellow Edwardians. Surely *little* is the burden word of the Victorian and Edwardian ages, compressing into six letters a sentimentality that glossed over the reality in which "little" children worked in the mines and cotton mills and begged for food in the streets. Emily Dickinson's lesser poems make constant use of the word, which is surprising when one considers the clear, cool gaze she bent on life and death in the finest of them.

Hans Christian Andersen, who could be as cruel as Barrie in such stories as "The Shadow" and "Little Claus and Big Claus," could also be appallingly sentimental, yet not, interestingly enough, in "The Ugly Duckling," the symbolic tale of his own life, and a small masterpiece, in which aesthetic distance is always kept. There is no violin playing. Unfortunately, that is what we hear again and again in "The Little Mermaid," in which poignancy slips over into the quality that Herbert Read, in contrasting sentimentality with art, speaks of "as a release, but also a loosening, a relaxing of the emotions." Of art, on the other hand, he says that it is a "release, but also a bracing. Art is the economy of feeling; it is emotion cultivating good form."

In Andersen's story "Lovely" he makes great fun of that word, using it throughout the tale and saying in the course of it: "Oh, yes, lovely she was: lovely it cannot be repeated too often." (His fellow Victorians would have agreed, however, and not seen the mischief in his story.) Oddly enough, Andersen was onto the word *lovely* long before Barrie apparently could not help scattering it throughout his descriptions. "Oh, lovely!" people cry. Mrs. Darling is "a lovely lady," Peter Pan "a lovely boy" with "the loveliest of gurgles" as his laugh. "Oh, the lovely," cries Wendy about Tinker Bell and thinks "it is perfectly lovely the way" Peter talks about girls.

Perhaps we can't take the psychically fractured Barrie as the Peter Pan who didn't want to grow up, but as the Peter Pan who eternally needed a mother figure in order to be fulfilled emotionally—as he was emotionally tied to Sylvia; the kind of being who wanted (like Peter Pan) to keep house and have children but who wanted above all to be free and gay and innocent (of the sexual act, at any rate) and heartless. The fact that Barrie was much of the time not gay at all does not change the truth that he could be amusing and enchanting, so that people remembered him long afterward for these qualities, but heartless in such a way that he could write *Tommy and Grizel* and *Peter Pan* as he did, uncaring whom he hurt. And it is fascinating that, despite Cynthia Asquith's maintaining that he "faced the painful facts," one of the most revealing proofs of Barrie's doubleness is that he confessed he had no recollection at all of having written *Peter Pan*. It was like a dream that his unconscious did not want disclosed to its creator, or which Barrie could not accept, as if he were ashamed of it because it revealed too much of the M'Connachie side of him and had therefore to be completely erased from his conscious mind.

But it doesn't matter what one notes about Barrie's work—his sentimentality, his cruelty (as bad a combination as sentimentality and violence)—what remains is the power there is in *Peter Pan*. A piece of advertising I got from the *New York Review of Books* had a surprising figure on the flap—surprising considering the tone of this journal, its point of view, its seriousness. Who but James Barrie? There is no way of knowing, but I think Barrie would have been amused.

III

To come down to the present in speaking of dreams, art, and the unconscious, I asked three writers for children and youth what part they believed the unconscious played in their work. One replied that if the unconscious was at work at all, it sent up "nothing but garbage," implying, I gather, that her conscious mind and imagination are responsible, as far as she is aware, for what she writes (and with outstanding success). Another said that she knew far too much about psychology to give any responsible statement about her unconscious. But Lloyd Alexander wrote me:

> I have a feeling that my unconscious indeed "knows" the answers but is reluctant to tell me! It knows the answer to the riddle but makes me labor enormously to solve it. Or, sometimes, perhaps out of pity, it gives me an occasional answer as a free gift. As for dreams, I don't think I've ever dreamed specifically of anything I would be working on—or been given a specific idea in a dream. . . . But the emotional effect, the feeling tone of my dreams is usually very strong; the mood and the emotions hang on for a long time and they must surely color what work you do when you're awake. . . . Inspiration tends to go slantwise, showing up long after any specific incident. The trigger isn't always direct and immediate. . . . The mechanism, I think, is more often like a sort of creative time bomb ticking away over a longer period.

E. B. White's "creative time bomb" was a dream, and heaven knows how long it had been "ticking away" inside him. White dreamed Stuart—not the whole novel itself, but Stuart. In a March 1, 1939, letter to Eugene Saxton at Harper, he wrote:

> You will be shocked and grieved to discover that the principal character in the story has somewhat the attributes and appearance

of a mouse. This does not mean that I am either challenging or denying Mr. Disney's genius. At the risk of seeming a very whimsical fellow indeed, I will have to break down and confess to you that Stuart Little appeared to me in a dream, all complete, with his hat, his cane, and his brisk manner. Since he was the only fictional figure ever to honor and disturb my sleep, I was deeply touched, and felt that I was not free to change him into a grasshopper or a wallaby. Luckily he bears no resemblance, either physically or temperamentally, to Mickey. I guess that's a break for all of us.[39]

After the dream, as White himself has written, he went on with Stuart, involving him in a story, episode by episode, "over a period of about twelve years, for home consumption. I had nephews and nieces who wanted me to tell them a story, and that's the way I went about it. Book publication was not in my mind."[40] The first two or three chapters were written in the early 1930s, Dorothy Lobrano Guth, the editor of White's letters, tells us, and the last two, says White, were "no dream, they were a nightmare: I wrote them doggedly and while under the impression that I was at death's door and should catch up on loose ends."[41] White so often felt this, as you will discover if you read his letters, which are funny in the inimitable White way, melancholy, tragic toward the end, engrossing, endearing, enchanting, and illuminating about himself and about life.

Now, White's awareness of Stuart's resemblance to a mouse right at the very beginning, and his devotion to his dream—as revealed in his firm statement that he would not feel "free to change him into a grasshopper or a wallaby"—sit oddly with his later protestations that Stuart is not really a mouse. These come *after* he had received the famous letter from Anne Carroll Moore (then newly retired from her position as head of work with children at the New York Public Library) in which she totally rejects the whole idea of the novel, saying that "it mustn't be published,"[42] and *after* he had read and heard appalled exclamations from various sources concerning the idea of a perfectly decent, normal, healthy American housewife being delivered of a *mouse*. Revolting! Before all this happened, in a letter to Eugene Saxton about a month and a half after he has sent Saxton the unfinished manuscript and they are thinking of fall publication, he is considering a possible illustrator and says: "It would have to be somebody who likes mice and men."[43] In other words, at that point he doesn't at all seem to be put off by Stuart's clear resemblance to a mouse. And in May of the publication year, 1945, when he is writing to Ursula Nordstrom, his editor, about the illustrations by Garth Williams, he speaks only of Harriet, of how her legs should look more attractive and her skirt be fuller, and that "Dr. Carey looks a lot like President Truman."[44] But there is no objection at all to Williams's depiction of Stuart, who is very definitely a mouse—you couldn't by any stretch of the imagination call him anything else.

And as late as 1965, he writes in a letter: "In 'Stuart Little' an American family has a two inch mouse. This is highly questionable and would be, I guess, bad if it were stated in any other than in a matter-of-fact way."[45] In 1969 he wrote Nordstrom that "Garth's Stuart was superb and did much to elevate the book."[46] And in a beautifully generous statement to Williams (in a letter expressing his great sorrow that Williams had, after all, failed to get the job of illustrating *The Trumpet of the Swan*), he speaks of Williams's characterization of Stuart, "which really blew life into him and was the start of the whole business. Without your contribution, I don't think Stuart would have traveled very far."[47] (We must, I think, be privileged to differ, as fine as Garth Williams's illustrations are.)

Apparently it was the period directly after the publication of *Stuart Little* that was the rough time for White as far as his notion of a woman being delivered of a mouse was concerned. For in November of the publication year, White wrote to Nordstrom that the Harper ads referring to Stuart as a mouse were "inaccurate" and had probably better be abandoned. Nowhere in the book (and I think I am right about this) is Stuart described as a mouse. He is a small guy who looks very much like a mouse, but he obviously is not a mouse. He is a second son. . . . (I am wrong, Stuart *is* called a mouse on Page 36—I just found it. He should not have been.) Anyway, you see what I mean.[48]

But, unfortunately, how *could* Nordstrom see what he meant, when he denies that Stuart is a mouse and yet he himself has called him one? What *is* obvious is that White's devotion to his unconscious, which had given him Stuart as a gift in a dream, is at war with all the horrified exclamations coming from the world of public opinion (to the point where the New York Public Library was reluctant to put *Stuart Little* on its shelves, for Anne Carroll Moore's presence and her opinions were very strongly felt even after she retired). White had an extremely low regard for Moore's letter, though he was generous enough to write Frances Clarke Sayers, who followed Moore as head of the children's department at the library, that he would continue to support the system by which librarians and book committees are free to select books without pressure from interested parties.

It is revealing that White seems, here and there in his life, to have been particularly aware of mice. In the midst of one of his depleting nervous spells (of which he had many), he spoke of having mice in the unconscious. And one of his favorite adjectives is *tiny*, as you will find in reading the letters and essays. A childhood experience just may have had something to do with his unconscious bringing forth the mouse dream (the "creative time bomb ticking away over a longer period"). Once when he was sick in bed, he tells us, he "had a mouse take up" with him. "He was a common house mouse and I think he must have been a very young one, as he was friendly and without fear. I made a home for him, complete with gymnasium, and he learned many fine tricks and was pleasant company."[49]

What led up to this story was his reply to a letter about a mouse who was visiting his friend Faith McNulty Martin, whom he instructs to find out whether her mouse is *Peromyscus maniculatus* (deer mouse) or *Peromyscus leucopus* (white-footed mouse). "Until you know *that,* you are enveloped in mysticism and are really not free to talk at all—except to a mouse."[50] He then goes on to make her what he calls "a horrid confession":

Not long ago I had a mouse visiting my desk at night. He came because I had a small crock of water with a sponge in it next to my jar of pencils, and it was obvious that the mouse was visiting this convenient little spring, for a drink. The sponge is yellow plastic, and my mouse would leave his tiny turds in the tiny craters of the sponge. I tired of this after a while, but kept hoping I would catch a glimpse of my visitor. I didn't, so I set a back-breaker trap, baiting it carefully with smoky bacon. Next morning the mouse lay there, his back broken, his eyes wide open, as though incredulous to the last. It was a Deer Mouse, very beautiful in death, and I could have slit my throat with remorse. But then I got wondering how prejudiced a man can get—why was I perfectly prepared to kill a house mouse but not a beautiful Deer Mouse with its soft white underbelly and white feet? I belong in Birmingham among the white supremicists.[51]

One more item about White and mice. I can't remember which of White's resemblances to Stuart came first for me, appearance or character. But let us take appearance first. This struck me when I was looking at the photographs of him in later years, which are interleaved with the letters—the slimness of his face, the effect of his mustache, the length and fineness of his nose. And then what did I find in the letters but one from White to his wife's children that reports the words of one Annie Parson, who had

knocked out a 14-page dissertation entitled "Characteristics of E. B. White as Shown through his Essays and Children's Books."

Annie is a powerful writer. "It is quite possible (she wrote) to believe that Stuart Little *is* E. B. White. Indeed, in real life, Mr. White physically resembles a mouse. He is about five feet six inches tall, with a little pointed face and sharp ears." (This puts a new light on my passion for cheese.)[52]

As to White's temperamental likeness to Stuart, you will recall that despite Stuart's family's love and concern for him, he simply takes off one fine day when he decides that he must make a quest for his beloved bird, Margalo, a symbol for the human quest for happiness, White often explained. Without so much as a word to his family, and stopping only at a department store to buy suitable clothes on their charge account, off he goes. What wretched anxieties they might suffer are, apparently, of no concern to him, and we never hear of them again throughout the rest of the book.

In a long, long letter to his wife, Katharine—which he writes because if he tried to tell her what he has in mind, he "would only stutter and grow angry at myself for inexactitudes of meanings (and probably at you, too, for misinterpreting my muddy speech)"—he lays out his plans that he has *already decided on* for his own freedom. He is going to take what he calls "My Year," or his "year of grace," in order to find himself and perhaps write a book, the book of his dreams; in other words, to go in quest of *his* Margalo, leaving Katharine to get on with her job as fiction editor at the *New Yorker*. He wants to make use of his talents, he says, "such as they are"; he isn't having any fun at his job, is in a rut, and he longs "to recapture something which everyone loses when he agrees to perform certain creative miracles on specified dates for a particular sum." All of this is to inform Katharine "of a new allegiance—to a routine of my own spirit rather than to a fixed household & office routine. I seek the important privilege of not coming home to supper unless I happen to. I plan no absences [but he *did* go off to Maine a good deal of the time], I plan no attendances. No plans." He realizes that the whole thing "sounds selfish and not much fun for you; but that's the way art goes. You let

yourself in for this, marrying a man who is supposed to write something, even though he never does. . . . Will be glad to answer any
questions, or argue the whole matter out if it fails to meet with your
approval or pleasure."[53]

Apparently it did meet with Katharine's approval, at least. Because
away went White. And, though White was far more thoughtful in
his leave-taking, still, we *are* reminded just slightly of Stuart.

Ursula Le Guin would understand perfectly what Lloyd Alexander
means by the "creative time bomb ticking," as would all the writers
included here. When she was a child, she says in her Library of
Congress lecture, "The Child and the Shadow," she read the tales of
Hans Christian Andersen. She "hated all of the Andersen stories with
unhappy endings,"[54] but one of them she hated especially, the one
called "The Shadow." Yet she reread it many times and remembered
it so clearly that after a gap of over thirty years when she was pondering
her talk, "a little voice suddenly said inside my left ear, 'You'd better
dig out that Andersen story, you know, about the shadow.' "[55] It is
a cruel one, as so many Andersen stories are cruel, but this one is
extraordinarily so, a "story about insanity, ending in humiliation and
death," as Le Guin puts it. In essence is is about a civilized, learned,
kindly, idealistic, decent man, who sounds like Andersen himself.
And the shadow in the story is "all that gets suppressed in the process
of becoming a decent, civilized adult. The shadow is man's thwarted
selfishness, his unadmitted desires, the swearwords he never spoke,
the murders he didn't commit. The shadow is the dark side of the
soul, the unadmitted, the inadmissible."[56]

With these words we are being taken back to Barrie's dream and
Mr. Lapraik, to his unremembered creating of Peter Pan/Hook, and
to all the rebellions and furies and cruelties and cold vengeances Lewis
Carroll so lightly, ironically, wittily, and comically wove into *Alice.*
It reminds us, too, of his *Pillow Problems,* a collection of exercises in
mental arithmetic, which Carroll recommended not only as amuse-

ments for sleepless nights but as a way of driving off negative and blasphemous reflections and those "unholy thoughts, which torture with their hateful presence the fancy that would fain be pure."[57]

Le Guin had already experienced the "time bomb" long before she gave her Library of Congress talk. Those who are familiar with the writings of Carl Jung know that the inferior being within us, that aspect of ourselves that wants to do all the forbidden things we never allow ourselves to do, who is everything that we, consciously, are not, he called the shadow. And Le Guin's *A Wizard of Earthsea* is a wonderfully gifted expression of man's having to turn and face his shadow and name it with his own name if he is to have any peace, indeed if he is to live at all. It is an extended metaphor concerning the necessity of coming to terms with the dark side of the unconscious, just as Jung described it in those words I quoted earlier: "Man becomes whole, integrated, calm, fertile, and happy when (and only when) the process of individuation is complete."[58] (Elsewhere Jung says of individuation that all these moments in the individual's life, when the universal laws of human fate break in upon the purposes, expectations, and opinions of the personal consciousness, are stations along the road of the individuation process. This process is, in effect, the spontaneous realization of the whole man.) And the truly astonishing part of the entire matter of Le Guin's writing *Wizard* in just the way she did was that she had never read Jung. No, but she *had* read, decades before, when she was a child, Andersen's story "The Shadow." And did Jung, too, perhaps, read it as a child and get his conception of the shadow from Andersen's story? It would seem a question worth asking, though it probably cannot be answered.

Meanwhile, the "time bomb" was ticking away in Le Guin's unconscious, coalescing the conception of Andersen's driven man into her own private conception of the wizard Ged, hunted almost to the brink of defeat by his own terrible shadow, which he had released into visible and powerful life in a moment of arrogant, hating, envious passion, a shadow that had the power to destroy not only Ged himself but any being it wished if left to wander Earthsea.

But here is something else. The first green shoot of the Wizard trilogy appeared in 1964, when Le Guin wrote the short story about magical transformations called "The Word of Unbinding," which takes place on an island. Yes, on an island, she was quite clear about that, one among many islands, even though she hadn't given much attention to place. However, later she had the distinct feeling that this island lay up to the north of Pendor, from which came the dragon Yvaud in "The Rule of Names," her second story set in this as yet almost totally unexplored world, which lay there waiting for her to create in words. And it is fascinating to find her saying in an essay, "Dreams Must Explain Themselves," that she is not sure even now what that particular island was called, and she speaks of "later voyages of discovery."[59] It would seem almost as if that world of Earthsea already lay, totally existent, in her unconscious and needed only her undivided attention, her complete absorption, to be uncovered and brought to the full light of day.

Some years after that another curious thing happened to Le Guin in the course of her writing—an intimation of the collective unconscious, that all-enveloping sea that surrounds our individual islands. In *The Word for World Is Forest*, she posits the Athsheans, a race of gentle forest beings on another planet, whose cultural tradition it is to use dreams and the telling of them as therapy, a way of releasing children from guilt and psychoses. When the psychologist Dr. Charles Tart asked Le Guin if she had modeled her conception on the Senoi people of Malaya, she asked in astonishment: "The who?" In the first place, for the Athsheans, Le Guin had written, the word for "dream" is the same as for "root," and this is the key to the kingdom of these forest people. They have Lord Dreamers, who dream the great, slow, deep-running dreams, who can "weave and shape, direct and follow, start and cease at will," and who can walk the road the dream goes.* Children dream only in sleep; the skilled adult Athsheans dream

---

*Here again we are reminded of Jung when he says that "The 'big' or 'meaningful' dreams come from this deeper level," the collective unconscious.

awake. Or rather, "their dream-state is neither sleeping nor awake: a condition that relates to Terran [or Earth human] dreaming-sleep as the Parthenon to a mud hut: the same thing basically, but with the addition of complexity, quality, and control." The Great Dreamers are also healers, and they use the unskilled dreamers' dreams to heal and to teach how to dream, so that there comes a moment for the initiate when there is no longer any difference between world time and dream time. And when once you have learned "to balance sanity not on the razor's edge of reason but on double support, the fine balance of reason and dream; once you have learned that, you cannot unlearn it any more than you can unlearn to think."

Now, as for the Senoi people of Malaya, writes Kilton Stewart in *Altered States of Consciousness,* edited by Dr. Tart:

Breakfast in the Senoi house is like a dream clinic, with the father and older brothers listening to and analyzing the dreams of all the children. . . . When the Senoi child reports a falling dream, the adult answers with enthusiasm, "That is a wonderful dream, one of the best a man can have. Where did you fall to, and what did you discover?". . . That which was an indwelling fear and anxiety, becomes an indwelling joy or act of will; that which was ill esteem toward the forces which caused the child to fall in his dream, becomes good will towards the denizens of the dream world, because he relaxes in his dream and finds pleasurable adventures, rather than waking up with a clammy skin and crawling scalp. . . . Dream characters are bad only as long as one is afraid and retreating from them, and will continue to seem bad and fearful as long as one refuses to come to grips with them.[60]

And the basic likeness between Le Guin's Athsheans and the Senoi of Malaya comes as a result of their basic philosophies: Neither of these peoples is warlike or violent. An Athshean, before the coming of the Terrans, could never have conceived of killing another Athshean, or any inhabitant of his planet. And, reports Kilton Stewart, "Within the tribe of the Senoi there has not been a violent crime or an inter-communal conflict for the space of two or three hundred years because of the insight and inventiveness of the Tohats [doctors who are both healers and educators] of their various communities."[61]

The "sublime spider," I've found myself calling the unconscious, which seems always to be at work. Thus, in my own case, when I return in my mind to some fiction I have a certainty I am going to write but which I have been letting rest in the dark, I am aware of being intensely grateful for the revelations awaiting me. I must struggle to express the story, when it comes to actual writing, in a way that will satisfy the inner ear, but I do not "carefully" (an adverb so often used by reviewers) *think out* such complex weavings as appear in *The Court of the Stone Children,* for example, or the patterns that emerge in other fictions. They weave themselves, seeming to grow naturally over a long period of time, sometimes with my conscious help, sometimes without it. And no matter how slow the progress or how many the moments of uncertainty, I know that it is well to recall the words of Martha Graham (already quoted in *Tree* but so apropos that I must repeat them here):

> There is a vitality, a life-force, an energy, a quickening that is translated through you into action and because there is only one of you in all of time, this expression is unique. And if you block it, it will never exist through any other medium and will be lost. The world will not have it. It is not your business to determine how good it is, nor how valuable, nor how it compares with other expressions. It is your business to keep it yours clearly and directly, to keep the channel open.[62]

In Jane Gardam's memorable novel for adults, *Crusoe's Daughter,* Polly Flint is talking with Lady Celia about Tennyson. Polly confesses that she loves Tennyson, but that she loves Daniel Defoe more. "Daniel Defoe?" cries Lady Celia. "You mean *Robinson Crusoe? Moll Flanders?*" "Yes," says Polly. "But, my child—no trace, no *trace* of poetry. No trace of poetic truth." And then Polly grows terribly angry and says in a fury: "*Robinson Crusoe* is full of poetic truth. And it is an attempt at a universal truth very differently expressed." "No form," cries Lady Celia, "no form." "It is wonderfully written," returns Polly. "It is true to [Defoe's] chosen form. Because of his verisimilitude it reads like reality. I have read it twenty-three times. In a novel, form is not always apparent at a first or second reading. Form is determined by hard secret work—in a notebook and in the subconscious and in the head."

Oh, to create something that would mean as much to someone throughout a lifetime as *Robinson Crusoe* meant to Polly Flint! But the mystery remains. We can objectively analyze and satisfy ourselves in part as to what in a deeply felt work makes it treasurable. Yet some indescribable quality lies there that eludes definition, a quality resulting from a perfect harmony and understanding between the conscious and the unconscious, between the writer as Crusoe on the island and all those mysterious intimations that come from we know not where. All the writer—and we—can do is to remember Graham's words: "Keep the channel open."

References

Preface

1. *Children's Literature Association Quarterly,* Fall 1982, pp. 33–60.
2. Ibid., p. 36.
3. Bloom, introduction to Burchfield, *Unlocking the English Language,* pp. xii–xv.

The Seed and the Vision

1. Woolf, *A Passionate Apprentice,* p. 282.
2. Woolf, *Moments of Being,* p. 81.
3. Wintle, Justin, and Emma Fisher, editors, *The Pied Pipers: Interviews with the Influential Creators of Children's Literature.* New York: Paddington Press, n.d., p. 223.
4. Woolf, *Orlando.* New York: Harcourt, 1973, pp. 189–90.
5. Gordon, *Virginia Woolf,* p. 6.
6. Sendak, with Virginia Haviland, "Questions to an Artist Who Is Also an Author," in *The Openhearted Audience,* edited by Haviland, p. 26.
7. Lanes, *The Art of Maurice Sendak,* p. 248.
8. Le Guin, in the Children's Book Council *Calendar* (now *CBC Features*), November 1977–June 1978.
9. Thirkell, *Three Houses,* p. 88.
10. Dillard, *An American Childhood,* p. 158.
11. Lopez, *Crossing Open Ground,* pp. 148–49.
12. Ibid., p. 150.

Matters of Character

1–11. Hoban, "Thoughts on a Shirtless Cyclist, Robin Hood, Johann Sebastian Bach, and One or Two Other Things," *Children's Literature in Education,* Spring 1973, pp. 5–22.
12. Dickey, *Self-Interviews,* p. 33.
13. Boston, *Memory in a House,* p. 117.
14. Moss, "The Adult-eration of Children's Books," in *Part of the Pattern: A Personal Journey Through the World of Children's Books, 1960–1985.* New York: Greenwillow, 1986, p. 117.
15. Poirier, *The Peforming Self: Compositions and Decompositions in the*

Languages of Contemporary Life.
New York: Oxford University
Press, 1971, p. 44.

The Fleas in the Cat's Fur

1. Oates, *(Woman) Writer,* p. 156.
2. Warner, *Letters,* p. 26.
3. Dillard, *Pilgrim at Tinker Creek,* p. 35.
4. Dickey, *Metaphor as Pure Adventure,* p. 8.
5. Perrin, review of Annie Dillard's *An American Childhood, New York Times Book Review,* September 27, 1987, p. 7.
6. Wills, review of Hedrick Smith's *The Power Game: How Washington Really Works, New York Times Book Review,* March 27, 1988, p. 1.
7. Barzun, "A Little Matter of Sense," *New York Times Book Review,* June 21, 1987, p. 27.
8. Dickey, *Metaphor as Pure Adventure,* p. 4.
9. Ibid.
10. Finch, review of Loren Eiseley's *The Lost Notebooks of Loren Eiseley, New York Times Book Review,* September 20, 1987, p. 4.
11. White, *Writings from The New Yorker,* p. 234.
12. Gregory, "If Education Is a Feast, Why Do We Restrict the Menu?" *College Teaching,* vol. 35, no. 3, pp. 101–6.
13. Dickey, *Metaphor as Pure Adventure,* p. 9.
14. Ibid., p. 4.
15. Warner, *Letters,* p. viii.
16. Ibid.
17. Dickey, *Metaphor as Pure Adventure,* pp. 8, 9.
18. Ibid., p. 12.
19. Ibid., pp. 12–13.
20. Ibid., p. 16.
21. Ibid., p. 17.
22. White, *Essays of E. B. White,* p. 17.
23. Ibid., pp. 20–21.
24. Ibid., p. 23.
25. Neumeyer, "The Creation of *Charlotte's Web:* From Drafts to Book," part 1, *The Horn Book,* December 1982, pp. 489–97; part 2, January 1983, pp. 617–25.
26. White, *Essays of E. B. White,* pp. 23–24.
27. Woolf, *The Letters of Virginia Woolf,* vol. 5, p. 432.
28. O'Connor, *Mystery and Manners: Occasional Prose.* New York: Farrar, Straus, 1969, pp. 58–59.
29. Garner, "A Bit More Practice," *London Times Literary Supplement,* June 6, 1968, p. 577.
30. Levin, *Enthusiasms,* pp. 167–69.
31. Pfeiffer, *The Creative Explosion,* p. 217.
32. Ibid.
33. Ibid., p. 218.
34. Ibid., p. 217.
35. Ibid.
36. Ibid.
37. Sacks, *The Man Who Mistook His Wife for a Hat: And Other Clinical Tales.* New York: Harper, 1990, pp. 184–85.
38. Greene, *The Lost Childhood and Other Essays,* p. 83.

One Woman as Writer and Feminist

1. Warner, *Letters,* p. 84.
2. *Proceedings,* 1990 Conference of

the Children's Literature Association, pp. 67–74.
3. Heilbrun, *Writing a Woman's Life,* p. 14.
4. Heilbrun, *Hamlet's Mother* and *Writing a Woman's Life,* acknowledgments.
5. Heilbrun, *Writing a Woman's Life,* pp. 56, 57, 58.
6. Spalding, *Vanessa Bell.*
7. Garnett, *Deceived with Kindness.*
8. Moers, *Literary Women,* p. 63.
9. Walker, "On Being Female, Black, and Free," in *The Writer on Her Work,* edited and with an introduction by Janet Sternberg. New York: Norton, 1981, p. 105.
10. Jong, "Blood and Guts," in *The Writer on Her Work,* p. 173.
11. Ibid., pp. 176–77.
12. Woolf, *A Room of One's Own,* p. 108.
13. Lehman, *Signs of the Times,* p. 52.
14. Laing, "The Massacre of the Innocents," *Peace News,* January 22, 1965, p. 6.
15. Priestley, *Man and Time,* p. 297.

The Inmost Secret

1. Bond, in a letter to *The Horn Book,* May 1983, pp. 283–84, with my answer following.
2. Cameron, *The Green and Burning Tree,* pp. 126–31.
3. Sayers (quoted from an article written by E. B. White entitled "The Librarian Said It Was Bad for the Children," which appeared in the *New York Times,* March 6, 1966), *Anne Carroll Moore,* pp. 242–43.

The Pleasures and Problems of Time Fantasy

1. Raverat, *Period Piece,* pp. 185–86.
2. De la Mare, "On the Alice Books," in *Aspects of Alice,* edited by Robert Phillips, pp. 60–67.
3. Chant, *The High Kings,* p. 16.
4. Ibid.
5. Le Guin, from a letter to the author.
6. Le Guin, *Always Coming Home,* p. xi.
7. Le Guin, from a letter to the author.
8. Cech, review of Betty Levin's *The Keeping Room, Christian Science Monitor,* March 16, 1981, p. 23.
9. Warner, *Letters,* p. 208.
10. Rees, *The Marble in the Water,* p. 195.
11. Lopez, *Arctic Dreams,* p. 246.
12. Ibid., pp. 246–47.

The Inimitable Frances

1. Edna Johnson, Evelyn Sickels, and Frances Clarke Sayers, editors.

On Criticism, Awards, and Peaches

1. Cole, *Remembering Laughter: The Life of Noël Coward.* New York: Penguin, 1978, pp. 370–71.
2. Ibid.
3. Carpenter, *Secret Gardens,* p. 126.
4. Ibid., p. 128.

5. Ibid., p. 126.
6. Ibid.
7. Briggs, *A Woman of Passion,* pp. xii, xx.
8. Lewis, *Surprised by Joy: The Shape of My Early Life.* New York: Harcourt, 1956, p. 14.
9. Kazin, *Contemporaries.* Boston: Atlantic-Little, Brown, 1962, pp. 495–96.
10. Pickering, Jr., "The Function of Criticism in Children's Literature," *Children's Literature in Education,* Spring 1982, p. 13.
11. Heins, editor, *Crosscurrents of Criticism,* pp. 92–125; *The Horn Book,* October 1972– April 1973.
12. Pickering, Jr., "The Function of Criticism in Children's Literature," p. 13.
13. Neumeyer, "The Creation of *Charlotte's Web,*" part 1, pp. 489–97; part 2, pp. 617–25.
14. Pickering, Jr., "The Function of Criticism in Children's Literature," p. 13.
15. Rahn, "Tailpiece: *The Tale of Two Bad Mice,*" *Children's Literature,* vol. 12 (1984), pp. 78– 91.
16. Pickering, Jr., "The Function of Criticism in Children's Literature," p. 13.
17. Woolf, *The Common Reader.* New York: Harcourt, 1925, p. 237.

With Wrinkled Brow and Cool Fresh Eye

1. Lowell, editor, *Randall Jarrell,* pp. 104–5.
2. *The Horn Book,* October 1972– April 1973; also in Heins, editor, *Crosscurrents of Criticism,* pp. 92–125.
3. Sayers, "Walt Disney Accused," *The Horn Book,* December 1965, pp. 602–7.
4. Heins, editor, *Crosscurrents of Criticism,* pp. 124–25.
5. Moore, from a letter to the author.
6. Genette, *Narrative Discourse: An Essay in Method.* Ithaca, New York: Cornell University Press, 1979, p. 266.
7. Cott, *Pipers at the Gates of Dawn: The Wisdom of Children's Literature.* New York: Random, 1983, p. 74.
8. Greene, *The Lost Childhood and Other Essays,* p. 109.
9. Ibid., p. 111, note.
10. McCarthy, *Cast a Cold Eye.* New York: Harcourt, 1950, p. 237.
11. White, *Letters of E. B. White,* p. 332.
12. Ibid., p. 373.
13. Ibid., p. 614.
14. Cameron, "High Fantasy: *A Wizard of Earthsea,*" *The Horn Book,* April 1971, pp. 129–38; also in *Crosscurrents of Criticism,* pp. 333–41.
15. Le Guin, "Dreams Must Explain Themselves," in *The Language of the Night,* p. 55.
16. Cameron, "With Wrinkled Brow and Cool Fresh Eye," *The Horn Book,* May–June 1985, p. 285.
17. Wintle and Fisher, editors, *The Pied Pipers,* p. 142.

18. Ibid., pp. 144–45.
19. Graham, "How the Story Was Told," in Carroll's *Alice's Adventures in Wonderland and Through the Looking-Glass,* p. 15.
20. Suvin, *Science Fiction Studies #7,* November 1975, p. 203.
21. Moore, *The Complete Prose of Marianne Moore,* edited and with an introduction by Patricia C. Willis. New York: Viking, 1986, p. vii.
22. Ibid., p. 170.
23. Bell, "Toward a Psychology of Telephone Conversations," in *Sociology and Everyday Life,* David Karp and William Yoels, editors. Itasca, Illinois: Peacock Publishers, 1986, p. 60.
24. Heilbrun, *Writing a Woman's Life,* p. 45.
25. Murray and Fulford, "When Jane Jacobs Took on the World," *New York Times Book Review,* February 16, 1992, p. 1.
26. Steiner, *Real Presences.* Chicago: University of Chicago Press, 1989, p. 116.
27. Dickinson, from a letter to the author.
28. Gordimer, "The Gap between the Writer and the Reader," *New York Review of Books,* September 28, 1989, p. 59.
29. Pritchett, *The Myth Makers: Essays on European Novelists, Including Russian, Spanish, and French.* New York: Random, 1979, p. 135.
30. Woolf, *The Diary of Virginia Woolf,* edited by Anne Olivier Bell (vol. 5, 1936–1941). New York: Harcourt, 1984, p. 347.
31. Forster, *Aspects of the Novel.* New York: Harcourt, 1956, p. 109.
32. Cameron, *The Green and Burning Tree,* pp. 80–81.
33. Cahill, editor, *New Women and New Fiction: Short Stories Since the Sixties.* New York: New American Library, 1986, p. xi.
34. Fuller, "Every Child Is Born a Genius," *Children's Literature,* vol. 9 (1981), p. 3.
35. Kaplan, *Mr. Clemens and Mark Twain: A Biography.* New York: Simon & Schuster, 1966, pp. 291–92.
36. Bell, *Old Friends: Personal Recollections.* New York: Harcourt, 1956, pp. 94–95.
37. Boston, *Memory in a House,* p. 140.
38. Howard, *Chaucer: His Life, His Work, His World.* New York: Dutton, 1987, p. xi.
39. Eliot, "The Cultivation of Christmas Trees," in *Collected Poems,* p. 107.
40. Bogan, *What the Woman Lived: Selected Letters of Louise Bogan, 1920–1970,* edited and with an introduction by Ruth Limmer. New York: Harcourt, 1973, p. 265.
41. Cooper, "In Defense of the Artist," in *Signposts to Criticism of Children's Literature,* edited by Robert Bator, p. 103.
42. Ibid., p. 105.
43. Ibid.
44. Ibid.
45. Ibid., p. 108.

Into Something Rich and Strange

1. Brontë, *Wuthering Heights*, p. 12.
2. Faulkner, *Selected Letters of William Faulkner*, edited by Joseph Blotner. New York: Random, 1977, p. 348.
3. Brontë, *Wuthering Heights*, p. 72.
4. Greene, *The End of the Affair*. New York: Penguin, 1977, p. 3.
5. Aiken, "Between Family and Fantasy," in *The Openhearted Audience*, edited by Virginia Haviland, p. 66.
6. Bowen, *Seven Winters and Afterthoughts*. New York: Knopf, 1962, p. 153.
7. Schorer, *The World We Imagine, Selected Essays*. New York: Farrar, Straus, 1968, p. 153.
8. Ibid.
9. Ibid.
10. Ibid., p. 8.
11. Wescott, *Images of Truth*. New York: Harper, 1962, p. 159.
12. Le Guin, from a letter to the author.
13. Woolf, *Moments of Being*, p. 81.
14. Lehmann, John, *Virginia Woolf and Her World*. New York: Harcourt, 1975, p. 12.
15. Woolf, *Moments of Being*, p. 81.
16. Bowen, *Seven Winters and Afterthoughts*, p. 158.
17. McCullers, *The Mortgaged Heart: The Previously Uncollected Writings of Carson McCullers*, edited by Margarita G. Smith. Boston: Houghton, 1971, p. 275.
18. Nabokov, *Strong Opinions*. New York: McGraw, 1973, p. 31.
19. Greene, *Collected Stories*. New York: Viking, 1973, p. vii.
20. Arieti, *Creativity, the Magic Synthesis*. New York: Basic Books, 1976, pp. 345–46.

Of Dreams, Art, and the Unconscious

1. Freeman, introduction to Jung, *Man and His Symbols*, p. 14.
2. Ibid.
3. Woolf, *Moments of Being*, p. 69.
4. Ibid.
5. Jung, *Dreams*, p. 77.
6. Woolf, *Moments of Being*, p. 68.
7. Carroll, *The Complete Sylvie and Bruno*. San Francisco: Mercury House, 1991, p. x.
8. Ibid.
9. Aiken, "Between Family and Fantasy," p. 62.
10. Carroll, *The Annotated Snark*, p. 22.
11. Gattégno, *Lewis Carroll*, p. 99.
12. Ibid., p. 3.
13. Ibid., p. 113.
14. Ibid., pp. 252–53.
15. Ibid., p. 256.
16. Ibid., p. 26.
17. Ibid., p. 257.
18. Carpenter, *Secret Gardens*, p. 59.
19. Ibid., p. 60.
20. Ibid., pp. 60–61.
21. Ibid., p. 61.
22. Ibid., p. 62.
23. Ibid.
24. Ibid., p. 64.
25. Birkin, *J. M. Barrie and the Lost Boys*, p. 255.
26. Ibid.
27. Asquith, *Portrait of Barrie*, p. 26.

28. Egan, "The Neverland as Id," *Children's Literature*, vol. 10 (1982), p. 40.
29. Birkin, *J. M. Barrie and the Lost Boys*, p. 1.
30. Ibid.
31. Ibid., p. 4.
32. Ibid., p. 5.
33. Ibid., p. 6.
34. Ibid., p. 37.
35. Ibid.
36. Ibid., p. 22.
37. Asquith, *Portrait of Barrie*, p. 218.
38. Ibid., p. 219.
39. White, *Letters of E. B. White*, p. 193.
40. Ibid., p. 644.
41. Ibid., p. 313.
42. Ibid., p. 267.
43. Ibid., p. 194.
44. Ibid., p. 265.
45. Ibid., p. 253.
46. Ibid., p. 584.
47. Ibid., p. 592.
48. Ibid., p. 270.
49. Ibid., p. 512.
50. Ibid., p. 511.
51. Ibid., p. 512.
52. Ibid., p. 564.
53. Ibid., pp. 153–56.
54. Le Guin, "The Child and the Shadow," in *The Language of the Night*, p. 61, and in *The Open-hearted Audience*, p. 104.
55. Ibid.
56. Ibid., p. 60 (*The Language of the Night*), p. 103 (*The Open-hearted Audience*).
57. Carroll, *Pillow Problems and a Tangled Tale*. New York: Dover, n.d., pp. xiii–xiv.
58. Jung, *Man and His Symbols*, p. 14.
59. Le Guin, "Dreams Must Explain Themselves," in *The Language of the Night*, p. 50.
60. Stewart, "Dream Theory in Malaya," in *Altered States of Consciousness*, edited by Dr. Charles Tart. New York: Doubleday, 1969, pp. 163, 164, 165.
61. Ibid., p. 162.
62. De Mille, Agnes, *Dance to the Piper*. New York: Da Capo, 1989, p. 335.

Bibliography *

Adams, Richard. *Watership Down*. New York: Macmillan, 1974.

Aiken, Joan. *Midnight Is a Place*. New York: Dell, 1985.

Alexander, Lloyd. *The First Two Lives of Lukas-Kasha*. New York: Dutton, 1976.

———. The Prydain series. New York: Dutton.

———. *The Remarkable Journey of Prince Jen*. New York: Dutton, 1991.

Andersen, Hans Christian. *The Complete Fairy Tales and Stories,* translated by Erik Christian Haugaard, with a foreword by Virginia Haviland. New York: Doubleday, 1974.

Anno, Mitsumasa. *Anno's Counting Book*. New York: Harper, 1977.

Asquith, Cynthia. *Portrait of Barrie*. New York: Greenwood Press, 1972.

Babbitt, Natalie. *Tuck Everlasting*. New York: Farrar, Straus, 1985.

Barrie, James M. *Peter Pan*. New York: Holt, 1987.

———. *Peter Pan and Wendy*. New York: Crown, 1988.

———. *Peter Pan in Kensington Gardens*. New York: Buccaneer, 1981.

Barthes, Roland. *New Critical Essays*. Berkeley: University of California Press, 1990.

Bator, Robert, editor. *Signposts to Criticism of Children's Literature*. Chicago: American Library Association, 1983.

Birkin, Andrew. *J. M. Barrie and the Lost Boys: The Love Story that Gave Birth to Peter Pan*. New York: Clarkson N. Potter, 1979.

Blishen, Edward. *The Thorny Paradise: Writers on Writing for Children*. London: Kestral Books, 1975.

Bond, Nancy. *A String in the Harp*. New York: Macmillan, 1976.

———. *The Voyage Begun*. New York: Macmillan, 1981.

---

*This is a rather unexpected collection of titles for a volume on children's literature. But the explanation lies in the fact that it is a very personal one, including works —whether or not they have directly to do with children's literature—that have been of particular interest to me as writer of both fiction and criticism.

Boston, Lucy M. *The Children of Green Knowe.* New York: Harcourt, 1955.

————. *Memory in a House.* New York: Macmillan, 1973.

————. *Perverse and Foolish: A Memoir of Childhood and Youth.* London: Bodley Head, 1979.

————. *The River at Green Knowe.* New York: Harcourt, 1989.

————. *The Stones of Green Knowe.* New York: Atheneum, 1976.

————. *A Stranger at Green Knowe.* New York: Atheneum, 1961.

————. *Treasure of Green Knowe.* New York: Harcourt, 1958.

Briggs, Julia. *A Woman of Passion: The Life of E. Nesbit, 1858–1928.* New York: New Amsterdam Books, 1987.

Brontë, Charlotte, *Jane Eyre.* (Many editions)

Brontë, Emily. *Wuthering Heights,* edited by William Sale, Jr. New York: Norton, 1963.

Brooks, Bruce. *The Moves Make the Man.* New York: Harper, 1984.

Bryson, Bill. *The Mother Tongue: English and How It Got that Way.* New York: Morrow, 1991.

Burchfield, Robert. *Unlocking the English Language,* with an introduction by Harold Bloom. New York: Hill and Wang, 1989.

Butler, Francelia. *Sharing Literature with Children: A Thematic Anthology.* Prospect Heights, Illinois: Waveland Press, 1989.

Byars, Betsy. *The Cartoonist.* New York: Viking, 1978.

————. *The Pinballs.* New York: Harper, 1977.

————. *The Summer of the Swans.* New York: Viking, 1970.

Cameron, Eleanor. *The Green and Burning Tree: On the Writing and Enjoyment of Children's Books.* Boston: Atlantic-Little, Brown, 1969.

Carpenter, Humphrey. *Secret Gardens: The Golden Age of Children's Literature from Alice in Wonderland to Winnie-the-Pooh.* Boston: Houghton, 1985.

Carroll, Lewis. *Alice's Adventures in Wonderland and Through the Looking-Glass,* with an introduction by Eleanor Graham. New York: Puffin, 1962.

————. *Alice's Adventures under Ground: A Facsimile of the Author's Manuscript Book with Additional Material from the Facsimile Edition of 1886,* with a new introduction by Martin Gardner. New York: Dover, 1965.

————. *The Annotated Snark: The Full Text of Lewis Carroll's Great Nonsense Epic The Hunting of the Snark,* with an introduction and notes by Martin Gardner. Harmondsworth, England: Penguin, 1962.

Cassedy, Sylvia. *Lucie Babbidge's House.* New York: Harper, 1989.

Chant, Joy. *The High Kings: Arthur's Celtic Ancestors.* New York: Bantam, 1983.

————. *Red Moon and Black Mountain.* New York: Dutton, 1976.

Childress, Alice. *A Hero Ain't Nothin' But a Sandwich.* New York: Avon, 1977.

Clark, Kenneth. *Civilisation: A Personal View.* New York: Harper, 1990.

Clarke, Pauline. *The Return of the Twelves.* New York: Dell, 1986.

Cleary, Beverly. *Dear Mr. Henshaw.* New York: Morrow, 1983.

————. *A Girl from Yamhill.* New York: Morrow, 1988.

————. The Ramona books. New York: Morrow.

Collodi, Carlo. *The Adventures of Pinocchio*. (Many editions)

Cooper, Susan. *The Dark Is Rising*. New York: Macmillan, 1973.

———. *Greenwitch*. New York: Macmillan, 1973.

———. *The Grey King*. New York: Macmillan, 1975.

———. *Over Sea under Stone*. New York: Harcourt, 1966.

———. *Silver on the Tree*. New York: Macmillan, 1977.

Curry, Jane Louise. *The Bassumtyte Treasure*. New York: Atheneum, 1978.

———. *Poor Tom's Ghost*. New York: Atheneum, 1977.

———. *The Watchers*. New York: Atheneum, 1975.

De la Mare, Walter. *The Best Stories of Walter de la Mare*. London: Faber & Faber, 1989.

———. *Collected Stories for Children*. London: Faber & Faber, n.d.

———. *Peacock Pie*. (Many editions)

———. *Selected Poems*. London: Faber & Faber, 1973.

Dickey, James. *Metaphor as Pure Adventure*. Washington, D.C.: Library of Congress, 1968.

———. *Self-Interviews*. New York: Delta, 1970.

Dickinson, Peter. *The Dancing Bear*. New York: Dell, 1988.

———. *Eva*. New York: Doubleday, 1989.

———. *Merlin Dreams*. New York: Delacorte, 1988.

———. *Tulku*. New York: Ace, 1984.

Dillard, Annie. *An American Childhood*. New York: Harper, 1988.

———. *Pilgrim at Tinker Creek*. New York: Harper, 1988.

Eager, Edward. *Knight's Castle*. New York: Harcourt, 1990.

Edel, Leon. *Stuff of Sleep and Dreams: Experiments in Literary Psychology*. New York: Harper, 1982.

Egoff, Sheila, G. T. Stubs, and L. F. Ashley. *Only Connect: Readings on Children's Literature*. New York: Oxford, 1969.

Eliot, T. S. *Collected Poems, 1909–1962*. New York: Harcourt, 1971.

———. *Old Possum's Book of Practical Cats*. New York: Harcourt, 1982.

Farmer, Penelope. *Charlotte Sometimes*. New York: Dell, 1987.

Fleischman, Paul. *Graven Images*. New York: Harper, 1982.

———. *Half-a-Moon Inn*. New York: Harper, 1980.

———. *Joyful Noise: Poems for Two Voices*. New York: Harper, 1988.

Fleischman, Sid. *Humbug Mountain*. Boston: Little, Brown, 1988.

———. *Mr. Mysterious and Company*. Boston: Little, Brown, 1962.

———. *The Whipping Boy*. New York: Greenwillow, 1986.

Fox, Paula. *How Many Miles to Babylon?* New York: Bradbury, 1980.

———. *Lily and the Lost Boy*. New York: Orchard, 1987.

———. *One-Eyed Cat*. New York: Bradbury, 1984.

———. *A Place Apart*. New York: Farrar, Straus, 1980.

———. *The Village by the Sea*. New York: Orchard, 1988.

Gardam, Jane. *Bilgewater*. New York: Greenwillow, 1977.

———. *Crusoe's Daughter*. New York: Atheneum, 1986.

———. *A Few Fair Days*. New York: Greenwillow, 1988.

———. *The Hollow Land*. New York: Greenwillow, 1982.

———. *A Long Way from Verona*. New York: Macmillan, 1971.

Garner, Alan. *Elidor*. New York: Walck, 1967.

———. *The Owl Service*. New York: Walck, 1968.

———. *Red Shift*. New York: Macmillan, 1973.

Garnett, Angelica. *Deceived with Kindness: A Bloomsbury Childhood*. New York: Harcourt, 1985.

Gattégno, Jean. *Lewis Carroll: Fragments of a Looking-Glass*, translated by Rosemary Sheed. New York: Crowell, 1976.

Golding, William. *The Lord of the Flies*. New York: Putnam, 1962.

Gordon, Lyndall. *Virginia Woolf: A Writer's Life*. New York: Norton, 1984.

Greene, Graham. *The Lost Childhood and Other Essays*. New York: Viking, 1951.

Hamilton, Virginia. *A Little Love*. New York: Putnam, 1984.

———. *M. C. Higgins the Great*. New York: Macmillan, 1987.

———. *The People Could Fly*. New York: Knopf, 1985.

———. *The Planet of Junior Brown*. New York: Macmillan, 1971.

———. *Zeely*. New York: Macmillan, 1967.

Haviland, Virginia, editor. *The Openhearted Audience: Ten Authors Talk about Writing for Children*. Washington, D.C.: Library of Congress, 1980.

Hazard, Paul. *Books, Children and Men*. Boston: The Horn Book, 1983.

Heilbrun, Carolyn G. *Writing a Woman's Life*. New York: Norton, 1988.

Heins, Paul, editor. *Crosscurrents of Criticism: Horn Book Essays 1968–1977*. Boston: The Horn Book, 1977.

Hoban, Russell. *The Mouse and His Child*. New York: Harper, 1967.

———. *Turtle Diary*. New York: Avon, 1982.

Howker, Janni. *Badger on the Barge and Other Stories*. New York: Greenwillow, 1985.

———. *Isaac Campion*. New York: Greenwillow, 1987.

Hunter, Mollie. *The Kelpie's Pearls*. New York: Funk & Wagnalls, 1966.

———. *A Sound of Chariots*. New York: Harper, 1972.

Jansson, Tove. *Finn Family Moomintroll*. New York: Farrar, Straus, 1989.

———. *Moominpappa at Sea*. New York: Walck, 1967.

———. *The Sculptor's Daughter*. London: Ernest Benn, 1974.

———. *The Summer Book*. New York: Pantheon, 1974.

———. *Tales from Moominvalley*. New York: Walck, 1964.

Jarrell, Randall. *The Animal Family*. New York: Pantheon, 1985.

———. *The Bat-Poet*. New York: Macmillan, 1964.

———. *Fly by Night*. New York: Farrar, Straus, 1976.

———. *Randall Jarrell's Letters, an Autobiographical and Literary Selection*, edited by Mary Jarrell. Boston: Houghton, 1985.

Jung, Carl G. *Dreams*, translated by R. F. C. Hull. New Jersey: Princeton University Press, 1974.

———. *Man and His Symbols*. New York: Doubleday, 1964.

————. *The Spirit in Man, Art, and Literature,* translated by R. F. C. Hull. New Jersey: Princeton University Press, 1966.

Kipling, Rudyard. *The Jungle Books.* (Many editions)

————. *The Just So Stories.* (Many editions)

————. *Puck of Pook's Hill.* New York: Penguin, 1987.

Kocher, Paul H. *Master of Middle Earth: The Fiction of J. R. R. Tolkien.* Boston: Houghton, 1972.

Kozol, Jonathan. *Death at an Early Age.* New York: New American Library, 1985.

————. *Savage Inequalities: Children in America's Schools.* New York: Crown, 1991.

Lane, Margaret. *The Tale of Beatrix Potter: A Biography.* New York: Warne, 1968. Revised editon.

Lanes, Selma. *The Art of Maurice Sendak.* New York: Abrams, 1984.

Langton, Jane. *The Diamond in the Window.* New York: Harper, 1973.

Le Guin, Ursula K. *Always Coming Home.* New York: Harper, 1985.

————. *The Beginning Place.* New York: Harper, 1990.

————. *Dancing at the Edge of the World: Thoughts on Words, Women, Places.* New York: Grove, 1989.

————. *The Farthest Shore.* New York: Atheneum, 1971.

————. *The Language of the Night: Essays on Fantasy and Science Fiction,* edited and with introductions by Susan Wood. New York: Putnam, 1979.

————. *Tehanu: The Last Book of Earthsea.* New York: Atheneum, 1990.

————. *The Tombs of Atuan.* New York: Atheneum, 1971.

————. *A Wizard of Earthsea.* Berkeley: Parnassus, 1968.

Lehman, David. *Signs of the Times: Deconstruction and the Fall of Paul de Man.* New York: Poseidon, 1991.

Levin, Bernard. *Enthusiasms.* New York: Crown, 1984.

Levin, Betty. *Brother Moose.* New York: Greenwillow, 1990.

————. *The Keeping Room.* New York: Greenwillow, 1989.

————. *The Trouble with Gramary.* New York: Greenwillow, 1988.

Lewis, Richard, collector. *Miracles: Poems by Children from the English-Speaking World.* New York: The Touchstone Center for Children, Inc., 1992.

Linder, Leslie. *A History of the Writings of Beatrix Potter.* New York: Warne, 1971.

Lively, Penelope. *The Ghost of Thomas Kempe.* New York: Dutton, 1973.

————. *The House in Norham Gardens.* New York: Dutton, 1974.

————. *A Stitch in Time.* Boston: G. K. Hall, 1988.

Lopez, Barry. *Arctic Dreams: Imagination and Desire in a Northern Landscape.* New York: Scribner, 1987.

————. *Crossing Open Ground.* New York: Vintage, 1988.

Lowell, Robert, editor. *Randall Jarrell, 1914–1965.* New York: Farrar, Straus, 1967.

Lurie, Alison. *Don't Tell the Grown-ups: Subversive Children's Literature.* Boston: Little, Brown, 1990.

Mabinogion, translated by Jeffrey Gantz. New York: Penguin, 1976.

MacLachlan, Patricia. *The Facts and Fictions of Minna Pratt.* New York: Harper, 1988.,

———. *Sarah Plain and Tall.* New York: Harper, 1985.

MacNeil, Robert. *Wordstruck: A Memoir.* New York: Viking, 1989.

Mahy, Margaret. *The Changeover: A Supernatural Romance.* New York: Macmillan, 1984.

———. *Memory.* New York: Macmillan, 1988.

Mayne, William. *Earthfasts.* New York: Peter Smith, n.d.

———. *A Game of Dark.* New York: Dutton, 1971.

———. *Gideon Ahoy.* New York: Delacorte, 1989.

———. *It.* New York: Greenwillow, 1977.

McKinley, Robin. *Beauty: A Retelling of the Story of "Beauty and the Beast."* New York: Harper, 1978.

Moers, Ellen. *Literary Women: The Great Writers.* New York: Doubleday, 1976.

Nesbit, E. *The Enchanted Castle.* (Many editions)

———. *The Five Children and It.* (Many editions)

———. *The Story of the Amulet.* New York: Penguin, 1986.

Nodelman, Perry. *Words about Pictures.* Athens: University of Georgia Press, 1988.

Norton, Mary. *The Borrowers.* New York: Harcourt, 1953.

———. *The Borrowers Afield.* New York: Harcourt, 1955.

———. *The Borrowers Afloat.* New York: Harcourt, 1959.

———. *The Borrowers Aloft.* New York: Harcourt, 1961.

———. *The Borrowers Avenged.* New York: Harcourt, 1982.

Oates, Joyce Carol. *(Woman) Writer: Occasions and Opportunities.* New York: Dutton, 1988.

O'Dell, Scott. *Island of the Blue Dolphins.* (Many editions)

———. *The King's Fifth.* Boston: Houghton, 1966.

———. *Sing Down the Moon.* Boston: Houghton, 1970.

Oneal, Zibby. *A Formal Feeling.* New York: Penguin, 1982.

———. *The Language of Goldfish.* New York: Penguin, 1990.

Opie, Iona and Peter. *The Classic Fairy Tales.* New York: Oxford, 1974.

Park, Ruth. *Playing Beatie Bow.* New York: Macmillan, 1982.

Paterson, Katherine. *Bridge to Terabithia.* New York: Harper, 1977.

———. *The Great Gilly Hopkins.* New York: Harper, 1978.

———. *Jacob Have I Loved.* New York: Harper, 1980.

———. *Lyddie.* New York: Lodestar, 1991.

Pearce, Philippa. *Tom's Midnight Garden.* New York: Harper, 1984.

———. *The Way to Sattin Shore.* New York: Penguin, 1985.

Peyton, K. M. *The Flambards.* New York: Penguin, 1977.

———. *A Pattern of Roses.* New York: Crowell, 1973.

———. *Pennington's Seventeenth Summer.* New York: Crowell, 1971.

Pfeiffer, John E. *The Creative Explosion.* New York: Harper, 1982.

Phillips, Robert, editor. *Aspects of Alice: Lewis Carroll's Dreamchild as Seen Through the Critics' Looking-Glasses, 1865–1971.* New York: Vanguard, 1971.

Pickering, Samuel, Jr. *John Locke and Children's Books in Eighteenth-Century England.* Knoxville: University of Tennessee Press, 1981.

Postman, Neil. *Conscientious Objections: Stirring Up Trouble about Language, Technology and Education.* New York: Random House, 1992.

———. *The Disappearance of Childhood.* New York: Dell, 1982.

Potter, Beatrix. *The Art of Beatrix Potter,* with an appreciation by Anne Carroll Moore. New York: Warne, 1955.

———. *Beatrix Potter's Letters,* selected and introduced by Judy Taylor. New York: Warne, 1989.

———. *Letters to Children,* with a foreword by Philip Hofer. New York: Walker and Company, 1992.

———. *Letters to Children from Beatrix Potter,* collected and introduced by Judy Taylor. New York: Warne, 1992.

Priestley, J. B. *Man and Time.* London: Aldus Books, 1964.

Raverat, Gwen. *Period Piece: A Cambridge Childhood.* London: Faber & Faber, 1961.

Ready, William. *The Tolkien Relation: A Personal Inquiry.* Chicago: Regnery, 1968.

Rees, David. *Marble in the Water: Essays on Contemporary Writers of Fiction for Children and Young Adults.* Boston: The Horn Book, 1985.

———. *Painted Desert, Green Shade: Essays on Contemporary Writers for Children.* Boston: The Horn Book, 1984.

Sayers, Frances Clarke. *Anne Carroll Moore: A Biography.* New York: Atheneum, 1972.

———. *Summoned by Books.* New York: Atheneum, 1965.

Scholes, Robert. *Structuralism in Literature: An Introduction.* New Haven: Yale University Press, 1974.

Segal, Lore, and Randall Jarrell, translators. *The Juniper Tree: And Other Tales from Grimm.* New York: Farrar, Straus, 1973.

Sendak, Maurice. *Caldecott & Co.: Notes on Books & Pictures.* New York: Farrar, Straus, 1988.

———. *In the Night Kitchen.* New York: Harper, 1970.

———. *The Nutshell Library.* New York: Harper, 1962.

———. *Outside over There.* New York: Harper, 1981.

———. *Where the Wild Things Are.* New York: Harper, 1988.

Sewell, Elizabeth. *The Field of Nonsense.* London: Chatto & Windus, 1952.

Shelley, Mary. *Frankenstein: Or, the Modern Prometheus.* (Many editions)

Shepard, Ernest H. *Drawn from Memory.* New York: Penguin, 1985.

Shlain, Leonard. *Art and Physics: Parallel Visions in Space, Time and Light.* New York: Morrow, 1991.

Spalding, Frances. *Vanessa Bell.* New York: Ticknor & Fields, 1983.

Spinelli, Jerry. *Maniac Magee.* Boston: Little, Brown, 1990.

Staples, Suzanne Fisher. *Shabanu: Daughter of the Wind.* New York: Knopf, 1989.

Stegner, Wallace. *On the Teaching of Creative Writing: Responses to a Series of Questions,* edited by Edward Connery Lathem. Hanover, New Hampshire: University Press of New England, 1988.

Steig, William. *Abel's Island*. New York: Farrar, Straus, 1985.

———. *The Amazing Bone*. New York: Farrar, Straus, 1986.

———. *Sylvester and the Magic Pebble*. New York: Simon & Schuster, 1969.

Stevenson, Robert Louis. *Dr. Jekyll and Mr. Hyde*. (Many editions)

Sutcliff, Rosemary. *Blue Remembered Hills: A Recollection*. New York: Oxford, 1988.

———. *The Light Beyond the Forest*. New York: Dutton, 1980.

———. *The Mark of the Horselord*. New York: Dell, 1989.

———. *The Road to Camlan: The Death of Arthur*. New York: Dutton, 1982.

Taylor, Mildred. *The Gold Cadillac*. New York: Dial, 1987.

———. *Let the Circle Be Unbroken*. New York: Dial, 1981.

———. *Roll of Thunder, Hear My Cry*. New York: Bantam, 1987.

Thirkell, Angela. *Three Houses*. London: Robin Clark, Ltd., 1931.

Tolkien, J. R. R. *Tree and Leaf*. Boston: Houghton, 1965.

Townsend, John Rowe. *A Sense of Story: Essays on Contemporary Writers for Children*. Boston: The Horn Book, 1973.

———. *A Sounding of Storytellers*. New York: Lippincott, 1979.

———. *The Visitors*. New York: Lippincott, 1977.

Twain, Mark. *The Adventures of Huckleberry Finn*. (Many editions)

———. *The Adventures of Tom Sawyer*. (Many editions)

Udry, Janice. *The Moon Jumpers*. New York: Harper, n.d.

———. *A Tree Is Nice*. New York: Harper, 1956.

———. *What Mary Jo Shared*. New York: Scholastic, 1970.

Uttley, Alison. *A Traveler in Time*. New York: Viking, 1964.

Verne, Jules. *The Mysterious Island*. (Many editions)

Voigt, Cynthia. *Dicey's Song*. New York: Atheneum, 1982.

———. *The Homecoming*. New York: Macmillan, 1981.

———. *A Solitary Blue*. New York: Macmillan, 1983.

———. *Tell Me if the Lovers are Losers*. New York: Macmillian, 1982.

Walsh, Jill Paton. *A Chance Child*. New York: Farrar, Straus, 1978.

———. *Gaffer Samson's Luck*. New York: Farrar, Straus, 1984.

———. *Grace*. New York: Farrar, Straus, 1992.

———. *A Parcel of Patterns*. New York: Farrar, Straus, 1983.

———. *Unleaving*. New York: Farrar, Straus, 1986.

Warner, Sylvia Townsend. *Letters*. New York: Viking, 1982.

———. *Scenes of Childhood and Other Stories*. New York: Viking, 1981.

Wells, H. G. *The Time Machine*. (Many editions)

Welty, Eudora. *One Writer's Beginnings*. Boston: Harvard University Press, 1984.

Westall, Robert. *Blitzcat*. New York: Scholastic, 1989.

———. *Devil on the Road*. New York: Greenwillow, 1978.

———. *The Haunting of Chas McGill*. New York: Greenwillow, 1983.

———. *The Machine Gunners*. New York: Greenwillow, 1976.

White, E. B. *Charlotte's Web*. New York: Harper, 1952.

———. *Essays of E. B. White*. New York: Harper, 1979.

————. *Letters of E. B. White,* collected and edited by Dorothy Lobrano Guth. New York: Harper, 1976.

————. *Stuart Little.* New York: Harper, 1945.

————. *Writings from The New Yorker, 1927–1976,* edited by Rebecca M. Dale. New York: Harper, 1990.

Wilder, Laura Ingalls. The Little House books. New York: Harper.

Woolf, Virginia. *The Letters of Virginia Woolf,* in six volumes, edited by Nigel Nicholson and Joanne Trautmann. New York: Harcourt, 1975–1980.

————. *Moments of Being: Unpublished Autobiographical Writings of Virginia Woolf,* edited and with an introduction and notes by Jeanne Schulkind. Sussex, England: The University Press, 1976.

————. *A Passionate Apprentice: The Early Journals 1897–1909,* edited by Mitchell A. Leaska. New York: Harcourt, 1990.

————. *A Room of One's Own.* New York: Harcourt, 1989.

————. *Three Guineas.* New York: Harcourt, 1963.

————. *To the Lighthouse.* New York: Harcourt, 1989.

𝒫ermissions

The author wishes to express her thanks to the following authors, executors, agents, representatives, and book publishers for permission to quote from copyrighted works:

Atheneum Books, an imprint of Macmillan Publishing Company, for material from *The Tombs of Atuan*, by Ursula K. Le Guin, © 1970, 1971 by Ursula K. Le Guin. And for material from *Tehanu*, by Ursula K. Le Guin, © 1990 by the Inter-Vivos Trust for the Le Guin children. And for material from *A Solitary Blue*, by Cynthia Voigt, © 1983 by Cynthia Voigt.

Keith Basso, for material by Keith Basso from *The Creative Explosion*, by John E. Pfeiffer, © 1982 by John E. Pfeiffer. Also published in *Western Apache Language and Culture: Essays in Linguistic Anthropology*, by Keith Basso, © 1991 by Keith Basso.

Georges Borchardt, Inc., for material from *Real Presences*, by George Steiner, © 1989 by George Steiner.

Chatto and Windus, Ltd., for material from *Old Friends: Personal Recollections*, by Clive Bell, © 1957 by Clive Bell.

James Dickey, for material from *Metaphor as Pure Adventure*, by James Dickey, © 1968 by James Dickey.

Faber & Faber, Ltd., for material from *Collected Poems, 1909–1962*, by T. S. Eliot, © 1963, by T. S. Eliot. And for material from *Period Piece: A Cambridge Childhood*, by Gwen Raverat, © 1961 by Gwen Raverat.

Farrar, Straus & Giroux, Inc., for material from *Randall Jarrell, 1914–1965*, edited by Robert Lowell, Peter Taylor, and Robert Penn Warren, © 1967 by Robert Lowell, Peter Taylor, and Robert Penn Warren.

Grove Weidenfeld, for material from *Passing On*, by Penelope Lively, © 1989 by Penelope Lively.

Harcourt Brace Jovanovich, Inc., for material from *A Passionate Apprentice: The Early Journals, 1897–1909*, by Virginia Woolf, edited by Mitchell A. Leaska, text

343

Index

Acceptance quotient, 165n, 221
Adams, Richard, 77, 243, 256
"Adult-eration of Children's Books, The" (Moss), 69
Adventures of Huckleberry Finn, The (Twain), 223, 284–85
Adventures of Tom Sawyer, The (Twain), xv, 107
Aesthetic belief, importance of, by author, 53
Aesthetic distance, 5, 143
After the First Death (Cormier), 226
"Against Interpretation" (Sontag), 239
Aiken, Joan, 171, 276, 295
Alcott, Louisa May, 171n
Alexander, Lloyd, 22–23, 314, 320
Alexander, Peter, 297
Alice's Adventures in Wonderland (Carroll), 22, 106, 212, 223, 240, 243, 293, 294, 296, 297–303, 320
Alice's Adventures Through the Looking-Glass (Carroll), 240, 293, 300
Alice's Adventures under Ground (Carroll), 294
Allegory, 240
Altered States of Consciousness (Tart), 323
Always Coming Home (Le Guin), 175–76

Andersen, Hans Christian, 12, 32, 220, 224, 256, 272, 312–13, 320
Animal Family, The (Jarrell), 77, 95, 253
Anno, Mitsumasa, xvi
Anno's Counting Book (Anno), xvi
Antar and the Eagles (Mayne), 253–56
Anthology of Children's Literature (Johnson, Sickels, and Sayers), 210
Apache Indians, 110
Arctic Dreams (Lopez), 26, 203
Arieti, Sylvano, 287
Arilla Sundown (Hamilton), 36
Art and Physics (Shlain), 121n
Art, Herbert Read's definition of, 312
Arthurian legend, influence of, 18, 32, 33, 170, 174
"Artists in Uniform" (McCarthy), 239
Art of Beatrix Potter, The (Potter), 34
Art of Maurice Sendak, The (Lanes), 258
Ascent of Man, The (Bronowski), 73
Aspects of Alice (Phillips, editor), 240, 293–94
Aspects of the Novel (Forster), 163n
Asquith, Cynthia, 310, 313
Asquith, Herbert H., 304
Attitudes toward characters, author's, in relation to feminism, 121–27

Auden, W. H., 130
Author's point of view, 35–36
Autobiography, use of in novel writing, 9

Babbitt, Natalie, 22, 95
Barker, Eric, 187
Barrie, David, 306
Barrie, James M., xx, 13, 224, 243, 303–13, 320
Barthes, Roland, xvi, 122n, 248–50, 251
Barton, Todd, 175
Barzun, Jacques, 83
Basso, Keith N., 110
Bassumtyte Treasure, The (Curry), 171n
Bastable books, the (Nesbit), 220
Bat-Poet, The (Jarrell), 77
Bawden, Nina, 86
Beardsley, Aubrey, 91, 92
Beatrix Potter's Letters (Potter), 34
Beginning Place, The (Le Guin), 169, 182–84, 202, 203, 224
Behn, Aphra, 117–18
Bell, Angelica, 129
Bell, Clive, 129, 258, 259
Bellow, Saul, 35
Bell, Vanessa, 129
Beneath the Hill (Curry), 171n
Bergman, Ingmar, 177, 263
"Between Family and Fantasy" (Aiken), 276, 295
Between the Acts (Woolf), 245
Beyond Silence (Cameron), 104, 119, 124, 172–73, 251
Bilgewater (Gardam), 87–88
Birkin, Andrew, 243, 306
Bishop, Elizabeth, 131
Blitzcat (Westall), 201
"Blood and Guts" (Jong), 130
Bloom, Harold, xvi
Blue Remembered Hills (Sutcliff), 21n

Bogan, Louise, 131, 262
Bond, Nancy, 95, 152, 158, 162, 171n, 174
Böök, Fredrik, 272
Books, Children and Men (Hazard), 210
Borges, Jorge Luis, 70
Borrower books, the (Norton), 263
Borrowers, The (Norton), 252
Boston, Lucy M., 21n, 45, 47–48, 151, 169, 194, 196, 259
Bowen, Elizabeth, 276
Bowman, Isa, 298
Briggs, Julia, 220
Brombert, Victor, 250
Bronowski, Jacob, 73
Brontë, Charlotte, 270
Brontë, Emily, 270, 272, 277
Brookner, Anita, 35
Brooks, Bruce, 88, 103, 106
"Brush Up Your Shakespeare" (Taylor), 109n
Bryson, Bill, 121n
Budge, Wallis, 153
Burchfield, Robert, xvi
Burden words, 65, 68–69, 106, 225–26, 312
Burke, James, 73
Burns, Robert, 214
Burnt-out Case, A (Greene), 276
Burroughs, William, 132
Bushmen, the, 276
Byars, Betsy, 36
Byatt, A. S., 265

Calendar, The (Children's Book Council), 17
Canham, Stephen, 86n
Carnegie Medal, the, 45n
Carpenter, Humphrey, 2: 226, 299, 300
Carroll, Lewis, xx, 106–7, 170, 243, 244, 296–303, 320
Carson, Rachel, 265n

Cartoonist, The (Byars), 35, 36–40
Cassedy, Sylvia, 40, 221
Cat, The (Colette), 201
Cay, The (Taylor), 125
CBC Features (Children's Book Council), 17
Cech, John, 185–86
Celts, the, 174
Center for the Study of Children's Literature at Simmons College, 234n
Cézanne, Paul, 259
Chagall, Marc, 13
Chance Child, A (Walsh), 169, 171, 184–85, 193
Changeover, The (Mahy), 55
Chant, Joy, 170, 174, 178, 180, 181, 203
"Characteristics of E. B. White as Shown through his Essays and Children's Books" (Parson), 318–19
Characterization, 27–71: Alfie in *The Cartoonist,* 36–40; Alice in *Alice in Wonderland,* 298–99; Arha, SEE Tenar; Brontë, Emily, and, 270, 277; by means of metaphors, 54, 87–89; Carrie in *The Language of Goldfish,* 89–93; clichés and, 100–6; feminist, 121–27; Ged in the Earthsea books, 136–41; Gilly in *The Great Gilly Hopkins,* 56–61; Hanno in *A Stranger at Green Knowe,* 45–48; importance of, 34; initiation of, 27–32, 277; Jeff and his father in *A Solitary Blue,* 61–69; Lucie in *Lucie Babbidge's House,* 40–45; Manny Rat in *The Mouse and His Child,* 29–32; Melody in *A Solitary Blue,* 61–69; Peter Pan, 303–13; sexist view of characters, 121–27; Shabanu in *Shabanu, Daughter of the Wind,* 133–36; Sophie and Jonny in *Memory,* 48–56; Stuart Little in *Stuart Little,* 315–20; Tenar in the first and last Earthsea books, 136–

41; Trotter in *The Great Gilly Hopkins,* 56–61; unconscious, power of the, in, 270, 277, 279, 280, 283–84, 293, 315–20
Charlie and the Chocolate Factory (Dahl), 232–33
Charlotte Sometimes (Farmer), 194–96
Charlotte's Web (White), 98, 151, 155, 156, 165, 223, 231
Chaucer, Geoffrey, 167, 259, 260
"Child and the Shadow, The" (Le Guin), 320
Childhood: idea of, in fiction writing, 3–26; influence on writer, 3–26, 32–33; reading and, xvii–xviii, 16–25, 32–33; recovery of, in fiction writing, 218, 220, 260–62; spirit of, in reviewer and critic, 260–62; writer to come, the, and, 3–26
"Children in the Woods" (Lopez), 26
Children of Green Knowe, The (Boston), 151, 152, 153–54, 192, 196
Children's Book Council, the, 16
Children's Literature, xv, 224n
Children's Literature Association Quarterly, 118n
Children's literature, criticism of, SEE Criticism
Children's Literature in Education, 173n, 224n
Childress, Alice, 252
Ciardi, John, 70
Cixous, Helene, 133n
Clarke, Pauline, 22, 121
Clark, Kenneth, 73
Cleary, Beverly, 252
Clichés, 72–78, 100–8, 113, 114–16: current slang and, 102, 105–6; influence of, 75; Shakespeare and, 108–9; within dialogue, 100–6; within first-person novel, 100–6
Clitoral hermeneutics, 132
"Clitoral Imagery and Masturbation in Emily Dickinson," 132

Clockwork Orange, The (Burgess), 49

Colette, 72, 100, 114, 127–28, 131, 201

Collected Stories of Eudora Welty, The (Welty), 127n

Collective unconscious, the, 275, 289, 322

Colwin, Laurie, 78

Comedy, 39

Complete Prose of Marianne Moore, The (Willis, editor), 244

Conrad's War (Davies), 197

Conscientious Objections (Postman), xviin

Conviction, importance of, in writer, 48, 53

Cooper, Susan, 170, 171n, 174–75, 178–80, 181, 262–65

Cormier, Robert, 223, 224n, 226, 252

Cott, Jonathan, 237

"Country of the Mind, A" (Cameron), 173n

Court of the Stone Children (Cameron), 7, 273, 279–80, 324

Coward, Noël, 217, 218

Creation of character through metaphors, 89–94

"Creation of *Charlotte's Web*, The," (Neumeyer), 223

"Creation of E. B. White's *The Trumpet of the Swan*, The," (Neumeyer), 223

Creative time bomb, the, 314, 317, 320, 321

Critic as author, 251–53

Criticism, xv, xvi, xix–xx, 205–65: academic, 262–65; acceptance quotient in, 221; change in children's literature of its, since 1960s, xv–xvii; close reading, importance of, for, 223–24; deconstructionist, 236n; destruction of reader's pleasure through, 231–32, 263–64; emotion in, 215, 231, 235; forcing

according to theory in, 236–37; Freudian theory in, 237–39, 240, 242–43, 247; historical research in, 223, 226, 227; intuition in, 236; judgment in, 215; psychological, 240, 295; rereading, importance of, in, 215, 223–24; shallowness in, 219; spirit of childhood in children's literature and, 260–62; subjectivity of, 215, 218, 220–21; textual scholarship in, 223, 226; theory in general and, 236; writing of, 221–23

Cro-Magnon man, 109–10

Crosscurrents of Criticism (Heins, editor), 225n

Crossing Open Ground (Lopez), 26

Crusoe, Robinson, 289

Crusoe's Daughter (Gardam), 324

Cuckoo Clock (Molesworth), 219

Cunard, Nancy, 118

Curry, Jane Louise, 171n, 177

Cushman, Marilyn and Harvey, 29

Dahl, Roald, 232–33

Dancing at the Edge of the World (Le Guin), 264n

"Darkening of the Green, The" (Hollindale), 45n

Dark Is Rising, The (Cooper), 179

Dark Is Rising, The, sequence (Cooper), 170, 174, 178, 202

Darkness Visible (Styron), 74n

Daughter of Time, The (Tey), 79

Davies, Andrew, 197

Davis, Boyd, xvi

Davis, Linda, 84

"Day the Universe Changed, The," 73

Dead Poets Society (Keating), 221n

Death and Life of Great American Cities, The (Jacobs), 246, 265n

"Death of a Pig" (White), 99

"Death of the Moth, The" (Woolf), 113

Deconstruction, 236n, 247

Defoe, Daniel, 325

De la Mare, Walter, 95, 113–14, 170, 272, 274–75, 281

De Lauretis, Teresa, 246

DeMott, Benjamin, 232

Denis, Maurice, 91

Derrida, Jacques, xix

DeSalvo, Louise, 293n

"Desublimating the Male Sublime," 132

Devil on the Road (Westall), 194, 197–201, 203

Dialogue, 294: clichés and, 100–6; communication of individuality through, 36–45, 100–6

Diamond in the Window, The (Langton), 171n, 202

Dicey books, the (Voigt), 263

Dickens, Charles, 27, 171

Dickey, James, 46, 81, 83, 85, 95, 96, 97–98

Dickinson, Emily, 132–33, 171n

Dickinson, Ken, 76, 77, 78

Dickinson, Peter, 174, 247, 252

Dick, Philip K., 243

Didion, Joan, 131

Dilation around an image, 96

Dillard, Annie, 24, 80–82, 128

Dinesen, Isak, 220

Disappearance of Childhood, The (Postman), xviii

Discovery, aesthetic, xvi

Disney, Walt, 16, 17, 212, 315

Dispossessed, The (Le Guin), 18

DNA, 290

Dodgson, Charles Lutwidge, SEE Carroll, Lewis

Donnée in novel writing, the, 27–29, 314–17, 321–22

Doubleness in the writer: Barrie, James M., 13, 303–13; Carroll, Lewis, 296–303; Stevenson, Robert Louis, 11–13, 293, 304n; White, E. B., 319–20

Drabble, Margaret, 130

Dragon in fantasy, the, 137, 139, 141, 182–83, 240–41, 322

Drawn from Memory (Shepard), 21n

Dreaming: Adams, Richard, and, 243; Aiken, Joan, and, 276; Alexander, Lloyd, and, 314; Barrie, J. M., and, 13, 303–4; Brontë, Emily, and, 272; Bushmen, the, and, 276; Cameron, Eleanor, and, 271–72, 273–74, 276; de la Mare, Walter, and, 272, 274–75; *Diamond in the Window, The,* and, 202; donnée for novel through, 314–15; Eager, Edward, and, 202n; flying in, 14; Fowles, John, and, 28–29; Greene, Graham, and, 275–76; *House in Norham Gardens, The,* and, 202; Jung, C. G., on, 322n; Le Guin, Ursula, and, 322–24; premonitory, 290–91; revelations of writers through, 272; Sendak, Maurice, and, 14, 16; Stevenson, Robert Louis, and, 11–13, 304; unconscious, the, and, 11–13, 322–23; White, E. B., and, 315; Woolf, Virginia, and, 292

Dreams, "big," "meaningful" (Jung), 322n

"Dreams Must Explain Themselves" (Le Guin), 241

Dr. Jekyll and Mr. Hyde (Stevenson), 12–13, 110, 293, 304n

Dustland series, the (Hamilton), 36

Eager, Edward, 202n

Earthfasts (Mayne), 152, 157–58, 162, 170, 172

Earthsea books, the (Le Guin), 223

Edel, Leon, 122n
Egan, Michael, 14, 237, 243, 304
Einstein, Albert, 149n, 170
Eiseley, Loren, 84
Elidor (Garner), 102, 172, 177
Eliot, George, 120
Eliot, T. S., 130, 261–62
Elizabeth I of England, 117
Emily Dickinson (Sewall), 234
Emotion in criticism, 215, 231, 235
Enchanted Castle, The (Nesbit), xv
End of the Affair, The (Greene), 276
Endurance of children's literature, 70
Eternal Moment, the, 168, 189
Eva (Dickinson), 252
Evil, 33, 55
Ewing, Juliana Horatio, 218
"Excellence in Children's Books,"
    210–12

Fairy tales, influence of, on writer,
    19–20, 32, 56, 97, 272
Fairy tales, magic and, 151, 255
Fantasy (SEE ALSO Time fantasy): caus-
    ative agent in, 150–51; character-
    ization in, 136–41, 182–84;
    conception of, 168, 294–95; defini-
    tion of, by E. M. Forster, 163n;
    dragons in, 137, 139, 141, 182–
    83, 240–41, 322; early reading of,
    effect on writer, 17–18, 19–20; en-
    largement of understanding of ex-
    perience through, 19, 45–48, 169,
    182–83; farce in, 163; inner logic
    in, 149–66, 201, 253–56; mechan-
    ical manipulation in, 196–97, 200–
    1; paradoxes of, 152–54, 169; par-
    ents in, 152–53, 182–84; premise,
    importance of, in, 149–66; reality,
    particular kind of, in, 162, 253–
    56; rules in, 149–66; secret ambig-
    uously kept in, 155–62; secret not
    kept in, 162–65; secret unambigu-

ously kept in, 152–54; symbolism
    in, 91, 92, 182–85; toughness in,
    197; unconscious, creative, in, 163,
    182–84, 294–95
Farce, 162–64
Farmer, Penelope, 194–96
Farthest Shore, The (Le Guin), 279
Father: influence of on fictional protag-
    onist, 67–69, 133–36; influence on
    writer, 4–5
Father-son relationship, novelistic, 67–
    69
Faulkner, William, 220, 270, 275
"Female Oedipal Complex in Maurice
    Sendak's *Outside over There*, The"
    (Reed), 237
Feminine Mystique, The (Freidan), 265n
Fenichel, Otto, 237
Few Fair Days, A (Gardam), 83
Field of Nonsense, The (Sewell), 302
Fight for Mr. Lapraik (Barrie), 303–4
Figures of speech (SEE ALSO Imagery):
    confusion in, 78–79, 83; creation
    of, 81, 97–98, 100, 107, 110–11,
    112; exaggeration or distortion of,
    81–82; logic, aesthetically satisfy-
    ing, in, 79–80, 89–94; three ways
    of misfiring in, 78–83
Finch, Robert, 84
Finnegans Wake (Joyce), 100
First-person telling: characterization
    developed through, 103–5; clichés,
    use of, in, 103–5; *Turtle Diary* and,
    105
First Two Lives of Lukas-Kasha, The
    (Alexander), 23
"Fisherwoman's Daughter, The" (Le
    Guin), 142
Five Children and It, The (Nesbit),
    219
Flambard series, the (Peyton), 187
Flaubert, Gustave, 270
Flying: in dreams, 14; in fantasy, 14,
    16

Forcing: according to critical theory, 236, 240, 263; in novel writing, 283

Forster, E. M., 163n

Fowles, John, 28–29

Fox, Paula, 86, 87, 96

"Frances Clarke Sayers" (Heins), 208n

Frankenstein (Shelley), 28n, 293, 304n

French Lieutenant's Woman, The (Fowles), 28–29

Freudian theory, 237–38, 240, 242, 247, 290, 305

Freud, Sigmund, 133n, 290, 304

Friedan, Betty, 265n

Fry, Roger, 129, 258

Fulford, Robert, 246, 265n

Fuller, Buckminster, 258

"Function of Criticism in Children's Literature, The" (Pickering, Jr.), 223

Furniss, Harry, 296

Game of Dark, A (Mayne), 93–94, 95, 169, 182–84, 202, 240

Gardam, Jane, 83, 87, 95, 252, 257, 260, 324

Gardner, Martin, 295

Garner, Alan, 9–10, 102–3, 170, 172, 174–75, 224, 287

Garnett, Angelica, 129

Gathering of Gargoyles, A (Pierce), 176–77

Gattégno, Jean, 297–99

Generalizations, 128, 129–31, 142

Genette, Gerard, 236

Genius, 257–60

Ghost of Thomas Kempe, The (Lively), 151, 152, 155–56, 189, 191–92

Girl in a Swing, The (Adams), 77–78, 80

Gondal Saga (Brontë), 277, 278

Goodman, Paul, 265n

"Good News from the Land of Bronty-fans" (Kuznets), 121

"Good Oyster, A" (Smedman), 224n

Gordimer, Nadine, 248

Gordon, John, 79

Gordon, Lyndall, 11

Grahame, Kenneth, 226

Graham, Martha, 324, 325

Grant, Duncan, 129

Great Gilly Hopkins, The (Paterson), 56–61, 62, 263

Green and Burning Tree, The (Cameron), xv, xix, 19, 34n, 168

Greene, Graham, 113, 238, 275–76, 284

Gregory, Marshall, 85

Grey King, The (Cooper), 179

Group, The (McCarthy), 105–6

Growing Up Absurd (Goodman), 265n

Guth, Dorothy Lobrano, E. B. White's note to, 315

Hamilton, Virginia, xvi, 35, 36, 224, 242, 252

Hamlet's Mother (Heilbrun), 118, 128

Hampden, John, 167

Hanley, Mary, 287

Hardy, Thomas, 246

Haunting of Chas McGill, The (Westall), 201

Haviland, Virginia, 13

Hawkes, Jacquetta, 120

Hazard, Paul, 210

Hazzard, Shirley, 35, 78

Heart Is a Lonely Hunter, The (McCullers), 283–84

Heideggerian theory, 247

Heilbrun, Carolyn G., 118, 127, 128, 129, 246

Heins, Ethel, 208n

Heins, Paul, 225n

Hero Ain't Nothin' But a Sandwich, A (Childress), 106, 252

Heroic fantasy, SEE High fantasy

High fantasy, 170, 174, 176, 253

"High Fantasy" (Cameron), 225n

High Kings, The (Chant), 174

High King, The (Alexander), 23

Hill, David R., 246

Historical criticism, 221, 226–27

History of the Writings of Beatrix Potter, A (Linder), 34

Hoban, Russell, 29–32, 85, 88, 95, 105, 223, 253

Holbrook, David, 237

Hollindale, Peter, 45n

Hollow Land, The (Gardam), 252

Hopi language, the, 203

Hopkins, Gerard Manley, 287

Horn Book Magazine, The, 208n, 212n, 223, 232, 234

House in Norham Gardens, The (Lively), 87, 169, 185, 189–92, 202, 203

House of Arden, The (Nesbit), 219

Howard, Donald R., 259

"How It Strikes a Contemporary" (Woolf), 227

Howker, Janni, 82, 101

Hoyle, Karen Nelson, 234n

Huckleberry Finn, SEE *Adventures of Huckleberry Finn, The*

Humphreys, Josephine, 74

Hunter, Mollie, 225

Hunting of the Snark, The (Carroll), 295, 296

I Am the Cheese (Cormier), 40, 44, 223, 224n, 252

"If Education Is a Feast, Why Do We Restrict the Menu?" (Gregory), 85

Illuminations, xvi, 9, 56–69, 225

Imagery (SEE ALSO Figures of speech), 54, 67, 78–116: extended, 89–94, 99, 321; reason for, 89–94, 112–13; Western Apache Indians', 110; working out of, 89–94, 98, 99, 100; work of the unconscious in creation of, 98–99, 113–14, 321

"In Defense of the Artist" (Cooper), 262–65

Individuation, 321

Initiation of a creative work, SEE Donnée in novel writing, the

Innocence, xviin

Interpretation in literary criticism, 239

In the Night Kitchen (Sendak), 15

Intruder in the Dust (Faulkner), 220

Intuition in criticism, 236

Irigaray, Luce, 133n

Isaac Campion (Howker), 101

Jacob Have I Loved (Paterson), 223

Jacobs, Jane, 246, 265n

Jacob's Room (Woolf), 113, 293

James, Henry, 70, 113, 176, 180, 238

Jane Eyre (Brontë), 22

Japanese fairy tales, 19–20

Jarrell, Randall, 16, 77, 95, 130, 230–31, 235, 246, 247, 253

Jeans, Sir James, 19, 25

Jennings, Peter, 144n

Jersey Shore, The (Mayne), 282–83

Jesus Christ, 33n

"Jim Jay" (de la Mare), 254

J. M. Barrie and the Lost Boys (Birkin), 243

John Locke and Children's Books in Eighteenth-Century England (Pickering, Jr.), 221

John the Baptist, 91

Jong, Erica, 130–31

Journal of Beatrix Potter, The (Potter), 34

Journey from Obscurity (Owen), 188

Julia and the Hand of God (Cameron), 119

Jungian theory, 240, 242, 271, 275, 276, 290–91, 292, 321, 322n

Jungle Books, The (Kipling), 20
"Juniper Tree, The" (Grimm), 16
Juniper Tree, The (Segal and Jarrell, translators), 16
Just So Stories, The (Kipling), 20

Kafka, Franz, 13, 291
Kaplan, Justin, 258
Kazin, Alfred, 125, 221, 222
Keating, Tom, 221n
Keeping Room, The (Levin), 186
Kerlan Collection, University of Minnesota, the, 234n
Kermode, Frank, 235
"Kiddy Lit.," 209
"Killer and the Slain, The" (Edel), 122n
Kim (Kipling), xvi
King Arthur, SEE Arthurian legend
King's Fifth, The (O'Dell), 24
Kingsley, Charles, 218
Kipling, Rudyard, xvi, 20–21, 32, 168
Klee, Paul, 13, 232
Knight's Castle (Eager), 202n
Kozol, Jonathan, 130
Kristeva, Julia, 133n
Kuznets, Lois, 121, 262n

Lacan, Jacques, 133n
Laing, R. D., 144
Lancelot, 33, 88
Lane, Margaret, 35
Lanes, Selma, 11, 14, 258
Langton, Jane, 171n, 202
Language of Goldfish, The (Oneal), 89–94
Language of the Night, The (Le Guin), 224n
Lawrence, D. H., 130

Left Hand of Darkness, The (Le Guin), 18
"Left in the Dark" (Gordon), 79
Legend: Arthurian, 18, 32, 33, 170, 174; nontraditional, 32, 170, 175–76
Le Guin, Ursula K., 17–18, 115, 128, 131, 133, 142, 169, 175–76, 180, 182–84, 202, 223, 224, 227, 240, 241–42, 243–44, 253, 264n, 320–24
Letters of E. B. White (White), 315
Levin, Bernard, 108, 109n
Levin, Betty, 186, 237–38
Lewis Carroll (Gattégno), 297–99
Lewis, C. S., 220, 235, 238
Light Princess, The (MacDonald), 16
Lily and the Lost Boy (Fox), 96
Limberlost novels, the (Stratton-Porter), 20–22
Linder, Leslie, 34
Lion and the Unicorn, The, xv
Literary criticism, 205–65: historical, 221, 226–27; Sayers, Frances Clarke, and, 215; textual scholarship and, 223; writing of, xv, 217–29
Literary Women: The Great Writers (Moers), 129
Literature, a definition of, xviii
Literature, effect of, on child, xvii–xviii
"Little Matter of Sense, A" (Barzun), 84
"Little Mermaid, The" (Andersen), 312
Little Minister, The (Barrie), 312
Little Pig Robinson (Potter), 239
"Little," use of: in hypocrisy, 62; in sentimentality, 62, 312
Little White Bird, The (Barrie), 312
Lively, Penelope, 87, 95, 151, 155, 169, 185, 191

Llewellyn Davies, Arthur, 306, 310
Llewellyn Davies, Peter, 306
Llewellyn Davies, Sylvia, 306, 308, 310
Long Way from Verona, A (Gardam), 257
Lopez, Barry, 26, 203–4
Lord of the Flies, The (Golding), 42
Lord of the Rings, The (Tolkien), 17
Los Angeles Times, the: librarians, letter about, to, 207; Sayers, Frances Clarke, letter to, 212n
"Lose Not the Nightingale" (Sayers), 208
Lost Notebooks of Loren Eiseley, The (Eiseley), 84
Love in the Time of Cholera (Márquez), 36
"Lovely," use of in sentimentality, 312–13
Lowell, Robert, 230
Lucie Babbidge's House (Cassedy), 35, 40–45, 53, 221

Mabinogion, 170, 174, 177–78
MacDonald, George, 16, 218
Machine Gunners, The (Westall), 199, 252
MacLachlan, Patricia, 70
Madame Bovary (Flaubert), 270
Magic, 149, 150–52, 165, 179, 192, 262
Mahy, Margaret, 48, 55
Man and His Symbols (Jung), 290
Man and Time (Priestley), 144
Maniac Magee (Spinelli), 227, 228
Mansfield, Katherine, xvi, 276, 283
Man Who Mistook His Wife for a Hat, The (Sacks), 111
Marble in the Water (Rees), 189
Margaret Ogilvie (Barrie), 308
Markheim (Stevenson), 12

Márquez, Gabriel García, 36
Martin, Faith McNulty, 318
Marxist theory, 247
"Massacre of the Innocents, The" (Laing), 144
Maturation, 36–71, 89–94
Maxwell, William, 96
Mayne, William, 93, 152, 155, 169, 170, 172, 182–84, 202, 203, 224, 240, 253
McCarthy, Mary, 105, 130, 131, 239
McCullers, Carson, 131, 283–84
M. C. Higgins the Great (Hamilton), xvi, 242, 252
McLuhan, Marshall, 265n
"McLuhan, Youth and Literature" (Cameron), 223, 232, 234
Melville, Herman, 132
Memory (Mahy), 48–56
Merlin Dreams (Dickinson), 174
Metaphor as Pure Adventure (Dickey), 84, 95
Metaphors, SEE Figures of speech
Midnight Hour Encores (Brooks), 106
Midnight Is a Place (Aiken), 171
Milosevic, Peter, 77
Miracles (Lewis, collector), 76
"Modern Fiction" (Woolf), 246
Modern Language Association, the, 132
Moers, Ellen, 129
Molesworth, Mary Louisa Stewart, 219
Moomintroll novels, the (Jansson), 263
Moon Jumpers, The (Udry), 15
Moon Tiger (Lively), 191
Moore, Anne Carroll, 34, 165, 315, 317
Moore, Marianne, 244–45
Moore, Susan, 236
Mordred, 33
Morrison, Toni, xv, 131
Moss, Anita, xv, 224n
Moss, Elaine, 69

Mother-daughter relationship, novelistic, 7–9, 56–61

Mother, influence of, on writer, 7–10, 74n

Mother-son relationship, novelistic, 36–40, 61–69

Mother Tongue, The (Bryson), 121n

Mouse and His Child, The (Hoban), 29–32, 35, 88, 223, 226, 253

Moves Make the Man, The (Brooks), 88–89, 103, 106

Mozart, Wolfgang Amadeus, 237

Mr. Fortune's Maggot (Warner), 76, 96

Murray, Joan, 246, 265n

"Muse of Masturbation, The," 132

Mushroom Planet books, the (Cameron), 25

My Mother's House and Sido (Colette), 128

Mysterious Island, The (Verne), 248–49

Mystery, 40–45

Myth Makers, The (Pritchett), 250

"Myth Today" (Barthes), xvi

Nabokov, Vladimir, 284

Nader, Ralph, 265n

Naming: of characters, 38, 62, 122, 175; of places, 174–75, 176

Nesbit, E., xv, 151, 168, 169, 217, 218–20

Neumeyer, Peter, 99, 223, 242

"Neverland as Id" (Egan), 224n, 237, 243, 304

Newbery Award, the, 227–28

New Critical Essays (Barthes), 122n, 250

New Theory, 247–50: style in writing of, 245–50

New Women and New Fiction (Cahill), 258

New York Review of Books, the, 313

New York Times Book Review, the, 78, 109n, 165, 265

Nodelman, Perry, xv, 224n

Nordstrum, Ursula, 316, 317

Norton, Mary, 252

Oates, Joyce Carol, 75, 130, 131, 233, 293

O'Connor, Flannery, 101, 131

O'Dell, Scott, 22, 24, 210–11

Oedipus complex, the, 237

Ogilvie, Margaret, 306–7

Old Possum's Book of Practical Cats (Eliot), 261–62

Oneal, Zibby, 89, 93

One-Eyed Cat (Fox), 86, 87, 96

One Writer's Beginnings (Welty), 127

"Only Good Author?, The" (Le Guin), 264n

Optimist's Daughter, The (Welty), 101, 105

Orlando (Woolf), 292

Orwell, George, 130

Outside over There (Sendak), 237, 242, 295

Ovarian hermeneutics, 132

Owl Service, The (Garner), 10, 102, 170, 174–75, 177, 224

Ozick, Cynthia, 78, 130

Parallels in données of novels, 56, 61

Parents: in fantasy, 152–53; in reality, 56–69

Parson, Annie, 318

Passing On (Lively), 191, 192

Paterson, Katherine, 22, 56, 223

Pattern of Roses, A (Peyton), 185, 187–89, 203

Peacock Pie (de la Mare), 114

Pearce, Philippa, 152, 185, 234n

Pedantry: reviewing of children's books and, 261; scholars and, 263–64

Performing Self, The (Poirier), 70
Period Piece (Raverat), 21n, 167, 168
Perrin, Noel, 81–82
Personal experience, author's use of, 9, 19, 23, 24–25, 260–61
Perverse and Foolish (Boston), 21n
Peter Pan and Wendy (Barrie), 310n
Peter Pan (Barrie), 14, 224, 242, 256, 293, 303–13, 320
Peyton, K. M., 185, 187, 188
Pfeiffer, John E., 109, 110
Phallic connotation, 92
Phillips, Robert, 293
Picasso, Pablo, 258
Pickering, Samuel, Jr., 221–22, 226–27
Pictures in an Institution (Jarrell), 77
Pied Pipers, The (Wintle and Fisher, editors), 9
Pierce, Meredith Ann, 176–77
Pigeon Post (Ransome), 238
Pilgerman (Hoban), 32
Pilgrim at Tinker Creek (Dillard), 80–81
Pillow Problems (Barrie), 320–21
Pinocchio, 212
Pipers at the Gates of Dawn (Cott), 237
Place, sense of, 21–22, 34–45, 87, 101–2, 171n, 173–76, 278, 279, 280, 285–86
Planet of Junior Brown, The (Hamilton), 35
Playing Beatie Bow (Park), 192–93
Plot, complexities of, 40–45
Pluralism, 249n
Poirier, Richard, 70
Ponder Heart, The (Welty), 104–5
Pooh books, the (Milne), 21
Poor Tom's Ghost (Curry), 171n
Popularity and literary qualities, 232
Possession (Byatt), 265
Postman, Neil, xviii
Potter, Beatrix, 15, 34–35, 70, 218, 238–39

Powell, Lawrence Clarke, 209, 215
Predictability in fictional structure, 93–94
Price, Reynolds, 71, 74–75
Priestley, J. B., 144
Prince and the Pauper, The (Twain), 16
Pritchett, V. S., 130, 250, 251
Private vision, power of, 201–4, 288, 289
"Proust and Names" (Barthes), 122n
Prydain series, the (Alexander), 23
Psychic disorders of fictional characters, 89–94
Psychoanalytic approaches, 69, 237
Psychoanalytic Theory of Neurosis, The (Fenichel), 237
Psychological criticism, 237, 240
Puck of Pook's Hill (Kipling), 168

Rafferty, Max, 212n
Rahn, Suzanne, 226
Railway Children, The (Nesbit), 219
Ramona and Her Father (Cleary), 252
Ramona books, the (Cleary), 263
Ransome, Arthur, 238
Rape, 143, 144n
Raverat, Gwen, 21n, 167, 168
Read, Herbert, 37
Reading, childhood influence of, on writer, 16–24
Reality: kinds of, in fantasy, 186–87; treatment of, in fantasy, 253–56
Real Presences (Steiner), 247, 248
Red Moon and Black Mountain (Chant), 170–78, 180–82, 202, 203
Red Shift (Garner), 10, 224, 287
Reed, Michael D., 237
Rees, David, 189
Remarkable Journey of Prince Jen, The (Alexander), 23
Rembrandt van Rijn, 167
Renaissance, the, xvii
Renault, Mary, 131

Rereading, value of, in literary criticism, 223–26
Return of the Twelves, The (Clarke), 22, 121, 149, 152, 164–65, 221
Reviewing, 257
Rhys, Jean, 126
Rich in Love (Humphreys), 74
Riddley Walker (Hoban), 32
Rise of the Red Alders, The (Rogers), 17
River at Green Knowe, The (Boston), 45
"Robert Cormier Does a Number" (Nodelman), 224n
Robinson Crusoe (Defoe), 325
Room Made of Windows, A (Cameron), xix, 4, 8, 123–24
Room of One's Own, A (Woolf), 118, 131–32
"Root of All Evil, The" (Greene), 276
Roth, Philip, 78
Rotten Reviews (Henderson, editor), 20n
Roxburgh, Stephen, xvi
Rukeyser, Muriel, 109
"Rule of Names, The" (Le Guin), 322

Sacks, Oliver, 111
Saki, 217
Sarah Plain and Tall (MacLachlan), 70
Saussure, Ferdinand de, xvi
Savage Inequalities (Kozol), 130
Saxton, Eugene, 314, 316
Sayers, Frances Clarke, 207–16, 232, 317
Scarlet Pimpernel, The (Orczy), 22
Scenes of Childhood and Other Stories (Warner), 128
Scholes, Robert, 251
Schorer, Mark, 277
Schwartz, Albert, 125
Science fiction, 172, 175–76, 243, 252
Science Fiction of Ursula K. Le Guin, The (Suvin and Muller, editors), 243
Secret Gardens (Carpenter), 219, 299

Segal, Lore, 16
Self-Interviews (Dickey), 46
Semiotics, xvi
Sendak, Maurice, 11, 13–16, 237, 242, 258, 295
Senoi people of Malaya, the, 322–24
Sense of place, 21–22, 45, 87, 101–2, 171n, 173–76, 278, 279, 280, 285–86
"Sense of Reality, A" (Greene), 276
Sense of wonder, 24–25
Sentimentality, 48, 62, 127, 220, 311–13
"Settling the Colonel's Hash" (McCarthy), 239
Sewell, Elizabeth, 302
Sexist tradition, 121n
Sexuality, xv, 14, 28, 33, 51–52, 55, 56, 63–65, 89–94, 110, 132–33, 134–36, 238, 241–42, 299, 308, 311
Shabanu (Staples), 133, 227
Shadow Dancers, The (Curry), 177
"Shadow, The" (Andersen), 224, 320, 321
Shakespeare, William, 33n, 108, 109, 117, 230, 260, 269–70
Sheed, Wilfred, 130
Shelley, Mary, 28n, 293, 304n
Shepard, Ernest H., 21n
Shlain, Leonard, 121n, 149
Shock of recognition in imagery, 95
Shock-receiving capacity of writer, 11
Signal, 45n
Signposts to Criticism of Children's Literature (Bator, editor), 262n
Silent Spring (Carson), 265n
Silver on the Tree (Cooper), 179, 181
"Sketch of the Past, A" (Woolf), 291–92
Slang, 105–6
Sleepers, The (Curry), 171n
Smedman, Sarah M., 224n
Smith, Hedrick, 83

Smith, Lillian, 210
Snow White, 212
Solitary Blue, A (Voigt), 56, 61–69, 225, 281
Song of Solomon (Morrison), xv
Sontag, Susan, 130, 131, 239
Sound of Chariots, A (Hunter), 225, 226
Space fantasy, 19
Spain, metaphorical stone carvings in, 110
Spear and the Piccolo, The (Steig), 223, 224n
Spectator Bird, The (Stegner), 107
Spinelli, Jerry, 227
Stahl, John Daniel, xix–xx, 133
Stakenas, Paula, 234
Staples, Suzanne Fisher, 133, 227
Stegner, Wallace, 107
Steig, William, 223, 224n
Steiner, George, 247, 248
Stevenson, Robert Louis, 11–13, 293, 304n
Stewart, Kilton, 324
Still Life (Byatt), 265
Stitch in Time, A (Lively), 189
Stone carvings, metaphorical prehistoric, 110
Stones of Green Knowe, The (Boston), 194, 196–97
Story, 69–70
Story of the Amulet, The (Nesbit), 151, 152–53, 168, 169, 219
Story of the Treasure Seekers, The (Nesbit), 219
Stranger at Green Knowe, A (Boston), 45–48
Stratton-Porter, Gene, 21–22
Strauss, Jean, 78
String in the Harp, A (Bond), 149–50, 152, 155, 158–62, 171n, 174, 193, 203, 234
Structuralism, xvi, 248
Structure, novelistic, 33, 182–84, 201

Stuart Little (White), 165, 315–20
Stuff of Sleep and Dreams (Edel), 122n
Style, 243–46: feminism and, 121; Kipling, Rudyard, and his, 20–21; New Theory, sound of, in critical writing, 245–50; pedagogic, 245–50; personal sound in, 240; pretentiousness in, 245–50; television writing, effect on, 102–3; Thoreau, Henry David, and his, 75; tour de force, 244–45; Voigt, Cynthia, and her, 63–64; White, E. B., sound of, 98–100, 240
Styron, William, 74n
Summoned by Books (Sayers), 208
Surprised by Joy (Lewis), 220
"Susan Cooper" (Kuznets), 262n
Suspension of disbelief, 45–56
Sutcliff, Rosemary, 21n, 88, 181
Suvin, Darko, 243
Swallows and Amazons series, the (Ransome), 238
Sweet Whispers, Brother Rush (Hamilton), 36, 86
Sylvie and Bruno (Carroll), 294, 295
Symbol hunting, 237, 239–40
Symbolism in children's literature, 67–68, 89–94, 182–84, 224, 237, 239–42, 319

"Tailpiece" (Rahn), 226
Tale of Beatrix Potter, The, 35
Tale of Jemima Puddle-Duck, The (Potter), 238
Tale of Mr. Tod, The (Potter), 239
Tale of Tom Kitten, The (Potter), 226
Tale of Two Bad Mice, The (Potter), 226
Taliesin, 174
Tapestry Room, The (Molesworth), 219
Tart, Charles, 322
Tate, Allen, 262
Taylor, Gary, 109n

Taylor, Judy, 34
Technique, 278
Tehanu (Le Guin), 133, 136–41, 180, 227
Telephone conversation, 245
Television, xvi, 76, 102–3
Television writing, effect on style, 102, 106
Tennyson, Alfred Lord, 325
Textual scholarship, 223, 226
Tey, Josephine, 79
That Julia Redfern (Cameron), 24
Theme, novelistic, 125, 142–43, 226
Theory, literary, 247–51, 265
Thirkell, Angela, 20, 21n
Thomas, D. M., 78
Thoreau, Henry David, 75, 171n
Thorny Paradise, The (Blishen, editor), 287
"Thoughts on a Shirtless Cyclist, Robin Hood, Johann Sebastian Bach, and One or Two Other Things" (Hoban), 29–30
Three Guineas (Woolf), 131
Three Houses (Thirkell), 21n
Three Royal Monkeys, The (de la Mare), 281
Thurber, James, 85
Time bomb, creative, 314, 317, 321
Time fantasy, 149–204: history, use of, in, 170–72; legend, use of, in, 170; science fiction, use of, in, 172–73
Time: Hopi conception of, 203; idea of, 168
"Time Is a River without Banks," 273
Tir na n-Og Award, 174
Titular colonicity, 246
Tolkien, J. R. R., 180, 269
Tolstoy, Leo, 260
Tombs of Atuan, The (Le Guin), xvi, 141–42, 224, 225, 241–42
Tommy and Grizel (Barrie), 313

Tom Sawyer, SEE *Adventures of Tom Sawyer, The*
Tom's Midnight Garden (Pearce), 152, 154, 185, 192, 197
Tongues of Angels, The (Price), 74
To the Green Mountains (Cameron), 8, 121, 125, 142, 273
To the Lighthouse (Woolf), 3, 4, 7, 8, 114, 281–82
Townsend, John Rowe, 172, 257, 263, 287
Traveler in Time, A (Uttley), 173, 202n
Travers, Pamela, 220
Treasure Island (Stevenson), 22, 24
Treasure of Green Knowe (Boston), 169, 196
Treasures of Time, The (Lively), 191
Treasure Seekers, The, SEE *Story of the Treasure Seekers, The*
Tricks in time fantasy, 184–87
Trilling, Lionel, 130
Trumpet of the Swan, The (White), 151–52, 162–64, 223, 231, 316
Tuck Everlasting (Babbitt), 95
Turtle Diary (Hoban), 85–86, 88, 105
Twain, Mark, xv, 27n, 258, 284–85

Udry, Janice, 15
"Ugly Duckling, The" (Andersen), 212, 224, 312
Ulysses (Joyce), 100
Unconscious, the, 269–325: Alexander, Lloyd, and, 314; Barrie, J. M., and, 293, 303–13; Brontë, Emily, and, 270, 272; Cameron, Eleanor, and, 324; Carroll, Lewis, and, 293; character creation and, 278, 279, 293–320; coalescing of novelistic events and, 277; collective, idea of the, 289; criticism and, 236; dreaming and, 11–13, 16, 27–

29, 271–72, 274–75; learning from, 274–79; Le Guin, Ursula K., and, 279, 322–24; metaphors, imagery, symbols, and themes, creation of, through, 98–99, 113–14, 279; opening one's self to, 287–88; recollections of apparently forgotten events through, 286; symbolism and, 225, 269; White, E. B., and, 314–20; writing, power of, imbued through, 225n, 277, 279, 283–87
Unconscious Before Freud, The (Whyte), 270–71
"Undercurrents" (MacLeod), 173n
Understanding Media (McLuhan), 265n
University of California at Los Angeles: "Excellence in Children's Literature," tour financed by, 210; Powell, Lawrence Clark, head of library at, 209; Sayers, Frances Clarke, at, 208; study of creative thinkers by, 236
Unleaving (Walsh), 86, 223
Unlocking the English Language (Burchfield), xvi
Unreluctant Years, The (Smith), 210
Updike, John, 130
Uttley, Alison, 173, 202n

Vanessa Bell (Spalding), 129
Verne, Jules, 248–49
Vidal, Gore, 130
Virginia Woolf (DeSalvo), 293n
Vision, power of private, the, 201–4, 288, 289
Visitors, The (Townsend), 172
Voigt, Cynthia, 225, 281
Voyage Begun, The (Bond), 95

Wales, as place for time fantasy, 170, 173–74, 177–78

Walker, Margaret, 130
"Walk on the Wild Side, A" (Westall), 201
Walsh, Jill Paton, 86, 169, 171, 184–85, 202, 252, 257
"Walt Disney Accused" (Sayers), 212n, 232
Warner, Sylvia Townsend, 76, 85, 95, 114, 115, 118, 128, 188
Watchers, The (Curry), 171n, 177
Waves, The (Woolf), 100, 113, 189
Way to Sattin Shore, The (Pearce), 234n
Weisenberg, Charles W., 212n
Wells, H. G., 254
Welty, Eudora, 34, 71, 101, 104, 127
Wescott, Glenway, 278
Westall, Robert, 194, 197, 199, 201, 203, 252
When a Man's Single (Barrie), 308
"When Jane Jacobs Took on the World" (Murray and Fulford), 246, 265n
"Where to Begin" (Barthes), 248
White, E. B., 70, 85, 98–100, 128, 151, 155, 165, 223, 314–20
White, Katharine, 319–20
Whorf, Benjamin Lee, 204
Whyte, Lancelot Law, 270
Wilde, Oscar, 217
Wilder, Laura Ingalls, 70, 126
Wild Strawberries, 177
Williams, Garth, 316
Williams, Joan, 270
Williams, Robin, 221n
Willie Bea and the Night the Martians Came (Hamilton), 36
Willis, Patricia C., 244
Wills, Garry, 83
Wilson, Edmund, 130, 220
Wilson Library Bulletin, 224n
Wind in the Willows, The (Grahame), 22, 226

Wind's Eye, The (Westall), 200

Witch's Brat, The (Sutcliff), 95

Wizard of Earthsea, A (Le Guin), 224, 225, 240, 253, 279, 321

Wolves of Aam, The (Curry), 177

Woman of Passion, A (Briggs), 220

(Woman) Writer (Oates), 293

Wonder, sense of, 24–25

Woolf, Leonard, 211

Woolf, Virginia, xx, 3, 7–8, 10–11, 74, 100, 113, 114, 117, 130, 131–32, 189, 211, 227, 246, 247, 252–53, 258, 281–82, 291

Word for World Is Forest, The (Le Guin), 322

"Word of Unbinding, The" (Le Guin), 322

Writer-critic, SEE Critic as author

Writing a Woman's Life (Heilbrun), 118, 127, 128, 129, 246

Writing over the heads of children, 311

Writing the body, 133n

Wuthering Heights (Brontë), 22, 270, 272, 277–78

Yeats, William Butler, 95, 234

Yosemite National Park, 24–25, 26

Yourcenar, Marguerite, 131

Zaturenska, Marya, 131

Zeely (Hamilton), xvi

Zen, 105

Zola, Emile, 259